THE TRAVELLER'S GOOD HEALTH GUIDE

Ted Lankester is InterHealth's Director of Health Care. Previously a GP in London, Ted has travelled extensively and lived for a number of years in the Himalayas, setting up community health programmes and looking after the health needs of travellers. He was previously a board member of Tearfund, and Assistant Editor of the journal *Tropical Doctor*. Currently he is a Trustee of People in Aid; a part-time lecturer on global health at London University; the author of books on community-based health care; and is on the advisory panel of the UK government's National Travel Health Network and Centre (NaTHNaC). He is also a fellow of the Faculty of Travel Medicine at the Royal College of Physicians and Surgeons of Glasgow, and is co-founder and director of Community Health Global Network (see <http://www.communityhealthglobal.net>).

D1098974

THE TRAVELLER'S GOOD HEALTH GUIDE

Some reviews of previous editions:

'It is always a delight to review a book that one really enjoys and finds informative. This excellent compact publication is a guide for backpackers, travellers, volunteers and overseas workers, and I would also recommend it as an excellent pocket companion for all travel health advisers.'
Travelwise: The British Travel Health Association

'Those who feel they need specific information before setting off for exotic climes are catered for in *The Traveller's Good Health Guide* which takes a comprehensive look at every aspect of staying healthy when travelling.'
The Overseas Jobs Express

'The excellent cartoons add spice to the excellent text.'
Newsletter of the Voluntary Agency Medical Advisors Group

'I found it easy to read, clear and accessible.'
Interserve Go Magazine

'The book is great value particularly in view of its highly affordable price.'
Journal of the International Society of Travel Medicine

'I would regard this as a vital bench book for a travel clinic.'
London-Calling, Royal College of General Practitioners

'Goodness knows how many times I have referred to this book over the years.'
Aid worker with Save the Children

The Traveller's Good Health Guide

A Guide for Those Living, Working and Travelling Internationally

Dr Ted Lankester
and members of the InterHealth team

With a chapter on stress by
Dr Ruth Fowke

sheldon **PRESS**

First published in Great Britain in 1993 by InterHealth in association with Gospel Communication under the title *Healthy Beyond Heathrow*. Second edition published in Great Britain in 1995 by Hodder & Stoughton under the title *Good Health, Good Travel*

First published by Sheldon Press in 1999

Sheldon Press
36 Causton Street
London SW1P 4ST

Second edition published 2002
Third edition published 2006

The author and publisher have made every effort to ensure that the external website and email addresses included in this book are correct and up to date at the time of going to press. The author and publisher are not responsible for the content, quality of continuing accessibility of the sites.

British Library Cataloguing-in-Publication Data

A catalogue record for this book is available from the British Library

ISBN-13: 978–0–85969–991–4
ISBN-10: 0–85969–991–9

1 3 5 7 9 10 8 6 4 2

This book has arisen largely out of the experience of InterHealth and its staff of 15 travel health specialists. InterHealth is a registered NGO based on Christian foundations, with its headquarters in London, that specializes in the health needs of those working internationally. Its clients include aid workers, corporate travellers, diplomats, volunteers, missionaries and anyone living or working long term overseas, regardless of their religious affiliation. Services include medical and psychological assessment before travel, and detailed health examinations on return, including psychiatric support, counselling and debriefing. InterHealth provides a comprehensive range of travel health supplies, and provides a 24-hour round-the-clock advisory service by phone or email for its members and the agencies to which they belong. Individuals and organizations are invited to become members in order to enjoy the full range of services and supplies at discounted prices. See <www.interhealth.org.uk>.

Typeset by Deltatype Limited, Birkenhead, Merseyside
Printed in Great Britain by
Ashford Colour Press

Contents

v

CONTENTS

CONTENTS

Illustrations

Acknowledgements

For the original edition

I would like to thank a number of people for their helpful comments on reading through the draft of this manual. They include the late Dr A. J. Broomhall, Mr Stuart Buchanan of the Church Mission Society, Dr Denis Roche, previously of Interserve, Dr Mark Evason, previously of Crosslinks, Dr Marianne Janosi, previously VSO medical adviser, Dr Mike Jones of Edinburgh International Health Centre (Care for Mission), and Mr Steve Price-Thomas, formerly of VSO, and Jean Sinclair. In addition Mr Frank Tovey OBE and Jackie Fenwick, formerly of InterHealth, have given invaluable advice. I am indebted to Jason Carter for livening up the text with his cartoons.

For the current edition

I would like to thank all my friends and colleagues at InterHealth for their valuable contributions and advice. This book is increasingly becoming a team effort. Dr Ruth Fowke, formerly consultant psychiatrist at InterHealth, has contributed a chapter on stress, and Annie Hargrave a section entitled 'A stress self-help tool'. Drs Simon Clift and Evelyn Sharpe, and Margaret Lancaster have made important contributions to the text. I would also like to thank Dr Vanessa Field, Diane Parsons and Cathy Travis for considerable time taken in reading through the text and making many useful suggestions. And a big thank you also to Malcolm Livingstone for additional illustrations and to Joanna Moriarty, commissioning editor at Sheldon Press, for her support and encouragement. And, lastly, my thanks go to the members of the editorial and production teams: Liz Jones, Kathryn Wolfendale, Rhona Pipe, Monica Capoferri, Ruth McBrien and Louise Clairmonte.

Information sources and disclaimer

Information in this book is based on authoritative UK and international sources including the World Health Organization, the UK Advisory Committee on Malaria Prevention, the National Travel Health Network and Centre, Health Protection Scotland, the Health Protection Agency, the Centers for Disease Control and Prevention, USA, and a large number of research papers and reviews published in international journals.

As far as possible information was correct at the time of publication. However, recommendations on travel medicine frequently change, especially with regard to immunization and antimalarial advice. For this reason the latest edition of this book should be used, and in addition a travel health adviser should be consulted.

Although every effort has been made to ensure accuracy, neither the author nor the publisher can accept any liability for unforeseen errors or omissions, or for any illness or event resulting from advice or information given in this book.

Author to traveller

A medical friend of mine recently said he preferred working at the top of the cliff, rather than at the bottom. In reply to my puzzled look he explained: 'It's just my way of saying prevention is better than cure.'

The purpose of this book is to help you take sensible precautions and then stop worrying about all the things that may but probably won't happen to you. Many people living internationally keep in better health than their friends back home, and the commonest conditions are often the same, including 'accidents', which can happen anywhere. You will probably have bouts of diarrhoea, and you may get malaria, but body-devouring parasites and giant creepy-crawlies are more likely to be met in your dreams than in reality.

So this book is mainly about how to prevent getting ill in the first place, but with plenty of tips about what to do if you're not lucky or successful. Think back to any time you've been abroad and got sick. Could it have been prevented? Being a bit more faithful with the antimalarials and mosquito nets? Declining more of those alluring salads? Working – or playing – that bit less hard and long?

The basic message is this: have your jabs, take your antimalarials, set up rules for sensible eating and personal hygiene, and lead a balanced lifestyle. If it prevents extra trips to the hotel toilet or your personal long-drop, and increases the odds that your holiday, mission or posting is not ruined by bugs, stress or accidents, it will be worth it.

I've tried to write the book in as logical an order as possible – Before, During and After:

Section 1 Before you go

Skim through this weeks before leaving, because it's all about getting prepared. It will only take a few minutes but it could save you a lot of 'if only' thoughts when you get to Destination X. It also guides you about important travel health items you may want to take with you.

Section 2 While abroad

Read through this before you leave and again when you arrive.

Section 3 When you return

It is better to read this before you head back homewards.

Section 4 Notes on important conditions

This can't possibly cover everything but it tries to look at the commonest travel-related problems and illnesses you may experience, with tips on how to prevent them and treat them. If you developed some intriguing illness or picked up an impressive parasite which is not mentioned, do write and tell me.

And don't forget the series of useful appendices which include a stress self-help tool, details on each individual travel vaccine and contents of first-aid and medical kits.

Like any book, this health manual will be largely useless if left at home, or lost among the novels and 4×4 manuals in the back of beyond. I hope it travels with you and that its pages, made from sustainable forests, soon start looking well-thumbed.

This is the third incarnation of the book. The first was called *Healthy Beyond Heathrow*, a title people from the south of England liked, the Scots and Irish were less sure about, and which puzzled many travellers from other countries.

Please let me know if I've left out any mention of your favourite diseases or most hated parasites. With travellers coming and going from a million destinations, and each having vastly different risks, shapes, ages and immune systems, it can never be right for everyone. But I would value your comments on how to make any improvements.

This book is dedicated to
my favourite fellow travellers
who also happen to be my wife and children,
Joy, Rachel, Heather and Debbie

SECTION 1
Before you go

Checklist for before you leave

There is a great deal to do just before leaving and it's all too easy if you are normally healthy, or very laid back, to leave health matters to the last moment. By planning well ahead, especially for immunizations, you actually save yourself time – and a lot of last-minute hassle. For all except the shortest journeys to the healthiest places you will need to do the following:

- Complete all necessary *immunizations* (see pages 6–12).
- Obtain any *certificates* that may be required, e.g. yellow fever. Some countries need an HIV certificate or medical form, especially for residence permits.
- Select and buy appropriate *first-aid, medical or needle and syringe kits* (see pages 13–17 and Appendix D).
- If going to a *malarious area*, take a mosquito net, insect repellent, standby treatment kit and sufficient malaria prevention tablets and start them before leaving (see pages 17–22).
- Take other *personal supplies*, including medicines or inhalers you normally use, contraceptives, spare glasses and contact lens-cleaning fluid (see pages 22–7).
- Find out your *blood group*, and keep a written record with you (see page 169).
- Visit a *dentist* and have all dental work completed.
- Consider visiting an *optician* for a routine eye check (see page 267).
- Find out about any *reciprocal health arrangements* in the country you are going to (see page 70).
- If you live in the UK and are going to a country in the *European Economic Area (EU) or Switzerland*, obtain a European Health Insurance Card (EHIC) from a post office or phone 020 7210 4850. This has replaced the E111 form (see page 70). The EHIC covers only a proportion of costs, so in addition take out comprehensive travel insurance.
- Consider having a *medical examination*, especially if you have any known health problems, are over the age of 50, are going on a difficult or high-risk assignment or are going to a developing country for longer than six months (see pages 28–63, especially pages 61–3).
- Take out *health insurance* unless arranged by your company or agency (see pages 69–70).
- Women should be up to date with their *cervical smear tests*, and if over the age of 50 with a recent mammogram (40 or 45 in some countries).

3

- Discover any particular *health or security hazards* of the country you are visiting or special precautions that are recommended.
- Consider going on a *first-aid course*, especially if going to a remote area or leading a team or expedition.
- Check all *travel documents* and work out a *safe system* for keeping them – and money (see page 227).
- Consider making a *will*.

What are the main risks of travelling abroad?

These will obviously vary a great deal depending on your length of travel, where you are going, what you will be doing and perhaps above all your personality, and especially whether you are cautious or a risk-taker. International travel is not necessarily any more dangerous than spending the equivalent time at home, especially if you take sensible precautions.

The list below is not supposed to frighten you or put you off your planned posting, mission, or trip of a lifetime but it points out the commonest risks.

An article in the *Lancet*[1] published a table of risks drawn from a variety of sources. Of 100,000 travellers going to the developing world for one month:

- 50,000 will develop some sort of health problem during their trip;
- 8,000 will consult a doctor;
- 5,000 will be ill enough to stay in bed;
- 110 will be incapacitated in their work abroad or on returning home;
- 300 will be admitted to hospital;
- 50 will have to be air-evacuated;
- 1 will die.

If you are wondering what the commonest causes of serious illness or death are, the evidence is a bit limited. Among aid workers, road and other accidents come top, stress and depression second and malaria third. Among older travellers (50 or over) one large study showed that heart problems accounted for half of all deaths. Among all travellers, diarrhoea is the commonest problem – a major nuisance but rarely life-threatening.

---

[1] A. Spira, *Lancet* (2003) 261:1368–81.

CHECKLIST FOR BEFORE YOU LEAVE

- *Photocopy important documents*, including the main page of your passport and any outward or return air tickets, and keep the photocopies separately, along with numbers of travellers' cheques. Also leave copies at home with your next of kin.
- Plan ahead for *self-entertainment* and *professional update* if going to a remote area or prolonged assignment (see pages 67 and 218–19).
- Be *well prepared medically* but don't allow worries about health to cast a shadow over your time abroad.

1
Arranging your immunizations

A visit to a clinic or your local doctor leaving you with a slightly sore muscle is a small price to pay for protection from several nasty diseases. It is, however, worth noting that fewer than one disease episode in ten when overseas is preventable by a vaccine. This means that following antimalarial precautions, advice on food and water, and accident prevention is just as important as being jabbed at your local health centre or travel clinic. *But the vaccines are still essential.*

Appendix J gives details on all the commonly used travel vaccines, and a summary of minor vaccine reactions.

What travel jabs will I need?

The menu of jabs gets longer every year. It's possible to get over-immunized – i.e. go for everything just because it's on a comprehensive list – or, worse, be inadequately protected. Unless you are going on a straightforward trip to a low-risk destination, ask your travel health adviser to draw up a list of what is appropriate for your particular trip. This will take into account your age, how healthy you are, and what previous immunizations you have had (try and find a record of these so you have only the jabs you really need).

Your health adviser will also need to know the area of the country you will be living in, any job you may be doing, the length of time you may be staying and the sort of lifestyle you are likely to follow. Settle for just one opinion from a travel health adviser you trust who is well informed about the risks you are likely to face – otherwise it's confusion all round. Table 1.1 shows some guidelines based largely on current UK recommendations.

Group 1

Immunizations recommended for *all* countries outside western Europe, North America, Japan and Australasia, for which you should be in-date before leaving:

Adults

- Hepatitis A
- Polio, tetanus with diphtheria (Revaxis)
- Typhoid

6

Table 1.1 Commonly used travel vaccines

Name	Original course	Boosters due	Takes effect after	Side-effects	Usual lowest age
Hepatitis A	One	After 6–24 months, then every 10–20 years	Fully within two weeks, probably earlier	Nil serious	Adult form from 16 years Junior from one year
Hepatitis B	Three at months 0, 1 and 6*	*	At once after third dose or booster	Serious reactions rare	Birth
Japanese encephalitis (Biken brand)	Three at days 0, 7–14, 28	At two years then every three years	14 days after third dose, immediately after any booster	Occasionally more serious, sometimes a few days or weeks after immunization	12 months, occasionally six
Meningitis **ACWY	One	Every five years	Ten days	Serious reactions rare	Two years
Polio	Three at monthly intervals	Every ten years	At once after third dose or booster	Serious reactions rare	Birth
Rabies	Three at days 0, 7, 21–28	First after three years, then every five	At once after third dose or booster	Serious reactions rare	One year
Tetanus with diphtheria	Three at monthly intervals	Every ten years	At once after third dose or booster	Serious reactions rare	Variable, usually seven years
Tick-borne encephalitis	Two, from 4 to 12 weeks apart	5–12 months after second dose, then every three years	At once after third dose or booster	Serious reactions rare	Obtain advice
Typhoid (injectable)	One	Every three years	7–10 days after first, at once after booster	Occasionally pain and fever in first 48 hours	Two years
Yellow fever	One	Every ten years	Ten days after first, at once after booster	Occasionally fever 5–10 days after injection	Usually nine months

Notes: There are now so many vaccines, different manufacturers and different schedules that for many vaccines the table above represents only a selection of commonly used dosage regimes. Different countries also have differing schedules so there are many variations. There is more on all these and other vaccines in Appendix J.

* Accelerated course available (see page 385 for more information; no booster considered necessary if titre is over 10 iu/ml).

** See pages 389–91 for more details. Various other meningitis vaccines are used, all with their own schedules.

Children

See UK immunization schedule on page 243.

- Diphtheria, pertussis, tetanus, inactivated polio, Hib (Pedicel)
- Hepatitis A (Junior) for children 1–15 years (depending on risk)
- Meningitis C (either as conjugate vaccine or combined vaccine against Groups A and C)
- Pneumococcus (Prevenar)
- MMR (mumps, measles, rubella)
- Typhoid (not usually under two years)

Group 2

Immunizations needed for *some* countries depending on your location, occupation and length of time abroad:

All those listed for adults in Group 1 plus for both adults and children:

- Cholera
- Hepatitis B
- Japanese encephalitis
- Meningitis ACWY
- Rabies
- Tick-borne encephalitis
- Yellow fever (you also need a certificate)

Group 3

Immunizations needed only in special circumstances:

- anthrax for those working with animals in affected areas;
- BCG for tuberculosis;
- chickenpox;
- influenza for travellers to northern or southern hemisphere winter aged 65 or over or at special risk (annual);
- measles for adults without immunity, in some war and relief situations, usually given as MMR;
- mumps, usually given as MMR;
- plague (special circumstances only);
- pneumococcal vaccine for those 65 or over (one only), and other high-risk groups;
- rubella (for women of child-bearing age with no immunity, usually given as MMR).

In addition, Anti D immunoglobulin may be needed by Rhesus

negative women who become pregnant or who plan to give birth while overseas (see pages 236–7).

There are two situations where you need an international certificate: for any yellow fever immunization and for meningitis ACWY if you are going on the Hajj pilgrimage to Saudi Arabia.

How should I arrange having my immunizations?

Here are some guidelines:

Discover which immunizations you will need

If you are travelling independently, ask your doctor or practice nurse for advice, or visit a travel clinic (see Appendix G).

If going with a company or agency, you will normally be provided with a list of recommended immunizations for your trip. If not, ask for one.

Work out a time schedule

Do this with the doctor or nurse likely to be giving you the majority of your immunizations. If you have been given a recommended list, take this along. Let the clinic work out a schedule with you, rather than spending too much time working out your own. Usually immunizations can be completed in two or three visits to the health centre or travel clinic.

Allow plenty of time to fit them all in

If going to a developing country, try to allow three months unless you have travelled in the past three years. This way you will be able to complete courses without having to take vaccine with you. If you don't have this much time, your schedule can usually be accelerated.

Understand which are the live vaccines

These include BCG (for tuberculosis), measles, MMR, mumps, polio (oral), rubella, typhoid (oral) and yellow fever.

Stricter precautions apply to live vaccines. There are rules which govern their spacing, they should be avoided in pregnancy and pregnancy should ideally be avoided for 28 days after a live vaccine is given. Some are best avoided when breastfeeding, especially yellow fever (see page 398). They should be used with caution in those who are immunocompromised (i.e. those who have diminished immunity, see pages 48–51).

9

Taking booster doses with you

Sometimes it is not possible to complete a course of immunizations before you leave. In this case, discover whether the immunizations you need are available in the country you are going to. If not, or you are unable to be certain, you can consider taking certain vaccines with you. Although most vaccines will keep for a short time unrefrigerated, it is better to carry them in a chilled vacuum flask, but they must not freeze so the flask should contain no ice. For the same reason they should not be put in the aircraft hold. Place them in a fridge on arrival. Yellow fever vaccine cannot be taken with you: it is against international health regulations.

Some doctors or travel clinics will provide supplies for you to take abroad. When you reach your destination the vaccines should be administered by a doctor or nurse using a sterile syringe and needle. They must be kept reliably cold between 2° and 8°C unless otherwise specified.

Where should I go for my travel jabs?

You will need to weigh up the three considerations of availability, convenience and cost. In the UK you will have two main choices: your NHS health centre or GP surgery, or a travel clinic.

Your NHS health centre or GP surgery

There are great differences between GP surgeries, clinics and health centres, both in terms of what jabs they have available and in the amount they charge. Some carry out a lot of travel medicine, others give very few vaccines. Find out what is available and how much different vaccinations will cost. Only a few health centres are licensed to give yellow fever immunization. Some may be able to order less common vaccines for you or give you a private prescription to collect one from a chemist.

In the UK and at the time of writing, the following are usually available free on the NHS for those who are eligible to use the National Health Service:

- hepatitis A vaccine
- hepatitis B for accredited health workers
- polio
- tetanus with diphtheria
- typhoid
- all normal childhood vaccinations (see page 243).

A *travel clinic*

In the UK there are various types of travel clinic: first, those run by hospitals with travel health or tropical health departments; second, networks of private travel health centres, of which the best-known are MASTA health clinics throughout the UK, the British Airways travel clinic in London, and Nomad travel clinics in London, Bristol and Southampton; third, specialist medical charities, of which InterHealth and EIHC are examples, see Appendix G). Most of these clinics are convenient to use and keep all immunizations in stock. Prices vary considerably. Some medical charities, for example, offer reduced rates for those working abroad with aid agencies, missionary societies and voluntary organizations.

Arrangements are different in other countries, but all developed countries will have the vaccinations available that you need, and most developing countries will have the most usual ones available from private clinics in major cities or those specializing in travel medicine. Children's vaccination schedules differ widely from country to country but are nearly always available.

For more details about health facilities worldwide see details under IAMAT on page 371, and the website of the International Society of Travel Medicine, <http://www.istm.org>.

Differing advice!

It can be bewildering (and annoying) when different doctors seem to give different advice. It helps to understand some of the reasons: new vaccines are being developed, there are differing country-by-country recommendations because experts do not always agree; advice from UK sources is not always the same as that from European, North

American, Australian or World Health Organization sources. Also, for many immunizations risk and benefit have to be weighed, so there are often no clear answers.

It is usually simplest to follow the advice of one informed health adviser. If going with a company or agency, follow their medical adviser's recommendations; otherwise follow advice from a travel clinic or your GP or practice nurse, after asking about the source of their information.

Pregnancy and breastfeeding

Live vaccines (see page 9) should be avoided in pregnancy. Non-live vaccines are generally considered safe but should only be given if, in discussion with your health adviser, you decide that benefit outweighs any possible risk. Gammaglobulin and tetanus (without diphtheria) appear to have no pregnancy-related risks, but these are not generally available in the UK.

Most vaccinations except yellow fever can be given when breastfeeding (again based on weighing risk and benefit), so discuss this with your travel nurse.

Special note for parents

Children going abroad need even more jabs than their friends staying back home. By following a few simple rules, the trauma for them (and for you) can be reduced.

- Be relaxed when going with them to the doctor.
- Tell them, preferably on the way to the clinic and almost in passing, that they will be having a jab. Mention it may hurt a little, but not very much.
- Don't build up to the event, and don't pile on sympathy.
- Have a sweet or treat ready to encourage the last-minute falterer or to use as a bribe or reward.
- Follow the doctor's or nurse's instruction, and hold your child firmly.
- Try not to let your child see the nurse preparing the injection.
- Use paracetamol suspension (Calpol, Tylenol) over the next few hours and during the first night if your child seems fretful.

Special note for experienced travellers

As a seasoned traveller or long-term expatriate, you may assume that your hard-won immunity removes the need for immunizations. Your risks are no less than for the first-time traveller. Follow standard immunization advice like everyone else.

2

Kits, medicines and health supplies

Before deciding what to take

As you will soon discover, travel health supplies is a growth industry. There are dozens of kits, medicines and items of equipment you could take, and a bewildering mix and match of needles, first-aid items and medicines. Before coming to any decision, ask yourself these questions:

- *Location*: will you be based for the majority of your trip in a country with good, medium or poor health facilities? Will you be near a large city or off the beaten track? What is the remotest area you are likely to visit, for example on holiday, and how far will it be from good health care?
- *Your basic health*: do you have any medical conditions likely to put you at greater risk when travelling? What is your age and what is your level of physical fitness? Are you overweight?
- *Your lifestyle*: where will you come on the spectrum between living in air-conditioned limos and lounges and roughing it in the outback?
- *Length of time abroad*: are you on a short-term visit, a longer-term assignment, or not sure when you will come back?
- *Occupation*: does this put you at special risk, e.g. as an aid worker, missionary or volunteer, anthropologist or journalist; a water engineer, vet or healthcare worker; a dedicated adventure traveller?
- *Your personality*: do you feel uncomfortable unless prepared for almost any situation, or do you tend to go with the flow?
- *The practicals*: space, luggage allowance. How much health kit would you put in your case or rucksack when travelling out from your overseas home or hotel?
- *Cost*: are you having to pay for supplies yourself or is your company or agency able to foot the bill? Ideally this should not be your major consideration. You should decide to take those items you feel will be genuinely useful for your particular trip.

Thinking these through will help you decide what's worth taking.

Needles and syringes

The World Health Organization estimates that worldwide a staggering 12 million people or more catch hepatitis B or C from unclean needles every year. Tens of thousands also become infected with HIV. About one injection in three is potentially contaminated.

Having packed a needle and syringe kit, you must remember to have it with you when you need it. Rather more difficult is to insist that the doctor or nurse uses it. This may require courage and tact, but if you fail to ask you may worry about it afterwards. In fact, an increasing number of clinics used by travellers are careful to use clean needles and if you see the doctor or nurse open these in front of you there is no need to use your own supply. But still have it with you in case.

Customs officials rarely seem to object when they come across medical supplies in your personal luggage. However, you should always have a signed doctor's note with you – preferably in your travel documents – which states

These medical supplies are for the personal private use of
.... (your name)

and is then signed, stamped and dated by your doctor and written on official paper. Some travel kits have a similar non-personalized message written in two or more languages, and this is usually adequate.

Those travelling to a few countries, e.g. Malaysia, Singapore and occasionally Thailand, should be cautious taking needles and syringes because of the risk of being misidentified as a drug addict.

> ### General recommendation for needle and syringe kits
> If going to a developing country for all but the shortest, lowest-risk trips, take clean needles and syringes, ideally as part of a first-aid kit.

First-aid kits

These come in a wide range of contents, combinations and cost (see Table D.1 on page 362). Here are some guidelines:

Basic first-aid supplies

Basic supplies include plasters, scissors, bandages, safety pins and tape. It is always sensible to have these, regardless of where you travel. For simple trips you can merely add to any supplies you have at home by buying the extras you need. For longer trips it may be easier to buy a simple kit. When flying, scissors or tweezers should ideally be kept in the hold, not your hand luggage. Kits in general are best packed in your

14

main luggage unless they contain any medical supplies which might be harmed by freezing, such as insulin. If you are carrying personal medicines (including malaria prevention tablets) it is worthwhile carrying at least some of these in your hand luggage in case your main luggage is delayed or goes missing.

More advanced supplies for higher-risk travel

You will need more than the basics if you are going abroad for a longer time or taking up an assignment, also if you are travelling extensively on dangerous roads or planning adventure pursuits. Your kit will need to include equipment for suturing and for putting up intravenous drips, and a wider range of first-aid items for more serious injuries. It will probably be better to buy a ready-made kit. You can save money if travelling in a group or team by sharing one or more kits between you.

HIV and hepatitis B protection kit

This contains transfusion substitutes for extensive travel in high-risk areas. You should consider taking a kit if travelling extensively on dangerous roads or by light aircraft in countries where HIV/AIDS (or hepatitis B and C) are common (see pages 153 and 301).

Blood transfusions are a serious risk for HIV and hepatitis B and C in many developing countries. In much of sub-Saharan Africa, South and Southeast Asia and parts of Latin America, blood is often obtained through private suppliers who may buy blood from those living on the streets, many of whom will be HIV positive or hepatitis B or C carriers. Screening is often inadequate or non-existent.

You should therefore avoid a 'blind' blood transfusion in a developing country except in a life-threatening emergency. The purpose of the HIV and hepatitis B protection kit is to enable one litre of intravenous fluid to be administered, either to avoid the need for blood altogether or to buy time until safe blood is available (see page 168). Until recently, fluids known as plasma expanders were the preferred choice (e.g. Haemacell or Gelofusine), but recent evidence suggests that simple intravenous fluids such as Hartmann's solution are a better choice, used early before veins have collapsed from too much blood loss. Normally we can survive blood loss of about 20 per cent before needing fluid replacement.

The HIV and hepatitis B protection kit can only be used by someone familiar with putting up an intravenous line, such as a medical travelling companion or sometimes by a trained onlooker at any accident. This does mean there is a possibility that the kit cannot be used at the time you need it. Any colleagues travelling with you should know that a kit is available. Many experts still consider it is better to have one with you, in case it can be used, than not to have one at all. The worst scenario is to be in an accident, need your kit, have a trained health worker on site but to have left your kit in the cupboard at home.

General recommendations for first-aid kits

- For short low-risk trips buy a simple first-aid kit or make up your own.
- If going to live abroad, taking up an assignment or planning adventurous travel, obtain a more comprehensive kit, including needles and syringes, an intravenous giving set, a needle and suture kit and a wider range of dressings.
- If planning to travel extensively by road and light aircraft where HIV or hepatitis B are prevalent, consider taking one litre of intravenous fluid as part of an HIV and hepatitis B protection kit.

Medicine kits

Although many countries sell a huge range of medicines, good-quality essential supplies may be harder to obtain. In some countries many medicines are substandard, fake or expired. Here are some options to consider if you are planning to travel in a developing country.

- A medicine kit you can put together yourself. For simple destinations and short trips you can obtain a collection of the medicines you are most likely to need – for example, painkillers, antihistamines, travel sickness pills and antiseptic cream.
- A medicine kit containing a wider range of medicines, some of which will need a prescription in the UK and some other countries. A range of these kits is available from suppliers in developed countries and is often the best option.
- A diarrhoea treatment kit, used by an increasing number of travellers. This usually contains the extremely useful antibiotic ciprofloxacin (or an equivalent such as azithromycin), in addition to oral rehydration salts and loperamide (Imodium).
- A standby malaria treatment kit, in case you cannot reliably get good medical advice and reliable malaria treatment within eight hours of coming down with a fever in a malarious area. (See below and pages 129–33.)

- An emergency dental kit. Consider taking one of these if you are living for any length of time in remote areas where dentists are few and far between, or where there is a high level of HIV infection (see page 152).

In all cases you will need to follow guidelines carefully when buying these kits and only obtain them from ethical suppliers that follow established protocols. Also carry a doctor's letter and list of contents in case either foreign customs or, on return, your own customs raise any questions. A similar doctor's letter, as described on page 14, must be included with the medicines.

General recommendations for personal medicines and medicine kits

Consider taking a medicine kit if you will be travelling in remote areas, living in a country where good-quality supplies are not easily available or living at a distance from good health facilities. Medicine kits are also useful for families or those travelling in groups, teams or expeditions, when contents can be shared.

Avoiding mosquitoes and preventing malaria

Malaria tablets

Although this section starts with the tablets you need to take, remember that preventing yourself from being bitten is just as important.

There are two types of tablet which people frequently confuse. First, there are malaria prevention tablets, also known as antimalarials or as malaria (chemo) prophylaxis. You can read more about them on pages 125–8. Second, there are tablets to treat malaria, which are sometimes supplied in malaria standby treatment kits.

If you are travelling to a malarious part of the world *it is essential to take antimalarials*. Usually it is easier to take these from the UK or from your home country rather than buying them abroad, though good-quality antimalarials are becoming available in an increasing number of countries.

In most malarious areas you should also take a standby treatment kit. This is necessary if you are going to be in the area for more than one week and you may at any time be more than eight hours from good-quality health care or a reliable supply of an effective medicine to treat malaria. These kits are especially useful for sub-Saharan Africa. Remember that malaria can occur any time from seven days after being bitten by an infected mosquito. Some antimalarials (e.g. chloroquine and proguanil (Paludrine)) are available without a prescription from chemists in the UK, but these are only effective in a very few countries. In the UK all other antimalarials have to be prescribed by your GP (there is usually a charge) or obtained from travel clinics – see Appendixes E and G. All anti-malarials and malaria treatment tablets are available from InterHealth.

In many countries a variety of antimalarials can be bought direct from pharmacists, but make sure you obtain the correct antimalarials, as described here, which are based on current international advice.

Remember: no antimalarial gives you full protection, so avoiding bites is also essential. If you are going to an area where malaria is common, you may still get malaria even if you take your tablets regularly, though it is less likely to be so severe. It is really important that you take your recommended antimalarials according to the instructions you are given, that you do not miss any doses and that you continue taking them for the full length of time recommended.

Mosquito nets

If you are travelling to a malarious area, it's important that you use a mosquito net even if there don't seem to be many mosquitoes round. Just a single bite is enough to cause malaria, especially in parts of Africa where so many of the mosquitoes carry malaria. Sleeping under a net will stop the mozzies biting you as you sleep at night and are most vulnerable. It will also keep out bed-bugs and other creepy crawlies, so you can sleep without the fear of what might crawl (or drop) on to you during the night. And as well as protecting you from malaria, sleeping under a mosquito net will also help protect you from a number of other insect-borne diseases.

Find out whether there will be a mosquito net at your destination, or whether you need to take your own. If there is a net that you can use, check that there are no holes in it. Also make sure it has been impregnated with an appropriate insecticide such as permethrin or deltamethrin; if not, obtain permethrin and soak it yourself according to instructions. Permethrin is an insecticide that kills mosquitoes and other insects. Sleeping under a net that has been treated with permethrin greatly increases your protection from malaria compared to using an untreated net. The net also acts as a mosquito killer, so reducing the number of insects in the room.

Most mosquito nets available in the UK have been treated with a formulation of permethrin that will last for about six months but gradually loses its effectiveness, especially when the net is put up and taken down frequently or when it is washed. Newer formulations are becoming available which last longer, and in parts of Africa under the Roll Back Malaria programme Long Lasting Impregnated Nets (LLINs) are available.

Permethrin is lethal to invertebrates, so when treating your net be careful not to let any solution run into rivers, lakes or ponds.

If there is unlikely to be a mosquito net present or easily available at your destination you should buy your own before leaving. There are many different types of nets on the market in a variety of shapes and sizes. Some nets can be converted to different shapes, making them suitable for a range of different environments. To decide which type of net is best for you, think about whether you are staying in the same place for a substantial length of time or will be moving around frequently.

Things to consider when choosing a mosquito net:

Shape

- *Box nets* are suspended at four corners and are the standard net used in many homes, guest houses and hotels. They are ideal if you are staying in one place for a substantial length of time, because they provide the greatest internal living space, meaning that you are less likely to brush against the edge of the net as you sleep. They are available in single and double sizes and can often be adapted to form other shapes if you are moving around from place to place.
- *Wedge nets* hang from two points above your head (they can also be hung from one point as a pyramid) and tend to pack down smaller than a box net, making them easy to carry and suspend if you are travelling around a lot. However, they can be a bit claustrophobic.
- *Bell nets* suspend from a single point and use a spider frame or built-in sprung hoop to form a bell shape. As they only require one hanging point, they are very easy to suspend and are flexible for use at home and when travelling. They are available in single, double or cot sizes.
- *Freestanding nets* are convenient if you want to sleep outside, as many contain a built-in groundsheet and, as the name suggests, they are freestanding so do not require hanging. There are some kinds that are designed for indoor use over a bed.

Mesh size, strength and material

Mesh size is generally measured in holes per square inch, and the current WHO minimum is 156 holes/inch^2 (or 25 holes/cm^2). All manufacturers must meet or exceed these guidelines. A mesh size of 156 holes/inch^2 will keep mosquitoes out but does not guarantee protection against sandflies (however, treating the net with the insecticide permethrin gives added protection).

Nets come in various strengths, but manufacturers do not always advertise the strength (or denier). Generally speaking, the finer the mesh size, the stronger the material. Also, hexagonal mesh is stronger than square mesh.

In terms of material, most nets are made from synthetic fibres, which are more durable than cotton. Most UK-manufactured nets are made of polyester. Cotton nets are often available overseas and can still be soaked with permethrin, but tend to rot in humid conditions.

A final tip: many mosquito nets come with a hanging kit, which includes hooks and some cord, but it is useful to take some extra string.

Insect repellents

Insect repellents act by masking the body scents, carbon dioxide and lactic acid to which mosquitoes are attracted from as far away as 30 metres. Repellents produce a vapour that repels mosquitoes and thus stops them landing on your skin and biting you. Repellents come in various forms (e.g. sprays, creams, roll-ons) to suit your personal preference.

The most effective insect repellents on the market are those that contain DEET (diethyl-toluamide). DEET has been available for over 40 years and has a remarkable safety profile.

A small number of severe reactions associated with DEET have occurred, but these have been mainly associated with misuse or overuse of repellents (including ingestion). DEET is considered safe for use in adults, pregnant women, and children over two months of age. Current evidence suggests that there is no need to use a reduced concentration DEET in children over two months, and that they can safely use a 50 per cent concentration. DEET very occasionally causes an allergic reaction and it is not recommended for use in babies under two months of age, nor in those with serious skin complaints. In the rare case of DEET causing an allergic reaction (e.g. itching, swelling or blistering), stop using it immediately and take an antihistamine. If you tend to have sensitive skin, test DEET on a small patch of skin and leave for a few hours before using it more widely. Care should be taken when applying DEET to young children and it should not be applied to children's hands.

DEET repellents are available in various concentrations. Research has shown that the higher the concentration of DEET, the longer lasting the level of protection. However, as repellents wear off as you sweat, the effect of increased concentrations seems to level off above 50 per cent concentration. Therefore, we recommend that you apply a concentration of 50 per cent DEET to all exposed skin (except the lips and eyelids). A new type of repellent (Expedition PLUS) combines 50 per cent DEET with natural pyrethroid insecticidal oils to stop insects that land on your skin from biting.

There is some evidence that DEET can reduce the protection offered by sunscreen products by 33–50 per cent if applied to the same area. We therefore recommend that you use a higher factor sunscreen and reapply it more frequently to prevent sunburn. Apply sunscreen first and allow a few minutes for it to be absorbed into the skin before applying DEET.

For those who are unable to use DEET-based insect repellents (i.e. children under two months of age or anyone with serious skin complaints), the next most effective repellents are those which contain extract of lemon eucalyptus (e.g. Mosiguard). This is the most effective of the natural insect repellents that are available. However, it does not give as much protection as DEET and should be reapplied more frequently.

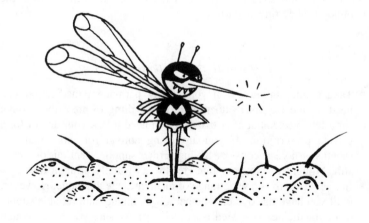

Anti-mosquito clothes spray

You can spray clothes with permethrin, using Nomad's Bug Proof Clothing Treatment, which acts as a contact killer if a mosquito does land on your clothes and tries to bite through. One treatment lasts about two weeks, but in the UK it is not licensed for use on children's clothing. Alternatively 90–100 per cent DEET can be used on clothing, but take care as DEET can damage synthetic fabrics and plastic. Use DEET-soaked clothing with caution in children and do not use with babies.

DEET repels mosquitoes but does not kill them; permethrin kills but does not necessarily repel them.

Wrist and ankle bands

Mosquitoes particularly like the wrists, ankles and feet so make sure that these parts are well covered with DEET (or, better still, with clothing). You may also want to consider using repellent wrist and ankle bands, which are either pre-treated or can be sprayed with DEET before use. These are useful if you are out on safari or having a romantic evening outside – but they do *not* offer full protection.

Mosquito coils, electric plug-ins and knockdown sprays

Using a quick-acting knockdown insecticide (e.g. allethrin) repels and kills insects that are around.

Mosquito coils should only be used outdoors or in well-ventilated rooms. If you have a reliable electricity supply you can use an electric mosquito killer, which releases an insecticide vapour overnight. There is in fact little evidence that either coils or plug-ins reduce the likelihood of getting malaria.

Personal medical supplies

- Take ample supplies with you of any permanent medication you need. In the UK, NHS doctors *may* be willing to prescribe enough for a few weeks, but after that you will need to ask your doctor for a private prescription. If you are going abroad for more than six months or a year, consider having further supplies sent out or, better still, brought out to you. InterHealth can usually arrange this.
- In many countries a wide range of medicines are available. However, until you have discovered whether a high-quality and reliable supply of the medicines you need is available, make sure you have enough supplies with you.
- Remember that all medicines have both a trade name (usually in bold

22

print), which varies from place to place, and a generic name (usually in small print), which is the worldwide scientific name. You should get used to recognizing and using the generic name. Take the packaging with you of any medicine you need, as this may make it easier to identify an equivalent overseas.

- In the case of asthma medication or other supplies you may need in an emergency, keep one set of supplies with you at all times and another in a different part of your luggage or storage place in your house, in case of loss or theft. The same goes for adrenalin (epinephrine, EpiPen) to use in case of a serious allergic reaction. EpiPen in addition has a short expiry date, so check it regularly.
- It is better to take medicines as blister packs or in bottles well packed with cotton wool, to prevent transit damage, especially when backpacking. Make sure the tops of ointment tubes are firmly done up, especially at high altitude. Having arrived at your destination, keep your supplies in a cool place, out of direct sunlight and away from the reach of rats, ants – and children.
- If you use contact lenses, take plenty of cleansing fluid as well as a pair of glasses.
- If you are a diabetic take all the supplies you may need with you (see pages 38–40).
- Women should take a supply of tampons unless your enquiries confirm that reliable and acceptable supplies are available where you are going.
- A note on expiry dates. Many medicines have a use-by date two to four years from the date of manufacture. This means some items in your medical kit are likely to pass their expiry date if your assignment is long term. Check the dates at the time of purchase.

Always carry a note of all the medication you are taking – the generic name, the dose and how often you take it. Your doctor should sign this, and your next of kin should have a note of this at home. You should keep it in a safe place along with your medical records.

Contraceptives and their uses

Because you usually need to take supplies with you it is worth deciding well ahead about what sort of contraception you may be needing. If you are using the pill for the first time, try to take two or three cycles before you go abroad to make sure it suits you.

If there is any chance at all you may need condoms, take a supply with you. If buying condoms in the UK use only the kite-marked brands. It is usually better not to rely on local supplies. Keep condoms in a cool place, away from the light, and check the expiry date. Latex perishes in hot climates. For more details see pages 157–8.

If you are planning to live abroad it is worth considering other forms of contraception, such as an injectable contraceptive or an intra-uterine device (IUD/IUCD) or Mirena. Talk this over with your family planning clinic or doctor, several months before you leave.

Suggestions for those taking the pill when travelling

- *Ample supplies* Take plenty with you unless you know the pill of your choice is available overseas. There are many brand names for each pill, so keep a packet cover with you with both the brand name and the exact formulation written on it. Split your supply between different parts of your baggage in case of theft. In the UK your GP may be willing to prescribe enough for up to three months, your family planning clinic possibly for longer. Otherwise you can obtain a private prescription from your doctor or from some travel clinics. Contraceptives are usually available over the counter in developing countries. Make sure all your supplies expire after the latest date you might need them.

- *Time zones* When crossing these make sure you take a pill at least every 24 hours, preferably at the same time, until you gradually adjust to your new timetable. During this adjustment the time between pills can be less than 24 hours but should ideally not be longer, though some advisers extend this to 27 hours (not for the minipill or progesterone-only pill). Check the Patient Information Leaflet in the supplies you have.

- *Forgetting a pill* Check the instructions in your packet, which will explain exactly what to do if you forget a pill or are late taking it – both easy to do when you are travelling.

- *Diarrhoea, stomach upsets and courses of antibiotics* Take the pill as usual, and avoid having sex or in addition use a barrier method during these risk periods and for seven days afterwards, or according to the specific instructions with your pill. Antibiotics, in particular ampicillin and tetracyclines, can reduce absorption of the pill. (There are more details about the pill and the antimalarial doxycycline on pages 142–3, which are complex and need reading thoroughly.)

- *Vomiting* If this occurs within three hours of taking a pill, take another. If vomiting then continues, use additional protection and follow the seven-day rule, as above: again also check the manufacturer's instructions.

- *Avoiding periods when travelling* You can do this for at least two or three cycles by taking the (fixed dose) pill continuously. If you plan to do this, remember to take extra packs with you. It may be possible for you to use this method even if you do not take the pill for contraception – discuss with your doctor well before leaving. If you are not taking the pill you can delay your period by taking norethisterone 5 mg, one tablet three times daily, starting three days before your expected period. Periods usually start two or three days after stopping. Of course, you can get side-effects from this, and in the UK it has to be prescribed by a doctor.

- *Types of pill* A fixed combination oestrogen-progestogen pill is probably the most appropriate. This is usually known as the combined contraceptive pill. The progestogen-only pill is less appropriate for travel and gives less good protection, especially when crossing time zones or with stomach upsets. Biphasic and triphasic pills with dose formulations that vary with the time of the month are less flexible for travelling.
- *Hepatitis* If you go down with this it is best to avoid the pill for six months.
- *Hot climates* Pills should remain effective provided your pack is within the expiry date, it remains intact and you keep it in as cool a place as possible.
- *Emergency contraception* If there is a serious chance you may have become pregnant against your wishes, you can take oral contraceptive pills within the first 12 hours, the sooner the better and not later than 72 hours. There are four ways of doing this:
  - The standard method is to take two pills, 12 hours apart, each containing 0.75 mg of levonorgestrel. This combination, Levonelle-2, is available in the UK.
  - The Yuzpe method is to take two doses of a preparation, 12 hours apart, each containing ethinyloestradiol 100 micrograms and levonorgestrel 0.5 mg. This is equivalent to taking two Ovran contraceptive pills, and a further two after 12 hours.
  - A third alternative is simply to take two combined fixed-dose contraceptive pills of whichever brand you use, followed by two more 12 hours later. This is *not* an ideal solution.
  - A fourth alternative is to have a copper-containing IUD (intra-uterine device) inserted within 120 hours (five days) under sterile conditions by an experienced health worker. Some women will have religious or moral objections to this method.

It is important to realize that occasional side-effects, sometimes serious, can occur. Report any lower abdominal pain immediately None of these regimes fully guarantee pregnancy will be prevented. If your periods do not rapidly return to normal, get medical advice and remember to use a barrier method of contraception until your next period, unless you have an IUD fitted.

Other health supplies

Most regular travellers keep a list in their head or in their top drawer. If you don't, start making one now:

- *A hat* This is an essential item if you will be regularly out in the sun as part of your job or when on holiday.
- *Sun cream* Buy cream with a sun protection factor (SPF) of at least 15 if you do not burn easily or factor 24 or more if you do. Also use a high SPF if you are using the antimalarial doxycycline, or need sun cream for children. In addition, consider taking a sun-protecting lipsalve.
- *Sunglasses* In sunny climates and high altitude these help to prevent cataracts forming in the lenses of the eye. If trekking, skiing or mountaineering above the snow line, wear goggles or sunglasses with side panels or of 'wrap-around' design.
- *Water filters or purifiers* If you will be living abroad in an area where boiling is not an easy option (e.g. fuel supplies are in short supply), consider buying a domestic water filter unless good brands are available locally. If you will be travelling extensively, decide whether to buy a portable water purifier for the road (see pages 93–4).
- *Water sterilizing tablets* Iodine (the most effective) or chlorine tablets are always worth taking with you.
- *A rehydration measuring spoon* so you can make up your own salt–sugar solution when traveller's diarrhoea finally opens the flood gates.
- *A water bottle*, such as a Platypus.
- *A thermometer*, either a mercury one – accurate but breakable – or Zeal disposables, easy to use and unbreakable. Thermometers are very useful to confirm whether you or your travelling companion actually have a fever – vital to know, for example, in suspected malaria or meningitis.
- *Appropriate clothing* to stop you from getting too hot, cold or wet and that will not offend the local population.
- *Gloves* Ideally, take a packet of latex gloves unless allergic. They have many uses including giving hands-on care for people living with HIV.
- *Special rubber-soled shoes* to avoid electrocution in the shower and to protect your feet, e.g. when walking on the beach. Merrell is a well-known supplier.

- A *torch* to avoid hazards in the dark such as snakes, or for village latrines. Head torches such as Petzl lamps are especially useful.
- A *travel adaptor* so that vital pieces of equipment aren't left lying useless on the chair.
- A *money belt*.
- A *MedicAlert bracelet or pendant* if you have any severe allergies or serious conditions that others need to know about (see pages 29–31).
- A *wide-mouth vacuum flask* either to store vaccines or to keep food and water cold.
- A *skipping rope* or other method for keeping fit if going to an area where regular forms of exercise are not possible.
- Don't forget to take this book with you!

See Appendices B, C and D for more details on the contents of kits and supplies.

3

Travellers with specific health risks

The basic questions

More and more people are travelling today who even a few years ago might have been advised by their doctor, friends or relatives against exchanging suburbia for the Sahara.

If you are concerned about a health problem and whether it might affect your overseas travel, seek medical advice before dreaming of an exotic holiday or planning any job, posting or assignment.

If you are going abroad as an employee or volunteer, the organization will need to know that you are likely to be fit enough for the travel you will be doing and the occupation you will be carrying out.

Obviously if you are travelling independently or simply for leisure, you will want to be confident you are well enough to travel. Also when it comes to travel insurance, the company may either refuse to insure you for any health problem that arises from a pre-existing condition, or, more likely, add an extra premium (see pages 69–70).

There are three main sources of medical advice you can tap into: first, your own GP or family doctor; second, your specialist if you are attending a hospital clinic or have recently done so; third, a travel medicine specialist or occupational health physician with experience in travellers' health.

You will need answers to the following questions.

- Should I go at all?
- What extra precautions should I take?
- Are my plans, itinerary and activities safe and appropriate?
- What medicines should I take with me?
- Will I have enough medicines for the trip, and if not, how will I obtain further supplies, at my destination or sent from home?
- Will any routine medical care or follow-up tests be available at my destination?
- Will there be adequate emergency care at my destination if my condition suddenly worsens?

The information given below on different medical conditions does not replace the specific advice you should obtain from one of the sources mentioned above. This list covers many of the commonest and most important conditions but is not fully comprehensive.

Allergies and anaphylactic reactions

What is anaphylaxis?

Anaphylaxis is the name given to a severe allergic reaction, which affects your whole body. It typically involves an itchy rash, swelling of the lips and tongue, and breathing difficulties. Anaphylaxis is life-threatening and so you need to take immediate action. Fortunately it is rare in travellers, but the secret is to be well prepared and well informed so if it occurs you know what to do. This will involve two things: using your adrenalin self-injection kit, and then seeking medical help as soon as you can.

Many allergies are becoming more common. In the UK peanut allergy now affects one in 70 children. The most common causes of anaphylaxis are insect stings, medication especially penicillin, latex, peanuts and tree nuts (e.g. walnuts, hazelnuts, almonds, cashews, pecans and pistachios), sesame seeds, fresh fruit, shellfish and fish, milk, eggs and wheat. In practice, insect stings and nut allergies are the most important for travellers.

What guidelines should I follow?

If you have had a severe allergic reaction follow these guidelines:

1 Arrange through your doctor to see a specialist, if you have not already done this, well ahead of your overseas travel, ideally several months.

2 Before travelling, check out the likelihood of being re-exposed to whatever it is that causes your allergy. For example, it is hard to avoid traces of nuts while eating local food in much of sub-Saharan Africa and Asia. Food will often not be labelled. In discussion with your specialist consider whether your travel plans are safe and, if not, consider changing them. Being near to a good health facility is one important factor.

3 Ask your GP or allergy specialist for a prescription for an adrenalin (epinephrine) self-injection kit, e.g. EpiPen. Take two self-injection kits with you, kept in different parts of your luggage, but with one always with you for immediate use. Check with the doctor that you do not have any contra-indications for using it and that it will not interact with any other drug you are taking. Be sure to read carefully the Patient Information Leaflet which comes with the syringes so that you are clear about how to give yourself the injection. Also be prepared for the feeling of anxiety or your heart racing which are normal side-effects of the medication. The doctor

29

might also prescribe other stand-by emergency drugs such as an antihistamine, e.g. chlorphenamine (Piriton).

4 Make sure you have your specific allergies clearly written in your vaccination booklet or other official document which you carry with you at all times.

5 Ask your doctor for a letter explaining that the medication you are carrying is for your own personal use in the event of an allergic reaction. The letter should be on headed notepaper and be stamped with the doctor's name, address, qualifications and date.

6 Wear a MedicAlert bracelet or pendant (website: <http://www.medicalert.org.uk>).

7 If you have a food allergy, contact the airline you are travelling with, to pre-order meals according to your requirements. If you have any doubts take your own food to eat on the flight(s).

8 Make sure you carry your emergency drugs on board in case you have a severe reaction during the flight(s). You may need to explain why you have these when checking in your hand luggage. Always have a doctor's letter in case you are asked for it.

9 If you are travelling as an employee or volunteer, inform your team leader or manager (and any other key people who are taking responsibility for you, e.g. local host or placement supervisor) of your allergy so that you have an action plan just in case it occurs.

10 Find out as early as possible details of the best medical facility to use in the areas where you will be travelling. Your local host, coordinator or some other expatriate is the most likely to know.

11 Make sure you have your emergency drugs on your person at all times.

12 Make sure your travel insurance includes this pre-existing condition.

13 Invest time in learning some useful phrases in the local language (or writing them down), e.g. 'I am allergic to . . . ', 'I would like to eat . . . '

14 If you are allergic to bee, wasp or other insect stings, consider the following advice:
   (a) Avoid the use of perfumes or hygiene products that include perfumes, particularly floral scents, as these attract pollinating insects.
   (b) Also avoid brightly coloured clothing, which attracts bees and other pollinating insects.
   (c) Avoid locations of known hives or nests, and avoid using equipment that disturbs the hive.

(d) Wear effective insect repellent.

How do I treat a severe reaction?

1 The first signs are usually large raised itchy patches on your skin, swelling of the lips or tongue, wheezing and vomiting. These symptoms may occur very suddenly or come on gradually.

2 At the first sign of a reaction, inject adrenalin with your EpiPen, then go immediately to the nearest good health facility. The injection is mainly to buy you time.

3 Remain under medical care for up to 24 hours, as commonly symptoms recur and you may need further treatment with adrenalin or an antihistamine.

Note on less severe reactions

If your previous reactions have only caused itchy patches on your skin and there has been no swelling of your lips and tongue, no wheezing and no vomiting, you will not usually need to use adrenalin. You should, however, take a supply of antihistamines (chlorphenamine (Piriton) is usually considered the most effective), and have these with you at all times. Take one at the first sign of any reaction, repeating within one or two hours if necessary, or doubling the dose if you are heavy or strongly built. Remember, the tablets may make you feel drowsy so you should not drive or operate machinery within a few hours of taking them.

If you are in doubt about how severe your allergy is, talk to your doctor.

Anxiety and depression

Most of us will have some experience of these feelings and usually we will have learnt how to deal with them. However, when we travel the additional stress can sometimes make symptoms worse or bring out underlying feelings or problems we have been struggling with.

Feelings of anxiety and depression often go together, so this section is about both.

What are the symptoms?

These will be quite familiar. As well as having a low mood or feeling tensed up we may lose sleep, have a change in our appetite and find it harder to relax, concentrate or work. Life may be less enjoyable and we may lose our sense of humour. Our sex drive may become less, or occasionally more. Sometimes too we may have physical symptoms such as palpitations, sweating, muscle tension and pains, breathing problems, dizziness, faintness, indigestion and diarrhoea. In order to avoid such unpleasant symptoms people tend to steer clear of situations which may trigger them, meaning their activities can become somewhat restricted. This may be harder to do when overseas or working in a team.

How are symptoms graded?

Symptoms of anxiety and depression are classified as mild, moderate or severe, depending on the extent to which they interfere with the normal way we function. Mild symptoms are commonly linked to a stressful life event and resolve with little, if any, treatment; moderate symptoms may respond to psychological help alone; severe symptoms usually require medication and sometimes hospital admission as well.

What can trigger these symptoms?

Anyone, whatever their age, gender or background, can be affected by anxiety or depression. There are some factors which make us more vulnerable to developing these disorders, including our genes, family background and childhood experiences. So can chronic physical ill health and the misuse of alcohol or drugs, including marihuana.

A specific event may trigger an episode of anxiety or depression. If we have experienced these symptoms before, especially recently or severely, they may come back without any obvious cause or be brought on by something we would usually be able to deal with. In general, the longer we have gone since we had any significant problems, the more likely it is we will be able to cope.

How can we deal with depression and anxiety?

There are various ways of dealing with these things, and there are sections on pages 173–80 and 350–3 which give ideas of how we can help to prevent and manage them overseas.

Before going, there are some things we can do. An approach known as Cognitive Behaviour Therapy (CBT) works well for many people with mild to moderate conditions and can give skills in dealing with problems which might otherwise be a bit beyond us. Unfortunately it is not always easy to get access to CBT, but there are several self-help resources that use this approach. Information can be obtained from the Oxford Cognitive Therapy Centre at <http://www.octc.co.uk>.

Counselling can also be helpful in understanding how the condition came about and addressing some of the factors that may have contributed. Sometimes psychotherapy can help if there are more major issues needing to be dealt with from the past, but it is better not to start this if you are feeling depressed.

Sometimes medication can be very helpful. For anxiety, tablets called benzodiazepines, e.g. diazepam, are good at relieving symptoms but should only be used for a short time. Antidepressants are the drugs most commonly used for both anxiety and depression and of these the group known as SSRIs, e.g. fluoxetine or paroxetine, are the most commonly used. There are many people working overseas (and at home) who have found that these enable them to carry on with their normal activities. Current guidelines recommend that these drugs should be continued for a period of four to six months after recovery, both to reduce the risk of illness returning and because additional symptoms can occur when we start reducing the dose. Paroxetine should not normally be used in those under 18 years of age. Staying on antidepressants may be helpful in some cases to keep anxiety under control or to prevent recurrent depression.

When depression is part of a recurring condition such as Bipolar Disorder (swinging from being very elated to quite depressed), drugs known as mood stabilizers are often helpful, e.g. lithium, carbamaze-pine and valproate. With some of these drugs regular monitoring by blood tests is needed; this can often be arranged in main cities abroad. Again, these drugs can enable many people to continue working in overseas situations.

Going abroad

A history of anxiety or depression doesn't stop you from being able to undertake travel or work abroad, but you will need to think carefully about whether or not it is wise to go on certain projects or for long periods of time. Jobs can be demanding and require long working hours, and many team projects, though exciting, can be stressful and may trigger a recurrence of symptoms or make existing symptoms worse. Often it is harder to get help if a problem does recur.

If you have recently been severely depressed or anxious and have suffered from a psychosis, or felt suicidal, it is worth having a period of at least two years before going on an overseas assignment. Discuss this with your doctor or specialist.

If you are on medication, don't stop this just before going abroad. This is for two reasons: first, because of symptoms which often occur when reducing the dose, and second, because of the risk of relapse. You and your medical adviser will need to make a decision about this well before the proposed trip, so as to establish whether you should gradually come off the drugs before you go, or to decide how to obtain supplies if you continue to take them. In some countries antidepressants can be bought over the counter. If this isn't the case, it is usually possible to get them sent out from home.

It's important that you 'know yourself', come to recognize the warning signs and take appropriate action – whatever works best for you and eases tension. If you are going on an assignment or a gap-year programme, it is a good idea for your team leader or programme director to know about the problem: that takes the pressure off everyone, including you, and means you can get quicker support if problems do arise.

Finally, it is essential you do not use the antimalarial mefloquine (Lariam), which can make symptoms worse.

Asthma and breathing problems

Is my asthma likely to get worse?

Asthma is often better overseas, but this is not always the case. For example, if you are staying in large cities such as Cairo, Lagos, La Paz, Mumbai, Kathmandu or Mexico City where pollution levels are high, your symptoms may get worse. Sometimes dust associated with dry climates, the pollens of certain plants or crops, or moulds associated with monsoon rains can trigger an attack.

If one or more of the following applies to you, follow the guidelines listed below.

- You are on inhaled steroids on a regular basis, e.g. Becotide, Pulmicort, Flixotide or Seretide.
- You require your bronchodilator, e.g. salbutamol (Ventolin), terbutaline (Bricanyl), at least once per day.
- You have been admitted to hospital for asthma over the last five years.
- You have needed a nebulizer or spacer device (e.g. Volumatic, Aerochamber) over the last five years.
- You have been prescribed a course of oral steroids over the last five years.

What guidelines should I follow?

1 Discuss a self-treatment plan with your asthma specialist. This is especially important, as you may not have access to reliable health care when abroad. Your plan should include:
   (a) assessing the likely risks from pollution, different climate and other variables;
   (b) agreeing how to assess your asthma, usually by using a peak flow meter;
   (c) setting appropriate thresholds for increasing your treatment, e.g. deciding what symptoms or peak flow reading would cause you to double your inhaler dose.

2 Take adequate supplies of all your medications (including spacer devices and stand-by courses of steroids and/or antibiotics if you have needed them over the last three years) to cover *the whole duration* of your stay overseas, unless this is longer than six months or you know they are available where you are going. Keep one set of supplies with you at all times.

3 Check immunizations. You should normally be covered for both flu and pneumococcus, in addition to immunizations required for your journey. Discuss this with your doctor.

4 Obtain a doctor's letter explaining that all the medication you are carrying is for your own personal use as an asthmatic. This should be on headed notepaper and signed, dated and stamped by your doctor.

5 Divide your asthma supplies between your hand luggage and the rest of your luggage in the hold to guard against the unlikely event of lost luggage. If your supplies are stolen or you start running out, try to obtain supplies from the best locally available pharmacy, or email home.

6 If travelling as an employee or volunteer, inform your team leader of your condition (and any other key people who are taking responsibility for you, e.g. local host or placement supervisor) in case you have a severe attack and require emergency treatment.

7 As soon as possible after arrival, identify the most appropriate local health facility. The most likely people to know are your team leader, employer, local host and expatriates.

8 Be aware of the effects of altitude. As a rule, people with well-controlled asthma cope well at altitude. However, dry air, cold, dust or exertion may trigger an attack. Take extra care if you have a respiratory infection, and start antibiotics early. Consider travelling by land rather than flying direct into a high-altitude airport, e.g. La Paz, or fly into a lower airport and acclimatize for a day first. Altitude sickness itself (see pages 188–93) is no commoner in those with asthma than in anyone else.

9 Be aware of the effects of pollution. This is also variable. High levels of particles in the air, sulphur dioxide or ozone can worsen asthma. Monitor symptoms carefully. In some cases you may need to plan your day so as to avoid the higher pollution levels, which build up during the day. For example, you could exercise indoors and arrange visits for the mornings only. Make use of local weather information, which may include a daily pollution indicator. The exact location of where you live can be important, as levels of pollution vary. If there is an industrial area to the city, try and live up-wind of the prevailing wind direction.

10 You won't usually need a nebulizer as large-volume spacing devices, e.g. Volumatic, usually work as well. Discuss this with your asthma specialist if you have needed to use either in the past five years. Nebulizers can be adapted to work on car batteries or mains. Dry powder inhalers sometimes get clogged in humid climates but this is unlikely with closed systems such as Turbohaler. If using a spacer device, follow instructions carefully to keep it clean and functioning.

11 Make sure that your health insurance covers any pre-existing conditions, including asthma.

Chronic Obstructive Pulmonary Disease (COPD)

Many of the guidelines for asthma also apply for COPD. You will need to plan your trip with special caution. If you need oxygen, this can usually be arranged in discussion with your specialist and with the airline. Rest times, good-quality hotels, having access to good health care and taking all the supplies you need will be especially important.

Backache

Background

As we all know, backache has a large number of causes, so if you have any significant problems see your doctor before planning your trip. In practice, travel puts the back at greater strain. There are several reasons for this: standing in queues, carrying luggage, being in a hurry, and travelling in a variety of vehicles, trains and planes, some with uncomfortable seats. Travelling with young children who need to be lifted or restrained can be an additional risk. Often, but not always, pre-existing back problems can become worse when travelling. Try to imagine how your back will stand up to bumping along rough roads in a 4×4 or visiting an offshore island in a small boat on a rough sea.

Some people have back problems that are largely predictable, i.e. they know that certain activities or movements are likely to cause pain. Others have unpredictable backs which suddenly 'go' at the most unexpected times, such as when turning, bending over or cleaning teeth. Those in this latter group need to take special care when travelling.

What can I do to prevent it?

Follow strictly the advice you have been given or which you know is effective for your particular problem. This will always include good posture, sitting up straight, avoiding sagging chairs, sleeping on a firm mattress, lifting with a straight back and taking care to avoid any situation or movement which makes your problem worse.

If your back suddenly goes or worsens before travel, see a doctor. The best way of treating backache is to move and walk slowly and carefully (known as gentle mobilization), rather than going to bed, unless the pain is excruciating. Severe pain can be treated by using a painkiller such as co-codamol up to eight per day, along with a muscle relaxant such as diazepam 5–10 mg, especially useful at night. Anti-inflammatory drugs such as ibuprofen 400 mg three times daily can help the pain. Diclofenac (Voltarol) up to 100 mg three times daily is another option, providing you have no stomach pain or indigestion.

When should I see my doctor?

If you have had any of these symptoms in the past year, see your doctor for advice before you travel:

- severe back pain which has 'locked' your back, making it almost impossible to move;
- persistent pain or numbness down one or both legs (sciatica);
- weakness in either leg or unsteadiness when you walk;
- difficulty passing or controlling urine;
- numbness around your back passage or genitals.

In addition, see your doctor if you have had recurrent back pain over several years, which has been enough to significantly restrict your normal activities or which has caused you to lose time from work.

If any of these apply to you, it is worth discussing the possibility of seeing a specialist or having an MRI scan, especially if you are going abroad for a significant length of time or are planning remote or adventurous travel.

Severe back pain is one of the commonest causes of having to return early from an assignment or being medically evacuated (medivacced) home.

Diabetes

Many diabetics manage to travel with little difficulty provided they are well controlled, well advised and well supplied. However, if you use insulin you would need to be in reach of good medical facilities and in the company of someone who is well informed about diabetes and how to manage it. Some of you reading this may be seasoned travellers, who are used to managing your diabetes in different parts of the world, but it may still be worth reading this section through.

What guidelines should I follow?

If you are planning to travel overseas take note of the following, especially if you are on insulin.

Before leaving

1 Make an appointment with your GP, hospital consultant or diabetic nurse to review your diabetes and to discuss your self-treatment plan in the light of your overseas trip. Agree together your schedule for monitoring your diabetes and set strategies for changing your insulin dosage. You will need to take the following into consideration:
   (a) Change of climate.
   (b) Change of food and drink:
       (i)   What different drinks will be available?
       (ii) What is the staple food?
       (iii) When do people eat their regular meals?
       (iv) What will you do when you are invited to someone's home for a meal?
   (c) Change of routine and activity levels:
       (i) Will you take more or less exercise?
       (ii) What about field trips into remote rural areas?
   (d) Change of time:
       (i) How will you manage your diabetes during a long-haul flight, especially when you cross time zones?
       (ii) What food will you eat during the flight?
   (e) Change in your exposure to infection – in general you will be more likely to get a gastrointestinal upset while overseas and may be exposed to unfamiliar tropical infections, e.g. malaria.
2 Check before travelling that there are good local health facilities

in the event of an emergency. If you are going abroad as an employee or volunteer, discuss this with your team leader or manager. Once you arrive, visit the local health facility to confirm arrangements.

3 Take adequate supplies of insulin with you and all the other supplies you need, e.g. needles, lancets, test strips, etc., to cover *the whole duration of your stay overseas*, unless this is longer than six months. Ideally, take considerably more than you need in case of loss or theft or to cover an increase in dose or frequency of testing.

4 Take a back-up, low-tech system for monitoring your blood glucose on top of your automated system, e.g. lancets and a box of blood glucose sticks with visual analogue scale.

5 Have all travel vaccines in plenty of time before leaving.

6 Take appropriate medication. If travelling to a malarious area be very strict about taking malaria prevention tablets and avoiding mosquito bites (malaria can upset diabetic control). Also take standby ciprofloxacin, an antibiotic which cures most cases of traveller's diarrhoea (normal adult dose 500 mg daily for three days, see page 103): diarrhoea can lead to dehydration. Take anti-sickness pills, again because vomiting may affect your control.

7 Take a first-aid kit to treat minor injuries.

8 Obtain a doctor's letter explaining that all the medication you are carrying is for your personal use as a diabetic. It should give details of your insulin dosage. Wear a MedicAlert bracelet or pendant, and if insulin-dependent obtain a Diabetic Identification Card from Diabetes UK or your national diabetes organization (<http://www.diabetes.org.uk>).

9 Make sure that your health insurance covers pre-existing medical conditions, including diabetes.

During travel

1 *Transporting insulin* Keep all your insulin in your hand luggage; it will freeze in the aeroplane's hold. Keep some of your other supplies in a different part of your luggage in case of loss or theft.

2 *Treating hypos* Avoiding hypos is a top priority. Always carry a form of sugar, e.g. dextrose tablets, in case of hypo attacks. Running 'a bit high' for a few days is unlikely to cause any harm; however, hypos are much more serious and need immediate action. Hypos commonly occur when flying and if a meal is delayed. Avoid drinking alcohol on an empty stomach.

3 *Airline meals* Many experienced diabetics suggest it is usually better not to order a diabetic meal (they can be too low in carbohydrate) but to pick and choose from a normal meal.

4 *Unexpected delays* Always carry a good supply of food and drink, and be prepared for stopovers, re-routing and cancellations.

At your destination

1 *Awareness* If you are an employee or volunteer, make sure that whoever is responsible for your health and welfare knows you are diabetic, in case you run into problems with your diabetes and require emergency treatment. If you are going for a longer trip, check out local reliable supplies you may be able to obtain.

2 *Foot care* Take special care of your feet, treating any fungal or other infection immediately. Keep your toenails short and wear in new shoes before travelling. Inspect your feet regularly.

3 *Storage* For trips over a month long, take with you an unbreakable stainless steel vacuum flask if your supplies will be outside the 1°–25°C range. Never put insulin into a glove compartment or the boot (trunk) of a car. Keep your insulin in the fridge (but don't allow it to freeze) or in as cool a place as possible, out of direct sunlight – consider purchasing FRIO Cooling Wallets, which help to keep insulin cool when out of a fridge (<http://www.friouk.com>).

4 *Fever, malaria and diarrhoea* You will probably need more insulin than usual. Monitor your blood sugar more frequently and immediately see a doctor if you suspect malaria or develop severe diarrhoea or vomiting.

5 *Dehydration* Take extra precautions to prevent and treat dehydration caused by diarrhoea, heat or exercise. Take strict precautions to minimize your risk of diarrhoeal disease. Maintain a high fluid intake when in hot climates. Drink plenty of fluids.

6 *Sunburn* Take care to avoid sunburn, especially to feet and legs.

7 *Local food and drink* Obviously, this may be different from what you are used to. In many countries normal drinks such as tea have large amounts of pre-added sugar.

8 *Hypos in hot climates* Because insulin is often absorbed more quickly when it's hot, you may be at slightly greater risk of getting hypos as a result. If you are going to a remote area or are prone to attacks, as well as taking dextrose or your favourite equivalent take glucagon or Hypostop Gel, but make sure your travelling companion knows how to use these. Tell them it is usually better to make sure you take something sweet by mouth unless you are unconscious.

For further information in the UK see Diabetes UK Travel Advice, tel. 020 7323 1531, Careline 020 7636 6112, <http://infodiabetes.org.uk>.

Eating disorders

Here are some questions to think about if you have had an eating disorder and are planning to undertake a placement overseas with a company or an agency.

Does a history of eating disorder mean I shouldn't work overseas?

No, provided you are now well, your weight is normal and you know how to maintain a healthy eating pattern. However, if the problem is very recent or still present then there is a real risk of it resurfacing or getting worse overseas, as there are new stresses and your normal supports are not readily available. If you are currently seeing a doctor or therapist, then it is a good idea to talk this through with them.

What problems could I experience while overseas?

Physically, you are unlikely to have major difficulties unless you are very underweight or overweight or are vomiting or using laxatives. However, stamina can be a problem if your weight isn't right. Also, vomiting and laxative use can cause dehydration and electrolyte imbalance (a disturbance of chemicals in the body, which can affect the functioning of the heart and other organs).

There are other difficulties which can arise from the changes in thinking and behaviour that accompany an eating disorder. Preoccupation with food and weight can make interaction with others more difficult, and you may feel inclined to avoid certain activities, such as eating with others. For some people there is a problem with impulsive behaviour in addition to the eating problem, especially in bulimia. If you have a strong need to keep the problem hidden, then that too distracts from the ability to enter into team life and the activities of the placement.

I am better now so presumably it's OK to go

This might well be the case, but eating disorders can come back, especially under stress, and although going overseas is normally an enjoyable experience it can also be a highly stressful one. An added problem is that you may be served food you find unappetizing. Adjustment to a new culture, relationships within the team or with a co-worker, separation from family and friends and from those who have provided support and help in dealing with the eating problem are additional stresses you may face.

Sometimes people hope that going overseas will help them get over an eating disorder because it will give them new experiences to focus on. Family and friends can think the same, but this is not usually the case. You take yourself with you overseas, and the problem comes too!

Finally, as a general rule, if recovery is recent, i.e. less than a year, it is likely to be inadvisable to go on an overseas placement, as the risk of relapse is high. There may be exceptions to this if the eating disorder lasted for only a very short time or was related to a particular situation. You will also need to consider factors such as the length of the trip and the confidence the team leaders or your employers have in dealing with any issues you may have.

Epilepsy

Can I travel if I have epilepsy?

Many people with epilepsy manage to travel with little difficulty provided they are well controlled, well advised and well supplied. However, some situations encountered overseas may disrupt your control and put you at a greater risk of further seizures. In addition, you will probably be unfamiliar with the health services available and may not be able to have the same medical back-up as you would at home. Flying in itself does not itself increase the risk of a seizure.

If one or more of the following applies to you, follow the guidelines later in this section:

- You have grand mal seizures resulting in a loss of consciousness.
- You have experienced seizures or any form of epilepsy in the last six months.
- You have been diagnosed as having epilepsy within the last 12 months.
- You require the use of stand-by emergency medication.
- You are considering taking up an overseas placement which may involve dangerous activities, e.g. adventure travelling or building work.
- Your overseas placement is based in a remote setting without easy access to appropriate health care.

What situations may increase my risks?

The following situations *may* increase your risk of seizures while overseas:

- crossing time zones and the need to adjust the time when you take your medicines;
- extreme tiredness, including jet lag;
- missing meals so that your blood sugar levels drop;
- the anxiety and stress of adapting to a new situation;
- taking other medication, e.g. you will need to avoid some anti-malarials (see below);

42

- gastrointestinal upsets, either vomiting or severe diarrhoea, meaning you may not absorb your medication so well;
- any fever, including malaria, dengue and typhoid.

What guidelines should I follow?

1 Make an appointment with your doctor, hospital consultant or epilepsy nurse several months before you are due to leave. Review your trip in the light of where you will be travelling, what you will be doing and whether there is access to good health care. If your control is less good, e.g. you have had seizures within the last six months, you may be advised to postpone your trip or consider an alternative placement with easy access to good health facilities.

2 Seek specialist advice about malaria. It is especially important to prevent this as malaria may increase your risk of seizures. You should not use either mefloquine (Lariam) or chloroquine (Nivaquine, Avloclor). Doxycyline or Malarone is the best malaria prevention treatment to use, but doxycycline is rendered slightly less effective with phenytoin, carbamazepine and primidone.

3 Before you travel, check there are good local health facilities available in the event of an emergency. If you are going as an employee or volunteer, your team leader, manager, local host or placement supervisor can advice you. Once in location, make contact with the health facility to confirm arrangements.

4 Take adequate supplies of your anticonvulsant medicines to cover *the whole duration of your stay overseas*, unless this is longer than six months. Ideally, take more than you need in case you have to increase your dose or your return home is delayed.

5 Remember to keep the majority of your tablets in your hand luggage, and a supply in another part of your luggage in case of loss or theft.

6 Carry a doctor's letter giving details of your medication, written on headed notepaper and signed and dated by your doctor. Wear a MedicAlert bracelet or pendant (website <http://www.medicalert. org.uk>) or obtain a free identity card from the National Society for Epilepsy (website: <http://www.epilepsynse.org.uk>) or any equivalent in your own country.

7 Inform anyone responsible for you overseas that you have epilepsy and agree an action plan in the event of seizures. This should include appropriate first-aid measures and administering emergency treatment if required. You may also want to inform your travelling companion, or a member of the airline staff if you are taking a long-haul flight on your own.

8 On arrival at your placement, carry out a risk assessment of both

where you live and where you work to keep yourself safe and minimize the risk of serious injury as a result of a seizure.

9 Avoid dangerous activities such as swimming alone or rock climbing. If you do decide to go swimming, go with someone who knows what to do if you have a seizure while in the water. Tell a swimming pool lifeguard or first-aider about your epilepsy.

10 Make sure that your health insurance covers pre-existing medical conditions including epilepsy. (In the UK, further information is available from the National Society for Epilepsy helpline on 01494 601400.)

Headaches and migraine

Both *migraine* and *tension headache* often become worse overseas, especially when under stress, when dehydrated or with frequent changes in altitude such as when travelling or trekking in mountains. If you have significant headaches it is worth consulting your doctor to discuss how best you can manage these. Take with you a supply of your favourite painkillers and work out an appropriate lifestyle (see also pages 177–9).

Heart problems

Background

Increasing numbers of patients with heart problems are travelling internationally. The great majority do this with no ill effects, but one research study does show that half of all Americans who die while travelling abroad do so from heart-related causes.

The type and severity of heart problems is so wide that if you have any cardiac condition you should talk to your doctor and get specific advice on both where, when and how safe it is to travel, and what activities you can reasonably carry out. A number of people who have had successful bypass operations are running international marathons and climbing the highest mountains. On the other hand, those with unstable angina or uncontrolled blood pressure have substantial risks.

What general guidelines should I follow?

For most travellers with recent or existing heart problems, these guidelines can be followed:

1 See your doctor, and in discussion draw up sensible travel plans.

2 Obtain a letter from your doctor, with details of the medical problems you have had, any important recommendations, and a list of the medication using the generic names of drugs and their doses. Take with you a recent ECG and any done at the time of any acute heart problem in the past. This can be very useful in case you need to see a doctor overseas.

3 Take enough medication to last the duration of your trip unless this is more than six months. Keep most of your medicine with you in your hand luggage, but always have spare supplies in a different part of your luggage in case of loss or theft.

4 If you have significant symptoms or risks and you are working abroad as an employee or volunteer, it is sensible to let your team leader or manager know about your condition.

5 Before travelling find out details of good health facilities at your destination, and when you arrive check them out yourself.

6 During the flight drink plenty of water to avoid dehydration, and avoid excessive coffee, alcohol or salty meals.

7 Ensure that any medication you are on does not interact with any medicines you need for travel, including malaria prevention and treatment tablets such as mefloquine.

8 Be covered for flu and pneumococcal immunization in addition to the other immunizations you need.

9 Prioritize air-conditioned rooms and offices where possible, to reduce dehydration and tiredness.

10 If you plan to visit altitudes over 2,000 metres or plan any climbing or exercise at altitude, see pages 188–93 and talk to your specialist.

What specific guidelines should I follow?

This obviously depends on the nature of your problem. Here are some basic guidelines for the commonest conditions:

- *Angina* It is not safe to fly with uncontrolled angina (angina that has not been investigated by a doctor and is not controlled by medication). If your angina is controlled you should plan your activities and your itinerary with common sense and immediately report any worsening of symptoms. Always have with you a supply of any medication you take to control symptoms.

- *Angioplasty or stent* Advice varies greatly depending on your exact health problems, so talk to your specialist about this.

- *Anticoagulants* See your specialist before you travel, taking ample supplies of medication with you. Keep your INR (blood-clotting measure) in the standard range between 2.5 and 3.5. Check your INR one month before travel and regularly when overseas, either through a reliable clinic or self-testing using the CoaguCheck (see <http://www.coagucheck.co.uk>). Various effects of travel, including climate and diet, may make the INR less stable. Consider taking ampoules of vitamin K in case the INR becomes unusually high.

- *Arrhythmias (irregular heartbeats)* Because there are so many forms of irregular heartbeat, obtain an ECG and see your GP or specialist before travelling. You must not travel if you have *uncontrolled* ventricular or supraventricular arrhythmias, including supraventricular tachycardia (SVT).

- *Cardiac pacemakers or Implantable Cardioverter Defibrillators (ICDs)* There are a variety of models. Carry details of the exact model with you. Ideally you should have a certificate for fitness to travel. Obtain specific advice from the manufacturer or your specialist regarding the safety of airport security systems, especially hand-held magnetic security devices and metal detector archways. In practice, such devices hardly ever set off metal detectors or cause your device to malfunction because of radiation or magnetic fields. If in doubt or nervous, explain you have an ICD and request to be manually searched.

- *Coronary artery bypass graft* Obtain clearance from your doctor before flying. The minimum time between surgery and air travel is two weeks, but you may wish to leave it considerably longer.

- *Heart attack (coronary thrombosis)* Obtain medical clearance from your doctor before flying. The minimum length of time between an uncomplicated heart attack and air travel is two to three weeks. It may be much longer before you feel like travelling or living or holidaying abroad.

- *Hypertension (raised blood pressure)* Ensure this is adequately controlled: blood pressure levels should not normally exceed 140/90 taken during average conditions. Be sure you never run out of tablets or discontinue taking them. Have your blood pressure regularly checked when you are abroad, or take a self-monitoring device.

Also see pages 72–4 for details on deep vein thrombosis (DVT).

Kidney and bladder problems

Background

Kidney and bladder problems are both common, and do not usually prevent you from travelling or working abroad. However, there are some conditions which require investigation and special advice before leaving home. Some guidelines on the more important ones are shown below (also see pages 346–7).

What precautions should I take?

Blood in the urine

There are many causes for this including bladder infections, kidney stones, bilharzia (see page 277) and occasionally more serious problems in the kidney or bladder. If significant blood is present on routine urine testing on two or more occasions and there is no obvious cause, discuss with your doctor whether any further investigations are needed if you are planning to go abroad for any length of time.

Kidney and bladder stones

These occur quite commonly and are more likely to occur or recur in hot climates and if you drink insufficient fluids. If you have previously experienced the agony of passing a stone, mention this to your doctor before travelling abroad. If this has been in the past five years and you had no scan to prove that no further stone was present, then for all but the shortest trips you should ask your doctor about having an abdominal ultrasound scan. In any case, drink plenty of fluids – enough to keep your urine pale.

Malaria tablets

Only proguanil (Paludrine, and also present in Malarone) passes through the kidney. Proguanil should not generally be used if your creatinine level is above 150 micromol per litre, but your specialist will guide you and provide further advice. In practice, proguanil is used much less than it used to be, as it is ineffective in sub-Saharan Africa; Malarone, which contains half the dose of Paludrine, is increasingly being used. Doxycyline can be used cautiously: discuss this with your doctor.

Prostate problems

Men with significant symptoms, such as previous urinary obstruction or the need to pass urine urgently, should see their doctor for advice before travelling abroad. In addition, over the age of 45 it is important to make sure either by a manual examination or a PSA blood test that there is no serious cause for these problems.

Recurrent urinary tract infections

These are very common, especially in women. If men have had two or more in their lifetime or women have had recurrent infections in the past year, they will need to discuss this with their doctor if going abroad for any length of time. Women who develop recurrent urinary tract infections abroad can consider taking prophylactic low-dose antibiotics. Travelling on bumpy roads, dehydration and sexual activity make these infections more likely. Drinking large amounts of extra fluid, enough to keep the urine pale, is the most important precaution. There are more details on pages 346–7 and 157–60.

Severe renal impairment, dialysis or previous renal transplant
If any of these apply to you, discuss your trip in detail with your specialist.

Liver problems

The liver can be under pressure when travelling, meaning you should treat it with care and get advice if you have ever had a serious liver condition in the past.

The following factors during overseas travel can put the liver at greater risk:

- drinking more alcohol than usual;
- taking the antimalarials doxycycline or mefloquine, which occasionally affect the liver;
- using statin drugs to control cholesterol, which again can sometimes increase the level of liver enzymes;
- being seriously overweight or with a high cholesterol: this can add further strain through fatty deposits in the liver;
- past hepatitis: many people travelling internationally who were brought up in a developing country may have had hepatitis earlier in life; hepatitis A rarely leads to any problems, but hepatitis B and C more commonly do so (see pages 300–304);
- tropical conditions such as some forms of bilharzia or amoebic liver abscess, which can damage the liver.

Lowered immunity

Background

The posh name for this is being immunocompromised. With travel becoming so routine, even for those with major health problems, more and more people with reduced immunity are visiting, living or working in developing countries.

Those severely compromised will not be able to travel, those with some loss of immunity can travel with care, and many of those previously considered to be at risk can in fact travel with few restrictions.

Need for and purpose of a travel consultation

If you consider you may have lowered immunity or have been told this is the case, you will need a careful travel health consultation before any trip to a developing country. The purpose of this is, first of all, to assess your risks and, second, to make sure you get accurate advice about the precautions to take to minimize your risk of becoming ill while overseas.

The two main risks are a worsening of your condition when travelling, and the greater likelihood of picking up an infectious disease which may cause you more severe symptoms.

Travellers considered to have no increased risk

Medical experts no longer consider the following travellers to have any significant risk from lowered immunity:

* those on short-term steroids (i.e. for less than two weeks) at a dosage of prednisolone 20 mg daily or less; or if one month or more has passed since being on doses higher than 20 mg;
* people living with HIV with more than 500 CD4 cells/m^3 and asymptomatic;
* those who have had three months or more (some experts recommend six months) since completing chemotherapy for leukaemia or lymphoma or cancer, with the malignancy in remission;
* most autoimmune diseases that are under control; if you have one of these conditions you will need specific advice from the specialist looking after you, as guidelines are not yet clarified.

Those with a degree of risk who need to take extra precautions

This group includes:

* those with chronic kidney or liver disease, diabetes or no spleen (see under separate headings in this chapter);
* those with asymptomatic HIV infection with CD4 counts between 200 and 500.

Those at high risk who should not normally travel to developing countries or resource-poor areas

This includes:

* people living with HIV who have clinical symptoms of AIDS and/or CD4 counts of less than 200;
* those with active leukaemia, lymphoma, generalized malignancy, aplastic anaemia or a recent transplant, or who have had recent or current whole body irradiation;
* those taking high-dose corticosteroids (the equivalent of more than prednisolone 20 mg daily) or transplant-related drugs to reduce tissue rejection, including methotrexate, azathioprine and cyclophosphomide. However, short trips to areas with good-quality medical back-up are sometimes possible. This list is not complete, and

anyone taking any immunosuppressive drugs or with a recent history as described above will need a detailed discussion with their specialist.

Precautions for those travelling with reduced immunity

1 Identify reliable medical care at your destination.
2 Avoid changes in your medication shortly before travel to ensure no side-effects or complications develop while travelling.
3 Ensure you have comprehensive travel health insurance, including, if possible, cover for conditions which may arise from your illness, even though a higher premium will be charged.
4 Take full medical details with you, with a signed letter from your doctor on headed notepaper recording the medication you are on and any special precautions you need to take.
5 Have adequate supplies of all the drugs you need for the full length of your journey, unless longer than six months, keeping the majority in your hand luggage, with some spares in other parts of your luggage in case of loss or theft.
6 Ensure there are no interactions between the drugs you are taking and any medication recommended to prevent or treat malaria, diarrhoea or other illnesses you may pick up abroad.
7 If HIV positive, ensure there are no travel restrictions on the country you are going to.

Malaria

See pages 114–50.

You will need to take strict precautions to avoid being bitten and report any fever at once. Malaria does not appear to be more frequent in those with HIV infection, unless severely immunocompromised. If you have had any illness affecting your liver or kidney you will need specialist advice about which antimalarials to take.

Diarrhoea and bowel infections

See pages 100–13.

The risk of food- and water-borne disease is much greater, so take extra care in all the recommendations given on pages 85–9. Be sure to take ciprofloxacin or an equivalent with you to treat any bout of traveller's diarrhoea early on, but check there are no drug interactions between this and any medication you may be taking. Report to a doctor if you develop severe or worsening symptoms.

Other illnesses

You need to take care to minimize your risk of tuberculosis (consider having a baseline tuberculin test before you go). Visceral leishmaniasis poses a risk in a few countries (see pages 315–16).

Certain fungal infections inhaled by mouth are a danger, e.g. coccidioidomycosis in the Americas.

Vaccinations

The situation is complex, and there is not yet full agreement among specialists. Arrange a consultation with a travel health specialist and also speak with your own specialist about what they recommend. Those severely immunocompromised should avoid live vaccines. Other vaccines (i.e. those that are inactivated) may be less effective, so booster doses are sometimes needed earlier.

Recommendations

If you come into any of the categories above, including those listed as having no appreciable risk, you should still arrange a travel health consultation and obtain details regarding travel risks, special precautions and vaccine advice from your own specialist. Do this in plenty of time, e.g. at least three months before travel.

Overweight

Background

In western Europe it is estimated that 13 per cent of men and 16 per cent of women are significantly overweight or obese, where obesity is defined as having a Body Mass Index (BMI) greater than 30 kg/m^2. This figure is increasing. There is strong evidence that obesity increases the risk of developing high blood pressure, coronary heart disease, diabetes, arthritis and heartburn.

What are the additional risks when travelling?

These include:

1 *Heat exhaustion, dehydration and fatigue* Being overweight means you will adapt more slowly to heat and altitude. You may get tired more easily. Therefore you will need to give yourself more time to adjust to the new climate. Learn to take life at a more leisurely pace, conserve your energy where you can, and make sure that you drink plenty of fluids. These measures will reduce your risk of developing heat exhaustion, becoming dehydrated or seriously fatigued.
2 *Skin infections* Take special care of your skin, treating any fungal or other infections promptly. Folds of skin are ideal areas for infections such as Candida (see page 332) to thrive, particularly in hot and humid environments.

3 *Musculo-skeletal problems* Excess weight puts extra pressure on knees, hips and lower back, increasing your risk of sustaining an injury which could temporarily put you out of action. Think carefully about how you can look after your back, neck and other joints during your stay overseas.

4 *Deep vein thrombosis (DVT)* Being overweight adds to your risk of developing a deep vein thrombosis when travelling, especially during long-haul flights. See pages 72–4 for ways you can reduce this risk.

What can I do about it?

We would strongly encourage you to lose weight over the months leading up to your departure date, although it is not necessary to get down to your 'ideal weight'. In fact, you benefit most from losing your first 5–10 kg. Don't try and lose weight too quickly, either. It is best to aim at reducing your weight by 0.5–1 kg a week (1–2 lb). To do this, you need to reduce your calorie intake by 500–1,000 calories per day. If you manage to keep this up for three months, you can expect to lose 6–12 kg (1–2 stone). There are numerous weight reducing programmes available, but most rely on a combination of dietary changes and an increase in regular physical exercise. Start these measures now, before you go, rather than assuming it will happen automatically when you head off overseas. Many people find they actually put on weight while overseas.

Here are some practical tips on losing weight that some people find helpful, but some of these are difficult to carry out while travelling:

- Always put food on your plate yourself rather than letting others do it for you. They often put on more than you need or want.
- Try and reduce the size of each helping by about one quarter.
- Avoid second helpings.
- If you feel you can't easily manage all the food on your plate, leave it – either keep it for another occasion or throw it away (I know, against what we were brought up to do).
- Reduce in particular high calorie foods such as butter, cheese and oily foods.
- If your cholesterol is raised, follow the extra advice you are given in reducing foods high in cholesterol and saturated fats.

Finally, having lost weight, take great care not to put it back on again!

Pregnancy

There is a full section on this on pages 230–9.

Previous splenectomy

Background

Although many people don't know where their spleens are located, we need them to help fight off infection. For those who have no functioning spleen or have had their spleen removed, infections can be harder to fight off and their effects can be more serious

What are the extra dangers during travel?

These include:

- There is a greater risk of infection. Several infectious illnesses are more likely to occur and more likely to be serious. These include meningitis (meningococcal, pneumococcal and Haemophilus), and streptococcal infections and influenza.
- There is a greater risk from falciparum (malignant malaria), the commonest form found in Africa.
- These and other infections can progress rapidly, meaning that you may need good-quality health care within a few hours.

- Travel health insurance is likely to be more expensive.

In practice it is usually possible for those with no functioning spleen to travel abroad providing they take extra precautions.

What recommendations should I follow?

Vaccinations

You will need the following:

1 pneumococcal vaccine every five to ten years;
2 meningococcal vaccine ACWY every three years (a quadrivalent vaccine against forms A, C, W135 and Y);
3 Haemophilus vaccine if not previously immunized; guidelines have yet to be developed on this but three injections at monthly intervals are known to confer good immunity in children and could be used in unimmunized travellers;
4 flu vaccination annually;
5 all other vaccines recommended for the area of travel.

Malaria

Avoid areas where falciparum malaria is known to be common. If this is not possible, take every precaution to avoid being bitten; be absolutely strict in taking the recommended malaria prevention tablets for the area being visited; report any feverish illness at once; self-treat with standby medication if you cannot immediately access good health care or if reliable supplies of an effective treatment are not available.

Antibiotics

Take a daily antibiotic to reduce the likelihood of catching a bacterial infection. This should be phenoxymethylpenicillin (250 mg daily) for those who are not allergic to penicillin or erythromycin (250 mg daily) for those who are.

Also take an adequate supply of a broad-spectrum antibiotic to treat any infection. Amoxicillin is suitable for those not allergic to penicillin (normal dose 500 mg three times daily for one week), or erythromycin (normal dose 500 mg four times daily for one week).

Fever overseas

Report any feverish illness at once, especially if you are in or have come from a malarious area.

Lifestyle

Avoid becoming overtired, or setting up an over-ambitious work or travel target.

Information

Carry written information about your condition, the medication you have with you and instructions on how to take it. Also arrange a MedicAlert bracelet or pendant to wear at all times.

Skin care

Treat any cut, bite or injury to the skin with care, cleaning carefully with soap and clean water, using an antiseptic cream, and reporting at once if any infection develops, using your standby antibiotics if immediate medical care is not possible. Animal bites need caution and must always be reported to a doctor.

Going as a volunteer

If you are going abroad as an employee or volunteer, it would be sensible to tell your team leader or manager about your condition.

Insurance

Take out comprehensive travel insurance, which must include cover for any conditions that might arise from or be more serious because of having no spleen.

(These guidelines are based largely on those issued by the British

Committee for Standards in Haematology in 2002, which at the time of writing represent current best practice.)

Skin conditions

The skin is at increased risk when abroad because of the heat, greater likelihood of boils, minor injuries and bites, and of course sunburn. There is a section on pages 329–35 which is worth reading before you go, especially if you suffer from any skin problems.

Eczema may flare up in hot or humid climates or with swimming, and is more likely to become infected. However, it often improves with the sun. Widespread, infected eczema is a dangerous condition in hot and especially in humid climates. Ensure your eczema is well controlled before travelling and take a copious supply of all the creams you are likely to need, plus a broad-spectrum antibiotic such as amoxicillin (see page 357). It is worth seeing your doctor if you have severe eczema or psoriasis, and talking through an action plan.

Fungal infections, especially of the skin between the toes (athlete's foot) and of the groin, commonly get worse. Take appropriate cream or powder with you (see also pages 332–3). *Fungal infections of the toenails* may get worse or start for the first time.

Psoriasis improves in the sun but can worsen under stress. The antimalarial chloroquine occasionally makes it worse.

If you have *diabetes* take special care (see page 40).

Stomach and digestive disorders

What conditions should I be concerned about?

The main danger for travellers comes from inflammatory bowel disease (IBD).

Background to inflammatory bowel disease

There are two forms of IBD: Crohn's disease, which in the UK affects about one person in 1,200, and ulcerative colitis, which affects about one in 600.

Both these conditions are unpredictable in terms of how and when symptoms can change. This makes it difficult to draw up guidelines for overseas travel. At the time of writing there are no official guidelines from the British Association of Gastroenterology on managing IBD during travel.

If your condition is well controlled, there is a good chance you will be able to live and work abroad, and to travel in developing countries, providing you take certain precautions.

What are the dangers of overseas travel?

- *Unpredictability* Because we are largely unsure of the causes and triggers of these conditions it is hard to predict how symptoms will change when travelling abroad.
- *The effect of traveller's diarrhoea* There is some evidence that this can worsen or at times trigger either form of IBD. Dysentery (diarrhoea with blood and fever) can be dangerous in patients with poorly controlled ulcerative colitis and can precipitate very severe diarrhoea and bleeding.
- *Unreliable access to good-quality health care* If your symptoms worsen in developing countries, expert advice may not be easy to obtain except from specialists in major cities, and even then care and treatment may be less reliable.

How can I minimize my risk?

1 See your specialist well before making your travel plans. You will need to discuss:
   (a) whether the proposed trip is recommended;
   (b) any modifications you may need to make;
   (c) how to manage any flare-ups or worsening of symptoms. This must include instructions on how and when you should increase the dose of any medication you are taking, and how and when to use any additional standby medication.

2 Obtain a letter from the doctor managing your condition with details of the illness, advice on treatment and a list of any medications you are taking. This should be on headed notepaper and signed and dated by your doctor.

3 Decide on the nature of your travel. If well controlled, you should be able to travel in developed countries and in less remote or hazardous regions of developing countries, providing you have discussed this with your doctor.

4 Avoid travel to developing countries if your symptoms are not well controlled. In the case of ulcerative colitis, except for the shortest low-risk trips, you should have had at least six months with no visible blood loss from the bowel.

5 Take adequate medical supplies with you for the full duration of your trip, unless this is longer than six months. Keep spare supplies in a different part of your luggage in case of loss or theft.

6 Check out health care in advance. Discover the names and addresses of hospitals and specialists who can be consulted if symptoms flare up.

7 Carry your consultant's email address, or mobile number if he or she is willing to give it.

57

8 Take out comprehensive travel insurance, if possible to include emergency repatriation for conditions which might arise from IBD. This will usually be possible, though you may have to pay a much higher premium.

9 Take all precautions to avoid traveller's diarrhoea, and also serious tropical conditions such as malaria.

10 Treat diarrhoea promptly with ciprofloxacin 500 mg daily for five days or an alternative antibiotic.

11 In the case of Crohn's disease, consider taking standby budesonide tablets, starting at 9 mg daily for one month, then 6 mg daily for one month, then 3 mg daily for one month. You need to discuss this with your specialist.

12 Ensure that you avoid any foods known to make your symptoms worse and keep to foods you know have no adverse effects.

13 Avoid overwork or over-ambitious travel schedules, and plan your work–life balance with care.

14 Arrange a stool test on return, and a medical check if any symptoms have worsened or new ones have developed.

Further advice on IBD

- The National Association for Colitis and Crohn's Disease: <http://www.nacc.org.uk>.
- The Crohn's and Colitis Foundation of America: <http://www.ccfa.org>.

Other gastrointestinal problems

These include:

- *Bleeding from the rectum,* usually put down to piles. Have this checked before any lengthy trip, either if it has recently started or if you have not seen your doctor about it in the past.
- *Coeliac disease* This is rarely a reason for not travelling. Check out the availability of gluten-free products before travelling, take any favourite supplies with you or have them brought out. Take extra care to avoid diarrhoea.
- *Diverticulitis* If you have had this in the past it may recur. Sometimes a change of diet may trigger it. See your doctor for specific advice. Take a supply of ciprofloxacin and use this at a dose of 500 mg daily for five days if you develop what appears to be traveller's diarrhoea or if you recognize the tell-tale signs of diverticulitis. Also take an antispasmodic tablet to control the pain, such as hyoscine 10 mg (Buscopan) or mebeverine 135 mg (Colofac). If the symptoms do not settle quickly, see a doctor.
- *Heartburn* If you get frequent heartburn, see your doctor to discuss

treatment – and investigation if it has been going on for a long time. Again, medication, for example lanzoprazole 15 or 30 mg daily, usually prevents it. If you are overweight, try losing weight, as this often helps symptoms.

• *Hernia* This should normally be repaired before travelling.

• *Irritable bowel syndrome* may worsen, e.g. after repeated bouts of diarrhoea, but would not normally stop you travelling. If this is a nuisance, discuss it with your doctor. Try to arrange stool tests and specific treatment if your symptoms obviously worsen. Also see pages 108–9.

• *Peptic ulcers* (in stomach or duodenum) commonly recur overseas, especially under stress, but are easily treated with modern drugs such as ranitidine. If you have a history of peptic ulcer and are going on a lengthy overseas trip, ask your GP for a Helicobacter blood or breath test. This germ is a cause of many ulcers and can be eradicated with a week's course of triple drug therapy. Treating peptic ulcers is important because if they bleed profusely you may need a blood transfusion.

4

Travel health consultations and medical examinations

Before travelling to a developing country you will need a travel health consultation, usually with a nurse, and in certain situations you may need a medical examination, usually with a doctor.

A travel health consultation

Background

Travel to exotic destinations is not only becoming more common, in many areas it is also becoming less safe. There are various reasons for this, including a greater risk of road crashes, more widespread malaria and other tropical infections, increased alcohol abuse, the worry and reality of HIV infection, and greater risks to personal security.

> When people think of preparing medically for their trip, they tend to think only about immunizations. These are important, but less than one disease episode in ten can be prevented by a vaccine, so make sure that when you get your travel jabs you also find out about how to keep healthy abroad.

Subjects will include: defeating malaria, avoiding road crashes (the commonest cause of death in travellers), reducing risks of HIV infection and other sexually transmitted illness, and dealing with the almost inevitable nuisance of diarrhoea. Because so many clinics are busy you will need to make a point of asking about these things.

What should this cover?

If you are going to a developing country it is really important that you arrange a travel health consultation – unless your trip is short, low-risk and you are an experienced traveller. Of course, you will still need to make sure your immunizations are up to date and that you are prepared for any specific risks such as malaria. Here is a checklist of what you need to cover at a travel consultation:

- Check what vaccines you need and start having them.
- If going to a malarious area, discuss how malaria can be prevented and treated and obtain malaria prevention tablets, a standby kit if advised, an insecticide-impregnated mosquito net and insect repellent.
- Discuss the commonest health risks you are likely to come across, including those mentioned above and others specific to the area you are going to, such as dengue fever and bilharzia.
- Take away written information on how to keep healthy abroad and how to recognize and treat common conditions. This book will help; other shorter ones are also available, such as *Travel Health in Your Pocket* (for details see pages 401–4).
- Take details of websites where you can look up any information you need; <http://www.interhealth.org.uk> will provide you with much of this. See Appendix H, pages 372–7 for others.

A medical examination

Who should have this done?

In addition to a travel health consultation with a nurse, many people benefit from having a medical before going abroad.

Obviously this is not usually needed for the average holiday or short-term trip, but it can be useful if any of the following apply to you:

- You are going on an international assignment in a developing country for six months or more.
- You are going on an emergency or high-risk mission regardless of length of stay.
- You are planning dangerous or arduous activities including scuba diving or mountaineering, or are going on an expedition remote from good health care.
- You have a pre-existing medical condition as described in Chapter 3.
- You are aged 60 or over.
- You are required by your company, agency or health insurance to undergo a medical examination.
- You need to have a medical for a visa or work permit.
- You have been through a serious time of stress or bereavement in the past few months or have experienced significant psychological health problems. It may be worth having a psychological health check from a psychiatrist or clinical psychologist before you go.

> ### *Who needs health screening: summary*
> This is recommended for anyone going on an assignment to a developing country for six months or more, on an emergency or high-risk mission for any length of time, and for anyone with a significant pre-existing medical condition. It should be carried out by a doctor experienced in travel medicine.

Who can carry out a medical examination?

In the UK, some GPs will be able to arrange a medical if you book well in advance. However, busy doctors often do not have the time to carry out a detailed medical and arrange the necessary blood tests. You are not entitled to one on the NHS, and you will be charged for it. Some specialist travel clinics will carry out medicals, including InterHealth and the Edinburgh International Health Centre in the UK (see pages 369–71). Most major cities in developing countries have doctors with experience in travel medicine; see details in Appendix G. If you are going as an employee, missionary or aid worker, you will usually be advised where you should have your medical. If it is not a requirement, it may still be in your interest to have one.

Some organizations ask applicants to be seen by a psychiatrist or clinical psychologist. Sometimes psychometric testing is also included. Don't be taken aback by this. The main purpose is not to exclude people from going abroad but to help ensure that your own placement is consistent with your gifts and temperament.

When you do have a medical or have to complete a questionnaire, it is worth being open and honest. Holding back information isn't doing you a favour. Questions on the forms are designed to help protect your health in situations where good health care may not be available, and to make sure you are placed in a safe and appropriate location.

Note on blood groups

If you do not know your blood group or those of other family members, this is a good time to find out. If you are travelling to a developing country or living overseas for any length of time, it is probably a good precaution to know your group (see pages 168–72 for more information on this). Your doctor may be willing to arrange to have it tested, but will usually charge for it. Alternatively, you can become a blood donor, though it may occasionally take several weeks before your donor card, with a note of your blood group, is sent to you.

Certain conditions preclude you from giving blood in the UK. These regulations are complex and change from time to time. You should phone the National Blood Service on 08457 711711 for further details of how and where to become a donor, and what conditions past or present mean that you are not eligible.

5

Preparing for an overseas assignment

If you are planning to spend any length of time in a new country, it is worth learning as much as possible about its customs and lifestyle. Apart from being interesting in itself, this has two main benefits: it helps to reduce your own culture shock on arrival, and it also makes it less likely that you will cause offence to the local people by dressing or behaving in a way that is out of keeping with local traditions.

Here are a few suggestions:

Be prepared for culture shock

Of course, you may not experience this, especially if you love travel, have a laid-back temperament and are lucky enough to have a stimulating assignment; also if you are travelling or working with close friends, or manage to retain a large measure of control over your life and lifestyle.

However, you probably will come to recognize the four typical phases shown in Figure 5.1, and just being prepared for them can be helpful. You then realize it's probably normal to be feeling the way you are, rather than wondering what on earth is happening to you.

The four phases are often described as follows (though, of course, you may bounce from one to the other or have reactions that are quite different):

- *Elation* All the new sounds, smells, sights and experiences excite you.
- *Depression* The excitement and newness wear off. Irritation at the hassles and inefficiency and annoyance with your companions take centre-stage. You feel homesick, miss your friends, the parties and good times – and all your home comforts. You wonder whether you can possibly last out the rest of your assignment – and so do your friends and relatives, who get worried about what you say in your text messages, phone calls and emails.
- *Recovery or integration* You start to value the good experiences and cope with the bad. You are missing the people and places back home

much less. Of course, despite integrating these aspects of your life, you still have some bad days.

• *Acculturation* A rather ugly word meaning you are getting used to the culture and people, and are coming to accept and enjoy their company and culture, the good and the bad. You may start enjoying life to such an extent that the idea of leaving fills you with horror. And the more good friends you make and the greater the experiences you have, the better it all feels. Of course, if you've had a really stressful time, some bad experiences, a colleague you can't get on with or problems with your job or assignment, you may not feel this way at all (if that is the case, be sure to get a proper debriefing when you get home).

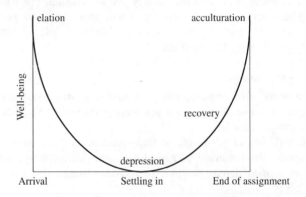

Figure 5.1 The U-curve pattern of adjustment to a new culture,
(Modified from *Social Work* (1993), 38 (6): 694–704,
after *International Science* (1955), 7: 45–51)

Meet people from the country you are going to before leaving home

There may be people from the country you will be visiting who are studying or living in your home country. It can be both useful and enjoyable to meet up and learn about each other's lifestyles, beliefs – and sense of humour.

It is also very useful to talk to anyone from your own country or background who has actually lived in or visited the area you are going to. By asking specific questions you will be able to prepare yourself both mentally and practically. It will give you a chance to find out what items are locally available, what clothes and personal belongings you should take with you, and what sports and leisure opportunities are available where you will be living.

Read

Time allowing, it is worth reading history books, travel books, novels and any literature covering your own profession or field of interest. Selective reading of a travel guide, e.g. Insight Guides, Footprint Guides, the Rough Guide or Lonely Planet series, helps to give ideas for leisure activities.

Look and listen

Watch films, DVDs and videos, TV programmes or cultural events (art exhibits, dances, drama) of the country you are visiting. The wider your background knowledge, the more you will appreciate and understand what you see – and the more you'll probably be able to contribute, which is satisfying for everyone.

Learn some language

A little of the host language can go a long way, stimulate interest and help give you a head start when you wander through the bazaar or join the language school.

You will probably be able to find someone in your home country who speaks the language you need to learn. Alternatively, select the most appropriate language guide or consider using a Linguaphone or BBC course.

Be realistic

Adjust your expectations to a sensible level, especially in terms of your job or assignment. This is especially important for goal-orientated professionals, who will need to learn that people are often more important than projects, and good local relationships of greater value than a list of achievements in newsletters home.

In terms of time management, it's helpful to realize that the process of living (e.g. shopping, cooking, communicating, travelling) may often take many times longer than at home, effectively reducing your 'productive' working life by half. You may need to spend a day each year, or even a day each month, sitting in an office to obtain a permit, visa or permission for something absurdly trivial. Being prepared for delays, inefficiency, corruption and red tape enables you to use time spent waiting productively (e.g. for language-learning, reading, working on your laptop), rather than prolonging the process by outbursts of anger and irritation – nearly always counterproductive in a developing country.

Discover ways to minimize cultural differences

You should select clothes and gadgets with care. Women's uncovered arms or legs may be quite acceptable in some countries but enough to cause stones to fly in others. Photographic and electronic wizardry may draw gasps of admiration from the local inhabitants, but at the expense of you being seen as a provider of foreign merchandise rather than as a straightforward friend.

Avoid gaffes

Customs, habits and clothes that we take for granted may cause offence or amusement in other cultures. Do some homework first so as to avoid social clangers that can put your local acceptance rating back to zero. Classic examples include eating or giving gifts with the left hand, baring your flesh in public (e.g. in Islamic cultures) and failing to remove your shoes when entering a local home or place of worship. In many countries, when sitting on the floor you must be careful not to point your toes at someone sitting opposite you. Passing wind may cause amusement or extreme offence – travellers with giardiasis (see pages 107–8) take special note!

Prepare for leisure

Before going abroad, decide to build into your lifestyle adequate leisure and time off. In practice this can be difficult if you live in a remote area, if travel is dangerous or if you are confined within the four walls of a hospital, training centre or compound. A few well-chosen books, games, raw materials for a creative hobby (e.g. oil paints) and a pair of binoculars can pay huge dividends. So can a skipping rope, an Ipod and music for aerobics, Pilates or Salsa. And, of course, your mobile phone.

Decide to keep a diary or record

Quite apart from being an amusing read in twelve months' time, or to children or grandchildren in future years, it helps you to see your life in perspective. Sometimes writing down a difficult, annoying or frightening episode can help to remove its sting. It also stimulates you to keep taking an interest in the country where you are living.

Go on an orientation course

Most agencies or large companies run training courses, briefing weekends or residential courses for preparation. If one hasn't been arranged, try to join one. By helping you to think through situations before they arise, they enable you to handle the human, emotional, physical and spiritual conditions you are likely to meet. Cross-cultural training is currently a trendy idea, and rightly so. More than ever, we need to learn what amuses or annoys people in the country we are going to, and the best ways to make friends, win the contract and avoid offending people.

Finally, consider doing a diploma for teaching English, a week on vehicle maintenance and, especially if you are going as a team leader, a first-aid course, run in the UK by the local branch of the British Red Cross (BRC) or St John or St Andrew's Ambulance (see Appendix H).

6

Health insurance for travel abroad

It is essential to take out travel health insurance, regardless of which country you are going to or what you will be doing.

You can obtain either single or multiple trip policies. Many regular travellers simply renew existing polices each year.

An adequate policy should cover the following:

- health insurance for all the countries you will be visiting, any activities you are planning and the full length of the trip;
- medical and emergency expenses abroad, including medical evacuation (medivac) when needed;
- 24-hour emergency assistance in case of accident or severe illness;
- availability of fully screened and tested blood within 24 hours (this can also be arranged via the Blood Care Foundation, see page 376);
- cover for emergency care in your home country if medically repatriated;
- personal accident to cover death and disability;
- personal liability to cover injury to third parties, including legal costs;
- cancellation and curtailment of trip due to ill health of traveller, family member or business associate;
- insurance to cover loss of money and damage to or theft of baggage, personal possessions, cash and documents;
- hijack.

If you are likely to become *pregnant*, make sure you know exactly what is covered and what is not, including any illnesses or accidents to the *newborn*. If there is any chance you may do *adventure sports* make sure these are covered: there are special policies for winter sports. Get specific advice if you are travelling in *war zones* or if you are a UK resident planning to visit a country which the Foreign and Commonwealth Office advises is not safe to visit.

Older travellers (i.e. those over 65) can usually get insurance cover if they shop around. Some policies will not cover problems arising from *pre-existing medical conditions*, but most will if you pay an extra premium. However, such conditions have to be declared and the company has to confirm in writing that they are accepted. See the list

69

below. If you are diabetic, contact Diabetes UK (see Appendix H).

As part of your travel insurance you will be give a medical emergency helpline telephone number which you or a colleague can phone at any time from anywhere in the world in case of serious illness or accident. This alerts the medical assistance company to whom the insurance agency contracts out any emergency care needed. They then start putting immediate plans in place, for treatment either in-country or in a neighbouring country, or for medical evacuation to a hospital which will offer the treatment needed.

If you are working for a company or an organization, or you are a volunteer, phone the person responsible in-country or back home, so that if necessary their medical adviser can coordinate with the medical assistance company. Keep the helpline number on you at all times and make sure any travelling companion also knows it.

If you are working overseas *with an agency or company*, health insurance will probably be arranged for you, but make sure that this is the case and that it is adequate. 'Self-insurance', i.e. the practice of a company or agency paying any expenses if they arise, is not sufficient. You need full travel insurance, which includes being given the medical emergency helpline. This on-the-spot advice, assessment and action can be life-saving. Ask your organization about its policy. For any visit to the USA you must have full health insurance (up to £5 million) to cover against potentially enormous medical fees.

For those resident in the UK, make yourself aware of any 'reciprocal health care' you may be entitled to in your host country. This covers only a few countries, but some in the Commonwealth and countries of the former Soviet Union are included. If you are visiting a country in the European Economic Area or Switzerland, make sure you obtain a European Health Insurance Card (EHIC) as well as private health insurance. This card entitles you to reduced cost, and sometimes free medical treatment, in most European countries. It has replaced the E111 scheme since 1 January 2006. You can apply online at <http://www.dh.gov.uk/PolicyAnd Guidance/HealthAdviceForTravellers/>. See Appendix F.

Health cover in Europe and other countries mentioned is less comprehensive than under the NHS in the UK, and some items will be excluded. Keep all receipts and proofs of purchase of medicines or treatment. In practice there are virtually no reciprocal arrangements with most developing countries. When travelling, make sure you have a readily available means of paying any hospital bills.

In terms of health insurance there are a very large number of travel health policies currently being offered. Shop around for exactly what you need, and get two or three quotes. Some insurers give special rates for older travellers and those with pre-existing conditions. (See page 376.)

7

The flight

Despite widespread fears of crashes, hijacks or terrorist attacks, the fact is that flying remains extremely safe. Usually any pre-flight nerves quickly settle as the plane takes off, and thoughts of distant places (or an impending hot bath at home) take over.

Cabin pressure and humidity

Cabin pressure

For most planes, pressure is maintained at that normally found at an altitude of 6,000 to 8,000 feet above sea level (1,800–2,400 metres). This explains why body gases expand, especially in stomachs and ears, and why the amount of oxygen slightly decreases, the latter being important only for those with severe heart or lung problems. Incidentally, if you do feel short of breath or wheezy you can ask the cabin attendant for oxygen, or – better – arrange beforehand with the airline to have this available.

You can ease stomach distension by wearing loose clothing, avoiding excessive carbonated drinks, eating slowly and avoiding large meals. Ear problems can usually be prevented by sucking a sweet during take-off and landing, or by regular jaw-opening or swallowing. Those with sensitive ears, including children with recent ear infections or catarrh, should have a combination of an antihistamine and pseudoephedrine known in the UK as Sudafed Plus (tablets or syrup) one hour before take-off and, on longer flights, again before landing (do not use in children under two). Alternatively, you can use ephedrine nasal drops 0.5 per cent, one or two drops at a time; these are safe for children over three months as well as for adults.

If you have had severe earache on previous flights, consider taking ibuprofen 400 mg and one Actifed or Sudafed tablet at the same time. In the UK all these products are available over the counter.

Cabin humidity

This is relatively low (about 20 per cent), which can lead to dry skin, sore eyes, and dry mouth and nose on a long flight. This causes no harm. Have plenty of soft drinks and consider a skin moisturizing lotion or a saline spray before the flight.

71

In-flight drinks and food

Alcohol, tea and coffee unfortunately make dehydration worse (they cause you to lose more urine than the fluid you take in) but by also drinking plenty of soft drinks or water you can easily put that right.

From the point of view of hygiene, aircraft food prepared or loaded in developing countries should carry the same health warnings as meals eaten out in the country of origin, although most well-known airlines have good levels of food hygiene. Keep to the rules on pages 85–6, taking care with salads, including lettuce and tomatoes.

Deep vein thrombosis
(The risk of blood clots when flying)

Background

For reasons we don't fully understand, the deep veins of the leg sometimes develop blood clots and these very occasionally break off and move upstream to the lung. A clot in the leg is known as a deep vein thrombosis (DVT) and a clot in the lung as a pulmonary embolism (PE).

There is a risk of DVTs and PEs after major surgery such as hip replacement, but any long-distance flights (often taken as five hours or longer) also increase the risk. Platelets (one of the blood cells) start to stick to the side of the vein and a small clot begins to develop.

There are several reasons why there is an increased risk of DVTs forming during long-distance flights:

- Dehydration leads to 'thicker' blood. The cabin air is dry, and drinking coffee, tea and alcohol increases dehydration further. Some travellers restrict the amount they drink before a flight because of the difficulty of accessing toilets.
- Immobility reduces the speed of blood flow, especially if we keep our legs still, don't move or walk about, or sit or sleep in a cramped position.
- Pressure interrupts blood flow in the legs, especially from the seat pressing on the back of the leg or behind the knee. This may be worse in short people.

Although travel-related DVT has been called 'Economy Class Syndrome' it can occur in any part of the plane, and your friends in club class or first class are almost as much at risk as you are, though more leg-room may slightly reduce their risk.

What factors increase the risk of DVTs?

Experts believe it is likely that any of the following may increase the risk, but further evidence is needed to give definite proof for some of those mentioned:

- previous DVT or PE; this is important and well established;
- history of DVT or PE in a close relative;
- taking the oral contraceptive pill or hormone replacement therapy;
- obesity;
- pregnancy, and the six to eight weeks following delivery;
- recent surgery or trauma, especially to the abdomen, to the pelvic region, including the hips, and to the legs;
- cancer, or a recent heart attack or stroke;
- being a heavy smoker;
- having significant varicose veins;
- being of short stature.

In addition, DVTs are more likely to occur in older people, 40 usually being taken as the cut-off point.

What precautions should all travellers take?

- Regularly stretch and flex the calf muscles when seated. Many in-flight magazines show the best way to do this.
- Keep legs as straight as possible and avoid storing hand luggage under the seat in front.
- Move around at least every two to three hours. Doing this more often is usually not practicable and the risk of injury from turbulence may outweigh the benefit.
- Avoid excessive coffee, tea or alcohol and drink plenty of water and soft drinks to avoid dehydration.
- Wear loose-fitting clothing, especially around the waist and thighs, and avoid wearing a broad or tight belt.

What extra precautions are needed for those with risk factors?

For those with any of the risk factors mentioned above:

- Follow all the above recommendations with care.
- Consider using below-knee compression stockings, also known as graded compression stockings. These need to be the right size and correctly fitted, or they may do more harm than good. See a pharmacist and, ideally, get measured.

For those who have previously had a pulmonary embolism or deep vein thrombosis:

- Follow all the recommendations above.
- In addition, discuss with your doctor using low molecular weight heparin as an injection (there are a variety of preparations and trade names). This is self-administered, and you will need instruction in how to use it if you are not already familiar with it. In the USA, fondaparinux is increasingly used instead. If you use any of these preparations, remember to take supplies for any subsequent long-distance flight, including the return flight home. Keep it below 25°C.

There is no clear evidence that taking aspirin reduces the risk of clots forming in veins, but current recommendations are not yet clarified. A sensible rule is that those already taking aspirin should continue to do so, but that there is no need for others to start.

Travelling by train, bus or car

The risks are probably less, but flexing the leg muscles, moving around as much as possible and avoiding dehydration are all important.

What are the symptoms of deep vein thrombosis or pulmonary embolism?

The commonest time for these to occur is after the flight, usually within the first two weeks.

The common symptom of a DVT is swelling of the ankle or leg, usually on one side, accompanied by pain in the calf. The commonest symptom of a PE is sudden pain in the chest, made worse by breathing in.

If you develop any of these symptoms, see a doctor without delay.

Jet lag

Background

All long flights cause you to feel tired, especially where you lose sleep, and this is as true for north–south flights as for transmeridian flights (east–west/west–east). But, in addition, after crossing time zones your body clock is disturbed. This is largely responsible for the downside of intercontinental flying, jet lag, which for most people tends to be worse going from west to east. Jet lag not only makes you feel tired but can affect your appetite and concentration, and can make you feel very out of sorts, both mentally and physically. Certain seasoned travellers claim they have learnt the secret of dealing with this, but for most of us it has to be endured, and perhaps helped to a degree by a few commonsense precautions.

Tips for beating jet lag

What works for one person may not work at all for another. The following guidelines are generally considered helpful, and until you work out your own routines are worth trying:

- Be as well rested as possible before departure.
- Try and take a flight that arrives at your destination in the evening.
- Take short naps during the flight, using earplugs and eyeshades if these help you.
- Eat light meals. Limit caffeine intake and don't drink excess alcohol (it reduces sleep quality).
- On arrival, especially if arriving early in the day, a shower and a short nap can be helpful; then ensure you use night-time at your new destination for your main sleep period.
- For very long flights it may be worth breaking your flight for 24 to 48 hours and catching up on sleep.
- The correct use of light can help adaptation. After a westward flight, try and stay awake while it is light at your destination, possibly after a short nap if you arrive very early. After an eastward flight, avoid bright light in the morning but be outdoors in the afternoon.
- Melatonin, a naturally occurring substance, helps to set our body clock. Our body makes melatonin in the evening and night, which acts as our own natural sleeping tablet. When we cross time zones, the time of its production gets out of synch. There is still a lot of dispute about whether taking melatonin helps to reduce jet lag, but there are many people who are sure it helps them. Melatonin is not packaged accurately into dosages, and often contains impurities. The USA and Hong Kong are probably the best places to try and obtain it. The best advice at the time of writing is that a dose of between 2 mg and 5 mg of the most reliable product you can find, taken at

bedtime on arrival and for the next two or three evenings, is the best way to use it. An alternative, almost as good, is to use a short-acting sleeping tablet (see page 77). Both melatonin and, of course, sleeping tablets can make you feel drowsy, so take extra care if driving within a few hours of taking either.

• As far as you can, allow at least 24 hours at your new destination before you take on any demanding meeting or vigorous activity, or have to make important decisions that may affect the future of the world, your project or your life.

Two final points. First, before you go: only bid into expensive lag-busting diets, massage regimes or computer programmes if you are very desperate or very rich. Second, on arrival: if you are feeling doped and gormless, try one or two sachets of oral rehydration solution (see pages 104–5). They can be very reviving, especially if you dried out on the flight.

Travel sickness

Travel sickness does not usually occur on planes unless there is a lot of turbulence. If you want to play safe or have previously had problems, the preparations listed below can be helpful. They can also be used for any other form of travel sickness.

As well as reaching for the travel pills, also try simpler methods. Pre-book seats near the middle of the plane and in the most central blocks of seats. This way there is less pitching and rolling. The same applies in boats.

Preparations to use

As most of us have discovered, taking sickness pills after you start feeling sick means you've probably lost the battle. However, you will be better motivated to start earlier next time round.

A hyoscine patch (Scopoderm TTS) can be applied on hairless skin behind the ear five to six hours before flying. This should not be used in children under ten.

For children (or adults) the drive to the airport is as likely to cause nausea as the flight itself. Give your favourite sickness pill in plenty of time, and take spares for any subsequent journeys overseas and the return flight. Hyoscine (Kwells) is a favourite brand, especially for children, and promethazine 25 mg (Avomine) (children 5–10 years half dose), and cinnarizine (Stugeron) (children 5–12 years half dose) – each have their followers.

Remember to take sickness pills at least two hours before their effects are needed, though one hour is sufficient for Kwells. All cause a degree of drowsiness, often manifested in children by either greater or lesser charm than usual. Adults using these tablets who are driving to the airport need to take special care.

In the UK all these preparations are available over the counter, apart from hyoscine patches.

Insomnia

Only the lucky few are able to sleep on a long flight and then to appear annoyingly fresh and enthusiastic on the day of arrival at the other side of the world.

For some people, lack of sleep during the flight and/or for a few nights after arrival can be a serious nuisance. This is especially true for those with important engagements or whose transworld responsibilities involve frequent crossing and recrossing of time zones.

No doubt you will be using earplugs, eyeshades and a comfy pillow. There is sometimes a place for the use of sleeping pills. The three golden rules are: use in the lowest dose that works; use for as few nights as possible; and choose a short-acting preparation with minimal after-effects. Current favourites are zolpidem 5 mg or 10 mg (Stilnoct), zopiclone 3.75 mg or 7.5 mg (Zimovane), or zaleplon 5 mg or 10 mg (Sonata), which is the shortest-acting of the three. In the UK they all have to be prescribed by a doctor (see Appendix C) and are best avoided in pregnancy and breastfeeding. Alternatively, just buy diphenhydramine 25 mg (Nytol) over the counter. Remember that sleeping in an aircraft seat for more than two or three hours may increase your risk of getting a DVT. Some experts therefore advise against the use of sleeping pills during flights.

Those unfit to fly

If in doubt about flying, you should discuss this with your own doctor or the medical officer of the airline. If you have any serious condition, be sure to notify the airline well in advance. You can advise the airline of medical problems using the MEDIF form which your doctor must complete. Obtain this from your airline. Talk to your travel agent about this.

Medical conditions that make flying unsuitable or unsafe

Except in special circumstances, international airlines will usually debar anyone with the following problems in the categories stated. However, if in doubt you should phone the airline(s) you are travelling

77

with, as there are many variations. The list below is more detailed than the broad guidelines issued by the World Health Organization. Some passengers with the conditions listed below may wish to leave longer than these minimum requirements before flying.

1 *Blood and bleeding disorders* Severe bleeding or clotting disorder within ten days; untreated deep venous thrombosis; unstable anticoagulation; anaemia with an Hb of 7.5 g/dl or less; sickle cell disease, especially with a history of sickling crisis within seven days.

2 *Decompression illness* Any cases with symptoms within ten days; any scuba-diving activity within 24 hours prior to the flight.

3 *Ear, nose and throat problems* Acute sinus or ear infection; middle-ear surgery within ten days; removal of tonsils within one week.

4 *Eye problems* Eye surgery or penetrating eye wound within seven days.

5 *Fractures* Fractures within 24 or 48 hours, depending on the site of the fracture and the type of plaster.

6 *Heart problems* Myocardial infarction (heart attack) within two weeks if uncomplicated, within two weeks of persistent recovery if initial complications; uncontrolled heart failure, angina or chest pain at rest; uncontrolled arrhythmia; open-heart surgery within two weeks; angioplasty within 14 days if stent used.

7 *Infants under seven days old.*

8 *Infectious illness* Any major infection in the infectious stage including TB, unless confirmed sputum negative.

9 *Major surgery or injury where trapped gas or air may be present,* including abdominal trauma or surgery, cranio-facial and ocular injuries, brain operations and eye operations involving penetration of the eyeball. No flying before 10–14 days.

10 *Mental health problems* Any acute problem, in particular psychotic illness, unless well controlled and/or escorted by competent trained escort and special permission granted.

11 *Neurological problems* Uncomplicated stroke within ten days; grand mal fit within 24 hours; brain surgery within ten days.

12 *Pregnancy and childbirth* After 36 weeks if no complications; after 32 weeks if multiple pregnancy; also no flight within seven days of delivery.

13 *Respiratory problems* Pneumothorax (collapsed lung) not fully inflated; major chest surgery within two weeks; unresolved pneumonia; shortness of breath at rest.

14 *Stomach and bowel problems* Bleeding from the gastrointestinal tract within ten days.

For more information, see <www.britishairways.com/travel/healthintro/public/en_gb>.

Risk of infection during travel

Although there is a much talk about the danger of picking up serious infections during travel, this seems to be relatively uncommon. However, there is evidence to show that infections can be passed on from someone sitting in the same row, or within three rows before and behind, and more rarely within five rows. This is because air-conditioning systems in most modern planes circulate air horizontally.

If you are suffering from an infectious illness, especially with a fever, it is best to delay your flight because of the small risk of passing this on to others.

More research is needed until full guidelines can be drawn up, but this is difficult because of the wide variety of aeroplane designs and ages.

Have children, will travel

Check with the airline what arrangements they have for children. You can probably pre-book a sky-cot near a bulkhead for children up to 12 or even 18 months. Some airlines let children under the age of two years or 18 months fly free; most make a reduced charge, but if you want them to have a seat in which to use your own safety carrier you will usually have to pay, unless the flight is fairly empty.

Many children feel sick going to the airport, so give your preferred antisickness pill (see page 76) at the correct time before leaving. Planes are exciting to start with but, especially for younger children, can become frustrating after a time. Take a supply of small, appropriate toys, books, puzzles and treats, which can be produced at magic intervals to treat, bribe or prevent boredom. You can be sensitive to the needs of others on the plane without hedging your own children in with too many prohibitions.

Children get very thirsty on planes – make sure they get plenty to drink as unrecognized thirst can make them bad-tempered. However, it is also possible to give too much breast milk or other fluid, which can lead to stomach ache as gas expands at altitude.

It is not usually a good idea to sedate your children on planes unless you know from previous experience that they are likely to be awkward or fractious. If you do use a sedative such as promethazine (Phenergan), make sure you have tried this at home first, as it stimulates some children rather than quietening them down.

Medical supplies in transit

Remember that anything placed in the aircraft hold is liable to freeze, especially on a long-haul flight. This means that any immunizations and insulin should be taken in your hand luggage, preferably in a cooled vacuum flask. Tubes of ointment can ooze because of pressure effects, so screw up all containers tightly. Put ballpoint pens in plastic bags.

In-flight emergencies

Although we read stories of in-flight heart attacks and cabin staff delivering babies, such events are rare. As far as you are concerned, they are rarer still if you avoid travelling against doctors' advice or avoid travel if you come in or near to any of the categories shown on page 78.

There are now specific guidelines which most long-distance carriers will adhere to. There are first-aid kits, which the crew are trained to use, and on most flights automated external defibrillators (AEDs) which on-board staff are trained to use. There is also a medical kit which can be used by any doctor who happens to be on board and is willing to use it. Specialist advice is available in the best carriers via electronic link-up to medical experts on the ground. However, it is always a matter of luck whether any doctor is on board, let alone any who are expert at dealing with in-flight emergencies.

Air rage

If someone else seems to be heading for it, keep a low profile and relax. Air rage is a big nuisance but only very rarely causes a safety problem. If you have a tendency to get highly stressed or angry on flights, consider taking a tranquillizer before going. Keep alcohol to the minimum, and if you are a heavy smoker use nicotine gum, as nicotine withdrawal can worsen the problem.

Fear of flying

Although this is very common, it may become so severe that it overshadows your trip or makes you want to cancel the flight.

If the fear is specific to a particular route or particular airline, then make arrangements that avoid these as far as possible. Sometimes discussing your fears with a friend or member of the family can help you to see it in perspective. For elderly travellers or those unfamiliar with flying, it helps to arrive at the airport in plenty of time, so avoiding last-minute panic and hassle, or even do a trial run from home to check-in a few days before.

It is worth remembering that a crash or hijack is extremely rare, and that even if there were many more air accidents than at present, flying on the majority of the world's airlines would still be considered safe.

If it's any comfort, you are more likely to be killed in a car crash going to the airport than be involved in a plane crash; the flight is likely to be the safest part of your whole overseas trip.

If the problem still seems to be getting on top of you, then in the UK Aviatours on 01252 793250 can help. At the time of writing (March 2006) they arrange courses at a variety of airports in England and Scotland for £235. See their website <http://www.aviatours.co.uk>. Most developed countries will have equivalent facilities.

SECTION 2
While abroad

8

Safe eating and safe drinking

This section is about how to keep healthy by eating the right foods and drinking safe drinks and, in the next chapter, about taking care with personal and domestic hygiene. In practice, of course, all this is mainly about how to prevent diarrhoea.

Diarrhoea in adults is rarely life-threatening but it is a big nuisance and probably the main downside of travel. Between one-fifth and one-half of travellers from developed countries visiting a developing one will suffer from traveller's diarrhoea. And although we often, sometimes correctly, put this down to a change in food, habit or time zone, in most cases it is likely to be infectious. Not surprisingly, fact and myth are often hopelessly mixed together on the vital topic of how to avoid Delhi Belly or Pharaoh's Revenge.

Safe eating

In trying to avoid the runs, it is helpful to steer a middle path between two extremes. On the one hand is the seasoned globetrotter, with an apparently cast-iron stomach, seizing any opportunity to eat local food, the more exotic the better. On the other is the obsessional worrier who produces plastic mugs, disposable cutlery and paper napkins at the first whiff of indigenous food.

In fact, avoiding diarrhoea depends on three things: constitution, good luck and taking sensible precautions. You can do little about the first two but quite a bit about the third.

By carefully preparing your own food at home you can eat virtually whatever you wish – and usually survive; the danger mainly arises when eating out. Restaurants are only as safe as the cleanliness of their kitchens and the personal hygiene of their food handlers; in this respect budget travellers in some countries, but not all, are at little more risk than the five-star hotel brigade. But sharing food in the homes of friends and colleagues and joining in local celebrations are probably the biggest risk of all.

In this chapter we are going to look first at food – how we can prepare and eat food as safely as possible – and then we shall look at what is safe to drink, and how we can make what is available to drink as safe as possible.

Foods – safe and unsafe

You are less likely to come to grief if you stick carefully to the following rules:

Safe to eat

- *Food, recently cooked and served still hot* Any food that has just been fried or cooked at above 60°C, providing it is heated right through or boiled or steamed at the boiling point of water for 15 minutes, is perfectly safe. Fortunately, much food comes into this category.
- *Fruit*, either sterilized (see page 87) or carefully peeled (see below).
- *Food (and drink) from sealed packs or cans.*

Unsafe

- *Shellfish, lobsters, crabs or prawns* In coastal areas known to be contaminated or where cholera is present, these should be avoided altogether. Otherwise they can be eaten *if you are sure* they have been boiled for at least 10 to 15 minutes (not easy to ascertain). Some specialists suggest they should always be avoided, not a popular option for most travellers. *Avoid raw fish and remember that sushi always carries a health warning.*
- *Salads* unless carefully home prepared.
- *Uncooked vegetables or fruit* unless known to have been carefully sterilized (see below).
- *Ice, ice cream, milk, cheese and yogurt* unless from a reliable, pasteurized source. Ice should never be put in drinks.
- *Food once hot but served cold*, especially if left in the open air where flies may have settled.
- *Food that has been reheated*, unless it is known to have been thoroughly recooked. This is especially important for rice.
- *Eggs*, unless cooked until the yolk goes solid.
- *Meat*, if any part of it remains pink.
- *Fancy, cold foods* that have involved much handling in their preparation.
- *Table sauces*, as they are often diluted with unclean water.

Children under six months should be exclusively breastfed. If this is not possible, use formula made up with boiled water.

(For more details on care needed with poultry, see the section on avian flu on pages 305–8.)

> *In summary*
> 'Cook it, peel it, clean it or leave it.'

Preparing food at home

Vegetables

Vegetables should be *cleaned* of gross dirt, *peeled* where appropriate and then either *cooked* thoroughly or *sterilized*.

If living overseas, consider planting your own vegetable garden, where you can grow leafy vegetables such as lettuce and spinach.

Fruit

Fruit should be *cleaned* of gross dirt, then *sterilized* and finally *peeled*. Peeling an unwashed piece of fruit is an excellent way of transferring germs progressively inwards. Mango-eaters will understand this. Bananas are an exception.

Milk

Milk should be *boiled* at a vigorous rolling boil for at least one minute, or for three minutes if above 2,000 metres (i.e. as for water), then *cooled* immediately and *kept covered and cool*. A glass disc (or something equivalent that does the job) placed in the milk prevents it from boiling over and is worth buying before you go abroad or improvising while there.

Sterilization

You can sterilize fruit and vegetables by adding tincture of iodine or water sterilization tablets at three times the dose normally used for decontaminating water (see page 94). Then *soak* for at least 20 minutes, drain, or – better – rinse over with boiled water to remove the iodine and the taste of chlorine (you can buy special neutralizing tablets that help mask the taste). Potassium permanganate is ineffective.

Separating cooked from raw food

Don't allow fresh or cooked food to come into contact with raw or contaminated food. This commonly occurs on surfaces and chopping boards and with knives. Beware of raw meat juice dripping in the fridge on to the shelf below. Keep all kitchen surfaces meticulously clean. Never use the same cloth on the floor and on clean surfaces (there are more specific details on this on page 97).

Storing cooked food

Leftover food should either be stored near or below 10°C or kept hot –

near or above 60°C. This is essential if you store food for more than four or five hours. Food for infants is better not stored at all. One word of warning: only place warm food in the refrigerator in small quantities – the centre may not cool and bacteria may explode in numbers.

Washing hands

Before eating or preparing food, *wash your hands* thoroughly with soap. If you are interrupted, need to change nappies, go to the toilet or touch any domestic animal or pet, wash your hands again. Young children's hands should be washed before meals and after going to the toilet, and their *nails kept clean and short.* There is strong evidence that regularly washing hands with soap and water if visibly dirty, or cleansing with an alcohol gel, reduces the likelihood of you, your friends and family getting diarrhoea. Surprisingly, it may also make it less likely that you will pick up a cold, flu or other respiratory infection.

Reheating food

All parts of the food must reach at least 60°C, or in other words be thoroughly recooked, to kill any organism that may have multiplied during storage.

Failed fridges

If the power supply fails, keep the door closed, cover the fridge with a soaked blanket and keep the blanket moist. Throw away any food that has returned to room temperature. Make sure your fridge has a thermometer.

Food storage

Protect your food from flies by netting or covers. A netted cupboard also protects from rodents. To keep ants away, the legs of such cupboards can be placed in cups containing oil or salty water (the salt in addition stops mosquitoes breeding).

Drainage

Plates and cutlery should be *drained* in racks after washing, and if possible protected from flies.

Cooks, houseboys and ayahs

Anyone you employ for cooking at home, in an institution or on an expedition should have *regular (e.g. six-monthly) stool tests,* as cooks are commonly carriers of Amoeba, Giardia or even typhoid. They should be encouraged to follow the same hand-washing habits as you insist on for other family or team members. *Anyone with diarrhoea or a stomach upset should not be on cooking duty.*

Local hospitality – beware

At home, and to a large extent when eating in restaurants, you have control over what you eat. This is certainly not the case when you are invited to a meal by friends, the tribal chief, an important political leader or the local bishop. Unless you think fast, you may have downed a whole range of suspect food (and drink) before you know it. As a guest your twin aim is to avoid offending both your host and your own digestion. Seasoned travellers can add their own suggestions to the advice given below.

- *Identify safe foods and concentrate on those.*
- *Identify and avoid* foods you consider suspect (including those you can't identify).
- If in serious trouble, *play with and pretend to eat your food* without actually doing so, or eat the smallest amounts possible.
- *Explain* that the part of the animal you have been handed is taboo in your 'tribe' – or honour your colleague with it instead!
- *Refuse* some of the food you are offered, politely or with an engaging smile.
- *Explain you are fasting* for religious or other reasons. Many cultures will readily understand this.
- *Play the eccentric* who is quaintly apologetic for his strange food habits and weak digestion.
- *Consider 'saying grace'* before meals. It was originally intended for gratitude – and protection.
- If really in a corner *play the health card*. Apologize that although you have always longed to eat what has been placed before you, your doctor has absolutely forbidden it.

Eating a balanced diet

It is nearly always possible to eat a balanced diet overseas, meaning you will not need to take extra vitamins or food supplements. There are a few exceptions:

- long-term travellers or volunteers who run low on money and skimp on proper food;
- those with chronic bowel problems which reduce the absorption of food, e.g. tropical sprue, especially in South Asia (see page 108);
- pregnant women and those considering pregnancy, who will need extra folic acid: 0.4 mg daily prior to conception, and 5 mg daily

when pregnant, especially if taking the anti-malarial proguanil (Paludrine), or Malarone as increasing numbers of advisers consider this to be safe in pregnancy;
- those who have a low body mass index of 19 or below, or are very thin;
- elderly travellers, especially if thin, or if they have been eating an inadequate diet before travelling, and especially if they have been living alone;
- vegetarians who do not reliably eat a healthy vegetarian diet or who find it hard to do so in the new culture in which they are living.

The golden rule of good nutrition is to maintain an adequate and balanced intake of the three main nutritional groups:

- *carbohydrates* or energy foods (the staple food crops mentioned below);
- *protein or bodybuilding foods* from two or more sources such as meat, fish, eggs, lentils and grains; if you are going to be involved in any strenuous pursuits, especially mountaineering, eat plenty of protein, preferably but not essentially meat;
- *vitamins* – protective foods – especially vitamins A (green, leafy vegetables and yellow vegetables and fruit), B (whole grains and meat) and C (citrus fruit and other fresh fruit and vegetables). Vitamin D is largely made in the skin, when exposed to sunlight. Folic acid is present in fresh vegetables and liver, and is important for women who are either pregnant or planning pregnancy.

In addition, *minerals*, especially iron, are also needed. Iron-rich foods include green leafy vegetables, eggs, fish and meat including liver. Children, pregnant women and breastfeeding mothers especially need calcium. It is found mainly in milk and dairy products.

Each part of the world has a staple crop – either rice, wheat, maize, millet or sorghum, or roots and tubers, e.g. cassava, potatoes, sweet potatoes and yams.

As well as eating enough of these staples each day, which will be your main supply of energy (calories), you will need to add a protein source and locally available foods containing the three main vitamins.

A reasonable rule of thumb is that a plateful of food containing three or more distinct colours (e.g. white or yellow for the staple food, green for vegetables containing vitamins A and C, and brown for meat containing protein, vitamin B and iron) is likely to be well balanced. Make sure, however, that vegetables are well (but not over-) cooked.

In many developed countries we are encouraged to eat five portions of fruit and vegetables each day. This is a good rule when living overseas, with one major proviso – that they must be safely prepared and not be eaten as salads prepared by others with different standards of hygiene. Many countries use large quantities of oil in cooking. Often these are composed mainly of unhealthy saturated fats, especially in southern Asia, and of palm oil, for example in West Africa and Indonesia. Apart from causing you to put on weight, these oils often raise your cholesterol level. Try to minimize the amount of fatty food you eat, and use healthy cooking oils such as groundnut, soya or olive oil.

Vegetarians

It is possible, but in practice not always easy, to be healthily vegetarian overseas. You must, however, ensure you are eating sufficient protein from several different sources, including a variety of beans and lentils. Many vegetarians are cheese-eaters; avoid cheese unless it is known to come from a safe pasteurized source. Consider taking Vegemite with you, which contains vitamin B. In practice, vegetarians tend to lose weight more easily, especially in the Indian subcontinent or after repeated stomach upsets. In these situations they are more likely to become anaemic and deficient in folic acid, and should consider taking iron and folate supplements.

Summary

A sensible aim for all travellers is to maintain normal (i.e. correct) body weight overseas. If you are overweight before departure, try to lose weight before leaving and during the first few months abroad. However, in many developing-world cultures a *minor* degree of overweight is a sign that you are a person of substance or success, and small reserves may be useful if you fall sick or find yourself in an appetite-depleting zone such as West Africa or monsoon Asia.

Safe drinking

Although drinking mineral water in the UK may be more a luxury than a necessity (and has been shown by recent research to be environmentally unfriendly), obtaining sufficient clean water in the tropics is a major health issue. In the heat and humidity we need a huge supply of fluids, and a safe supply has to be set up.

Contaminated water causes many diseases. These include hepatitis, diarrhoea and dysentery, typhoid, cholera and giardiasis, all caused by taking in organisms through the mouth. Germs come from food sources or fluids, or from fingers, contaminated by faeces. Some diseases, in particular bilharzia (schistosomiasis), are caught via the skin through swimming, splashing or washing in contaminated water (see pages 277–81). So is leptospirosis (see page 317).

Ways of making water safe

> The key rule for making water safe to drink is to boil it at a vigorous rolling boil for a full minute and for three minutes at over 2,000 metres.

This statement is an emerging consensus, even though experts still have some areas of disagreement.

Here are some more details, especially useful if living overseas for any length of time, or if setting up a house or base.

Step 1: Identify a source

If setting up home or base camp, find the nearest, cleanest source, such as a spring, a deep well or a rainwater tank (except where roofs are painted with lead or made of thatch). If using tapped water, identify where it comes from and make sure pipes and joints are sound. Hot tap-water left to cool is a useful source in a hotel. Treat with caution assurances from hosts that all their drinking water is boiled. Beware of shallow tube wells, which are often infected. Take special care with well water in Bangladesh and some other countries, as many are dangerously contaminated with arsenic. An ideal water supply is cool, clear and odourless.

Step 2: If cloudy, let it stand

Then decant it, or filter it through a cloth, fine gauze or Millbank bag.

Step 3: Sterilize it

There are three possible ways of ridding water of germs:

Boiling This is the most reliable method and kills all organisms, including viruses and amoebic cysts. Unless your water is known to be from a safe source or there is a serious lack of fuel, boiling is the method of choice.

As highlighted above, boil for one minute at a vigorous rolling boil and for three minutes if at over 2,000 metres. The additional boiling time over 2,000 metres is to kill viruses, some of which will not be killed by a minute's boiling at that altitude. There is no need to boil longer than this, and it wastes fuel and precious natural resources.

After boiling let the water cool and stand for a few hours to improve the taste, or shake it in a sterilized non-plastic container to mix it with air.

When making hot drinks at home, such as tea and coffee, remember to let the water boil for a good minute, which ideally means avoiding electric kettles that switch themselves off immediately on boiling.

Use boiled water for cleaning your teeth, keeping a separate supply in the bathroom. In an emergency just use toothpaste and saliva.

Filtering Water is filtered for one of two reasons:

- to remove suspended material prior to boiling (see Step 2 above);
- as a convenient alternative to boiling, and when there is a shortage of fuel or time.

Water should *not* be filtered after it has been boiled, despite some incorrect traditions among certain long-term expatriates. It risks recontamination.

The best filters, used correctly and cleaned regularly, are almost as reliable as boiling, though some viruses may not be excluded. There are usually three stages in the filtering process: charcoal activation, chemical treatment often with iodine resin, and actual filtration.

Water passes through a filter either by gravity or through an attached pump or direct from a tap through a special attachment.

There are two recommended materials used for filtration:

- Ceramic filters, using porcelain 'candles'. The pore size should be as small as possible, ideally 0.1 to 0.3 microns, and the filter impregnated with silver. This system kills most micro-organisms but not all viruses, Cryptosporidium or Giardia unless stated by the manufacturer. Katadyne is a well-known brand. Ceramic filters are suitable for home use.
- Iodine resin filters. Contact with iodine kills micro-organisms and releases a low level of iodine for continuing disinfection. These are ideal when on the road but should not be used long term (see page 95 for suggested models).

Check your filters carefully and maintain them according to the manufacturer's instructions. Ceramic candles should be regularly cleaned, handled with care and checked for any breaks or cracks, which will render them useless. Boil them once a week or according to instructions, unless impregnated with silver. Wash your hands carefully after cleaning or maintaining your water filters.

Disinfecting This is slightly less reliable than boiling and the best filtering.

- *Chlorine*-based disinfectants can be used. These kill most organisms but do not reliably kill all viruses, Giardia, Amoeba or Cryptosporidium. In the UK, Puritabs and Steritabs are well-known brands. Household bleach can also be used: add two drops of a 5–6 per cent solution of available chlorine to one litre, or add eight drops of a 1 per cent solution. (One drop is about 0.05 ml.) The water should smell and taste faintly of chlorine.
- *Iodine* is effective, killing most organisms but not Cryptosporidium. Buy Potable Aqua tablets and dissolve one in a litre of water, or according to the manufacturer's instructions. An alternative is to add five drops per litre of 2 per cent tincture of iodine (the normal concentration) to clear water, or ten drops per litre to cloudy or very cold water (below 5°C). Neutralizing tablets will help remove the unpleasant taste. (Cloudy water should first be strained through a cloth or allowed to stand and the clear water decanted.) After adding the tablets or solution to the water, allow to stand for 20 to 30 minutes at normal room temperature or for one or two hours if very cold.

Current advice is not to use iodine for longer than six weeks, and to use it only occasionally when pregnant, in those under six years of age, or if suffering from thyroid problems. If you do use iodine sterilization, including iodine-resin filters regularly for more than three months, have a thyroid blood test arranged at your next medical check.

Using the sun's heat If living in a sunny, remote area, you can fill transparent, clean containers with the cleanest water available and place them in the sun for at least five hours. This kills virtually all germs. Consider painting the lower half of the outside black or standing the containers on a black surface to increase heat absorption. Let the water cool overnight and use it the following day. Make sure the containers you use have not previously been used for storing chemicals or pesticides. This is known as the Sodis system and is increasingly used in developing countries. (See <http://www.sodis.org>.)

Step 4: Storing water

Boiled water should ideally be stored in the container in which it was boiled. Alternatively, it can be poured into a previously sterilized narrow-necked earthenware jar and placed on a clean, dry surface. The jar will need careful and regular cleaning and should be kept covered. No one should be allowed to dip into it.

Many people living abroad keep two large kettles, using each in turn first to boil, then to store. In this way there is a constant supply of cool, boiled water.

Water is best removed from its storage container through a tap or spout. Dippers are unsafe as they frequently get left on the floor and contaminate the whole supply. A good rule is 'Tap or tip, don't dip'.

Safe fluids – on the road

When you are on the road or in difficult conditions, boiling or filtering is not always possible. Thirsty travellers drinking what's offered and hoping for the best put their bowels at risk.

Here are some suggestions:

- Keep to *hot* drinks. Tea and coffee are usually safe, because the milk is usually added to the brew and boiled up together. Try to avoid any cup that is obviously cracked or has just been swilled out with dirty water. In parts of East Asia it is cultural to swill out cups and rice bowls with boiling tea and pour them out on the floor.
- Keep to *carbonated* soft drinks (or beer), from bottles with metal tops from reputable firms. Such drinks are usually clean and their slight acidity kills some organisms. Avoid bottles with loose or suspect tops, and soda or mineral water bottles whose contents may have been replenished from a tap.
- Bottles of mineral water are now available in many countries. Although some of them are clean and genuine, others definitely are not. It takes an experienced eye to tell them apart. *Only use those with unbroken seals*, and preferably bottles where both main label and bottle-top have identical names and appear to match up. If in doubt, ask an experienced expatriate about brands known to be reliable – or unreliable.
- Make sure all soft-drink bottles are opened in your presence. If drinking straight from the bottle, clean the rim with care, as it may have been resting in contaminated water to keep cool.
- Carry a *vacuum flask* or other container such as a Platypus bottle with a clean drink of your choice.
- Always have some *water sterilizing tablets* with you. They should be dry and reasonably fresh (yellowing tablets are losing their potency).
- If using a *plastic water bottle* for travelling or trekking, allow boiled water to cool first before pouring it into the bottle, otherwise the taste will be nauseating.
- Carry a small *portable water filter* such as a Pre-Mac Pocket Travel Well or Trekker Travel Well or other personal water purifier. Check the specifications from one of the suppliers in Appendix E to make sure it exactly fits your needs. Because they contain iodine, you

should follow the same precautions on restricted use mentioned under iodine tablets, above.

- *Avoid ice.* Freezing does not kill organisms and ice often comes from an impure source.
- *Avoid milk* unless just boiled.
- *Avoid excessive alcohol.* It lowers your inhibitions, dehydrates and does not sterilize, making it a low entry on the tropical drinks hit parade.

Swimming

Avoid swimming in contaminated *lakes, seas, rivers, pond or swimming pools.* First, disease-carrying organisms are likely to get into your mouth; second, you can catch skin infections through cuts and abrasions in your skin. This includes leptospirosis, especially in areas that have been flooded. In sub-Saharan Africa and some other areas, bilharzia is a risk (see pages 277–81). Crocodiles and sharks are not reported to have lost their appetites.

Avoid swimming on *beaches* near to cities if there is a known cholera outbreak, where the sea is obviously polluted, or where you know or suspect there is contamination with human sewage. Also take care where dog faeces are present on the beach (see pages 331–2).

Swimming pools that smell of chlorine are generally considered safe.

When babies and very young children swim or have a bath they often take in water. Make the bath as hot as possible, then let it cool to the right temperature for bathing.

9

Health and hygiene at home

This section looks at ways to minimize diarrhoea through good hygiene at home, and also how to help maintain good health among all those living in your house. If you live in a developing country, are on an expedition or set up your own home, there is a great deal you can do to prevent illness.

Wash frequently

In hot countries it is essential to wash frequently, not only because of the heat and dust but also because of the great number of germs that find your body surface a cosy environment. When the weather is hot, try to wash twice daily, at least once with soap, preferably using a shower. This will help prevent boils and skin infections. Water supply permitting, leave the shower to run briefly before getting under it, as this reduces the risk of getting Legionnaires' disease (legionellosis, which can cause severe pneumonia) from contaminated water tanks. Also try to avoid getting water into your mouth. To reduce the likelihood of getting intestinal worms, keep your fingernails, and those of your children, clean and short, and wear shoes when outside the house – this helps to avoid hookworm.

Clean and iron clothes

You should change your clothes regularly and keep them well laundered. This especially goes for underwear and socks.

Ideally dry clothes on a line, not on the ground, even though the local people may commonly do this. In areas where the tumbu fly is found (see pages 213–14), you should either dry all clothes in the house or, better still, hot-iron any clothes that may come into contact with the skin, including underwear and non-disposable nappies, making sure you thoroughly iron the creases and seams. This kills the tumbu fly eggs.

Domestic cleanliness

It is worth being very careful with domestic hygiene. Scraps of food left around quickly decompose or attract insects and animals. Take care that the house is swept regularly and the kitchen area is kept really clean. Make sure that any rag used for the floor is both separate and obviously different from any cloth used for wiping tables and wash both frequently (explain this carefully to anyone who works for you or visits you).

Toilets, whatever their type, easily attract flies, and you will need to have them regularly cleaned, especially where children are using them.

97

If you are building a latrine it should be 20 metres or more from any water source or river, and on a lower level. It should have a tight-fitting lid and ideally be based on a 'VIP' pit-latrine or water-seal model.

Well-cared-for surrounds to the house

Keep the *surrounds* of the house or camp clean, free from standing water (to reduce the risk of malaria, dengue fever and other mosquito-borne diseases) and free from thick or high vegetation (to reduce the risk of snakes getting into the house). Make sure you have a good *drainage system* for household water, keeping soakaways clean and de-slimed. Any *rainwater tank* needs to be well maintained, have a tight-fitting lid to prevent mosquitoes from breeding, and should be washed through by the first rains in areas where there are seasonal rains. Keep *windows, doors and screening* in a good state of repair to reduce the number of insects (especially mosquitoes) entering the house.

Keep the house cool

House temperature can be kept lower by making sure all outer walls are pale or white, and that you use a non-heat-absorbing roofing material. If this is not possible, paint the roof white. Other useful measures are overhanging eaves and insulating the roof by placing a layer of bamboo, grasses or thatch on top. Tall rooms with openings near the top and with large lower windows set opposite each other help air-flow. Of course, air conditioning is an option in many situations, not necessarily for the whole house but for one or two rooms, including the bedroom. For some travellers this will be too expensive and for some areas the electricity supply is too unreliable. A good alternative is a fast-moving ceiling fan.

Keep insects and animal pests at bay

You can keep flies to the minimum by good household hygiene, screening, swatting and the use of insecticides and fly-traps. Pyrethroid insecticides are effective against cockroaches. Ants should be killed with an appropriate ant-killer before they get established, otherwise it will be ants and marmalade for breakfast. Food should always be carefully stored, covered or screened so that no insect or animal can touch it.

Household rubbish

This needs to be appropriately disposed of. In rural areas you can separate it into material suitable for burning, composting and burial. Any rubbish dump, either household or communal, needs to be deep, a good distance from the house and kept covered with earth so that animals and children don't scatter the contents. Rubbish awaiting disposal should be stored in a strong container, kept raised off the ground, and should have its lid secured for protection against raiding animals.

Pets

Household pets can easily introduce diseases into the house. Take special care with dogs, which will need to be restricted in where they roam, and must be kept clean, carefully housetrained and have deworming medicine every six months. From the age of three months dogs and cats should be kept up to date with their rabies injections. Three-yearly boosters of a live attenuated vaccine are normally used, which if not available where you live can be brought out from the UK or your home country. Dogs should not be 'kissed', and after petting them or playing with them you should wash your hands (and those of your children when they have been touching them).

Health care of your employees

Finally, if you employ a house servant who is not used to working under the stricter hygiene rules suggested above, take care to explain the rules to them and gain their cooperation. This, along with a medical check and regular stool test, will help to keep the whole household more healthy. Encourage anyone you employ who has a persistent cough to have a sputum test or chest X-ray to exclude TB, especially if they work with you, regularly visit your house or have regular contact with your children. In areas where HIV is common, you can encourage anyone working with you to go for voluntary counselling and testing (VCT) to check for HIV infection, but you will need to do this sensitively, and unless too unwell to do the job they should never lose their job because of being HIV-positive.

10
Treating diarrhoea

'Travel broadens the mind but loosens the bowel.'

For most travellers in developing countries, diarrhoea is not a matter of if, but when. This section, which is therefore quite detailed, aims to help you deal with the almost inevitable, and to recognize and treat the more serious. It covers the following:

- Who is most at risk?
- What are the main types of diarrhoea?
- Action plan for acute diarrhoea (up to seven days)
- Action plan for persistent diarrhoea (over seven days)
- Amoebic infection
- Giardiasis
- Antibiotics to prevent traveller's diarrhoea
- Diarrhoea in the local population
- Cholera
- Typhoid fever (enteric fever)
- Constipation

Who is most at risk?

This depends on several factors: the area you are travelling to, your lifestyle, the precautions you take, natural resistance and good luck. Also your nationality: some recent large-scale research found that Brits caught diarrhoea more easily than other nationalities. Sadly, no explanation was offered.

Area being visited
We can broadly divide the world into three bowel zones:

- high risk: South and Southeast Asia (including China), Africa, Central America and the less developed countries of South America;
- medium risk: Russia and the former Soviet states, the Caribbean, southern and eastern Europe, the Near and Middle East, and the Pacific islands;
- low risk: North America, Australia, New Zealand, western Europe and Japan.

Within these countries you are generally more likely to get diarrhoea in hot and humid conditions and during the rainy season or monsoon.

Lifestyle and precautions
By being careful you are less likely to get diarrhoea but you can't

altogether avoid it – there are just too many ways in which germs can enter the body (e.g. on your fingers after shaking hands with local friends). The kitchens of five-star hotels may be no healthier than street vendors, especially if you buy something sizzling hot from the side of the road. Many downtown or seaside restaurants must be treated with care. The key to bowel calm lies more in the precautions you take than the lifestyle you lead.

Resistance

Some of us have more than others. We all know of those who seem to have cast-iron stomachs and others who fall to the first meal out in terra exotica. Medical sleuths in Nepal have recently discovered that expatriates living there for two years or more develop substantial resistance. Foreign travel within the previous six months may also give some short-lived protection. If you have a pre-existing condition, such as Crohn's disease or colitis, diarrhoea can hit you harder (see pages 56–9). Irritable bowel syndrome (IBS) can make your gripes worse. The use of some antacids may lower resistance. The very young and very old are at greater risk.

What are the main types of diarrhoea?

Although more than 40 different organisms are known to cause diarrhoea, experienced travellers find it helpful to divide the runs into one of three main types:

Acute watery diarrhoea

Acute watery diarrhoea, lasting a few days, with little or no fever, is the commonest form. The majority are caused by bacteria including, for example, E. coli (the commonest worldwide, and sometimes known as ETEC), Campylobacter and Salmonella. Viruses, especially noroviruses (also causing vomiting) and rotavirus, account for most of the remainder, especially in children. Malaria can sometimes cause diarrhoea. Ciguatera fish poisoning is becoming more common, and is caused by eating a variety of predatory tropical fish. Severe symptoms start within 24–48 hours, often with numbness in the limbs and itching. It usually subsides within a week, but may cause alarming symptoms.

Cholera (see page 110), rare in expatriates, can cause extremely severe, almost continuous watery diarrhoea (see below). Typhoid – much commoner – usually causes diarrhoea but not always at the start of the illness (see page 112).

Acute diarrhoea with blood

Acute diarrhoea with blood and usually fever is commonly known as *dysentery*. There are two common types:

- In *bacillary* dysentery (caused by Shigella) there is profuse bloody diarrhoea, usually with mucus (often 12 or more stools in 24 hours), with severe straining, griping and a feeling of doom. Fever is present.
- With acute *amoebic* dysentery the symptoms are usually less severe, with little or no fever and rarely more than 6–12 stools in 24 hours.

Other organisms can cause blood in the stools, including Campylobacter (similar to, though usually less severe than, bacillary dysentery, but giving joint pains in up to 10 per cent of those infected), typhoid (see below), rare forms of *E. coli* and schistosomiasis (see page 277).

Chronic diarrhoea

Chronic diarrhoea is taken here as diarrhoea lasting seven days or more. Any of the above can persist. However, Amoeba or Giardia, as well as more exotic germs such as Cryptosporidium, Cyclospora and possibly Blastocystis, often cause chronic diarrhoea. In many cases no cause is found (see below).

Action plan for acute diarrhoea including dysentery

Before reading this, remember it is always better to seek out medical help when ill overseas rather than self-treat. This is essential if you have more severe symptoms (see below).

Here are five broad categories. Treat according to which most obviously applies to you.

1 Mild symptoms

You have symptoms that do not interfere with normal activities; you feel generally well.

Treatment

- Keep up fluid intake (see 'Keeping up fluids in diarrhoea', page 104).
- Eat a light diet such as toast, soup, rice, bananas, in small amounts, chewing well, as soon as your symptoms start to improve. Encourage children to keep eating a light diet.

2 Moderate symptoms

Your symptoms threaten normal activities or travel; you feel reasonably well, and have no fever or dysentery.

Treatment

As in (1) above plus the following:

- loperamide 2 mg tablets (Imodium), two together, then if necessary one every four hours until symptoms improve (children under 12

102

should not generally use loperamide, unless their symptoms are troublesome or distressing, and it should never be used in children under four);

- ciprofloxacin 250 mg tablets, two together as a single dose; ciprofloxacin is most useful for short trips and should be used more sparingly for attacks of diarrhoea when you are resident overseas (children under 16 should not generally use ciprofloxacin or another quinolone antibiotic with a similar name, e.g. norfloxacin or ofloxacin).

3 More severe symptoms

You are unable to carry out normal activities, feel unwell, may have a fever but have no dysentery. See a doctor and give a stool test if your symptoms and general health are not rapidly improving.

Treatment

As (2) above except continue ciprofloxacin 250 mg tablets, two daily for a total of three days.

4 Dysentery

You have blood in your stool and/or fever and feel unwell, possibly seriously so.

Treatment

As (3) above, making absolutely sure you keep up fluids. Do not use loperamide or any other blocking medication in diarrhoea with blood or when there is a fever, or in travellers with ulcerative colitis.

You can occasionally get quickly and seriously ill with dysentery (and almost always feel ill and worried), so see a doctor and get a stool test. The stool must be fresh, preferably still warm, and examined without delay in a good-quality lab or doctor's clinic.

5 Treating according to stool test

Ciprofloxacin 500 mg daily for three days will usually be an effective treatment for Shigella, Salmonella and *E. coli*. The best treatment for Campylobacter is azithromycin 500 mg daily for three days; children between 15 and 25 kg, 200 mg once daily; between 26 and 35 kg, 300 mg daily; between 36 and 45 kg, 400 mg daily, all for three days. Alternatively, erythromycin can be used but the multiple doses are a nuisance. The normal adult dose is 250–500 mg every six hours for five to seven days.

Note that ciprofloxacin must be used with plenty of fluids, and is not suitable for those under 16 years of age, in pregnancy or during breastfeeding. It can occasionally affect driving ability and may cause slight temporary confusion in the elderly. For these and other side-effects of antibiotics, consult the Patient Information Leaflet.

Rifaximin is a relatively new antibiotic, effective, apparently free from major side-effects and largely unabsorbed from the bowel. At the time of writing (February 2006) it is not available in the UK, but it can be bought in a number of countries under various trade names (e.g. Normix, Redactiv, Flonorm and Zaxine). The dose is 200 mg three times daily or 400 mg twice daily for three days in moderate or severe diarrhoea where ETEC diarrhoea is suspected or proved. It should not be used in dysentery or in children under 12 years of age, or in pregnancy.

Treatment for children

Keeping up fluids is by far the most important treatment (see below). Drugs are less important and should not normally be used as a home remedy in children under four.

For children four and over with more severe symptoms and/or if there are essential journeys and no toilets available: loperamide (Imodium) as a blocking agent in the smallest dose which controls symptoms, e.g. age four to eight, 1 mg; age nine to twelve, 2 mg. Loperamide comes both as tablets and as a syrup, and can be repeated if necessary every four hours for up to a few doses.

Antibiotics are not always used in children, and the key is adequate rehydration until the infection self-cures. However, azithromycin (doses above) can be used if symptoms persist. Many drugs that are safe in children are now ineffective against many forms of traveller's diarrhoea because of drug resistance.

Treatment for pregnant women

Pregnant women should generally use rehydration only and avoid drugs unless seriously ill. Of the drugs mentioned above, only erythromycin is recommended. Both erythromycin and azithromycin can be used where necessary during breastfeeding.

Keeping up fluids in diarrhoea

You can use any appropriate non-alcoholic or non-milk-based fluid, such as soft drinks (e.g. Sprite, 7-Up, Fanta or Cola, shaken until flat), weak tea or light soup. A simple method is to buy packets of oral rehydration salts (ORS) and mix them with water as per instructions. Common brands are Dioralyte, Rehydrat or other sachets recommended by the World Health Organization (WHO).

It is also possible to make your own mixture. The methods and amounts recommended vary considerably. Current guidelines recommend adding eight level teaspoons of sugar plus half a teaspoon of salt to one litre of boiled water. One teaspoon equals about 5 ml. Children under two are spooned a quarter to half cup after each stool; those from two to ten sip half to one cup per stool; older children and adults have as much as they require, usually at least one cup per stool. Breastfed children should continue to receive breast milk.

If signs of dehydration occur – e.g. dry lips and tongue, inelastic skin, absent or highly concentrated urine – double the amount until these symptoms disappear. If vomiting also occurs, sips should be taken more slowly until the nausea improves.

Remember that after severe diarrhoea you can feel extremely weak and faint, especially on standing. As you take rehydration solution these symptoms will improve, sometimes dramatically. Continue to drink until your urine is no longer dark. Keeping up fluids is important in everyone, but life-saving in children and the elderly.

When to see a doctor

You should seek further help under the following situations:

- Your symptoms do not largely subside within 48 hours.
- You are seriously ill.
- You have blood in your stools.
- You have uncontrollable vomiting and/or marked abdominal pain.
- You (or your children) are severely dehydrated.

Don't forget that diarrhoea may mean you have malaria. If in doubt, get a malaria blood test.

Action plan for persistent diarrhoea

Diarrhoea lasting seven days or more (see page 102) tends to cause much concern and discussion among travellers. Before treating it or imagining a giant Amoeba eating away at your intestines, it is worth trying to identify the cause. There are two ways:

A stool test

Take a fresh stool in a labelled, waterproof container to a reliable laboratory and await the result. If the first is negative, try to arrange two further tests.

Often germs will not be identified, and even if they are, treatments you are given may not always be appropriate. Correct doses for germs showing up on stool tests in persistent diarrhoea include the following:

- *Amoeba and Giardia*: see separate section below.
- *Blastocysti*s *hominis*: adults, metronidazole 400 mg tablets, two tablets three times daily for seven days; children's doses as for

Amoeba. Blastocystis does not always cause symptoms (some specialists in Europe and America believe it rarely does), and metronidazole does not always cure them.

- *Cryptosporidium*: no treatment is reliably effective, but paromomycin 250 mg tablets, one twice daily for seven to ten days, may help. This must be given under medical supervision. A new drug called nitazoxanide is proving effective but is hard to get hold of and needs to be used under medical supervision. In those with normal immunity, 'Crypto' usually self-cures.
- *Cyclospora*: adults, cotrimoxazole 480 mg tablets, two tablets twice daily for seven days. This is frequent in Nepal and in some other areas of the tropics, especially in the rainy season.
- *Schistosomiasis (S. mansoni)*: adults, praziquantel 40 mg/kg as a single dose or in two divided doses for one day. For average-sized adults this approximates to 500 mg or 600 mg tablets, four tablets together or two tablets twice daily for one day (see page 280).
- *Strongyloides*: adults, albendazole 400 mg twice daily for three days (see pages 310–11). Children aged two or over, same dose. If Strongyloides is found on a stool test it is essential to seek medical advice.

Quite often stool tests in chronic diarrhoea will demonstrate an organism which causes acute diarrhoea (see section above), in which case use the recommended antibiotic mentioned in that section.

Inspired guesswork

If a stool test is negative, impossible to arrange or thought to be unreliable you will need to try to match cause to symptoms according to the descriptions below:

Amoebiasis (chronic amoebic dysentery)

This is common in most developing countries. *Symptoms* include mucus and sometimes blood in the stool, but these are often overlooked. Loose bowels may alternate with constipation; lower abdominal pain is common. There may be some weight loss. Chronic sufferers often become ill-tempered and withdrawn.

Occasionally amoebas travel upstream to the liver, causing amoebic hepatitis or an abscess. Suspect this if you develop a fever (often, but not always, high or 'swinging') or pain and tenderness in the upper right part of the abdomen or under the right rib cage. This must be treated urgently.

Treatment of amoebiasis is as follows: tinidazole 500 mg (Fasigyn), four tablets together after food on three successive evenings, or metronidazole 400 mg (Flagyl), two tablets three times a day for five days. If you suspect liver involvement, see a doctor urgently and take metronidazole 400 mg, two tablets three times a day for ten days.

Dosages for children are as follows. Tinidazole: 50–60 mg/kg daily for three days. Metronidazole: one to three years of age, 200 mg every eight hours; three to seven years of age, 200 mg every six hours; seven to ten years of age, 400 mg every eight hours; all for five days. There are slight variations to this on some packet instructions, in which case follow the Patient Information Leaflet. Metronidazole is available in the UK and several other countries as a syrup for children under the brand name Flagyl.

These drugs can make you feel ill, often causing headache, nausea, dark urine, a metallic taste and a conviction that the treatment is worse than the cure. Alcohol should be strictly avoided as it worsens the side-effects. Avoid in pregnancy. These drugs can make breast milk taste bitter, especially in high dosages, but are probably harmless to the baby. Tinidazole usually has less troublesome side-effects than metronidazole and is probably as effective.

After finishing your course of Fasigyn or Flagyl, you should ideally take diloxanide 500 mg (Furamide), one tablet three times a day for ten days (this kills the amoebic cysts). Children's dose is 20 mg/kg daily in three divided doses, for five days.

It is unwise to take *repeated* courses of amoeba treatment unless there is evidence on a fresh stool test of active motile forms (trophozoites) or you have very typical symptoms. Amoebic cysts on stool tests more often than not belong to a form of Amoeba that does not cause symptoms, known as *Entamoeba dispar*, but in most labs it is impossible to separate from the disease-causing *E. histolytica*. *E. dispar* is up to ten times more common in many areas than *E. histolytica*. Only treat for Amoeba if you have typical symptoms, not just because 'amoebic cysts' were found in the stool.

> Amoebas are sometimes overlooked; they are often also unfairly blamed for a variety of afflictions. An obsession with Amoeba is as common as an infection, and there comes a time when a self-imposed ban on 'The Amoebes', both in conversation and in letters home, is the most appropriate action.

Giardiasis

This is also common in many areas of the tropics, in eastern Europe and the former Soviet states. *Symptoms* include offensive wind ('eggy burps') and diarrhoea, loss of appetite, nausea and heartburn. It sometimes leads to milk (lactose) intolerance.

Treatment is as follows: *either* tinidazole 500 mg tablets (Fasigyn), four together after food, repeat same dose in two weeks; *or* metronidazole 400 mg tablets (Flagyl), three times daily for five days. Avoid alcohol while on treatment, and again be aware of the side-effects mentioned above. Giardiasis is common in young children. They may have few symptoms but still pass the infection on to others. Treatment in children is as follows: tinidazole 50–75 mg/kg as single dose, and repeated after two weeks; metronidazole: one to three years of age, 500 mg daily; three to seven years, 600–800 mg daily; seven to ten years, 1 g daily; all for three days. Metronidazole may be slightly more effective for Giardia in children than tinidazole.

Lactose intolerance

Giardiasis and some other bowel infections can lead on to *lactose (milk) intolerance*, which is one cause of persistent diarrhoea and flatulence. If you have symptoms suggestive of this you should see a doctor. One way of telling whether you might have this is to drink one to two pints of boiled milk and see if your symptoms of diarrhoea and flatulence obviously worsen over the following few hours. Alternatively, you can stop taking milk, yogurt and cheese for two or three weeks and see if your symptoms improve. If they do, consider avoiding dairy products for three months, then gradually reintroducing them. There are some preparations of lactase in encapsulated form in some countries which claim to help treat or speed up the healing of lactose intolerance.

Malabsorption and persistent diarrhoea

Sometimes, repeated bowel infections, including Giardia, Cryptosporidium, Cyclospora or Strongyloides, cause the lining of the small intestine to be less efficient in absorbing food. This is known as *tropical malabsorption* or *tropical sprue*. Typical symptoms are floating frothy stools, loss of weight, thinning muscles and decreasing energy. The condition is especially seen in those living, or budget travelling, in South Asia. If you suspect you have it, you must see a doctor.

A variety of other germs can cause persistent diarrhoea, including some that first cause acute symptoms and then remain as unwelcome visitors. They cannot be identified by guesswork and most will eventually disappear on their own. If you have had repeated or persistent bouts of diarrhoea you should have a stool test on your return home and see a doctor with experience in travel medicine, as persisting bowel problems are quite a medical challenge. Many of these will eventually be diagnosed as irritable bowel syndrome (IBS), better thought of as post-infectious or post-tropical IBS (PIIBS) if your symptoms only started after your travels. PIIBS is now a recognized medical condition; it is treated in much the same way as IBS.

If you have symptoms put down to IBS or PIIBS, you should try to arrange a special stool test to make sure there is no lingering organism causing these symptoms. A test known as an Enteric Organism Screen, based on antigen immunology, is probably the most effective (though only specialist labs perform this), or alternatively you can give stool tests on three successive occasions to a high-quality lab.

Probiotics and live bacteria such as lactobacilli have been shown to help restore healthy bowel flora, meaning bowel movements may return to normal more quickly, especially after using antibiotics. 'Live' yogurts, providing they are made safely and therefore not a source of infection, are an effective way of taking these.

Occasionally non-tropical bowel problems such as Crohn's disease, coeliac disease, colitis or bowel cancer first start or appear in the tropics or after returning home, meaning *you should always report any persisting symptoms to a doctor, especially if you feel unwell, unduly tired or are losing weight.*

Antibiotics to prevent traveller's diarrhoea

These, though quite effective, are not generally recommended for routine use for the following reasons:

• Their widespread use may lead to drug resistance.
• They may cause side-effects (which occasionally include diarrhoea).
• There are fewer medicines in reserve if you do need treatment.
• Modern drugs usually cure diarrhoea if you do develop it.

There are, however, two situations in which it is worth considering preventive antibiotics:

• Your trip is especially important and even a minor bout of diarrhoea might cause you to miss a crucial journey or cancel seeing the president.
• Your health is indifferent, you have bowel problems that could be worsened by diarrhoea, e.g. IBS (see page 59), or you consider yourself to be frail or elderly.

In these cases the best drugs to prevent diarrhoea are either ciprofloxacin 500 mg daily, norfloxacin 400 mg daily or ofloxacin 300 mg daily, starting each 24 hours before leaving, continuing for 48 hours after returning, and restricting the total length of treatment to no longer than 14 days.

Slightly less effective alternatives are trimethoprim 200 mg daily or doxycycline 100 mg daily, each of which can be taken for longer. None of these should be used in pregnancy. One minor advantage of using doxycycline as an antimalarial is that it gives some protection against traveller's diarrhoea.

Dukoral cholera vaccine gives about 50 per cent protection against ETEC diarrhoea for three months (see pages 381–2).

Diarrhoea in the local population

If you are living in a developing country, it is likely that diarrhoea will be one of the commonest causes of severe illness and death among children where you live. You should become familiar with the nationally recommended or local method of making oral rehydration solution (see pages 104–5) so that you can use and demonstrate this when you are consulted by your neighbours. It is better not to hand out routine antibiotics.

Cholera

Background

Cholera has become much more widespread since the 1990s and numbers are likely to remain high. There continue to be outbreaks in many countries, mainly in tropical Africa and Asia. A virulent strain, 0139 or Bengal cholera, is present in South Asia. Cholera often breaks out in the aftermath of civil war or during chronic complex emergencies but only rarely after natural disasters.

Cause

Cholera is caused by faecal contamination of water supplies and food, in particular fish and shellfish, raw fruit and vegetables. The germ that causes it is known as *Vibrio cholerae*.

Risk and prevention

Cholera is very rare in travellers. You can prevent it by taking care with personal hygiene and by following strict rules on drinking water and food preparation (see pages 85–8 and 91–6). Strictly avoid eating shellfish in any area where cholera is present. If travelling with a family or leading a group, make sure everyone knows and obeys basic rules of hygiene.

There is now an effective cholera vaccine (see pages 381–2), worth having if you are travelling to an area with a known outbreak, working in disaster relief or travelling to areas where cholera is endemic (i.e.

present year-round in the local population). This vaccine is not effective against strain 0139 found in parts of southern Asia. Discuss this with your travel health specialist.

Symptoms

Many cases of cholera cause nothing more than mild diarrhoea. However, typical life-threatening episodes have to be recognized and treated urgently as they can cause death from dehydration within just a few hours. They usually start suddenly, with massive painless watery diarrhoea, often resembling rice water. There is commonly vomiting. Dehydration occurs rapidly.

Treatment

This depends on immediate rehydration with oral rehydration solution or a suitable equivalent (see pages 104–5). Vomiting is best treated by drinking: start with small amounts at a time and increase as rapidly as possible. Slow sipping often eases the nausea. If vomiting continues and it is not possible to replace fluids rapidly, then intravenous fluids need to be given. This decision needs to be made by an experienced health worker.

If you strongly suspect cholera, the first priority is rehydration and, when any nausea has eased, either doxycycline 100 mg capsules/tablets three together, or ciprofloxacin 250 mg tablets four together. The treatment in children must be under medical supervision but usually consists of a three-day treatment course of either tetracycline or erythromycin. If you are going to an area where cholera often occurs or there is a current outbreak, take these tablets with you. Family doctors will usually be willing to give you a prescription, probably a private one, if you explain why you want them.

Even in an epidemic area you are in fact very unlikely to get cholera if you take sensible precautions. You may, however, get other forms of diarrhoea that you should manage according to the guidelines given. The main treatment of all forms of acute diarrhoea, including cholera, is oral rehydration solution.

If your symptoms or those of someone you are with suggest cholera, you should follow this procedure:

- Start oral rehydration solution at once and continue until the diarrhoea has improved and a good output of urine is produced.
- Take medication as recommended above.
- See a doctor or reliable health worker as soon as possible.

Typhoid fever (enteric fever)

Background

Typhoid fever is caused by a bacteria called *Salmonella typhi* and is spread by eating contaminated food and water. Shellfish from sewage-infected waters, direct spread from an infected person, eating salads and vegetables fertilized by 'night soil' (i.e. human faeces) or washed in unclean water are common ways of spreading it. Flies can spread it, and contaminated water supplies can cause large outbreaks. It is found virtually worldwide but is especially common in Asia and Africa. Paratyphoid fevers are also common, giving similar but usually less severe symptoms.

Typhoid is not uncommon in travellers, especially those living and working in poor conditions, such as gap-year students, missionaries and aid workers. The diagnosis of typhoid is sometimes missed, especially in those who have been immunized, as the symptoms may be less severe. It is probably also over-diagnosed because the standard blood test done in developing countries, the Widal test, is hard to interpret, and being immunized against typhoid can confuse this further.

Prevention

This is through strict food and water hygiene and through immunization (see pages 396–8).

Symptoms

Diarrhoea may occur with typhoid, especially after the first week, but constipation and cough are often present early. A typical attack of typhoid causes a severe and worsening illness, involving head and body ache and a temperature that rises higher each day, with the pulse staying relatively slow, often at about 80 beats per minute. After one or two weeks diarrhoea usually develops, often with blood, offensive breath and abdominal pain. In about 50 per cent of cases pale pink spots which fade on pressure appear on the trunk; these are known as rose spots. Untreated typhoid can occasionally be fatal, especially in those with poor health.

If you have been immunized against typhoid you can still get the illness, but symptoms may be less severe and harder to tell apart from other conditions. Typhoid may occasionally be the cause of persistent or intermittent diarrhoea, low-grade fever or worsening health.

Treatment

Diagnosis is often difficult (to confirm it you have to show the actual presence of the germs on a stool test or in a blood test) so treatment is often started without confirming the diagnosis. Typhoid and paraty-phoid are treated in the same way.

The best treatment for those aged 16 and over is ciprofloxacin 500–750 mg twice daily for ten to 14 days. An alternative is chloramphenicol 500 mg four times daily for 14 days, but this is not always effective, especially in Asia. These drugs are not appropriate in pregnancy, when you should use amoxicillin 500 mg three times daily for 14 days. Children should generally use amoxicillin, but resistance is occurring to many antibiotics and your doctor should advise as to the best antibiotic to use. Typhoid is not a disease which should be self-diagnosed or self-treated, and if you think you may have it, seeing a doctor is essential.

Even after typhoid is apparently cured it is still possible to be a carrier. Anyone preparing or cooking food who may have had typhoid should have a negative stool test before being allowed back into the kitchen.

Please also see Appendix J, pages 396–8.

Constipation

For many travellers, constipation is as much a problem as diarrhoea. Often they seem to alternate with annoying frequency, sometimes through overdoing the Imodium or because of underlying amoebic infection.

Methods of coping with constipation are obvious, though not always effective. Drinking enough to keep the urine dilute, especially during travel, is the most important. Keep eating a high-fibre diet with plenty of vegetables and fruit (hygienically prepared). When travelling, try not to suppress a bowel motion unless you really can't face the toilets or there are none available, as unrelieved traffic jams in your bowel will only make the problem worse. Finally, make sure you pack your favourite laxative to use either to treat the problem or to help prevent it in the first place. Senokot is a good choice; see Appendix C on page 359. Some people will need self-administered glycerol (glycerine) suppositories.

11

Preventing and treating malaria

Malaria is the most common and the most dangerous tropical illness for travellers. By knowing how to prevent it and how to treat it, you can save your life and that of your friends and family. Make sure you also read pages 17–22, which tell you the important medication and items to prevent mosquito bites which you will usually need to take with you.

This chapter looks at the following:

- Where is malaria found?
- What are your risks as an international traveller?
- Preventing malaria in those with pre-existing conditions
- What causes malaria?
- What are the symptoms of malaria?
- How can you prevent malaria?
  - Avoid mosquito bites
  - Take malaria prevention tablets (antimalarials)
- Preventing malaria country by country
- Preventing malaria in long-term travellers
- How do you treat malaria?
- Emergency standby treatment for malaria
- Where can you obtain medicines to prevent and treat malaria?
- Malaria after returning home
- Malaria and children
- Malaria, pregnancy and breastfeeding
- Notes on drugs commonly used for treating and preventing malaria
- Notes on additional drugs
- Summary

Where is malaria found?

At the present time malaria is found in over 100 countries and 2.4 billion people are at risk (see Figure 11.1). Malaria kills about one million people every year, including 3,000 children each day in sub-Saharan Africa alone. Each year 125 million international travellers visit countries where they are at risk of catching malaria.

Within individual countries, malaria may be common in some areas, absent in others. It is rarely found above 2,000 metres (about 6,500

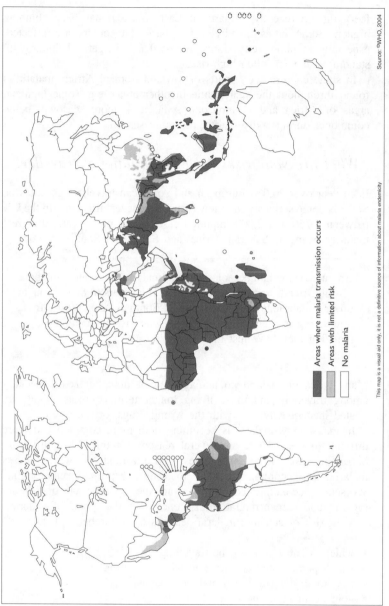

Figure 11.1 Areas where malaria is found (WHO, 2004)

Areas where malaria transmission occurs

Areas with limited risk

No malaria

This map is a visual aid only, it is not a definitive source of information about malaria endemicity

Source: ©WHO, 2004

feet), though recently in parts of East Africa it has been climbing higher. Some cities are free of malaria but others are affected, especially in poorer city slums. Forested and irrigated habitats with standing water are often high-risk.

In some countries, e.g. parts of lowland tropical Africa, malaria is found throughout the year, while in other areas, e.g. some highland areas of Africa and in monsoon Asia, it is more seasonal, being commoner during and just after the rainy season.

What are your risks as an international traveller?

Each year over 30,000 European and American travellers get malaria. Some become seriously ill; a few (usually unnecessarily) die. In the UK between 1,750 and 2,000 imported cases occur most years, the great majority from sub-Saharan Africa, and South and Southeast Asia.

> An increasing number of cases of malaria are found in those visiting friends and relatives (VFRs). This refers to those brought up in a malarious area, for example, South Asia or West Africa, now living in a non-malarious area, who visit their families, not realizing they have lost their immunity.

Many cases of malaria go undiagnosed or unrecognized, especially among travellers and those living longer term overseas. Many are treated inadequately, e.g. with the wrong drugs, or not at all.

In many areas malaria is becoming both more common and more difficult to treat. There are several reasons for this. Mosquitoes are becoming resistant to insecticides, and Plasmodium, which causes malaria, is becoming resistant to drugs, especially chloroquine. Worsening economic conditions, war, the opening up of frontier regions, and human migration also encourage the spread of malaria.

Your risk of catching malaria depends on a number of factors:

- which country you will be travelling to;
- which parts of the country you will be visiting;
- how long you will be in malarious areas;
- your occupation and style of travel;
- how effectively you take precautions to avoid being bitten by mosquitoes;
- whether you take your malaria prevention tablets (antimalarials) regularly, without missing doses and according to the manufacturer's instructions;

- whether you still have some degree of immunity from being brought up in a malarious country and have spent little time (under 6–12 months) away from it;
- your genetic make-up and inbuilt resistance.

You can't deal with all these factors, but by taking a few simple precautions and following them rigorously, you are much less likely to get malaria. Also, if you start treatment as soon as suspicious symptoms develop, you are very unlikely to become seriously ill.

Preventing malaria in those with pre-existing conditions

If you have any serious illness or have had one in the recent past, discuss this with your health adviser.

Here are a few guidelines about important medical conditions which may affect the type of antimalarial you should take.

Blood disorders

Two common illnesses found in many parts of the world, sickle-cell disease and thalassaemia, may give some protection from malaria, but equally malaria can lead to severe symptoms. So antimalarials are essential.

If you are taking anticoagulants, including warfarin, be aware that some tablets increase the INR; proguanil and Malarone are the most likely to do so, and doxycycline may occasionally. Check your INR regularly when travelling, especially if taking either of these antimalarials.

Cardiac conditions

Avoid mefloquine if you have any irregularities of your heartbeat and if you are taking any medication to control your heart rhythm. This includes beta-blockers, e.g. atenolol, as mefloquine may slow the heart further.

Epilepsy

Avoid both chloroquine and mefloquine if you have ever had a seizure or any form of epilepsy. Some experts suggest you should avoid these if your parents, siblings or children have ever had what is known as idiopathic epilepsy, i.e. epilepsy with no obvious cause.

G6PD deficiency

Also common is a condition known as G6PD deficiency. An increasingly used medicine to prevent and treat malaria called primaquine (see pages 146–7) is dangerous to take unless you have a blood test to make sure you do not have a deficiency of this enzyme.

Kidney problems

If you have kidney failure you are best not to travel, but if it is less severe and you are able to visit a malarious area, doxycycline (with caution) or mefloquine are the best to use and you should normally avoid proguanil or Malarone. Talk to your specialist.

Liver problems

If you have liver failure it is best not to travel to malarious areas at all, as no antimalarials are safe. If you have liver problems, including raised liver enzymes on a blood test, you should usually avoid chloroquine, mefloquine and doxycycline, apart from short trips and after discussion with your doctor. Malarone is generally the best to use.

Post splenectomy or no functioning spleen

(Also see pages 53–6.) Malaria can be severe and sometimes fatal, meaning that it is essential to take an effective antimalarial and strict precautions to avoid being bitten. Any antimalarial is OK to take, providing it is known to be effective in the area you are visiting. Ideally you should not be travelling to a malarious area.

Psychiatric illness

Avoid mefloquine. (See more details on pages 144–6.)

What causes malaria?

A single-celled organism called Plasmodium causes malaria. This is carried by the female Anopheles mosquito (see Figure 11.2), and is injected into the bloodstream through a bite. After an incubation period of at least seven days, and sometimes very much longer, the disease develops.

There are two main forms of malaria. *Malignant* malaria, caused by *Plasmodium falciparum*, is the more serious and in many areas, including Africa, the most common. So-called *benign* malaria, caused by *P. vivax*, *ovale* or *malariae*, tends to be more of a nuisance than a danger, is rarely fatal, but still needs to be diagnosed and treated promptly. It can only reliably be told from falciparum malaria by a malaria blood test (blood slide or special antibody test).

For the more technically minded, the form of the parasite which is injected into the blood is called a *sporozoite*. From your blood these pass into the liver where most become *liver schizonts*. When mature these burst, releasing *merozoites* into the bloodstream, and many of these enter your red blood cells. Here they develop into ring-shaped *trophozoites* (visible under the microscope) and then into *blood*

Figure 11.2 Anopheles mosquito (female 4–6 mm long)

schizonts. Finally these burst from the cells, releasing large numbers of *merozoites*, which can then enter new red blood cells. Fever coincides with the release of each batch of merozoites. Often red cells are destroyed in large numbers during this process. (See Figure 11.3.)

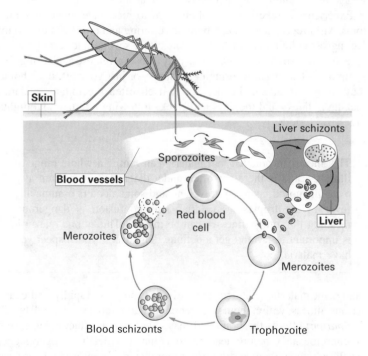

Figure 11.3 The life cycle of the malarial parasite
(Modified from a diagram by the Malaria Foundation, 2006)

What are the symptoms of malaria?

The typical symptoms of malaria are like severe flu: fever, headache, muscle ache and backache; nausea, vomiting and diarrhoea. The three classical phases of malaria are much less frequently seen, especially if you are taking your malaria prevention tablets, but this is a classic attack. First a sudden onset (the *cold phase*), when shivering and shaking start suddenly and last up to one hour. This is then followed by a *hot dry phase* lasting two to six hours, when the temperature may rise up to 40°C (104°F): there is headache, pains in the joints and often vomiting and diarrhoea. Finally comes the *hot wet phase*, lasting two to four hours, when the patient sweats profusely and then feels better.

However, as previously mentioned, *most attacks of malaria do not follow these phases*, especially if you are taking antimalarials. Malignant malaria in particular may cause a variety of symptoms, including continuous or, more often, irregular fever. Malaria in children under three months may not cause fever at all.

Experienced travellers can often learn to recognize malarial symptoms. Mild fever, headache, a bout of vomiting and diarrhoea or simply feeling off-colour may indicate an attack. A severe cold, an operation or a time of stress or exhaustion may cause a relapse and bring out symptoms. The strain of bringing a family, or just yourself, back home may trigger an attack. In fact, travel itself often precipitates malaria, making holidays and the days and weeks following international flights high-risk periods.

> This means in practice that malaria can mimic a whole range of illnesses, and is therefore often under-diagnosed. It is often also over-diagnosed, as many travellers and some doctors assume any fever in the tropics is malaria. This confusion is dangerous, meaning that other illnesses can be missed, This is one reason it is important to try and get a definite diagnosis if you suspect you have malaria.

Malignant malaria, if not treated early, can progress rapidly and cause serious illness within hours. Cerebral malaria (always caused by *P. falciparum*) affects the brain and may cause fits and fluctuating levels of consciousness before leading to coma and death. Danger signs, usually obvious, include drowsiness, confusion, absent urine, shortness of breath, jaundice and persistent fever. Repeated attacks of malaria may lead to exhaustion and contribute towards depression. The spleen may enlarge and anaemia can become severe.

How can you prevent malaria?

There are two ways, both essential.

- Avoid bites.
- Take antimalarials.

Taking malaria prevention tablets is highly recommended if you are travelling to an area of malaria risk. There are a number of different options, depending on your destination and medical history (see pages 125–8 for more information). None of the malaria prevention tablets are 100 per cent effective, and the best way to defeat malaria is to avoid getting bitten in the first place.

Avoid bites

There are lots of products available to help you keep the mosquitoes away (see pages 17–22 for more details). The Anopheles mosquito that spreads malaria starts biting just before sunset and continues to feed through the night until dawn. Here are some helpful ways that you can stop yourself getting bitten.

Sleep under a mosquito net that has been treated with the insecticide permethrin

This is essential if you are living or travelling in a malarious area. Remember to re-treat your net frequently. (See pages 18–20 for more information on mosquito nets.)

Use insect repellents

Mosquitoes are attracted to your body's heat and odour. Using insect repellents on all exposed skin (avoiding the eyes and mouth area) is an important way of preventing insect bites. There are a number of different repellents available, but the most effective ones are those that contain 50 per cent DEET (see pages 20–1 for more information). *Those who are likely to be outside from an hour before sunset onwards in malarious areas are strongly recommended to apply insect repellent thoroughly to all exposed areas of the skin, and reapply frequently, especially in hot or humid conditions, and also to cover up.*

- DEET should not be applied to the eyes and lips, nor to deep skin folds. Wash your hands after applying DEET.
- As well as applying DEET to the skin you can also apply it to cotton, linen or woollen clothing. However, DEET tends to destroy plastic, including spectacle frames, cameras, nail varnish and synthetic fabrics.

- DEET at a concentration of 50 per cent is now recommended by most experts as a safe and effective way of preventing mosquito bites, both in adults and in children over the age of two months.

Cover your skin

Wear light-coloured, long-sleeved clothing and long trousers to cover your skin so that the mozzies have more difficulty finding a tasty part of you to feed on. This may not always be pleasant in the heat of the tropics, but do think about covering up, particularly if going out in the evening. Mozzies particularly like the wrists, ankles and feet, so using impregnated bands on the wrists and ankles and wearing socks can help to keep them away. Remember that a determined mosquito can bite through socks, or even a pair of jeans, so covering up alone is not enough.

Here are some suggestions for areas where there is a severe mosquito or insect nuisance:

- When outside in the evening wear appropriate clothing, sprayed with permethrin, thoroughly apply a 50 per cent DEET-based insect repellent to your skin, and wear impregnated wrist and ankle bands and thick socks.
- Inside the house use permethrin-impregnated bed nets (and curtains), and screen windows and doors.
- When walking outside in highly affected areas, including trekking in tick- and leech-infested country, use DEET insect repellent on the skin and permethrin-sprayed clothing.

Soak or spray your clothes

You have two choices:

- *Use DEET-based products* Expedition 100 Insect Repellent Spray is an effective brand. A sprayed garment (e.g. a T-shirt or socks) remains repellent for a few days. Respray when you wash the garment, and do not wear it when wet from the spray. ONLY use it on cotton, linen or wool. (Alternatively you can soak appropriate clothes in a DEET solution.)
- *Use permethrin* You can spray clothes with permethrin, often marketed as Bug Proof. One treatment lasts about two weeks. It is better not to use this in children, and in the UK it is only licensed for use in adults. Bug Proof does not destroy fabrics.

Remember that DEET repels mosquitoes but does not kill them; permethrin kills but does not necessarily repel them.

Consider your accommodation

If you have the luxury of air conditioning or a fan, use it! Air conditioning means that the room is largely sealed: a fast-revolving ceiling fan blows mosquitoes away from you.

Also think about whether there are times when you are going to be at extra risk, e.g. camping by a lake or out in the evenings, and make sure that you take extra care with the insect repellent precautions at these times.

Screen your room

In areas with many mosquitoes, fix fine metal screening to your windows and doors, and make sure they are kept closed from about an hour before sunset to well after sunrise. Check for any holes or gaps in the screening. The netting should have six or seven threads per centimetre width. Where dengue fever is common (see page 287), keep your windows and doors closed throughout the day – especially during the morning and at least two hours before sunset, when the Aedes mosquito does most of its mischief.

Deal with the source

Try to eliminate breeding sites near the house. These include thick vegetation, ponds, areas of stagnant water including animal hoof-prints, rainwater tanks with poorly fitting lids, the axils of leaves, old vehicle tyres, pots on the veranda and the tops of bamboo canes. Mosquitoes can fly at least a mile, but eliminating the breeding sites within the immediate area of the house reduces the number. These measures also help prevent dengue fever, commoner in some areas than malaria, especially cities in Southeast Asia and South America.

Make sure that open water tanks are screened, using the same mesh size as for house screening.

Arrange for the government spraying team to visit your area. Consider stocking nearby ponds or paddyfields with larvicidal fish, e.g. guppy, or procuring polystyrene beads to put into wet pits and pit latrines.

Other precautions

Mosquito coils, electric mosquito killers (that release an insecticide) or a knockdown room spray all work in a similar way by killing mosquitoes and other insects that are in the room. Mosquito coils should only be used in a well-ventilated room. They are available cheaply in most countries, but beware of fake products. If using a knockdown spray, spray sleeping areas, being careful to include dark corners, hidden areas behind cupboards, under beds and – most important of all – the bath or shower room. Note that these sprays do not necessarily kill mosquitoes that arrive after you have finished spraying.

If your limbs rest against your net as you sleep, the mosquitoes can still bite you. Buy a roomy net and make sure that it is treated with permethrin for extra protection.

There is no evidence that electronic buzzers, vitamin B or garlic deter mosquito bites.

Take antimalarials

Many people get confused with the various terms used. Malaria prevention tablets are often known as antimalarials or as chemoprophylaxis. From now on we will use these terms interchangeably.

Although many short-term travellers to malarious areas take their prevention tablets, it is very common for those living or working longer term in malarious areas to stop their antimalarials after a few weeks or months. A recent survey of travellers to sub-Saharan Africa prescribed mefloquine tablets showed that only 32 per cent took their tablets reliably and according to instructions.

Good reasons for taking antimalarials

Here are some good reasons for taking antimalarials:

- They save lives – statistics prove it.
- Even if you get malaria it is less likely to kill you or be dangerous.
- Your health insurance may not cover you if you don't.
- If you don't take antimalarials your compliant colleagues may swear behind your back as they rush you to the nearest hospital at midnight.

If you *take the correct pills without missing doses* you are much less likely to get malaria, and even if you do, research has shown that it is likely to be less severe, which will allow you longer time to receive proper treatment.

Wrong reasons for not taking antimalarials
Here are some wrong and foolhardy reasons for not taking antimalarials, which we often hear in our travel clinic:

I/my friend took antimalarials and still got malaria.
But if you hadn't taken them the malaria would probably have been more severe. Did you miss a dose?

If you take antimalarials, when you get an attack there's nothing left to treat it with.
In fact there are several effective forms of treatment.

Everybody recommends a different tablet, so who should I believe?
Although advice can vary, there is a choice of two or three effective antimalarials depending on which country you visit.

We're expats and have lived here x years and we know best.
Unfortunately expats often get severe attacks of malaria, especially as new strains enter the area where they live.

I believe in garlic, vitamin B, yeast and homeopathic remedies.
These are unlikely to do you any harm, but there is no scientific evidence that they prevent or cure malaria. It is therefore dangerous to rely on them.

Guidelines on taking antimalarials

When it comes to choosing and using antimalarials, follow these suggestions:

- *Choose the recommended regime before you leave* by discussing your exact travel plans with a travel health specialist.
- *Don't change or stop tablets* unless there is a compelling reason such as unacceptable side-effects or clear evidence that malaria is rare or unknown in your immediate area. Advice from expatriates or the local population that pills are unnecessary, dangerous or useless should be treated with caution. So should pressure to change one type for another. An apparent absence of mosquitoes does not mean you cannot get malaria.

- *Don't forget your tablets* Try to take them at the same time each day (or week), and keep them in the same place as part of a regular routine. A bottle of pills on the dining-room table, above the house key rack, under your pillow or with your toothbrush are favourite memory-jogging sites.
- *Do not forget antimalarials when on holiday* Always keep a supply with you when you are travelling, plus a few extra for forgetful friends (but only after making sure they are using the same ones as you!).

How to take your tablets
Take tablets according to the instructions that come with the type of antimalarial you are taking. This will enable them to be absorbed most effectively and will help to reduce side-effects. (For more on this, see pages 141–7.)

When to start and when to stop
Start antimalarials well before travelling, and again according to the specific instructions with the medication you are taking. Continue them for the recommended time after you leave a malarious area. Apart from Malarone, which you only need to take for one week after leaving, continue your tablets for four weeks.

What to do if you vomit or have diarrhoea
Instructions vary depending on what tablet you are taking. Read the Patient Information Leaflet for the medication you are taking.

Preventing malaria country by country

Recommendations are continually changing. This is partly because malaria is becoming better controlled in some areas, less controlled in others. Resistance is emerging to commonly used antimalarials, especially chloroquine. New antimalarials are being recommended.

In previous editions of this book we published a table of recommended antimalarials for each affected country. We now recommend that you check this website from the World Health Organization: <http://libdoc.who.int/publications/2005/9241580364_country _list.pdf>, or, because websites change regularly, check the WHO website <http://www.who.int> under Health Topics; Travel and Health; Malaria.

For countries with chloroquine resistance, which includes all of sub-Saharan Africa, there are three recommended antimalarials: mefloquine, doxycycline and Malarone. Chloroquine and proguanil (Paludrine) are no longer recommended. This is by far the most likely area to cause serious illness in travellers. South Asia is also important, especially for those visiting friends and relatives (a group known as VFR) and at the time of writing a combination of chloroquine and proguanil is effective in Pakistan and most of India, excepting Assam, but resistance is spreading.

Some travel health advisers follow simplified charts as to whether malaria is present in a country or not. Although this works for some countries, e.g. for those where malaria is present throughout the country all year round, for many parts of the world malaria is present in some areas and at some times of year more than others. So the exact details of your journey are important in order for you to be given the best advice.

Preventing malaria in long-term travellers

There are not yet universally agreed guidelines. This is not through lack of trying – there is just not sufficient evidence to give watertight advice. However, as experience increases, antimalarials look increasingly safe in the long term.

Safety of long-term antimalarials

Current advice from the UK Advisory Committee on Malaria Prevention (2003) is as follows:[1]

- *Chloroquine and proguanil (Paludrine)* There are no problems with long-term use, but considerable concerns regarding their lack of effectiveness in many malarious areas including the whole of sub-Saharan Africa.
- *Doxycycline* There is no evidence of harm in long-term use. Evidence suggests that it may be used safely for periods of up to at least two years.
- *Malarone* There is no evidence of harm in long-term use. It is suggested it can be used confidently for travel up to three months, and possibly up to six months or longer, but only with caution until more evidence is available. Adverse effects, including attacks of malaria, should be reported.
- *Mefloquine (Lariam)* There is no evidence of harm in long-term use if tolerated in the short term, and it is suggested it can be used for up to three years in the absence of side-effects.

[1] There may be minor changes in the new guidelines due to be published in 2007.

Different countries have different guidelines. Many travellers have been using the above antimalarials for much longer than the times listed above, with no signs of harmful effects. Some countries put few or no restrictions on the length of time antimalarials may be used. For more details, see the information in the section below on pages 141–7.

Many international travellers staying abroad long term are reluctant to take antimalarials and the majority stop after a few weeks or months. You should only do this if you have worked out a careful strategy based on a risk assessment of your particular situation.

Some options to consider:

- One option is to take antimalarials during the time of year when malaria is most prevalent (in some countries it varies little between seasons) or when travelling away from home or to more seriously affected regions. Then at home, or during the dry season, you would not use antimalarials but would report any fever immediately. You would always have standby medication with you in case appropriate treatment was not available.
- For those living in cities with a limited risk and making a number of short trips each year to more affected areas, Malarone is a good option as it only needs to be started a day before travelling and continued for a week after returning. Other antimalarials need to be continued for four weeks, meaning that in practice you might be taking antimalarials most of the time.

It is always best to work out a strategy in discussion with an expert in travel medicine who knows the specific risks of the area you are living in. The two options described above are unsafe in a number of locations.

How do you treat malaria?

If you think you may have malaria, follow these steps:

1 See a reliable doctor or health worker and ask for a malaria blood test (malaria slide, ideally combined with a malaria antibody or antigen test to give greater accuracy). You should do this within eight hours of the start of fever or of other suspicious symptoms. To exclude malaria it is ideal to get three negative malaria slides from a reliable laboratory taken at different times, preferably when you have a fever, but this is often not possible in practice.
2 If the malaria slide is positive or the doctor believes you have malaria, make sure you receive treatment. If you are carrying your

own standby tablets, use these unless the doctor has medication available that you know is reliable and safe to use.

3 If the slide is negative or the doctor says you have not got malaria, or you continue to feel ill with a fever, self-treat anyway if *either* there is no obvious cause for your fever *or* your symptoms are not rapidly resolving within 24 hours.

4 If your symptoms continue or recur, whether or not you have been treated for malaria or had a positive blood slide, make sure you get expert medical help as quickly as possible.

If you are travelling off the beaten path you should always carry standby treatment with you. But if at all possible you should still see a reliable health worker, get professional advice and have a blood test.

A note on dipstick self-testing kits

There are now tests for malaria, which depend on obtaining a finger prick of blood, applying it to a test-strip and then reading the results. Current brands include the ParaSight F test, the ICT Malaria Pf test, and Optimal. These are already proving useful for teams and expeditions where there is someone medically qualified or a first-aider trained in their use. At the time of writing they are not recommended for individual use.

Malaria suspected or confirmed must be appropriately treated without delay.

Emergency standby treatment for malaria

Who should take a malaria standby treatment kit?

You should consider taking a standby treatment kit if you are going to a high-risk malarious area for more than one week, unless you know there is good-quality health care available within eight hours and that the recommended treatment for malaria is reliably available and of good quality.

In practice these kits are especially useful in sub-Saharan Africa.

When should you use the kit?

Wherever possible you should seek medical advice as soon as you can if you think you are going down with malaria – even if you are taking malaria prevention tablets.

You should only take a standby treatment kit with you if you have first read or received a careful explanation about how to recognize the symptoms of malaria, and how and when to self-treat. You also need to understand that standby treatment is not a substitute for seeking medical help but helps to buy you time until you can be under the best medical care available.

You should use this kit if you develop symptoms suggestive of malaria and

- *either* you are unable to have this confirmed and treated within eight hours;
- *or* you are able to have malaria confirmed by a health worker but the recommended malaria treatment of reliable quality is not available;
- *or* you have a negative malaria blood slide but are still suffering from the same or worsening symptoms.

In addition, standby kits can be used by travellers genuinely unable to take any malaria prevention tablets or who after careful explanation decide not to do so.

Which standby treatment should you use?

There are a number of treatments available but malaria specialists currently recommend those listed in Table 11.1. Options are listed in order of preference. You should usually use a different standby drug from the one you are taking for malaria prevention. Normal adult doses are given unless otherwise stated.

What should you do?

If you are likely to need a standby treatment kit, read through the options listed and decide which one is most suitable for you. Make sure you consult a travel health practitioner to discuss the use of the kit. You can order these from InterHealth and from some other travel clinics. Before you go overseas and again before taking the medication, read the Patient Information Leaflets and instructions enclosed with the kits. Always try and get medical care if you suspect malaria and ensure that after starting standby treatment you seek out good medical advice as soon as possible. There is a small chance that the standby medication may not be effective, and it is very possible that your symptoms will have another cause – both good reasons for seeing a doctor.

Table 11.1 Recommended malaria treatment options

Recommended malaria treatment (normal adult dose)	Children's doses	Who for and other important information
Option 1 **Malarone** tablets, four tablets taken together for three days (total 12 tablets). Malarone is atovaquone 250 mg plus proguanil 100 mg. Those weighing 40 kg and above should take the full adult dose.	11–20 kg: one adult Malarone tablet taken daily for three days (total three tablets) 21–30 kg: two adult Malarone tablets taken together daily for three days (total six tablets) 31–40 kg: three adult Malrone tablets taken together daily for three days (total nine tablets) For children 9–10 kg three paediatric Malarone tablets can be used, and 5–8 kg two paediatric tablets. Not to be used in children under 5 kg	Malarone is an effective treatment for adults and children in areas where there is chloroquine-resistant malaria, e.g. sub-Saharan Africa, the Amazon basin and Oceania. This is a very effective treatment against the most serious form of malaria, *P. falciparum*, but does not always cure so-called benign *P. vivax* and *P. ovale* malaria. It is not advised for those using Malarone as malaria prevention. If taking doxycycline for prevention, discontinue the doxycycline until treatment with Malarone is completed. Malarone is not currently recommended in pregnancy or for treatment when breastfeeding infants under 5 kg.
Option 2 **Co-artemether** (Riamet) tablets. The dose, which should ideally be taken with food containing some fat, is four tablets taken together followed by four further tablets after 8, 24, 36, 48 and 60 hours. Total 24 tablets. Co-artemether is artemether 20 mg plus lumefantrine 120 mg, and is one form of Artemesinin Combined Therapy (ACT), whose use is recommended by the World Health Organization.	There are currently recommended dosages given by the World Health Organization, but in the UK it is not currently recommended.	This is a useful and effective standby treatment and is ideal for use in sub-Saharan Africa. This is suitable whatever malaria prevention is being used, but malaria prevention tablets should be discontinued until treatment with Co-artemether is completed. Co-artemether should not be used in pregnancy and breastfeeding, except in an emergency. Not suitable for those with heart rhythm disorders. It interacts with certain medicines – seek advice from your doctor or InterHealth.
Option 3 **Quinine** tablets 300 mg, two tablets every eight hours for three days **plus** **doxycycline** 100 mg capsules, one twice daily for seven days started at the same time as quinine.	This combination is not suitable for children under 12.	This is an effective treatment in most areas where there is chloroquine resistance, e.g. sub-Saharan Africa, the Amazon basin and Oceania. This is best NOT used (unless you are under medical supervision) if you are taking mefloquine as malaria prevention, as occasionally quinine and mefloquine can interact. If you are using doxycycline to prevent malaria, ideally use Options 1 or 2; otherwise take two doxycycline per day for seven days instead of just one tablet. This combination is not suitable in pregnancy or in children under 12.

Table 11.1 Recommended malaria treatment options (cont'd)

Recommended malaria treatment (normal adult dose)	Children's doses	Who for and other important information
Option 4 **Quinine** tablets 300 mg, two every eight hours for three days **followed by Fansidar**, three tablets taken together.	**Quinine** (8 mg per kg of body weight) every eight hours for three days followed by a single dose of **Fansidar** as follows: 6 weeks to 4 years: $\frac{1}{2}$ a tablet; 5–6 years: 1 tablet; 7–9 years: $1\frac{1}{2}$ tablets; 10–14 years: 2 tablets; 15 or over: adult dose	This is less useful than Options 1–3 above because there is increasing Fansidar resistance, especially in Africa. We only recommend this if you are unable to use one of the preferred Options 1–3. This is best NOT used (unless you are under medical supervision) if you are taking mefloquine to prevent malaria, as quinine and mefloquine can interact. This combination should not be used in pregnancy, breastfeeding or children under six weeks.
Option 5 **Quinine** tablets 300 mg, two every eight hours for seven days.	**Quinine** (8 mg per kg of body weight) every eight hours for seven days.	Although this is effective few people can tolerate it because of increasing side-effects, worse the more quinine you take. However, this is the only safe standby treatment for pregnant women (who on the whole should not be travelling in remote areas in malarious zones). This is best NOT used, unless you are under medical supervision, or if you are taking mefloquine to prevent malaria as occasionally quinine and mefloquine can interact. Quinine is considered safe in pregnancy and breastfeeding. Indeed, it can be life-saving.
Option 6 **Mefloquine** (one brand name Lariam) WHO recommends a dose of 15 mg per kg followed by a dose of 10 mg per kg 6–24 hours later. Other dosages are sometimes used as are combinations of mefloquine with other malaria treatment drugs.	Not recommended in children under 5 kg. Read manufacturers' instructions carefully.	Although effective, this can cause unpleasant side-effects and should be used as a last resort and under medical supervision. Should not be used if you are taking mefloquine to prevent malaria.

Note: We **do not recommend** Halofantrine (Halfan) as a treatment even though it is available and widely used in many parts of Africa. It can cause fatal heart problems and the World Health Organization has issued a strong warning about its use. We also do not recommend chloroquine or amodiaquine as a treatment as there is increasing resistance throughout much of the world.

Unless advised otherwise, you should continue taking your malaria prevention tablets when using your malaria standby treatment kit. However, co-artemether (Riamet) should not be taken with other antimalarials, and doxycycline should not be taken while taking Malarone for treatment (see notes below).

> It is essential that young children with malarial symptoms are seen by a doctor.

Leaving a malarious region

If, after leaving a malarious area, you will not have access to expert advice if you fall ill (e.g. because you are going on holiday) take the standby kit with you.

Where can you obtain medicines to prevent and treat malaria?

This varies from country to country. Currently in the UK, chloroquine and proguanil can be bought from chemists, under the supervision of a pharmacist. Mefloquine, doxycycline and other drugs used for the prevention and treatment of malaria can be prescribed by doctors on a private prescription and obtained from pharmacies. Most doctors will make a charge for the prescription. Some travel clinics also have them available (see Appendix G on pages 369–71).

In many countries, especially in Africa, Asia or Latin America, if malaria tablets are available within the country they can be bought from a pharmacist without a prescription. Beware of fake or substandard products.

Unless you know of a reliable supply of good-quality antimalarials and tablets to treat malaria at your destination, it is better to take a supply from home.

Malaria after returning home

• A flu-like illness may be malaria for any time up to at least one year, and especially in the first three months of leaving a malarious area. It is rare for malignant (falciparum) malaria to recur after three months, but so-called benign forms can recur for a year or more, occasionally for a number of years after returning home.

• You are at special risk of developing malaria after leaving a malarious area, especially if returning from sub-Saharan Africa, or after visiting friends and relatives in South Asia or Africa. If you have been taking mefloquine it can delay the onset of malaria.

- Make sure you report any suspicious symptoms without delay, especially in children. You should either report to your normal doctor or go direct to the accident and emergency department of a main hospital, explain you have come from a malarious area and insist you have a blood slide. If this is negative and the fever persists or worsens, you should have a repeat test carried out, preferably at a tropical diseases centre.

- It is *not* safe simply to take the malaria treatment tablets you have in your back pocket and hope for the best. If the fever comes on in the afternoon or evening, don't wait till the following morning: get it checked at once. Even if you have your standby with you, still get a blood slide.

- Note that if you are in or near London you can go to the Hospital for Tropical Diseases or nearby University College Hospital at any time of the day or night, without a letter, if you think you may have malaria (see pages 369–71 for details of this and other centres).

- If you have had recurrent attacks of malaria and are now home for good or for a long leave, it is sometimes advisable to take a course of primaquine to eradicate the persistent forms of benign malaria that may otherwise plague you for months. You should discuss this at your tropical health check (also see pages 146–7).

- If you have been brought up in a malarious country, then come to study or live in the UK or other non-malarious areas, your immunity usually starts to wane rapidly, usually within six months to a year. This means you are at risk of getting malaria on return to a malarious area. It is worth taking prophylactics for at least six months after returning and being very careful then, and subsequently, to report and treat any symptoms that could be malaria.

Malaria and children

Babies and young children can quickly become seriously ill with malaria. Moreover, because their symptoms may not be typical, the diagnosis can easily be missed. Sometimes their main symptoms are diarrhoea and/or vomiting. Very young children may have malaria without a fever.

Ideally, children under three months should avoid areas where malignant malaria is common. This is both because their risk is greater than that of adults, and because the ideal antimalarial cannot always be used for children. This means they are at particular risk, especially in chloroquine resistant areas.

For prevention, children should start antimalarials from the earliest

134

age at which the advised antimalarial is safe and spend as much time as possible between dusk and dawn under a bed net impregnated with permethrin or another appropriate insecticide (see pages 18–20 and 121). It is most important to prevent mosquito bites.

Babies can safely take chloroquine and proguanil from birth, and mefloquine from a weight of 5 kg or above (i.e. from the age of about three months) (see Table 11.4 on page 139 and Table 11.5 on page 146). Doxycycline cannot be used until the age of 12 (eight according to US guidelines) and Malarone should not be used for prophylaxis in those under 11 kg. See Table 11.2.

Table 11.2 Malaria prevention dosages for paediatric Malarone

Anyone weighing over 40.0 kg	One Malarone adult dose tablet (equivalent to four paediatric tablets) daily
Children weighing 31–40.0 kg	Three paediatric tablets as a single dose daily
Children weighing 21–30.9 kg	Two paediatric tablets as a single dose daily
Children weighing 11–20.9 kg	One paediatric tablet as a single dose daily
Children weighing under 11 kg	Not currently recommended

In severely affected areas such as much of sub-Saharan Africa, chloroquine and proguanil will give some degree of protection to babies and very young children but should only be used if there are compelling reasons that more effective preparations are not suitable.

Chloroquine is available in the UK as a syrup (Nivaquine syrup). Some children prefer this to a crushed tablet, others are very suspicious. Maloprim (Deltaprim) is available as a syrup in Zimbabwe and some surrounding countries but only gives partial protection, and should no longer be used unless no other preparation is available.

Other antimalarial drugs are only available as tablets. They should be crushed and given on a spoon with jam, honey or something sweet, or flavoured with chocolate. Alternatively they can be dissolved with sugar in a little milk, or rolled in butter, peanut butter or a favourite salty savoury and placed near the back of the tongue. *As a last resort* a tablet can be crushed, added to sugary milk, drawn up in a clean syringe from which the needle has been removed and introduced slowly down the side of the tongue. Giving antimalarials to children is an acquired art.

For treatment, the dosages in Table 11.3 follow current expert recommendations. Unfortunately there is still not complete agreement between experts in different countries and manufacturers.

Table 11.3 Malaria treatment dosages in children for Fansidar, Malarone and quinine

Fansidar

6 weeks to 4 years	$\frac{1}{2}$ tablet
5–6 years	1 tablet
7–9 years	$1\frac{1}{2}$ tablets together
10–14 years	2 tablets together
15 years and over	3 tablets together

Malarone

Under 5 kg	Not recommended
5–8 kg	Two paediatric tablets daily for three days
9–10 kg	Three paediatric tablets daily for three days
11–20 kg	One adult tablet daily for three days
21–30 kg	Two adult tablets daily for three days
31–40 kg	Three adult tablets daily for three days
Over 40 kg	Four adult tablets daily for three days

Quinine

8 mg/kg every eight hours for seven days.

Malaria, pregnancy and breastfeeding

Pregnancy

Mosquitoes are attracted to pregnant women and those recently pregnant. In addition, an attack of malaria, in particular malignant (*P. falciparum*) malaria, can cause severe symptoms in pregnancy, including miscarriages and stillbirths. Ideally, if you are pregnant you should avoid areas where malignant malaria is common, especially in the first three months and the last three months of pregnancy.

If this is not possible it is essential to take *prophylactics* without missing tablets, as well as full precautions to avoid mosquito bites (see pages 121–4).

- Chloroquine and proguanil are safe in pregnancy but give very poor protection in areas where there is chloroquine resistance, including most of sub-Saharan Africa.
- Mefloquine is now considered to be safe in pregnancy by most experts.
- Doxycycline should be avoided in pregnancy.
- Malarone is not currently recommended in pregnancy.

For *treatment*, quinine is the treatment of choice and can be life-saving. Other drugs should be avoided if possible, including co-artemether (Riamet).

When taking antimalarials, pregnant women should take folic acid 5 mg daily – especially important if taking proguanil or Malarone.

Breastfeeding

Chloroquine, proguanil and quinine are safe during breastfeeding. Other antimalarial drugs, including co-artemether, should be avoided. Mefloquine and doxycycline are secreted in breast milk but are not thought to be harmful. Current advice is that breastfeeding mothers should not take Malarone for prevention if the child is under 11 kg or for treatment if the child is under 5 kg.

Deltaprim and Fansidar (or its equivalents) are harmful to newborn babies. They are also secreted in breast milk, and breastfeeding mothers should avoid both until at least six weeks after birth.

Any malaria prophylaxis being taken by the mother will not be effective in protecting the baby as insufficient is secreted in breast milk.

Notes on drugs commonly used for treating and preventing malaria

When in the tropics, probably sooner rather than later the conversation will turn to malaria. Details of the latest therapeutic fashion mingled with advice, good, bad and indifferent, will soon fill the room. It is helpful to know basic information about the medicines you may be using as well as those others are talking about. A large number of different trade names add further to the confusion.

Here is a simple field guide. Detailed summaries on the most important drugs used in malaria are included first. Shorter notes on less commonly used drugs follow them.

Chloroquine and proguanil (Paludrine) to prevent malaria

Background

Chloroquine (Nivaquine, Avloclor) combined with proguanil (Paludrine) is used to prevent malaria in areas where little resistance has developed to their effectiveness. This combination now only works for some areas in South Asia, in Central and South America, excluding the Amazon basin, and in a few other areas of the world where malaria is relatively uncommon. This combination (or each alone) is dangerously unreliable (but still often and incorrectly used) in sub-Saharan Africa, Southeast Asia, Amazonia, Papua New Guinea and other Pacific islands. Travellers to Africa should not use chloroquine and proguanil, the one exception possibly being pregnant women in the first trimester of pregnancy. Proguanil is not recommended or normally available in the United States.

What are their side-effects?

These two drugs are generally regarded as safe and you do not need a prescription in the UK to obtain them. In terms of side-effects, both can give minor stomach upsets, and chloroquine can give occasional headache, dizziness and blurred vision. Chloroquine can make psoriasis worse and should be avoided if there is a history of epilepsy. Prolonged use of chloroquine (e.g. over five years) can in rare cases affect eyesight, usually only if you have taken more than two tablets per week. If you are concerned, see an ophthalmologist for a check-up using a slit-lamp examination for greater accuracy. Chloroquine often causes itching in those with black skin.

Proguanil should be avoided in those with serious kidney problems. It can also cause mouth ulcers (common) and both chloroquine and proguanil (especially proguanil) can lead to thinning of the hair (less common and usually over a longer period of time). This combination of

138

drugs is regarded as safe to take during pregnancy and breastfeeding. It is also safe for children to take.

Current guidelines from the Advisory Committee on Malaria Prevention for UK Travellers (ACMP, 2003) concluded that there were no problems with long-term use over several years of chloroquine and proguanil.

Please consult the Patient Information Leaflet for a longer list of possible side-effects and interactions with other medicines.

How should they be taken?

Chloroquine should be taken weekly as two (150 mg base) tablets. Proguanil should be taken daily as two (100 mg) tablets. Both are best taken with food. Start taking chloroquine one week before entering malarious areas, and start taking proguanil 24 hours before entering a malarious area. Continue taking both while there and for four weeks after leaving.

Dosages

The information listed in Table 11.4 comes from the ACMP 'Guidelines for malaria prevention in travellers from the United Kingdom for 2003'. Variation in doses does exist between Patient Information Leaflets and other authoritative sources.

**Table 11.4 Malaria prevention dosages
for chloroquine and proguanil (Paludrine) (ACMP 2003)**

Children and adults 45 kg and over	Chloroquine 150mg base: 2 tablets per week and proguanil 100mg: 2 tablets per day
Children weighing 25.0–44.9 kg	$1\frac{1}{2}$ chloroquine tablets weekly and $1\frac{1}{2}$ proguanil tablets daily
Children weighing 16.0–24.9 kg	1 chloroquine tablet weekly and 1 proguanil tablet daily
Children weighing 10.0–15.9 kg	$\frac{3}{4}$ chloroquine tablet weekly and $\frac{3}{4}$ proguanil tablet daily
Babies weighing 6.0–9.9 kg	$\frac{1}{2}$ chloroquine tablet weekly and $\frac{1}{2}$ proguanil tablet daily
Babies under 6.0 kg	$\frac{1}{4}$ chloroquine tablet weekly and $\frac{1}{4}$ proguanil tablet daily

Chloroquine is available as a syrup (Nivaquine) for young children as well as tablets. Proguanil is only available in tablet form.

Chloroquine has a number of trade names, including Aralen, Avloclor, Chinamine, Delagil, Imagon, Malariquine, Malarivon, Nivaquine, Plaquenol, Resochin, Sanioquin, Shellyquine, Tresochin. Savarine is chloroquine 100 mg (base) and proguanil 200 mg in a single tablet. The dose is one tablet daily. Savarine may be slightly more effective than the normal combination of chloroquine two tablets per week, and proguanil two tablets per day. It is not available in the UK, but is commonly used in France.

Co-artemether to treat malaria

Background

Co-artemether is one of a new powerful group of combined malaria prevention tablets known as Artemesinin Combined Therapies or ACTs. Co-artemether, also known as Co-artem (Riamet is a common trade name), consists of two different preparations, artemether 20 mg and lumefantrine 120 mg.

Artemesinins are derived from the herb *Artemisia annua*, long used in China under the name *quinghoasu*. Artemesinins are considered to be highly effective in treating malaria, especially when combined with certain other malaria treatment drugs. Single artemesinin preparations are available in many countries under a large variety of names, e.g. Cotecxin, artesunate and Artenan. Unless combined with another drug they may not fully cure malaria, which can recur after a number of days.

How effective is co-artemether?

It is almost 100 per cent effective if taken according to manufacturer's instructions in the full and correct dose.

How do you take it?

As soon as malaria is suspected or diagnosed, start a three-day course taking four tablets together at hours 0, 8, 24, 36, 48 and 60 (total 24 tablets). It is better absorbed if taken with fatty food where possible.

At the time of writing it is not currently recommended for use in children by UK sources.

What are its side-effects?

These are usually minor and artemether is considered to be a safe drug.

However, it should be avoided in those with heart rhythm disorders. It can also interact with a number of drugs, including antifungal agents and erythromycin; therefore check with your doctor and read the Patient Information Leaflet if you are taking any other medication. Also consult this for a longer list of possible side-effects.

It should not be used in pregnancy or breastfeeding.

Doxycycline to prevent malaria

Why is it used?

Doxycycline (100 mg) has become increasingly popular for malaria prevention. This is because in many parts of the world, especially sub-Saharan Africa, the combination of proguanil (Paludrine) and chloro-quine (Nivaquine or Avloclor) is becoming increasingly less effective. There are two other types of malaria prevention tablet (prophylactic) which you can consider taking if you are unable to use doxycycline: mefloquine (Lariam) or Malarone.

How effective is doxycycline?

Evidence suggests that for most areas it is very effective.

How safe is it?

It is relatively safe. Since it is an antibiotic, however, there are a few precautions you need to take. *It should not be used in pregnancy or or in children under the age of 12 (the USA recommends under the age of eight).* Those allergic to tetracycline antibiotics should avoid it. Those with liver problems or with raised liver enzymes, or those who have poor kidney function, should use it with caution and discuss this with their doctor.

How do you take it?

Take one 100 mg capsule or tablet of doxycycline each day with or after food, ideally at the same time of day, without missing a dose. Start 24 hours before entering a malarious area; continue daily while there and for four weeks after leaving. The monohydrate form of the drug is reported as being slightly better tolerated than the hyclate.

Swallow the capsules or tablets with plenty of water and ensure you are standing or sitting up, otherwise it can cause inflammation of the oesophagus. Don't lie down shortly after taking it and never take it just before going to bed.

What are the side-effects?

Doxycycline makes some people sunburn more easily so *take extra precautions especially if you are pale, fair or freckled.* If despite avoiding the sun and using a sun cream of SPF 15 or more you still burn, it is better not to take it. Doxycycline can sometimes cause or worsen vaginal thrush (candidiasis), so women should consider taking treatment with them for this in case of need (Canesten pessaries or fluconazole (Diflucan) capsules). Some people develop a skin rash or sensitivity in the mouth and/or tongue. It sometimes causes nausea and diarrhoea, but more often it helps to prevent you from getting diarrhoea. Very rarely it causes a severe headache: stop at once and see a doctor. If you start getting any troublesome side-effects also consult a doctor.

Current guidelines from the Advisory Committee on Malaria Prevention for UK Travellers (ACMP, 2003) concluded that there was no evidence of harm in the long-term use of doxycycline. They suggest that doxycycline can be used safely for periods up to at least two years. (It is used for the treatment of acne at the same dose and up to the same length of time.) At InterHealth we recommend you ask yourself the following questions after taking doxycycline for a total of six months, and repeat this exercise at six-monthly intervals:

- Have you had a significant increase in sunburn or rash on light exposed areas?
- Have there been any changes to pre-existing moles?
- Have you experienced persistent diarrhoea or pain on swallowing?
- Have you had more frequent fungal infections, including vaginal thrush?

If you answer 'No' to all of these questions you can carry on taking doxycycline. If you answer 'Yes' to any question we recommend you seek medical advice.

Please read the Patient Information Leaflet giving more advice both on possible side-effects and on interactions with other medicines.

Doxycycline and contraceptives

For those taking the combined oral contraceptive pill or using a patch, the UK Family Planning Association has issued the following advice, which needs careful reading:

- You should take additional precautions to avoid pregnancy during the first three weeks of taking doxycycline. This is not necessary with the progesterone-only pill (mini-pill).
- If the pill-free interval or patch-free week coincides with the first three weeks of taking doxycycline, the pill- or patch-free week should be omitted.
- After using doxycycline for three weeks, additional contraception can be stopped.
- If you have already been using doxycycline for three or more weeks, you can start the pill or patch up to and including day 5 of the menstrual cycle without using additional contraception. If you start

after day 5, use additional precautions such as a condom, for seven days.
- If you have been using doxycycline for less than three weeks, you will need additional precautions when starting the pill or patch until you have been taking doxycycline for three weeks.

Two common trade names for doxycycline are Vibramycin and Nordox.

Malarone to prevent malaria

What is Malarone?

Malarone is a combination of two drugs, atovaquone 250 mg and proguanil 100 mg. Proguanil is familiar to many as Paludrine, which until recently was widely used with chloroquine as a malaria prevention (prophylactic) drug.

Malarone is very effective and relatively free from side-effects, but it is expensive. It is used both as an effective treatment and also for prevention of malaria. Because Malarone needs to be started only 24 hours before going to a malarious area and continued for seven days after leaving, it is especially useful for travellers making short or frequent trips.

Although the technical UK licence for Malarone is for 28 days, there is no evidence that long-term use is harmful, and in the USA Malarone is licensed for unrestricted long-term use.

Current guidelines from the Advisory Committee on Malaria Prevention for UK Travellers (ACMP, 2003) concluded that there was no evidence of harm in the long-term use of Malarone. The Committee suggested that Malarone could be used confidently for travel up to three months and, with caution, for periods of six months or longer. At InterHealth we supply up to six months at a time.

How effective is Malarone?

Drug trials, which are still continuing, indicate that Malarone is very effective in preventing malaria if taken correctly and regularly, and in particular for preventing falciparum (malignant) malaria.

How safe is it and what are its side-effects?

Malarone appears to be safe. Side-effects are infrequent and mild, headache and abdominal pain being the most likely. Mouth ulcers and hair thinning occasionally occur in longer-term use because of proguanil. Read the Patient Information Leaflet which comes with the tablets for more information on possible side-effects and interactions with other medicines.

Who should avoid it?

Women who are pregnant should not take Malarone. Women should not use Malarone when breastfeeding children under 11 kg. The adult tablet should not be used as prevention for children or those under 40 kg in weight, but a paediatric formula for children is available (see Table 11.2 on page 135). Malarone should not generally be used by anyone with seriously impaired kidney function. As Malarone may occasionally interact with other medications, you should always discuss its use with your travel health adviser. Taking tetracyclines (including doxycycline) at the same time reduces its effectiveness.

How do you take it?

For preventing malaria the adult dose is one tablet daily, starting 24 hours before entering a malarious area, taking it while there and continuing for seven days after leaving. The tablets should be taken at the same time each day with food or a milky drink to aid absorption and achieve good protective levels.

InterHealth recommendations

We recommend Malarone for preventing malaria for adults who are travelling to areas where there is chloroquine-resistant malaria and who are unable to tolerate other antimalarials such as mefloquine (Lariam) or doxycycline, or who have had attacks of malaria despite taking these drugs regularly. It is especially useful for short-term trips, when its expense is relatively less because it only needs to be taken for one week after return compared to four weeks with other forms of malaria prevention.

For use of Malarone in the treatment of malaria see pages 131 and 136.

Mefloquine (Lariam) to prevent malaria

Why is it used?

Mefloquine (250 mg) is currently recommended as one of the most effective malaria prevention tablets (antimalarials) for most of sub-Saharan Africa, the Amazon and many other parts of the world where there is chloroquine resistance. Although mefloquine has had a bad press, research shows that the majority of travellers will tolerate it quite well. There are two other types of antimalarials which you can consider taking if you are unable to use mefloquine: doxycycline and Malarone (see above).

How effective is mefloquine?

Evidence suggests that for most malarious areas mefloquine is very

144

effective. An exception to this is the remote forested areas in the border regions of Thailand, Laos, Cambodia and Myanmar.

How safe is it?

Mefloquine is generally safe for most travellers. About one-third of those who take it experience some side-effects, but the majority of these are mild. They include vivid dreams, some sleep disturbance, light-headedness and dizziness. More serious side-effects include increased anxiety, depression and mood changes. Dangerous side-effects are comparatively rare and include confusion, fits, heart irregularities and severe skin reactions. Most side-effects show up in the first three doses, but they can develop later and where this is the case you should not persist with this medication but seek further medical advice promptly. Make sure you read the Patient Information Leaflet which accompanies the tablets; this lists a full range of reported side-effects and interactions with other medicines.

Current guidelines from the Advisory Committee on Malaria Prevention for UK travellers (ACMP, 2003) advise that it can be taken for at least three years providing there are no significant side-effects. Liver function tests should ideally be checked each year.

Who should avoid it?

Anyone who has had symptoms of anxiety, depression, sleep disturbance, other significant psychiatric problems, heart irregularities or anyone with a history of fits, convulsions or epilepsy. Mefloquine appears to be tolerated best in those who have steady temperaments and are not liable to mood swings. Those with disturbed liver function or abnormal liver function tests should generally avoid using it, except for short trips. It should not be used if any significant side-effects have occurred when taken previously. Pilots, scuba divers and those requiring fine coordination in their jobs are usually recommended not to take mefloquine. It can mimic symptoms of altitude sickness and is best avoided at high altitude (e.g. after climbing on to the Altiplano or Andes after using it in the South American rainforest).

Mefloquine may interact with a number of medications. It is therefore very important that you should check this out in detail with your travel health adviser.

It is generally safe to use in children weighing 5 kg or over (around three months plus). Most experts now consider mefloquine safe to take during pregnancy, at the time of conception and during breastfeeding.

How do you take it?

The adult dosage is one (usually 250 mg) tablet weekly, taken with a main meal and plenty of water. Start taking mefloquine (250 mg) three weeks before travelling, as three-quarters of all side-effects show up during this period, giving you time to change to an alternative if they are severe. If you have taken mefloquine before and have not experienced side-effects you may start one week before travel. Continue taking mefloquine throughout the time you are in a malarious area and for four weeks after leaving.

For dosages, see Table 11.5. These guidelines follow the advice provided by the Advisory Committee on Malaria Prevention and they differ from those provided by the manufacturers of Lariam. If you are following a different but official regime from the one in Table 11.5, continue using it.

Table 11.5 Mefloquine prevention dosages for malaria

Children and adults weighing 45 kg and above	1 tablet (250mg) per week (adult dose)
Children weighing from 25 to 44.9 kg	$\frac{3}{4}$ tablet per week
Children weighing from 16 to 24.9 kg	$\frac{1}{2}$ tablet per week
Children weighing from 5 to 15.9 kg	$\frac{1}{4}$ tablet per week
Babies weighing under 5 kg	Not recommended

Primaquine to prevent and treat malaria

Background

Primaquine has been used for many years to kill off the liver forms of recurrent (benign) malaria caused by *Plasmodium vivax* and *ovale*, both of which may recur over a number of months or years after leaving a malarious area. Recently it has increasingly been used to prevent malaria, especially in those unable to take other effective forms of prevention.

What are its side-effects?

By far the most important is dangerous haemolysis – that is, bursting of the red blood cells in those lacking an enzyme called G6PD. G6PD deficiency is common in many parts of the world, including the Middle East and West Asia, and *everyone* who takes primaquine must first be tested to make sure they have adequate sources of this enzyme in their body.

It should not be used in those with active rheumatoid arthritis or lupus, nor in those allergic to primaquine.

Primaquine can cause gastrointestinal upsets including cramps, nausea and vomiting, especially if taken on an empty stomach. It should not be used in pregnancy, or in breastfeeding unless the child is known to have adequate levels of G6PD. It is important to read the Patient Information Leaflet which gives a full range of possible side-effects and interactions with other medicines.

How is primaquine taken?

1 To prevent or treat relapses of malaria, as described above, the usual dose is 30 mg daily for 14 days after departure from the malarious area. There are, however, a variety of recommendations about the best dose to use, some specialists recommending a daily dose of 0.5 mg/kg which equates to 30 mg daily for those weighing 60 kg. For children a commonly recommended dose is 0.6 mg/kg taken once daily for 14 days. It is not recommended in children under four years of age.

2 To prevent malaria during travel – and this should only be used if no other prophylaxis is suitable and in discussion with a travel health specialist – the adult dose is 15 mg tablets twice daily (i.e. 30 mg daily) starting one to two days before going to a malarious area, continuing daily while there and continuing for seven days after returning. Children's doses are 0.6 mg/kg daily from the age of four upwards.

Travellers should never share their supplies of primaquine with others because of the danger that those they share them with may have G6PD deficiency.

Notes on additional drugs

Many of those mentioned below are used in developing countries but unless starred ** are rarely used by international travellers. Before using any of these, read through the Patient Information Leaflet carefully for a full list of possible side-effects and interactions with other medicines.

Amodiaquine

(Camoquin, Flavoquine, Florquine, Miaquine)
Uses: Was used for prophylaxis, but is now largely discontinued owing to risk of blood disorders. Occasionally still used for treatment in chloroquine-sensitive areas, especially when combined with artemesinin.

**Artemesinin derivatives

(Co-artemether, co-artem, Riamet, Artenan, Cotecxin, etc.)

147

These effective antimalarials are derived from the herb *Artemisia annua*, and have been used in China for centuries under the name *quinghoasu*. The main artemesinin derivatives are known as artemether, arteether, dihydroartemesinin and artesunate. For further details on co-artemether, which is the most effective form, see page 140.

Chlorproguanil

(Lapudrine)
An alternative to proguanil (probably slightly less effective) taken as 20 mg tablet twice weekly or – better – daily.
Warnings: as for proguanil.

Deltaprim (Maloprim)

(One trade name for pyrimethamine 12.5 mg plus dapsone 100 mg) (Maloprim, Malasone (not to be confused with Malarone))
Uses: for prophylaxis. Maloprim is being superseded by other antimalarials, and it now only rarely used for travellers.
Warnings: unlikely to cause blood disorders if taken at normal dose of one per week. Avoid in liver or kidney disease, first three months of pregnancy and first six weeks of lactation. Those sensitive to sulphonamides sometimes develop an allergic reaction and should take it for a trial period of two weeks before deciding to use it long term. Those who are pregnant must take folic acid 5 mg daily in addition.

**Fansidar

(The trade name for sulfadoxine 500 mg plus pyrimethamine 25 mg)
Uses: for treatment of malaria as described on page 132. Should not be used for prophylaxis. There is increasing Fansidar resistance in Africa and other areas, and it is much less used than previously.
Warnings: generally safe if used for treatment. Should be avoided in those sensitive to sulphonamides or pyrimethamine, in pregnancy and during the first six weeks of lactation. Should not be used in children under six weeks. Sometimes causes skin rashes and allergic reactions.

Halofantrine

(Halfan)
Uses: *should only be used under medical supervision.* It is an effective treatment against most forms of malaria, including chloroquine-resistant strains, and the course of six tablets can be repeated after one week to prevent recurrences. As Halfan syrup it is an effective treatment for children, but it is not available in the UK.
Warnings: cases of serious cardiac effects, including deaths, have occasionally been reported. Halfan should only be used in travellers who have had a recent, normal ECG and no history of heart disease.

Avoid during pregnancy and delay conception for at least one month after completing a course of treatment.

It is not safe during lactation.

Halofantrine should not be used for treatment unless no other medication is available. The World Health Organization has issued a warning about its use.

Pyrimethamine

(Daraprim, Chloridin, Malocide, Tindurin, Syraprim)

Uses: this was widely used for prevention of malaria but is no longer recommended as its effectiveness is very low.

**Quinine*

(Quinidine (in USA), Quinimax, Quinoforme)

Uses: for treatment of all forms of malaria (see pages 131–2 and 136).

Warnings: may cause headache, tinnitus, dizziness, nausea and allergic reactions. Can be used in pregnancy and lactation, which is now its main use. Should ideally be used under medical supervision, especially if mefloquine has been used as a prophylactic. Quinine is generally considered a safe (though unpleasant) drug, and is increasingly being replaced as a treatment by other drugs, mentioned in the text, and by artesunate in acute falciparum malaria (hospital only).

Other drugs and combinations sometimes used

These include:

- Azithromycin (Zithromax) is a reasonably effective prophylactic occasionally used.
- Daraclor is pyrimethamine and chloroquine.
- Fansimef is sulfadoxine 500 mg, pyrimethamine 25 mg and mefloquine 250 mg, and is used for treatment under medical supervision.
- Lapoquin is chlorproguanil plus chloroquine.
- Metakelfin is sulfalene and pyrimethamine.
- Tetracycline (Achromycin, Cyclomycin, Panmycin, Tetracyn, etc.) is occasionally used for treatment in areas where there is chloroquine and Fansidar resistance. In these cases a course of quinine is followed or accompanied by tetracycline 250 mg four times daily for seven days. It should not be used in those sensitive to tetracyclines, in pregnancy and in children under 12. It has largely been superseded by a drug of similar composition but longer action, doxycycline (see pages 141–3).

Summary

Malaria is a serious nuisance at best and a fatal illness at worst. You can think of defeating malaria according to these four steps:

A **Awareness** Being aware of the risk and what you should do about it.
B **Bites by mosquitoes** Taking action to avoid them through the use of impregnated bed nets, insect repellent, cover-up and avoidance.
C **Compliance** Deciding on the prophylaxis to take and never missing a dose.
D **Diagnosis** Seeing a doctor or, if not possible, self-treating within eight hours of suspicious symptoms, both when in a malarious area and for 12 months after leaving it.

12

Avoiding HIV infection

Please read this chapter on HIV and AIDS and the following one on preventing sexually transmitted infections (STIs) together.

What are HIV and AIDS?

AIDS stands for the Acquired Immune Deficiency Syndrome. It is caused by the Human Immunodeficiency Virus (HIV), which attacks the immune system. Usually within three months of being infected with the virus, antibodies develop to HIV and the blood antibody test becomes HIV positive.

Without appropriate medical treatment, infection with HIV will eventually weaken the body's immune system, leading to AIDS. This can take months or years.

Initially, HIV infection will often cause no symptoms for many weeks or months but some people develop signs of a primary infection at three to six weeks after exposure. This may include fever, swollen glands and a flu-like illness, sometimes with a rash, joint pain and ulcers in the mouth or on the genitals. It can take up to 90 days after catching the infection before an HIV antibody test shows positive. This period is known as the 'window period' and is the time during which someone may be infected and infectious, but the immune system has not yet produced antibodies against HIV. There is great variation in the speed and the way in which immune deficiency develops as a result of HIV infection.

It used to be said that, once a diagnosis of AIDS has been made, the person would die within two years. This is no longer so. Recent advances with anti-retroviral drug therapy (ART), often known as Highly Active Anti-Retroviral Therapy (HAART), have greatly prolonged the survival time for those who can access them and who can tolerate the side-effects. Most people who need them in industrialized countries have access to them, but in the developing world only about 5–10 per cent of those who need them can access them because of cost and the lack of good healthcare infrastructures. However, they are now becoming more available in developing countries. Most international travellers who become infected with HIV should see this as a chronic infection which, if well managed, can still allow them to live with a good quality of life for many years and to engage in work.

However, avoiding HIV infection in the first place remains

supremely important as there is still no cure and it can still cause very serious problems, and lead to death.

How big is the problem?

The World Health Organization estimates (January 2006) that there are over 40 million people living with HIV. Worldwide, AIDS kills more than 8,000 people every day; that's one person every ten seconds.

HIV is present in all countries and is increasing in all areas of the world. Five million new cases were reported in 2005, over 60 per cent of these in Africa. Numbers in Asia, including Thailand and India, Latin America, eastern Europe and Russia are increasing rapidly. Sub-Saharan Africa is still the most affected area.

How is HIV infection spread?

- Through having unprotected vaginal, anal or oral *sex with an infected person*.
- Through *infected blood transfusions*, and other blood products such as immunoglobulins.
- Through *needles* which are contaminated by infected blood and from *anything else which pierces the skin*; this includes tattooing, acupuncture, body piercing, the use of razors and in dentistry.
- Occasionally through *infected blood and other body fluids* coming into contact with mucus membranes or inflamed, eczematous or broken skin.
- From mother to child at or during *birth*.
- Through infected *breast milk*.

You can't pick up HIV infection:

- through normal social contact, hugging, or sharing plates, dishes, glasses or communion cups;
- through mosquitoes, bed-bugs or any insects.

If you travel or live in a country where HIV is common you face a potentially greater risk than staying in areas where HIV is rare. However, by taking a few commonsense precautions your risk of becoming infected can be reduced to near zero.

How can you minimize your risk?

Before you travel

- *Decide to abstain* from casual sexual encounters.
- *Take condoms* with you unless you consider your principles and beliefs will *guarantee* your safe behaviour even at times of stress or loneliness. Condoms should be in-date and made of good-quality latex. There are more details on condoms in the section below on sexually transmitted infections.
- *Complete immunizations* so as to reduce the need for further immunizations when travelling.
- *Have a dental check*, so as to reduce the need for dentistry.
- *Find out your blood group* and keep a record with you, as this may make finding a compatible safe donor easier in an emergency.
- *Take a needle and syringe kit.*
- *Consider taking an HIV and hepatitis B protection kit* containing an intravenous giving set and bottles of plasma substitute if in remote highly affected areas.
- It is especially important for women to consider strategies to avoid unsafe situations (see pages 227–9).

When abroad

Avoid casual sex

The only way of being certain to avoid sexually transmitted HIV infection is to be completely loyal to one partner who is known to be HIV negative and also completely loyal to you. This means that only those who have always abstained from pre- and extramarital sex can be certain to avoid getting infected.

Condoms will considerably reduce your risk, but 'safe sex' only means 'safer sex'. Condoms, if used correctly, are more than 90 per cent effective. However, many travellers when tired, stressed or when drinking alcohol or using recreational drugs fail to use condoms or do not use them correctly. Taken together these risks greatly add to the dangers of becoming infected with HIV when travelling.

These realities mean that abstinence and fidelity should move up the menu for methods of avoiding HIV infection, without denying the importance of using condoms correctly.

Also avoid situations and lifestyles that might increase your risk of being sexually assaulted; be aware of how easy it is to be 'proposition-ed' in many parts of the world and to be caught unawares and unprepared.

Avoid road, domestic and industrial accidents

Road crashes are especially dangerous because occasionally you may need a blood transfusion or emergency medical treatment. Most road crashes can be prevented. This is the commonest cause of death in travellers and one of the commonest causes for being repatriated. (See pages 161–3.)

Avoid blood transfusions from an unknown source except in extreme emergencies

In most developing countries, blood, even if screened, is still not reliably HIV negative. If you need blood, try as far as possible to receive this from someone whose lifestyle you would trust, who is known to be HIV negative, and who has a compatible blood group. In practice a responsible friend may need to make this decision for you, or you may need to do so for a friend. See pages 168–72 and the website of the Blood Care Foundation <http://www.bloodcare.org.uk/>.

Avoid contaminated needles and syringes

It's worth carrying your own emergency pack and tactfully insisting that this is used unless you are extremely sure that the supplies used on you are safe. Avoid the use of multi-dose vials. In practice, many health facilities have reliable packs of sterilized needles – just make sure that you see these being opened in front of you.

Also avoid getting a tattoo, body piercing, acupuncture or any other activity which involves the skin being pierced.

Take every precaution to avoid malaria

Severe malaria may land you in hospital or necessitate a blood transfusion. By avoiding it you will therefore reduce a potential HIV risk.

Healthcare workers and others at occupational risk

Healthcare workers will need more detailed advice. It is important you discuss the full implications of working in an occupation where the risk of HIV cannot be entirely eliminated. You should consider taking a personal anti-retroviral medical kit with you, for immediate post-exposure prophylaxis, starting within one or two hours of a high-risk incident. Combivir (lamivudine 150 mg + zidovudine 300 mg), one tablet twice daily for 28 days, is a good option (one form of dual therapy). This is obtainable from InterHealth and other suppliers, along with detailed instructions on how and when to use it.

Some experts recommend the use of triple therapy, i.e. adding a third drug known as a protease inhibitor, such as nelfinavir or indinavir, but this may cause some side-effects and probably adds only marginal value. Side-effects may discourage you from completing the 28-day course, but it is important that you do so. You should get medical advice and counselling, and have an HIV test within the first week or so following exposure. This is to check that you were not already HIV positive before the injury, and to provide a 'base line' from which further testing will provide more meaningful information. You should then have a further test after three months (90 days). Similar procedures are appropriate after rape, accompanied by counselling and support.

When you get home

If you are working for a company or agency it is unlikely they will expect you to have an HIV test when you get back home, but you may wish to have one. If in any doubt it is worth having this: it reduces your risk to others if you are infected, and it also means you can start on HAART if further blood tests show this is necessary.

In the UK you can have a confidential HIV test done either through your GP, through a GUM (genitourinary medicine) clinic and at InterHealth. In many developing countries it can be carried out at a centre which offers Voluntary Counselling and Testing (VCT). Before having the test you will be given a chance to talk through any fears and questions, have counselling, and results can be conveyed to you quickly afterwards.

Remember that, if you are tested for HIV antibodies within three months of your last exposure, you may test negative because you are still in the 'window period'. It may therefore be worth delaying any test until 90 days after your last possible exposure in order to get the true picture. Remember that you should use a condom if you do have sex during this time, even if it is with your usual partner, just in case you did become infected. If you did, you could be highly infectious to someone else.

Unless you have been fully immunized or are known to have immunity, it is also worth being tested for hepatitis B infection, spread in a similar way and 100 times more infectious. Also consider having a check-up for other sexually transmitted infections (see Chapter 13).

Provided your HIV test is negative and you can record an occupational reason or specific non-recurring risk while abroad, you are extremely unlikely to be declined by an insurance company or charged a higher premium. If you are you can appeal. In the UK a statement of practice is available from the Association of British Insurers, 51 Gresham Street, London EC2V 7HQ, email: <Info@abi.org.uk>.

Note on entry certificates

A few countries require certificates stating that you have tested HIV negative. A negative test carried out not more than 90 days before entry and accompanied by a doctor's signed and stamped certificate stating this was carried out in a WHO-accredited laboratory is usually sufficient, though some countries will expect you to have a test after arrival if you are planning to reside in that country. Check with the embassy of the country in question if in doubt, or with a specialist travel clinic.

For those working internationally who are HIV positive or immuno-compromised, see pages 48–51.

13

Preventing and treating sexually transmitted infections

Sexually transmitted infections (STIs) are theoretically the easiest diseases to prevent, but in practice they are some of the most difficult. You can forget about them if either you reliably practise abstinence or you have sex only in the context of a stable, mutually loyal, long-term relationship with a partner known to be free of infection. Lifestyles or religions which promote life-long monogamous relationships are doing public health a big service. *But,* even with those committed to a risk-free lifestyle, it is easy to slip up during a time of stress, loneliness or celebration.

Why are STIs important?

For several reasons:

- People who travel tend to take more sexual risks than those who stay at home.
- They are extremely common – each year sees at least 340 million new infections in the world, and rising.
- They often show few or no symptoms in their early stages but you are still infectious to others.
- They often have serious long-term effects.

There are at least 25 infectious diseases transmitted wholly or in part through sex.

How can you avoid getting an STI?

Well, obviously, by not having sex or by practising 'mutual monog-amy', i.e. having sex only with one partner known to be free of infection.

Condoms, if used reliably, will prevent more than 90 per cent of infections. Make sure these are high quality, in-date and made of latex, unless you are allergic in which case obtain condoms made of polyurethane. You should use condoms for *any* casual sexual encoun-ter. Travellers and those working internationally are at high risk of becoming infected because stress, laziness, alcohol, drugs or tiredness means the condoms are left on a shelf, in a pocket unused, put on too late, or slip off too quickly, causing spillage – basically, because you make a mistake or have an accident.

You should ideally only use water-based lubricants with latex condoms, e.g. KY Jelly and glycerine, because oil-based lubricants can weaken the latex. Avoid using spermicides containing nonoxynyl 9.

Female condoms are becoming more widespread and empower women with a degree of extra protection.

What are the commonest forms of STI?

In developing countries, gonorrhoea, hepatitis B and syphilis are common, but vary depending on geographical area. HIV, though seriously common, especially in sub-Saharan Africa and among sex workers, is 100 times less infectious than hepatitis B. Any form of genital sore or ulceration may indicate you have an STI but this also makes picking up other infections easier, especially HIV.

Travellers are at high risk of Chlamydia. This is common but underdiagnosed in developing countries, meaning travellers are at risk both from local inhabitants and from within their own cultural group.

In practice all these factors mean that those working and living away from their own country are at high risk from a wide range of STIs.

What are the symptoms?

These differ with different STIs but you need to take the following symptoms seriously: urethral discharge, vaginal discharge (though this will often have other causes), genital ulcers and genital or pelvic pain.

Some STIs, especially chlamydia, often remain silent, and are only discovered later when symptoms of pelvic infection or infertility occur – the latter a largely preventable tragedy.

Typical symptoms of common STIs include the following:

- *Gonorrhoea* Pain urinating and pale yellow discharge from the penis or female urethra.
- *Chlamydia* The same, but usually symptom-free in early stages. This is the commonest STI in developed countries, and probably among developed-world travellers returning from a developing country, for the reason mentioned above.
- *Herpes* Sores and vesicles around the genitals, or sometimes around the mouth, accompanied by pain or itching, especially with a first infection. Symptoms tend to recur. It is commoner in women.
- *Genital warts* caused by human papilloma virus (HPV). These tend to develop on the skin in the genital or anal area. HPV infection is associated with an increased risk of developing cervical cancer at a later stage.
- *HIV/AIDS* See Chapter 12.
- *Hepatitis B* Many people, especially those brought up in developing countries, have this infection without realizing it. Over two billion people – that's almost one-third of the population – have had this illness. Among adult travellers it can cause serious and severe symptoms of hepatitis usually six weeks to six months after infection. Symptoms include jaundice, with tiredness, nausea and abdominal pain. Sex with a hepatitis B carrier, whether ill or not, and infected needles and needle sharing are the commonest causes of spread in travellers. It is especially common in Africa and Asia. See pages 300–4 and 384–6.

How can STIs be treated?

Some of the above infections can be treated by antibiotics. Those that are caused by viruses, such as HIV, hepatitis B, HPV and Herpes, do not respond to antibiotics but can be treated with antiviral agents, although these are only partially effective. The best thing to do is to see a competent doctor, and get properly diagnosed and treated as soon as possible. If this is not possible, e.g. you are in a remote location or there is no medical care, the following antibiotics may cure a bacterial STI:

- tetracycline 500 mg four times daily for seven days;
- doxycycline 100 mg twice daily for seven days (if you are taking doxy as an antimalarial, just take two for seven days, then continue as usual on one per day);
- ciprofloxacin 500 mg as a one-off dose;
- azithromycin 2 grams as a single dose.

These drugs are not suitable in pregnancy. There is also varying resistance to them, so they are not cure-alls and self-treatment must not replace getting checked out as soon as possible by a reliable doctor. Make sure anyone with whom you have had sex also sees a doctor and gets checked, and treated if infected.

And when you get home?

If you have symptoms or have been at risk, see your doctor. In the UK you can attend a GUM clinic. Make sure any sexual partner also gets checked. You can also speak to InterHealth for advice. Please don't leave it, or hope for the best, or hop on a plane for a holiday or the next assignment, without getting checked. And take greater care next time.

14

Preventing road crashes

Road crashes

Most road accidents are not accidents at all, but preventable events which occur through your carelessness or someone else's. Following the suggestion of the World Health Organization, we will use the term 'road crash' rather than 'accident'. Road crashes kill 1.2 million people each year and injure or disable 50 million more. In some countries one hospital bed in ten is occupied by the victim of a car crash.

Road crashes are far and away the commonest cause of death in travellers. In some countries the risk of being in a crash is between 20 and 30 times greater than in the UK. In developed countries it is mainly drivers who get killed, but in developing countries nearly as many pedestrians are killed as drivers and vehicle occupants. There is a great deal you can do to reduce the risk of being hurt or killed in a road crash and to avoid hurting or killing others.

Many seasoned travellers develop the attitude that the suggestions below are often not practicable and that living in a different culture means you have to change your expectations rather than act like a fussy foreigner. That attitude if anything increases the danger.

Ways to prevent road crashes

- *Fit and wear seat belts* in both front AND rear seats, and ensure that all, including children, use them. Unstrapped back-seat passengers can kill those in the front seat.

Wearing seat belts, even for the shortest journeys, is probably the single most important health precaution you can take when overseas (or at home).

161

- *Keep your vehicle in good condition* by regular servicing, and make sure tyres are adequate and brakes and lights working properly.
- Make sure any driver you employ, personally or for a project, is both *licensed and competent* to drive.
- Try to *avoid driving when tired*, feverish, jet-lagged or for prolonged periods, or overnight or without a co-driver.

- *Never drink or take recreational drugs and then drive*, or drive when taking medicines that make you drowsy.
- *Leave plenty of time* for journeys so you are not in a hurry.
- *Don't use mobile (cell) phones* or two-way radios when driving, or fiddle with other equipment.
- *Choose drivers, taxis and rickshaws with care*, and, as far as your ingenuity allows, make sure that lights, tyres and brakes are in good order before setting out. Ensure your driver is alert and not under the influence of drugs or alcohol. 'Close-face bargaining' can enable you to assess the driver's level of alertness – or intoxication.
- *Ride in the safest part of the vehicle.*
- Carry in the vehicle *a first-aid kit, torch and leather gloves* for pulling victims free. Also take food, fluid and blankets if going on longer journeys, and a warning triangle.

- Motorcyclists should *wear crash helmets* (or change to a safer form of transport), even for the shortest journeys.
- When *crossing the road* remember the direction of traffic flow. Take special care of children if visiting a city after living in a rural area.

For the procedure to follow in a serious road accident, see page 171.

15

Preventing accidents at home, leisure and work

Swimming accidents

After road crashes, accidents in the sea and swimming pool are the next most important thing which travellers need to be aware of. Again, the great majority are preventable.

By following these simple rules you will make these much less likely and help to save the lives of your family and friends as well as yourself.

- Find out about areas where you can swim which are known to be safe – from currents, sharks, crocodiles, poisonous fish and jellyfish, dangerous currents, bilharzia and other hazards.
- Swim only in areas known to be free of these dangers.
- Never swim after drinking alcohol, after taking recreational drugs, after a heavy meal or for too long in cold water.
- Always wear a life-jacket for off-shore water sports, when using inflatables, canoes or small boats.
- Keep a very close watch on children, and ensure they wear inflatable arm bands.
- Always swim with a companion.
- Never swim out of your depth, except possibly on beaches you are familiar with and if you are a strong swimmer.
- Take every precaution to avoid sunburn (see pages 197–200).
- In swimming pools take care not to do the following: running along the edge, diving into cloudy water, diving without being sure you know the depth of the pool.
- Avoid polluted areas when swimming in the sea and make sure swimming pools look and smell clean, have no vegetation around the edges and are regularly chlorinated.
- Avoid swimming during electrical storms, especially in swimming pools.

Household safety

Domestic accidents have been called 'the hidden epidemic', and this epidemic is most dangerous for children. Overseas children are at greater risk than in their home country, and so too are visitors, especially older visitors or anyone with a disability.

When you first arrive in your new house or location, whether it is temporary or permanent, carry out a risk assessment. This may sound complicated but can be very simple. Do it as soon as possible after you arrive, and look at your living arrangements from your own viewpoint and that of any children – yours and others who may visit, or those of any people you are working with. You will need to identify the hazards, identify who is most likely to be harmed, and decide what extra things you can do to minimize the risk.

Risk assessments should also be carried out at regular intervals. These are some of the areas to watch out for:

- *Slips, trips and falls*: look imaginatively at places where it is easy to slip and fall, and at uneven floor surfaces. Balconies are dangerous, especially when heavy relatives or friends lean against them, worse still if they have been drinking. Of course, it may be you. Flat roofs are also a hazard, especially when used for sleeping.
- *Electrics*: unsafe wiring, uncovered live wires, dangers in kitchen and bathroom and taking a shower because of old or incorrect wiring; also broken sockets and poorly earthed appliances such as immersion heaters.
- *Burns and scalds* from cooking pots with protruding handles (children especially), cooking fires, especially those on the floor (important when visiting local families), boiling water, milk or cooking oil.

- *Furniture*: check that beds and chairs, etc. are in reasonable repair and not likely to break or collapse during use.
- *Windows and doors*: consider cuts from glass, walking into doors, falling from windows.
- *Fire hazards*: always ensure you know the quickest and safest way to escape. If staying in a hotel, consider taking a room on a lower floor, security permitting.
- *Repairing cars or other vehicles or machinery*: take all precautions whether at work or at home, especially when working beneath them.
- *Household chemicals and medicines*: be aware of dangers from bleach, medicines in the reach of children, incorrectly labelled bottles.
- *Carbon monoxide poisoning*: this is a danger from coal and charcoal fires with inadequate ventilation, especially at night.
- *Poisonous scorpions, snakes or spiders*: be watchful. Also be careful of domestic animals, including pets of friends, which may not have been immunized against rabies.
- *Drowning* of infants and young children in a bath, paddling pool or water near the house is a constant threat.
- *Extra dangers* will be present during climatic extremes, or when you are stressed, tired or in a hurry.

Safety at work

The UN states: 'Every citizen of the world has a right to a healthy and safe work place and to a work environment that enables him or her to live a socially and economically productive life.'[1]

We need to be just as strict about our work place overseas as at home, even though this may be hard to achieve. This is very important if we are responsible for the facility where employees or volunteers are working.

The key to this is the risk assessment, which includes:

- identifying the hazards;
- identifying who may be harmed;
- deciding if the risks are adequately controlled and, if not, taking further steps to reduce them;
- recording the findings of the assessment;
- monitoring and reviewing the situation at regular intervals;
- educating and encouraging all colleagues to practise the same and take responsibility for their own health and safety.

[1] United Nations, *Global Strategy on Occupational Health for All* (WHO, 1995).

Key work hazards will include the following:

- personal security (see the book *Staying Alive* (ICRC, 2006), available from InterHealth);
- manual handling;
- accommodation;
- hazards from the work environment, especially building sites, water supplies, sanitation, broken or unsafe equipment;
- office premises, including the prevention of repetitive strain injury, common with incorrectly designed and sited chairs, computer screens and keyboards;
- any additional hazards in unstable political situations, chronic complex emergencies, natural disasters, war zones and refugee camps.

Again, remember that risk assessments need to be done on a regular basis, not just on first arrival or once a year.

An increasing number of volunteers from developed countries spend a few weeks in building projects abroad. Assessing the risks in these situations is especially important. Often hard hats will be needed, as well as sturdy boots and sensible clothing. Anyone working in these situations must not wear jewellery. If you are responsible for work assignments, you will need to plan ahead and know where appropriate clothing can be obtained.

Finally, having survived the journey, your home, the swimming pool and the work environment, don't take absurd risks in your leisure time or in adventure sports. For example: make sure the person who takes you white-water rafting is licensed and experienced, you are well prepared for the mountains, and you don't run or dance yourself into heatstroke when the ambient temperature is over 40°C.

These subjects are so important there is a special booklet (20 easy-to-read pages) published by People in Aid on how individuals can help to prevent crashes and accidents, and how organizations can draw up guidelines to make them less likely. See *Prevent Accidents*, details on page 372, Appendix H.

16

Knowing about blood transfusions

Occasions when you might need blood

The commonest reason for needing a blood transfusion when overseas is because of a road crash. Other causes include: bleeding during surgery; blood loss before, during or after childbirth; severe malaria; a bleeding peptic ulcer; getting caught up in a civil disturbance or war. You can minimize these risks by commonsense precautions, a healthy lifestyle and planning ahead.

Serious blood loss – of more than 25 per cent of the blood volume – means you will probably require emergency transfusion. However, for all but the most urgent situations you can start treatment using a plasma substitute to replace fluid lost until such time as you can reach a safe donor or obtain supplies of safe blood. Until recently plasma expanders such as Haemaccel were the best choice, but recent evidence shows that cheaper and simpler intravenous fluids such as Hartmann's solution work as well or better.

Making sure blood is safe and compatible

Any blood you receive must fulfil two conditions: first, it must be free from infection, and second, it must belong to the same or a compatible blood group.

Blood should be free from infection

This includes HIV, hepatitis B and C, syphilis and malaria. When you go to a UK blood donor clinic, tests are carried out on all the above except malaria, at which time your blood group is also ascertained. However, when you simply have a blood grouping arranged, tests for infection are not usually carried out. Blood supplies in developing countries are often inadequately tested or not tested at all. They may be infected not only with HIV, hepatitis B and C and other viruses, but also with malaria and, in parts of South America, with Chagas' disease.

There are three ways to reduce the risk of receiving HIV-infected blood when overseas:

- Only accept blood that has been HIV tested immediately before you receive it.
- Only receive blood from a donor whose lifestyle you trust. This is important because blood infected with HIV may still test negative for

168

a period of three months after becoming infected, and during this 'window' period can still pass on HIV disease. Also, it is easy to be over-optimistic about another person's lifestyle.

- Use intravenous fluids until you can reach a source of known safe blood (see below).

Blood should belong to a compatible group
(See Table 16.1 on page 172.)

Even when compatible blood groups are used, it is essential that blood from donor and receiver is cross-matched to reduce the risk of serious reactions. In this test, drops of blood from the person giving and the person receiving blood are mixed together. Cross-matching should ideally be done just before the transfusion is set up. If you will be travelling as a team in dangerous situations with poor medical facilities, group members with the same blood group can arrange to have their blood cross-matched before departure.

REMEMBER: blood from an unknown or untreated source in a developing country should be avoided except in life-threatening emergencies.

Practical steps you should take

1 Know your blood group before going abroad
If you will be living in a developing country or travelling extensively, make sure that you and all family members or group members know their blood groups. Each person should keep a written record with them at all times. Similarly, parents should keep a note of the blood group of all family members, and group leaders of all in their group. The value of families and teams knowing their blood groups is that in a serious emergency, when safe blood may not be available quickly enough from a reliable source, another team member may have a compatible group, likely (but not usually proved) to be safe.

Blood grouping can sometimes be arranged in the UK through your GP or local hospital; both will usually charge. Better still, you can become a blood donor and have it checked free (see page 373).

2 Check your health insurance covers the provision of safe blood and join the Blood Care Foundation

Make sure that your health insurance includes the supply of safe blood being available within a 24-hour period. Alternatively or in addition, individuals should consider joining the Blood Care Programme run by the Blood Care Foundation Travel Club, and organizations should consider taking out a corporate membership with the Blood Care Foundation (website <http://www.bloodcare.org.uk>, and see page 376 for further details). This international organization is usually able to provide safe blood anywhere in the world within 12 to 18 hours, subject to the availability of scheduled air services. It uses quality-assured sources (and is also able to provide Human Rabies Immunoglobulin in an emergency, page 326).

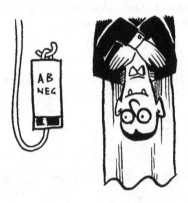

3 Consider taking an HIV and hepatitis B protection kit

(See pages 15–16.)

This is probably only necessary if you are doing extensive travel by road (or light aircraft) in areas where AIDS is common, or if you are travelling or living in remote and isolated areas. If you do take a kit, make sure it contains one or more intravenous giving sets and at least one litre of intravenous fluid. If young children will be travelling with you, take one or more 'butterfly' needles (see page 361). At the time of an accident, the use of a kit does depend on someone being present who knows how to set it up, though simple instructions are usually included. If you take a kit abroad, make sure you always have it with you on road journeys. It is no use having it under your bed if you've just had a road accident 100 kilometres from home. Plasma substitutes such as Haemaccel or Gelofusine should not be left for long periods in the boot of a car because of overheating. This is less important with simple intravenous fluids such as Hartmann's, which is now the recommended choice.

4 Know a transfusion procedure in case of an accident
This will include:

- *giving and receiving first aid*, and prevention of further bleeding where possible (see Further Reading, page 402);
- *setting up an intravenous line* as soon as possible and giving intravenous fluids if kit and health worker are available and if the injured person is losing blood or shows signs of shock (watch for concealed blood loss, with fast pulse, cold extremities, low blood pressure);
- *admission to a reliable health facility*;
- *arrangement for blood transfusion*, if needed, as soon as available, and from a safe source. This could include contacting your health insurance emergency line or the Blood Care Foundation without delay (see page 376).

Walking blood banks

These have been widely used in the past. A walking blood bank is a group of people, usually working long term in isolated areas, whose blood groups are known to each other so that in an emergency a member of the group who is seriously ill or injured and needing a transfusion can call on supposedly safe blood from a member of the bank with a compatible group.

Walking blood banks and 'trusted donor groups' are no longer considered either good or safe practice. This is largely because it is extremely hard to guarantee that blood is safe, especially after a member of the group has been overseas for any length of time. Also, there are now better and safer solutions in place, as described. However, this does not remove the value of families and short-term teams knowing each other's groups.

Compatible blood groups

Everyone belongs to group O, A, B or AB. In addition, everyone is Rhesus (D) positive or negative. Blood has to be compatible for both the group and the Rhesus sign, otherwise serious reactions can occur with transfusions. It is ideal to receive blood from someone with an identical blood group to your own, or who is O Rhesus negative (universal donor). However, blood can also be given and received according to Table 16.1, provided cross-matching is carried out before the transfusion is given.

Table 16.1 Compatible blood groups

Blood group	Can give to	Can receive from
O+	O+, A+, B+, AB+	O+, O–
O–	All groups	O–
A+	A+, AB+	A+, A–, O+, O–
A–	A+, A–, AB+, AB–	A–, O–
B+	B+, AB+	B+, B–, O+, O–
B–	B+, B–, AB+, AB–	B–, O–
AB+	AB+	All groups
AB–	AB+, AB–	AB–, A–, B–, O–

Note: Blood group O negative is known as universal donor

17

Coping with stress
by Dr Ruth Fowke

Stress or stimulus?

It sometimes seems that most people are either suffering from stress themselves or setting up seminars to help those who are. Stress is indeed an ever-present part of modern living, and few people will find that jumping on a plane for an overseas posting will automatically lead them to a stress-free nirvana. Indeed, for many working abroad, levels of stress are high. This means that learning to recognize, prevent and deal with stress is one of the most useful lessons you can learn, both before and during your time overseas. Please see pages 350–3 for some tips about how you can do this and help to prevent stress from getting on top of you.

Understanding your own personality and that of others can be a great help in reducing stress. If you have ever done a Myers Briggs Personality Typing in the past, remind yourself about it and any useful insights it gave you. If not and you have time before you go, consider doing one, especially if you are going on a long-term assignment and working in a team situation.

It's useful to understand that a situation that is of little consequence to one person may be highly stressful to someone else, and for a third person may be the very stimulus that leads to taking appropriate action (see Figure 17.1).

So a key way to minimize stress is to 'know yourself' – and to learn what situations are stressful to you.

Stimulation is necessary for effective living. No stimulation generally means no achievement.

The point in time or intensity when stimulation turns to stress is very much an individual matter. This means it is helpful for each individual, couple and family to find out the optimum level of stimulation for their own well-being.

173

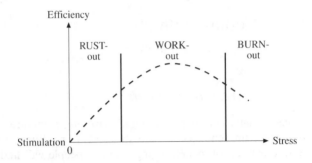

Figure 17.1 Personal efficiency curve

Specific overseas stresses

There are many stressors overseas, not necessarily more or greater than those experienced when living at home but often different and unfamiliar. Here are some important ones:

Living and working with expatriates and other colleagues

This can often be the biggest stress factor of all. Remember that what stresses one person or family may merely amuse or stimulate another. These individual differences to stress can in themselves cause tension, especially if you are living in confined circumstances, sharing homes, kitchens, work and leisure with little relief from one another's company. Just realizing this fact can in itself help the situation.

Some people can only recharge their personal batteries with plenty of people around them to join in the activity; others crave to be alone for a while. A routine lifestyle is essential for some; a random one is necessary for the health of others. Some people work best in sequential, even steps; others can only do so in bursts of energy with pauses between. The output of both may be similar, but the method of working is so different that each can mistrust and even come to dislike the other. It is difficult for larks and owls to agree on the best time to start work. But if this applies to you, even if you can't agree, try at least to accept that each person has a different metabolism (and that God created them both!).

Loneliness

This is a further cause of stress to many. It may be centred on absent friends, no kindred spirits or the longing for a personal or sexual relationship. It will strike people in various ways and at different times and is particularly hard to manage if friends, colleagues or other team members seem to be adapting well. The operative words here are 'seem to', because gentle discussion often reveals that others too are having or have had the same problems. Just knowing that others feel the same brings considerable relief. It is helpful also to pre-plan activities, ideally with others, during any festivals, birthdays or anniversaries of personal importance.

Inadequate skills

Many people get stressed by feeling they have inadequate skills for the job assigned, or have no clear role, job description or area of responsibility. Some are threatened by having no precedent to guide them, or conversely being expected to follow uncongenial or rigid procedures. Any of these factors may contribute to stress, which is best relieved by identifying the problem and talking it through with an appropriate person. As these situations are usually work-related, the best person may be your line manager, team leader, person visiting from your company or agency headquarters – or just a good friend. Often your employer needs to know and understand these issues, as expectations on you may be too high or you may have received insufficient induction or training.

Cross-cultural issues

There are a whole range of these which affect different people in different ways. Here are some common ones. They generally have to do with living and working in an environment where the following may apply:

- *Attitudes are different, especially professional ones* You may be working to different standards and a different timescale in a place with different ethics and values. Recognize these things and talk them through with someone.
- *Privacy and autonomy may be markedly reduced* You may be the subject of continual scrutiny wherever you go, and yet not be free to go where you choose. There are often small ways you can increase your range once you have recognized the problem.
- *Your role is very different* It may be unclear, unfamiliar and perhaps uncongenial. To go from being an established leader to finding yourself an insignificant newcomer can be hard, especially if the

skills you are bringing do not seem to be wanted or valued. Acknowledging this may help to take the sting out of it, but it may also be something you need to discuss within your work context.

- *Your sense of identity may be shaken* If you stay long enough to be at home in the new culture, you may feel you don't fully belong either to your new adopted country or to your country of origin. This can be very true for children and for adolescents. Bilingual children may in fact feel more at home in their host country than their 'home' one, which can be a real stress for their parents (see pages 264–6).
- *Violence, police surveillance and political uncertainty are common-place* To be living always in a state of maximum alertness is very hard on the nerves. Make sure you take all the rest and recreation you are entitled to.

Signs of stress

As stimulus turns to stress you will probably find your work output gradually lowers, but you may also feel a compulsion to keep on working in order to stay on top of things. Guidelines for healthy living, especially work–life balance and the need for rest and recreation are ignored 'just for once' or 'until I catch up'. Often, however, you don't catch up, so take this as a warning sign that you need to do something about it.

Healthy and unhealthy life patterns can be represented by the two triangles in Figure 17.2.

A person who slides into the second type of lifestyle continues to work harder and put in longer hours, with less overall effect. Warning signs include: losing concentration, having memory lapses, and becoming more irritable, less flexible and less humorous. This can lead on to feelings of anxiety or depression. All these things may be more easily detected by friends than by the person going through it.

These symptoms spell 'Take a break as soon as you can arrange it'. If you don't, it may take you time to recover, often by getting right away from the situation. Fortunately, you can avoid a decline into burn-out or breakdown by taking time away from work and the demands of others, and by absorbing yourself in some quite different activity. And you can take encouragement that many, if not most, people who have challenging jobs abroad, especially in cross-cultural situations, will usually have had many of these feelings and experiences.

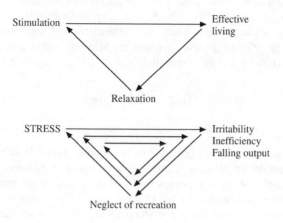

Figure 17.2 Stress triangles

Lifestyle review

Learn to recognize when your personal efficiency curve begins to decline. The aim of reviewing lifestyle is to help you generate options so that you can make appropriate choices and take charge of your life. It is designed to get you off that slippery slope and back towards peak performance. Look at the following:

- *Your lifestyle* Are your basic needs being met – do you get enough sleep, exercise and food? Have you any time for friends and fellowship – and don't forget to include some fun too. Is finance a problem?
- *Your relaxation* What do you do to 'switch off'? Chances are you have dropped your hobbies and interests – take them up again, quickly!
- *Your work satisfaction* If you are reasonably content with 70 per cent of your work time you can probably cope with the other 30 per cent. If the ratio is worse, try making some adjustments, and also consider in what other area of your life you can find some fulfilment.
- *Your relationships* Are they kept in good repair? You may need to give more time and attention to some of them.
- *Your expectations of yourself and of others* Perhaps you need to go for what is 'good enough', rather than perfect. This does not mean

accepting slipshod standards but simply doing things in a way that is adequate, i.e. good enough for the purpose of the task.

- *Areas of uncertainty* Check out any information that seems ambiguous or unclear. Make clear statements and requests yourself. Tell the relevant people that you are stressed – don't assume that they know – and tell them plainly.

Stress strategies

Just as one person's stress can be another person's stimulus, so patterns of relaxation differ greatly between different types of people. What one person finds relaxing may seem boring – or incomprehensible – to someone else. The answer is to discover your own coping strategies and find out what forms of relaxation will be both effective and possible in your overseas location.

Here are some further practical suggestions:

- Avoid self-medication with 'leisure' drugs, tranquillizers, nicotine, too much alcohol or casual sex.
- Do get enough sleep and change of occupation.
- Prioritize exercise, in a way you enjoy and of a type that works in your situation. For many people exercise is the best stress-buster of all, and once you put this in red ink in your diary your well-being really improves.
- Do talk your situation and feelings through with someone.
- Do develop an absorbing hobby or interest outside your work.
- Don't carry on working if you get sick – better to rest up before you really get laid up.

And finally . . .

Someone has worked out that we ourselves can help to solve 50 per cent of our problems, another 30 per cent can be eased if we have the courage to ask for help, and only 20 per cent will remain despite what we do. Although we can't alter this 20 per cent, we can change our own attitude by a combination of acceptance, prayer or spiritual discipline. When our attitude alters, our stress diminishes – especially if we take appropriate steps to deal with the 80 per cent we can do something about.

Most important of all is to keep a sense of proportion, to nurture a sense of humour, to avoid fatigue and to remember to switch off regularly by switching on to some form of recreation and relaxation. Even taking time to slow down, to do some deep breathing and to stretch, then relax every muscle group from toe to head, is beneficial, as are more formal relaxation tapes, at least for some people.

Anyone who has never been stressed has probably never lived life to the full. Only by living to our particular limits do we know what these limits are, but wise and healthy people, having discovered these, do not often, or for long, push themselves or allow others to push them beyond their threshold.

Learning to say no (in an appropriate way) to whatever requests push you over your personal stress level is a skill that is really worth learning.

Finally, with the subject of stress so topical in our culture, we need to make sure we do not get stressed about being stressed, or worry that we are about to have a nervous breakdown.

Some gentle humour, self-detachment and remembering friends who have been able to tough it out when circumstances demanded it, can help us to keep things in perspective and tide us over difficult times.

If despite all this you really feel that stress is getting the better of you, do let someone know. It is much quicker to put things right at this stage than to let them drag on. Consider having a personal debrief on returning home (see pages 262–4), and remember that it is no disgrace to be 'honourably wounded' when you are serving abroad, or at home, and that wounds do heal.

18
Tiredness and fatigue

Why am I so tired?

Feeling tired is extremely common in those living overseas (and at home), and there are many causes. Here are some common ones:

Lifestyle and work factors

Overwork, worry and failing to take regular time off are probably the commonest causes. You may have trouble getting on with a colleague, have frustration at work and too much, or too little, to do. You may be bored or homesick, losing sleep or beginning to suffer from stress without realizing it. You may be coping with a bereavement or finding it hard to make an important decision. If the reason is not obvious to you, ask your friends, who may have better insight than you. In our experience, these factors or a combination of them are much the commonest causes of persistent tiredness in those living or working internationally.

For those working at national or regional headquarters, making many trips away from home, and especially 'back-to-back' trips, leads to tiredness and demotivation after a while, unless good breaks are taken.

Many enthusiasts take on a job which they enjoy and then work long hours, without taking periods for holidays or rest and recreation. Very often they eventually lose energy or motivation, especially when the 'adrenalin tap' is turned off and the excitement or challenge of the job starts to decrease. One remedy: take all your annual leave, and time off in lieu (TOIL) from the start.

Physical conditions

A number of these can make you tired:

- *Anaemia* is a common one, for women often caused by heavy periods, and for all not eating enough iron-rich food or a balanced diet, having frequent attacks of malaria, or suffering from untreated hookworm or other bowel conditions.

- *Bilharzia* (see pages 277–81) can make you feel tired, and this is usually the commonest symptom in those infected.
- *Brucellosis*, especially if chronic or recurrent, usually caused from drinking unpasteurized milk (see pages 281–2), can make you feel tired.
- *Dengue fever*: the tiredness from this can persist for weeks or months and the original illness may not always show the typical symptoms described on page 286.
- *Depression* often first shows itself through tiredness and a lack of normal energy and enthusiasm.
- *Diabetes* may first present with a feeling that you lack your usual amount of energy.
- *Lyme disease* is a known cause of tiredness if untreated or undiagnosed (see pages 318–19).
- *Recurrent malaria*, either falciparum or 'benign', can cause this, sometimes for months or years after returning from a malarious area.
- *Q fever*, an uncommon but worldwide disease (see page 296) can cause persistent tiredness.
- *Thyroid problems*, especially producing too little thyroxin (hypothyroidism), are a common cause of tiredness, more common in women.
- *Sleeping sickness* (African trypanosomiasis) is a rare cause in travellers.
- *Undiagnosed heart, liver or kidney problems, HIV and certain forms of cancer* can occasionally produce tiredness as their first symptom, especially in older travellers.
- *Viruses* are a frequent cause. Two common ones are hepatitis, before, during and sometimes months after the illness, and glandular fever and related viruses (e.g. cytomegalovirus), common in younger travellers and often very persistent. Many other viruses, often undetected or unrecognized at the time, can lead to periods of tiredness and fatigue.

What action should I take?

If you feel abnormally tired or it seems a long time since you had your normal amount of energy, take the trouble of having an unhurried talk and examination from a doctor who understands your lifestyle. Various blood tests can be arranged that usually exclude serious or treatable causes, but many doctors in developing countries may be unfamiliar with the most important tests to carry out, or may not have the facilities. Glandular fever (infectious mononucleosis) is often little known about in developing countries. Also many other viruses are not revealed by normal blood tests.

Chronic fatigue syndrome (CFS)

Background

In our experience at InterHealth, CFS frequently occurs in travellers, or past symptoms recur during times of stress when overseas. For this reason this section looks at CFS in some detail. At any one time in the UK at least 1 per cent of the population are suffering from CFS, and similar levels are now being reported from other countries.

You should not diagnose chronic fatigue syndrome in yourself, but leave this to a sympathetic and experienced doctor who has made sure there are not other, commoner causes for the way you are feeling. Persistent undiagnosed tiredness, with possible CFS as a cause, usually means you should come home for further investigation and treatment. This is especially true if you have had this in the past, it has recurred overseas and a reasonable period of rest and time off work has not helped to restore your energy.

There is a strict case definition for CFS which has been agreed by health professionals, and only one-third of people with symptoms of continuing tiredness fit into the strict criteria for CFS. That is still quite a high proportion, but it does mean there are other causes you need to discount first.

What is CFS?

CFS is a puzzling and frequent illness that has become well known over the past decade. It goes under a variety of names, including myalgic encephalo-myelitis (ME), yuppie flu and the post-viral syndrome. Quite apart from its debilitating symptoms, those who have it often face further problems with doctors, friends and colleagues who may be ignorant or unsympathetic. People with CFS therefore often have to run their own 'public relations bureau'. This can be especially difficult among team members, family and overworked colleagues.

The symptoms of CFS

The chief symptom is profound tiredness and a sense of weakness or aching in the muscles, especially of the arms and legs. It has been described as 'flu, minus the fever, which doesn't go away'. These features usually date from a specific time, most often from a virus infection, glandular fever or flu-like illness whose symptoms persisted.

Mental exhaustion, poor concentration, memory loss, headache, dislike of bright lights and changes in sleep pattern are also common features. Vigorous or unaccustomed physical or mental exercise causes a relapse of symptoms. Because recovery is slow and cannot be hurried, those with CFS often develop symptoms of despondency or, less commonly, an actual depressive illness.

183

Normally CFS is only diagnosed in those with typical symptoms that have persisted for at least six months. It is different from a simple state of chronic tiredness or exhaustion (Tired All The Time or TATT syndrome).

The causes of CFS

CFS is commonly thought to be caused by a virus. The Epstein-Barr virus responsible for glandular fever is probably only one of several viruses normally rapidly fought off by the body's immune system, but which on occasions can persist, leading to CFS.

Although the cause of CFS is only partially understood, recent research has shown differences in gene expression in the immune cells between people who have CFS and those who do not. (This gives medical evidence that CFS is distinct from depression, even though the symptoms of CFS may on occasions lead on to it.)[1]

However, many CFS patients are found to have been living stressful or very energetic lifestyles at the time their illness started. Often this is through the outward circumstances of a difficult overseas posting or because past problems are reactivated by the stress of a tough assignment. Evidence suggests that the presence of stress, or persistent overwork, reduces the body's ability to fight off infection.

The treatment of CFS

See a doctor

Identify and then regularly consult a sympathetic doctor. If you think your symptoms fit into this category you should see a medic who has time, experience and sympathy with the condition, and access to laboratory tests. This may mean waiting till you return home or cutting short your assignment.

Because, as mentioned above, a number of illnesses, including some tropical diseases, can mimic CFS, it is important both medically and for your peace of mind that these are discussed and excluded, if necessary by further tests or a specialist referral.

Accept your diagnosis

Once CFS has been suggested as your likely diagnosis, accept this without any sense of guilt.

You will, however, need to get used to explaining your illness and symptoms to others. The use of a simple handout or article can be helpful. The term CFS, or post-viral syndrome, is preferable to ME, which may cause subconscious confusion with multiple sclerosis (MS), a totally different and usually more serious condition.

---

[1] *Journal of Clinical Pathology* (2005) 58: 826–32.

Set up an appropriate lifestyle

The suggestions below can sometimes be applied when overseas, providing you have consulted a doctor and carefully thought through the best location where you can maximize your recovery. These guidelines can also be modified to help you recover from any cause of severe tiredness, providing any serious cause has been excluded.

Pacing The key to recovery is learning to balance input (rest, encouragement, support) with output (physical and mental exercise and other activity). This in turn depends on learning to identify and carry out the maximum activity that does not worsen your symptoms over the following days. The amount of activity takes careful working out, and to start with it may be surprisingly little. It will also vary from day to day. This technique is known as pacing.

Your output will need to include the core priorities of life, plus any other activities you are able to add in without causing excessive tiredness or delaying your progress. Over-activity, often brought on by frustration, false guilt, an obligation carelessly agreed to or the expectations of others, can set you back days. Equally, under-activity can lead to further weakening and atrophy of the muscles.

Sleep In the early days of CFS, you may feel a need or even a hunger for sleep. At this stage extra sleep or rest is an important part of treatment. It can include a long lie-in, an afternoon nap or an early night. If night-time sleep is a problem, it is worth first reducing the amount of daytime sleep you take and/or gently increasing your amount of daily exercise. If that fails, consider short-term medication taken occasionally to help you sleep at night. As recovery starts, you should start rationing the amount of sleep you have, particularly during the day, or at least combining it with a gradually increasing exercise programme.

Work Work and responsibility need to be removed or reduced to a level at which gradual recovery is possible. This means that reduced hours, or time away from work, are usually necessary to begin with. You will also need to avoid situations where you need to pre-plan activities or make diary entries that may be hard to cancel. It is hard to predict how you will feel one day, week or month in advance, and it is helpful not to take on commitments that you are unable to cancel. As recovery takes place you can practise a lifestyle into which you can slot a gradual return to work. Of course, this will need to be negotiated carefully with your employer, and some will be more sympathetic than others. In the voluntary sector there is often more flexibility and understanding than if working with a company. Initially, any return to work should be for a few hours, once or twice a week, with a gradual increase as energy levels allow. *Do not rush this stage.* You will need your doctor's advice and, if necessary, explanation to help your employer understand your needs and provide flexibility in your working arrangements.

Exercise It is important, just as soon as you have the energy, to take some exercise to keep your muscles in trim. Walking is obviously sensible, to which swimming and a gentle exposure to a favourite sport can be added. Absorption in a sedentary hobby, reading or studying will provide useful mental exercise.

There is clear evidence that Graduated Exercise Therapy (GET), a fancy name for an exercise programme you can work out with your doctor or a sensible friend, can speed up your rate of recovery.

A *golden rule*: try to invest a proportion of energy 'in the bank' every day, rather than going till you drop.

Cognitive Behavioural Therapy (CBT)

This has also been shown to speed up recovery in many people. In some countries it is possible to be referred to specialists for this, but this is rarely possible in a developing country. CBT aims to help people with CFS understand their condition, learn to take control of their lives and manage their activities and lifestyle, thus lessening dependence on others. Of course, most of us would try to do this anyway, but structured CBT makes the process more successful. A useful website which helps you to do this is <http://www.kcl.ac.uk/cfs>.

Medication

Sometimes the symptoms of CFS and the change from a normally active lifestyle can cause clinical depression, in which case antidepressants can hasten recovery. Some research suggests that the drug sertraline, starting with 50 mg or less daily, then increasing the dose under medical supervision, helps restore energy in some people. Other drugs in this group, the SSRIs, are sometimes used. Short-term, mild sleeping pills may help to break any serious sleep disturbance.

Counselling and prayer

As already mentioned, counselling can sometimes hasten recovery, especially if you are aware of unresolved conflicts or difficult past experiences feeding into your fatigue. It is usually better to start it only when your energy levels have begun to recover. A counsellor needs to be chosen with care, and should be someone who understands CFS and who is in full sympathy with any religious outlook you may have. Some people find that various forms of prayer ministry are helpful.

Avoid too high expectations of 'magic remedies'

Some individuals claim that special diets or other inputs will help to bring recovery. Try these extras if you wish, but do not be disappointed if they are not as successful as you hoped. Some claim a daily cold bath improves their energy levels.

An unexpected bonus

Many have found that being forcibly set aside with CFS has deepened their spiritual life or helped them gain other valuable insights. Many active people need red traffic lights. It may, however, be only after your recovery that you begin to see the benefits of your illness.

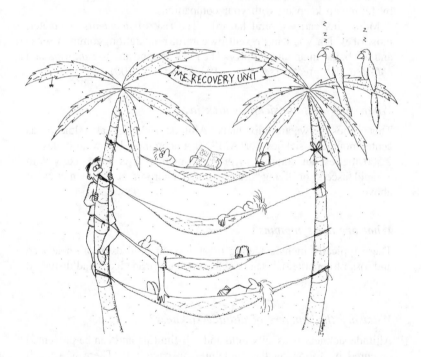

19

Height, heat, cold, sun

Altitude

Many travellers can't resist the temptation of
climbing a near (or distant) mountain peak or fitting in a high-altitude
trek while the opportunity is there. Although the rewards are great, so
are the potential risks, especially if your time available is short, your
preparation and equipment limited or you don't want to appear a wimp
by failing to keep up with your companions.

Mountains carry several hazards. The risk of *accidents* is greater,
most of which you can prevent by careful preparation, common sense
and not being in an undue hurry. The risks of exposure to *sun*, *wind* and
cold are also greater (see pages 193–5 and 197–200).

When does altitude sickness kick in?

This varies between individuals. Altitude sickness, also known as
acute mountain sickness or AMS, is uncommon below altitudes of
2,500 metres but common over 3,500 metres. It is more likely with
a rapid ascent or flying straight into an airport at 2,500 metres or
above.

What are the symptoms?

These typically include feeling breathless on mild exertion, headache
and loss of appetite, nausea or sickness, light-headedness and disturbed
sleep.

What are the dangers of altitude sickness?

Altitude sickness is usually mild and self-limiting and can be prevented
or cured by following the guidelines on page 190. There is a small
danger, especially if you rush your ascent, that it can turn into the
serious and potentially life-threatening complications HAPE or HACE.

HAPE

HAPE is High-Altitude Pulmonary Oedema, which means the lungs
gradually fill up with fluid. You are short of breath at rest, develop
bubbly or crackly breathing, usually with a cough. Your lips may look

blue, your pulse rate and breathing will be fast; you may develop a mild fever. HAPE often develops two to three days after being at altitude.

Who is at risk from high altitude?

The risk of developing altitude sickness is mainly due to individual susceptibility. It is hard to predict, and can affect those of any age and any degree of fitness.

For varied reasons the following need to be cautious at high altitude and get specialist advice:

- *Those with heart problems*: less oxygen and more exertion mean greater strain on the heart. Special precautions are needed for those with angina and hypertension, both of which must be well controlled.
- *Those with lung problems*: there is no increased risk of altitude sickness for those with asthma but altitude can cause other problems. Dry air may trigger wheezing, and developing a respiratory infection may add to the risk of breathing problems. More caution is therefore needed. Those with Chronic Obstructive Pulmonary Disease (COPD) are at higher risk.
- *The older traveller*, especially those over age 70, but this depends a great deal on the individual's state of health and physical fitness.
- *The overweight*: there is a slightly increased risk of altitude sickness, and in addition keeping up with others can be much more tiring.
- *Those taking the antimalarial mefloquine (Lariam)*: side-effects can sometimes mimic symptoms of altitude sickness and it is best not to take this at high altitude, e.g. climbing in the Andes after spending time in the Amazon jungle.
- *Children*: see pages 192–3.
- *Pregnancy*: see page 193. There is usually no significant risk to the foetus up to 3,000 metres.

HACE

HACE is High-Altitude Cerebral Oedema, where, put at its simplest, your brain becomes boggy. You develop a pounding headache which is hard to relieve, you may feel sick or vomit, you develop a staggering gait, may become drowsy or confused and can slip into coma. It can develop very rapidly.

How do you treat altitude sickness?

With simple altitude sickness this is what you should do:

- Move to a lower level or stay at the same height, monitor symptoms carefully and move lower if they do not improve.
- If there is no improvement after 24 hours you must descend.
- Take a painkiller such as paracetamol 500 mg, ibuprofen 400 mg or aspirin 600 mg, every four to six hours as needed.
- If you feel sick take domperidone 10 mg or another anti-emetic.
- Have plenty to drink; sweet drinks are best.
- Rest or take things very easy until symptoms improve.
- For HAPE and HACE get lower without delay. Use oxygen if available. If hyperbaric chambers are available, use them too. Rapid, immediate descent is the key.

How do you prevent altitude sickness?

- Acclimatize before going to 3,000 metres or above. Sleep at least one night at an intermediate altitude, and do climbs or uphill walks during the day, then come down to sleep.
- Above 3,000 metres spend each night not more than 300–600 metres higher than the night before.
- For every 1,000 metres climbed, try to take a rest day.
- Greatly increase your fluid intake, as dehydration quickly occurs and can worsen symptoms.
- Consider taking acetazolamide (Diamox), see below.
- Leaders of high-altitude expeditions should plan their treks to follow the above guidelines.

'Climb high but sleep low' should be your motto.

Other dangers of high altitude

- *Snow blindness*, especially if ice and snow are present: wear goggles to protect your eyes if walking in snow, dark glasses if not.
- *Sunburn*: keep covered, otherwise frequently apply high factor sun cream, 25 or above, to your skin, lipsalve to your lips.
- *Hypothermia*: this occurs rapidly at high altitude. Keep dry; wear several layers of loose-fitting clothes, including a vest to absorb perspiration with an open neck for ventilation, and an outer waterproof. Wear a hat and gloves or mittens. Recognize the signs of hypothermia – intense cold, shivering, listlessness, anger, and

confusion. If this occurs get dry, get out of the wind and warm up, e.g. with a companion's body heat and warm sugary drinks.

- *Respiratory infections*: if colds turn to coughs or bronchitis use an antibiotic, e.g. Augmentin 625 mg three times daily or, if allergic to penicillin, erythromycin 500 mg four times daily, each for a week.
- *Dehydration*: drink enough to keep up a good urinary output and to keep your urine pale.
- *Low blood sugar*: keep up your energy by regular snacking on something sweet. Kendal Mint Cake or chocolate are favourites.

Flying into high-altitude airports

You may have a headache and nausea when you arrive, or this may develop within two to three hours. You will feel breathless climbing stairs. You may have trouble sleeping. Your best bet is to travel lower as soon as you can, otherwise to rest, keep up your fluids and take painkillers and if necessary anti-sickness pills. Usually symptoms improve over one to three days. If they don't, get advice from your team leader or a health professional. Table 19.1 shows the height of some high-altitude airports.

Table 19.1 Heights in metres above sea level of some high-altitude cities and airports

Everest base camp	5,500
Lhasa, Tibet	3,700
La Paz, Bolivia	3,700
	(airport 4,000)
Cusco, Peru	3,300
Toluca, Mexico	2,900
Quito, Ecuador	2,800
Cochabamba, Bolivia	2,600
Addis Ababa	2,600
Bogota, Colombia	2,600

Is medication helpful?

Acetazolamide (Diamox) is the most useful. This usually helps to prevent or reduce the symptoms of altitude sickness. Take it either:

- for *treatment*: if you develop altitude sickness take 250 mg twice daily until you return to lower altitude;

- for *prevention*: take the same dose, starting 24 hours before flying into a high-altitude airport or climbing above 3,000 metres, especially if your climbing schedule forces you to climb at a rate higher than 500 metres per day. Continue until your symptoms subside or you return to a lower elevation.

Trial Diamox at home before leaving to make sure the side-effects are not troublesome, e.g. excessive urination and tingling sensations. Avoid it if you are allergic to sulfa drugs. Other medicines, e.g. dexamethasone or nifedipine, can be used but only under medical supervision, and for specific reasons.

Children at high altitude

There is not sufficient research into the dangers of children at altitude to draw up accurate guidelines. Current consensus suggests the following:

- Risks for healthy children are similar to adults. Some experts suggest these quite cautious rules: those under three months should not be *taken* above 2,500 metres; those from three months to two years of age should not *sleep* over 2,000 metres; three- to seven-year-olds should not *sleep* above 3,000 metres. It's OK to go higher during the day but best to return to lower altitude overnight.

- In children under about age three, symptoms are very non-specific and may include increased fussiness, poor appetite, trouble sleeping. Assume these are symptoms of AMS unless there is a good alternative explanation.
- There is an uncommon illness in children called symptomatic high-altitude pulmonary hypertension (SHAPH), which affects some children from low altitude living above 3,000 metres for more than a month. This can sometimes be triggered by viral infections. Symptoms include poor feeding, lethargy and sweating. Oxygen is needed and urgent descent. The slight risk of this should not prevent healthy children from living at high altitude but parents need to be aware of this condition.
- Children living long term at high altitude sometimes grow less fast, so monitor height and weight regularly.

Pregnancy and high altitude

There is little change in the amount of oxygen reaching the child until at least 3,000 metres so dangers are minimal for mother and child up to that altitude Those wishing to live or travel above that altitude, except for brief airport stop-overs, should discuss this with their doctor.

Further advice

If you are planning a high-altitude trek or climb, plan thoroughly and go extremely well prepared. If you have any pre-existing medical conditions get advice from a doctor before climbing.

Useful websites

- The British Mountaineering Council: <http://www.thebmc.co.uk>
- The High Altitude Medicine Guide: <http://www.high-altitude-medicine.com>
- The International Society of Mountain Medicine: <http://www.ismmed.org>
- The NHS public access website on travel health: <http://www.fitfortravel.nhs.uk>

More information

See *The High-Altitude Medicine Handbook*, A. J. Pollard and D. R. Murdoch, Radcliffe Medical Press, third edition 2003.

Cold

Cold injury (hypothermia) usually occurs either when there is a strong wind (wind-chill factor) or when you are wet through, or both. It can occur rapidly if you are injured or immobilized at high altitude. At lower altitude minor degrees are common, for example if you expose your skin to the sun when climbing in the hills during the day, and then become chilled overnight. Blood becomes diverted to the inflamed skin, so further reducing your body temperature.

Hypothermia occurs when the core body temperature falls below 35°C. Thin young men, children and the elderly are at greatest risk.

What are the symptoms of hypothermia?

Symptoms and signs that your body is seriously cooling often resemble drunkenness and include the following:

- A feeling of intense cold, uncontrollable shivering, tiredness and listlessness.
- Increasing effort when walking to keep going and to avoid stumbling.
- Slowness in responding to the comments and questions of companions, angry or confused responses, or denial that anything is amiss. Be alert for any companion who has stopped, rested or apparently fallen asleep.
- In the case of frostbite there is usually intense pain at the site, especially as the part warms up, and there is hard whitening of the skin. Commonly affected parts of the body are cheeks, chin, ears, nose, hands and feet. Check any area that has registered pain as soon as possible.
- In the case of frostnip, which can quickly lead to frostbite, there is numbness and whitening of the skin (most commonly on the cheeks) that may pass almost unnoticed.

How do you prevent hypothermia?

Follow these guidelines:

- *Keep dry* by wearing a waterproof outer layer, which will also protect against the wind. Prevent excessive sweating on the inner layer, e.g. by having an opening at the neck or sleeves except in extreme conditions.
- *Wear several layers of loose-fitting clothing* so that air between the layers gives extra insulation. The inner layer, ideally made of cotton, acts as a wick to help remove moisture; the middle layer(s) can be made of wool, fleece or insulate; and the outer layer, e.g. nylon, acts as a shell and waterproof.
- *Cover your head* using a hat with ear-flaps; wear a scarf and use warm mittens rather than gloves.
- *Set up a 'buddy system'* where each of a pair watches out for warning signs in the other.

How do you treat hypothermia?

- Treatment of hypothermia consists of gradual but sustained rewarming without delay.
- Remove your companion from the wind or wet, take off any wet clothes.
- Give warm sugary drinks.
- Share your body heat in a sleeping bag or use carefully wrapped heat-packs, taking care not to burn the skin.
- Do not give alcohol.
- Supervise for at least 24 hours. If symptoms are severe (e.g. incoherent, with clouded consciousness), arrange medical evacuation without delay and with extreme care.
- Treat *frostnip* by rewarming, e.g. with warm breath in a gloved hand, but do not rub the skin.
- Treat *frostbite* by protecting the affected part, rapid rewarming in water at, but not above, 40°C and evacuation as soon as possible. Avoid using dry external heat sources such as stoves. Strong painkillers will be needed, especially as rewarming starts. Some alcohol (which dilates the blood vessels) may help, providing any associated hypothermia has been treated. Frostbite is dangerous and can lead on to gangrene. A medical expert must always assess it.

Finally, remember to wear goggles at height to protect against intense ultraviolet radiation and snow-blindness, and to have plenty to drink to avoid dehydration.

If you are going on a high-altitude or extreme weather expedition, get detailed advice on this before leaving.

Heat

Your body normally takes 14 to 21 days to get used to a hotter climate. During that time the sweat glands become more efficient and water and salt regulation improves. These first two to three weeks are the toughest, especially if you are unfit or overweight. It can also be more difficult for older people, whose bodies adapt more slowly.

What are the risks?

There are two forms of illness caused by heat. *Heat exhaustion* is common and easily treated; *heatstroke* (also known as sunstroke) is rarer but much more serious (see Table 19.2).

Table 19.2 Types of heat injury

	Heat exhaustion	Heatstroke
Symptoms	Weak, exhausted, poor concentration, thirst, headache, possibly muscle cramps	Confused, drowsy, vomiting, sometimes convulsions, may lead to coma
Skin	Flushed, moist	Hot, usually dry
Temperature	Normal or slightly raised	High, usually above 39°C
Pulse	Normal or slightly raised	Fast, e.g. 100 per minute or above

Hot climates can also cause or worsen constipation and lead to the formation of kidney and bladder stones. Both these problems can be minimized if you regularly *keep up your fluids*.

Risks associated with heat are obviously increased during strenuous physical activity in the sun, or in a hot and humid atmosphere.

How do you prevent heatstroke?

The normal body temperature is 37°C (98.6°F) or slightly below. The normal fluid intake of an adult in a temperate climate is 2–2.5 litres per day. This can increase to at least 12 litres per day in a very hot climate.

Make sure you drink plenty of clean water or soft drinks. Tea, coffee and alcohol cause you to lose more fluid in urine than you actually drink, so although they may keep up your spirits they won't help to keep up your fluids.

Prevention is mostly common sense:

- Don't 'rush the tropics', i.e. take life at an easy pace.
- Wear cool, cotton, loose-fitting clothing, plus a hat in the sun.
- Keep up your fluid intake, so that your urine remains pale. This may mean drinking three, four or five times more than usual.
- Add salt to your food (but don't take salt tablets).
- Consider using Oral Rehydration Solution (ORS), see pages 104–5, when it's very hot or humid.
- Be cautious with exercise and don't spend long hours walking in the heat until confidently acclimatized.
- Stay in the shade whenever there is an option.
- Take extra care with children, including having adequate fluids. Keep them out of the sun and devise methods of shading in tropical traffic jams.

How do you treat heatstroke?

Ensure that you (or the victim):

- are placed in the shade, wearing the minimum of clothes;
- are gently fanned or sponged with a cool wet cloth;
- drink as much as possible without this causing nausea (soft drinks are ideal, plus one or two glasses of ORS);
- have the body temperature monitored;
- receive emergency medical care if not improving or if consciousness starts to cloud.

Remember, *heatstroke is a medical emergency.*

Finally, also remember that certain infectious diseases, especially malaria, can mimic or worsen heatstroke.

Sunburn

'Where's your suntan?' is about the most annoying thing your friends ask you when you get home, unless of course you have one. Usually if you go abroad to live or work, as opposed to having a holiday, you'll soon discover that the tropical sun is largely something to be avoided.

What effect does the sun have on my skin?

For most of us, some sun adds to our sense of well-being. It also has some beneficial effects. The sun makes vitamin D in our skin, which helps us to absorb calcium, and there is evidence that several forms of non-skin cancer are slightly less common if we have some exposure to the sun. The problem is that too much sun is dangerous, and because many of us enjoy the sun we are tempted to get too much of it.

Excessive sun is also harmful to our eyes, affecting both the outer layer – the cornea – and the lens, which is the reason cataracts are more common in people who spend a lot of time in the sun or live at high altitude.

There are two types of ultra-violet (UV) rays that reach us and can damage our skin. We don't actually feel either of them – it is not the UV rays that make the sun feel warm.

- UVA rays make up about 95 per cent of the rays that reach us but account for only a small part of the damage – they have some effect on the ageing of the skin.
- UVB rays account for only 5 per cent, but these are mainly responsible for sunburn, skin ageing and skin cancer.

How can I prevent getting sunburnt?

Research shows that four out of five cases of skin cancer can be prevented by what the Australians call 'sensible behaviour' or being 'sun-smart'. So follow the Aussie slogan: 'Slip on a shirt. Slap on a hat. Slop on some sun cream.'

- Avoid the sun between 11 a.m. and 3 p.m. The most severe burning usually takes place during these hours, and the higher above sea level you live, the greater will be the burning power (it increases by about 8 per cent for every 1,000 metres).
- Remember, the following all increase the burning power of the sun: water (by 25 per cent or more – rippling water reflects more than still), sand (15 per cent) and snow (up to 80 per cent).
- Take care when swimming or snorkelling, because the sun strongly penetrates water.
- If you have to walk or work in the sun, wear a wide-brimmed hat to protect your head, neck and face, and sunglasses, ideally of 'wrap-around' design or with side lenses; use an umbrella or headscarf and keep your arms, shoulders and thighs covered.
- Expose yourself very gradually: start with 15–20 minutes a day and only increase it by a few minutes each day. If the skin starts to look red or feels sore, go into the shade at once and avoid the sun the next day. *Make sure that you never burn.*
- Use a sunblock with sun protection factor (SPF) of 15 or above, 25 or above if you are fair or freckled and also for all children. Make sure it protects against both UVA and UVB. When using sun cream it's very easy to become an art exhibit in red and white by missing some areas out altogether, so make sure you cover all exposed parts.

Remember to give extra protection to those parts of you which are normally covered up, and to apply sunscreen to the backs of knees, top of feet, shoulders and tips of ears.

- Remember the lips – wear a lipsalve sun block.
- Wear sunglasses, ideally of 'wrap-around' design or with side lenses. Check that they protect against ultraviolet light, and if bought in the UK have a British Standard label or 'kitemark' – or the equivalent for the country where you buy them.
- Apply sunscreen 15–30 minutes before going out in the sun and reapply every one to two hours and again after swimming or heavy exercise. Follow the manufacturer's instructions.

- Beware of a cool seductive breeze as this can make you think you won't get burnt. Also remember you can get seriously burnt on a cloudy day.
- Think ahead to situations when you might get caught in the sun unawares, such as on field visits, travelling on a motorbike or in the back of a truck (not a sensible thing to do) or going on a boat trip.
- Children need rigorous protection, especially at the beach, swimming pool or garden. It's hard work getting the cooperation of the under-12s or under-18s, but well worth doing. Never place a baby in direct tropical sunlight.
- Some medicines increase the tendency of the skin to burn, especially tetracyclines, doxycycline, the heart drug amiodarone, oral hypo-glycaemic drugs for diabetes, and certain diuretics. So do some cosmetics.
- DEET-based insect repellents reduce the effectiveness of sunscreen – apply sunscreen before DEET (see pages 20–1).

How do you treat sunburn?

- If you're unlucky, or unwise, and get sunburnt, treat this with calamine or lacto calamine, rest and aspirin (paracetamol in those under age 16).
- Keep any blistered areas clean and see a doctor if the area burnt covers a large area or it starts to become infected. Learn from your mistake!
- If you suffer from cold sores on your face, the tropical sun can make them worse. Use plenty of sun lotion, including lipsalve. If they start to develop, apply acyclovir cream (Zovirax) at the first sign of trouble.

Checking your skin

Check your skin regularly if you have frequently been sunburnt in the past, especially as a child, or if you are fair-skinned or freckled, or if you have any moles. If you can't see them all, especially on your back, get a friend or partner to check them for you.

Show any of the following to your doctor:

- Any mole which enlarges, darkens, develops a less regular outline or appearance and any that itch, ooze, bleed or become painful. It just could be a malignant melanoma, usually curable if caught and removed early, but dangerous if left.
- Any patch of skin which becomes rough, itchy or bleeds, especially in areas which have had prolonged exposure. It could be a solar keratosis, which occasionally become malignant.
- Any skin nodule which arises, mainly on the face, with a pearly edge. It could be a rodent ulcer or basal cell carcinoma (BCC), and is best removed early.

Summary

It's best to avoid the sun by covering up or staying in the shade. If you must go out in the tropical sun take every care to avoid getting sunburnt, especially by using sun cream and wearing a hat. Take extra care with children.

20

Snakes and other creatures that bite and sting

Snakes

Serious snake bite is rare among travellers, though often common among the local population. Comparatively few snakes are poisonous, and more often than not they only manage to inject a small amount of venom. Even if venom has been injected, serious symptoms usually take hours, not minutes, to develop. A poisonous bite will usually show two fang marks, quite separate from a row of small tooth marks, which are not dangerous (see Figure 20.1).

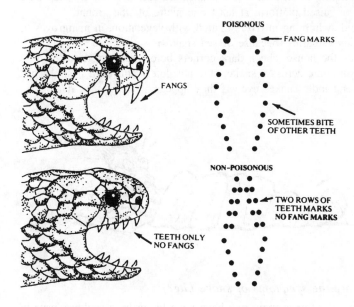

POISONOUS

FANG MARKS

FANGS

SOMETIMES BITE OF OTHER TEETH

NON-POISONOUS

TWO ROWS OF TEETH MARKS NO FANG MARKS

TEETH ONLY NO FANGS

Figure 20.1 Poisonous and non-poisonous snakes: telling the difference

How do you avoid being bitten?
By following a few rules snake bite can almost always be prevented.

Snakes attack when provoked, virtually never attacking if you keep still. One exception is sleeping on the ground in rural areas (especially in South Asia), when snakes may seek out your body warmth. If living in areas where poisonous snakes are known to live, follow these precautions:

- When walking outside, especially in long grass or thick undergrowth, carry a stick to beat the path in front of you. Wear boots or strong shoes and trousers. At night, carry a torch as well.
- Keep the grass and other vegetation short around your house.
- Never put your hand into holes, on to or under rock ledges or anywhere you cannot easily see if a snake is lurking.
- Wear gloves to collect firewood or logs if snakes are known to be common.
- Avoid climbing trees or rocks covered in dense foliage.
- Take care walking under overhanging trees or bushes.
- If camping in an area where snakes are common, try to sleep on a bed or raised platform at least one metre off the ground.
- Avoid swimming in rivers matted with vegetation, in mangroves or muddy estuaries (because of sea snakes).
- Inside the house, check dark corners before reaching into them.
- If you come across a snake, stay absolutely still until it slinks off.
- Never handle snakes even if they appear harmless – or dead.

What are the symptoms of snake bite?

Anyone who thinks they may have been bitten by a snake is usually very anxious, and signs of anxiety mimic the symptoms of certain forms of snake bite.

Poisonous snakes produce either neurotoxins (e.g. sea snakes, cobras, mambas) which cause symptoms of paralysis, or toxins which affect blood coagulation and cause bleeding (e.g. vipers).

Signs that suggest venom has actually entered the body include the following. From neurotoxins: drooping of the eyelids, difficulty swallowing or breathing, and paralysis. From toxins affecting blood coagulation: bleeding from the nose or areas distant from the bite, blood-stained vomit, dark urine, irregular pulse or falling blood pressure. Swelling spreading up the limb from the bite also indicates envenoming, and so usually does marked drowsiness or losing consciousness.

How do you treat snake bite?

Follow these guidelines:

- Give maximum reassurance and keep the affected body part *as still as possible*, preferably below heart level.
- Wipe any remaining venom off the skin with a cloth and then dispose of it.
- In the case of a bitten limb, apply a firm, broad bandage along its entire length, splinting the limb if possible, to limit the spread of toxin. This should not be too tight in the case of snakes that cause local swelling, such as vipers and rattlesnakes. A good technique is to apply a pad, ideally of bandaged rubber, over the bite and under the firm bandaging.
- The limb should not be moved or exercised.
- The use of tourniquets is not recommended, as they are likely to do as much harm as good. Also avoid incision, suction and compression, electric shock therapy or a traditional remedy known as 'The Black Stone'.
- Go to the nearest health facility known to have anti-snake venom, taking the dead snake if possible but not touching it with unprotected hands.
- The anti-venom should be given intravenously by an experienced health worker, and only if there are one or more signs of definite envenoming as listed under symptoms above, and if the anti-venom is strongly believed or known to be protective against the snake involved.
- Adrenalin must be on hand in case of an allergic reaction.
- Pain should be treated with paracetamol and not aspirin, which may worsen any bleeding tendency.
- Patients must remain under medical care until free of symptoms.

It is only worth taking anti-venom with you if you are going on an expedition or living in a remote area where poisonous snakes are known to be common. Even then you must be sure it will be effective against the snakes you are likely to come across, meaning it is usually best to obtain it in-country or from a regional manufacturer. Unfortunately there is a severe shortage of effective anti-snake venom for most of Africa, but recently an anti-venom has been developed which protects against the three most important poisonous snakes in sub-Saharan Africa. Snake anti-venom is hard to obtain and you will need to make special enquiries.

Aquatic animals

There are a number of poisonous aquatic animals in recreational waters enjoyed by swimmers, snorkellers and divers. Many areas are relatively safe, but a number of coastal waters – for example, off the coasts of northern Australia and the Philippines – have a variety of poisonous creatures.

How do you avoid being stung, punctured or attacked?

The key rule is to obtain local information about:

- the species that are present;
- the time of year, time of day and the weather conditions when they are most active;
- measures you can take to minimize risk;
- how to treat any injury that may occur.

What animals spell caution?

This is a list of known dangerous aquatic animals, but it is not comprehensive: conger and moray eels, stingrays, weeverfish, scorpion fish, stonefish, piranhas and certain seals. In addition, a number of species belonging to the Cnidarian group are poisonous, including jellyfish, fire corals, sea anemones and sea urchins. And, of course, crocodiles and many sharks and octopuses are dangerous.

What commonsense precautions should you take?

In particular:

- Avoid getting close to a venomous sea creature while bathing or wading.
- Take care to avoid treading on a stingray, weeverfish or sea urchin.
- Do not invade the territory of large animals when swimming or wading at the water's edge.
- Do not swim in areas used as hunting grounds by large predators, especially sharks and crocs.
- Do not interfere with or provoke dangerous aquatic creatures such as box jellyfish.
- Avoid swimming when danger notices are displayed.
- Wear shoes when walking on the shore or at the water's edge if dangerous aquatic animals are known to occur.
- Avoid contact with jellyfish in the sea and avoid handling jellyfish on the beach even if dead or apparently dead.
- When swimming in areas where sharks and other predators might be present, be especially careful if menstruating or bleeding from any injury.
- If swimming in areas where there is a risk of stings from dangerous jellyfish, consider wearing a Lycra stinger suit.
- Strictly avoid all waters at all times of year where crocodiles are ever known to be present, and be careful to keep your distance from infested waters so crocs are not tempted to snatch you from the bank when your gaze is elsewhere.
- Always seek medical advice after any sting or bite.

What are the danger signs of envenoming?

These vary greatly, but in serious cases there will be pain (often very severe), diarrhoea, vomiting, sweating and difficulty breathing. All these symptoms spell 'Get urgent medical help without delay'.

What treatments are available?

Obviously this is extremely variable and depends not only on the animal that has injured you but the extent to which it has bitten, punctured or injected venom.

Treatment from envenoming will depend on whether there is a puncture wound or a skin rash.

- Punctures caused by spiny fish require immediate immersion in hot water, extraction of the spine, cleaning of the wound, antibiotics and, in the case of stonefish, anti-venom as soon as possible. If the puncture was made by an octopus or sea urchin, the treatment is the same but without exposure to heat.

205

- Rashes or linear lesions are usually due to contact with poisonous Cnidarians. Use 5 per cent acetic acid (e.g. vinegar), steroid cream and tablets under medical advice, and in the case of the box jellyfish, *Chironex fleckeri*, immediate anti-venom.
- Sea urchin fragments can easily become embedded in the sole of your foot in tropical seas. Smaller ones gradually absorb and disappear; others can be removed by forceps after paring down the skin, having first softened it with salicylic acid.

Bed-bugs

These can be up to 10 mm long and usually bite at night, often leaving a scattering or a line of intensely itchy bites on exposed parts of the skin. They also hide in benches, for example at railway and bus stations, sometimes leading to a line of bites on the back of the thighs.

Prevent them by choosing clean accommodation. Bed-bugs gradually disappear if you put your bed in the sun or outside during the day. Keeping a light on at night discourages them from biting, and sleeping under a well-tucked-in permethrin-impregnated bed net will stop them from reaching you.

Treat bites by *not scratching* them and with an antihistamine by mouth (e.g. chlorphenamine or loratidine; see page 358). Bed-bugs do not spread any serious diseases, and although a major nuisance and common in budget accommodation, rarely cause any harm. The bites only rarely become infected.

Bees, wasps, hornets and ants

There are two potential dangers for travellers from these insects, all members of the group known as Hymenoptera. One is the rare attack by swarms of bees, usually in thundery weather (run fast, get inside a house or vehicle, dive into water). The other more common danger is being stung if you are allergic to bees, wasps, hornets or (less commonly) ants, in particular the fire ant of South America. (See pages 29–31 for details on anaphylaxis and treatment with adrenalin [epinephrine].)

Treatment

If in the past you have had a severe reaction to a sting (e.g. difficulty breathing, swelling of lips or tongue) or have developed progressively worse reactions, take and keep with you at least two self-injectable ampoules of adrenalin (epinephrine) such as EpiPen, available in the UK on prescription. Also wear a MedicAlert bracelet or necklet (see page 375).

Hives – large raised itchy patches on your skin accompanied by swelling of the lips or tongue or wheezing – are signs that you should use adrenalin straight away. In addition, take a double dose of an antihistamine, e.g. chlorphenamine (Piriton).

Fleas

Fleas are small jumping creatures 2–3 mm long, compressed sideways. They cause itchy bites, often in children, and are found anywhere on the body but commonly around the ankles. They are usually found in association with domestic pets, but those working with children in developing countries and with poorer members of the local population can be bitten by human fleas. See also under Jiggers, below.

Prevent flea bites by applying flea powder regularly to dogs and other domestic mammals. Where living accommodation is infested with fleas, carry out the following:

- Apply flea powder to all areas where fleas are found.
- Air all bedding and mattresses.
- Soak your sheets in permethrin (see pages 18–19 and 22).
- Sleep at least 60 cm above the floor (or at a height at which none of the fleas present on the floor can hop on to the bed), having first checked your bedclothes, body clothes and body surface for fleas, so that none get into the bed.
- Treat any animals as described above.
- Never allow animals on to the bed.
- Be patient – flea populations detached from their animal hosts eventually die out.

Apart from plague and certain forms of typhus fever – rare and only found in a few parts of the world – fleas are more of a nuisance than a danger.

Jiggers

These sand fleas are found in many parts of Africa, and in parts of South America and the Caribbean.

Symptoms

Jiggers burrow into the toes or feet, forming pea-sized swellings that may ulcerate. The condition they cause is medically known as tungiasis. Travellers usually only develop one or two lesions, but poorer members of the local population may have large numbers.

Prevention

You can prevent them by wearing good shoes or boots when walking in areas where they are known to occur. Spraying footwear with DEET solution probably helps. Inspect your feet regularly, as extracting them early helps to lessen infection. It is not known whether applying insect repellent to the skin has any effect.

Treatment

Treatment from a locally experienced member of the local community or health worker is to remove them, but make sure the needle they use is sterile, preferably from your own needle and syringe kit. Apply antiseptic afterwards to help prevent infection and report to a doctor if you develop any redness, pain, pus or swelling. Jiggers pose a tetanus risk so make sure your tetanus injections are up to date (see pages 394–5).

Leeches

These are common in jungle areas and monsoon forests, usually lying in wait by the path. The writer, when a medical student, once had over 50 leeches attached at one time when trekking in monsoon Nepal. Leeches are dangerous only when attached in numbers over a period of hours, when they can cause marked loss of blood.

Avoid swimming in forest lakes or rivers where water leeches are known to occur.

Prevention

Prevent leeches from biting you by wearing stout footwear and trousers tucked in at the ankles to boots or thick socks. Apply a DEET-containing insecticide to your skin and soak trousers and socks (only cotton or wool) in DEET, or spray them with a 100 per cent solution. Alternatively, spray permethrin in the form of Bug Proof (page 22) to your clothes before venturing out on to the forest paths.

Treatment

Salt or industrial spirit will cause a leech to detach itself in anguish, but the wound bleeds and itches for some time afterwards and occasionally gets infected if the biting part of the leech remains in the skin. Some experts suggest it is better to allow the leech to fall off naturally, but if a number of leeches are present this can lead to blood loss; in any case, few people are prepared to wait.

Leeches are not known to spread any illnesses but leech bites can get infected, especially if parts of the leech remain in the skin, meaning antibiotics are sometimes needed.

Lice

Lice are crawling insects 2–3 mm long found in the scalp, body hair or pubic region (crab lice).

They lay eggs, known as nits, which are dandruff-like objects attached firmly to the hair shafts. Head lice are very common worldwide, but especially in developing countries, often affecting expatriate and local children. They may give few symptoms, or alternatively cause severe itching and scratching with local infection and swollen lymph nodes.

Prevention

Lice are prevented by good personal hygiene, but even with care it is sometimes impossible to prevent children from catching head lice. Avoid crab lice by avoiding intimate contact, including sex, with those infected – not, of course, easy to ascertain in advance!

Treatment

Head lice can be treated with permethrin 1 per cent cream rinse, or 1 per cent lindane lotion and shampoo. After washing and drying your hair, apply according to manufacturer's instructions, leave for ten minutes, then rinse and dry. In many parts of the world lice have developed resistance to these. Alternatives are 0.5 per cent malathion lotion or 1 per cent malathion shampoo (USA) or carbaryl. Phenothrin 0.5 per cent liquid is widely used in the UK and a new treatment, dimeticone 4 per cent lotion, is proving effective. Whichever you use, follow instructions carefully. Most preparations should be repeated after seven days, to kill any lice that hatch out after the first treatment.

In addition to using these treatments, remove all viable nits by carefully combing wet hair, ideally using plastic combs. Olive oil is a good way of 'wetting' the hair. Also wash and dry all bedding, hats, etc., which come into contact with the hair and could be infected, including combs and brushes. Use the maximum heat they will tolerate.

For pubic lice (crab lice) use malathion, carbaryl, permethrin 5 per cent dermal cream or other preparations mentioned above. Apply to all body hair, not just the pubic area; include the beard but exclude the scalp. Encourage your partner to also get treatment. With all these preparations, avoid contact with eyes and mucous membranes. Make sure you and any partner who has had crabs also get tested for other sexually transmitted infections.

Increasingly ivermectin is being used to deal with lice. The dose is the same as for scabies, 0.2 mg/kg, with the same dose repeated after ten days; it is not safe in pregnancy.

Lice on clothing can be dealt with by washing the clothes in hot water (over 55°C) or sealing clothes in a bag for two weeks, when all the lice will die out.

Mites (causing scabies) and chiggers

Scabies

Mites are tiny creatures that cause this common skin condition. Scabies is frequently caught by expatriate children who go to a local school, or by health workers and others in close contact with the local population.

Symptoms

These include severe itching, especially at night. Scabies quickly spreads to other family members.

Treatment

Treat scabies by applying permethrin 5 per cent dermal cream or a 0.5 per cent malathion preparation. Apply to the whole body up to the neckline, leave for 12 to 24 hours, and then wash off. Avoid contact with eyes and mucous membranes. Benzyl benzoate may be the only preparation you can buy in remoter areas. Use it in the same way but remember it can sting, especially if the skin is chapped or cut. A single dose of ivermectin 0.2 mg/kg (the same drug as is used to treat river blindness), repeated after ten days, is effective in scabies. It is not safe in pregnancy.

Anyone else in the household or any sexual partner, whether or not they have symptoms, should be treated at the same time. Sheets, blankets, linen and clothes with which your skin has been in direct contact should be washed in hot water and dried, if possible in full sun. Itching may persist for at least two weeks and sometimes much longer after the scabies is cured. If it still continues, treat again or see a doctor.

Post-scabies itching often responds to Crotamiton cream, with or without the use of 1 per cent hydrocortisone cream and antihistamine tablets, e.g. chlorphenamine (Piriton).

Chiggers

Chiggers (not to be confused with jiggers) are small red mites that cause skin irritation. They are common in East Asia, the Pacific islands and South America. They often favour areas with shrubby overgrowth, such as areas cleared of forest or forest margins. They can cause scrub typhus (see page 344), especially common in Thailand. To prevent them getting on to your skin, use DEET insect repellent and tuck trousers into socks where chiggers are known to occur. You can also spray your socks and shoes with permethrin (Bug Proof).

Scorpions and spiders

Scorpions

There are more than 1,500 scorpion species in the world but comparatively few are really poisonous. Scorpions usually only bite if startled or annoyed, and the majority of bites therefore occur on the feet and hands.

Prevention

Prevent bites by never reaching into unlit corners, and always shaking shoes before putting them on. Don't walk barefoot in the house or anywhere else if scorpions are known to be present. Check your bedding.

In scorpion-infested areas, camp sites should be checked and cleared of scorpion tunnels before pitching tents.

Symptoms

Most scorpion bites are very painful, and dangerous scorpions usually produce neurotoxins which in addition to causing local pain and irritation can cause similar symptoms as described under snake bite, though not usually so serious. In practice children, especially, can develop a wide range of symptoms from poisonous species.

Central and South American, North African and some Indian species are the most poisonous.

Treatment

Treat bites by strong painkillers or an injection of local anaesthetic (e.g. lignocaine 2 per cent). A local anaesthetic cream, such as EMLA or Ametop, also reduces the pain. Specific anti-venom is available in some countries (e.g. South America), and if you are living in an area where poisonous species are commonly found, search out a clinic or hospital where this is available.

Spiders

Spiders, with a few exceptions such as the Black Widow or Australian Redback, are rarely dangerous. Prevent and treat in the same way as for scorpions, and take any locally advised precautions to avoid known poisonous species.

Ticks

If you notice a small nodule or dusky-coloured bump on your skin not apparently there a few hours or days before, this could be a tick. They attach themselves to the body, usually after you have been walking through vegetation or in close proximity to animals. Ticks feed on blood, gradually enlarging and eventually falling off.

They can, however, cause disease (e.g. tick-borne encephalitis, tick-bite fever, some forms of typhus and Lyme disease, see pages 396, 338–9, 345–6 and 318–19).

Prevention

Use DEET insect repellent on the skin, or soak trousers (cotton or woollen only) in DEET solution or spray with 100 per cent DEET or permethrin in the form of Bug Proof. Tuck your trouser legs into thick socks, and wear strong shoes or boots.

Removal

Where ticks are known to occur, check your skin or that of your companion each evening. Remove them by grasping the head-end (if recognizable) near your skin with blunt curved tweezers and gently pulling, if necessary with a rocking motion, to detach the head-parts. Be patient and try not to squeeze the tick's body, as this can enhance any disease transmission which may be occurring. Having removed the tick, apply alcohol to the skin (whisky, gin or any spirit will do). Keep an eye out for the symptoms of any tick-borne illness that is known to occur locally.

Tumbu flies (mango or putsi flies)

If you live in tropical Africa or, less commonly, in South America (the home of the similar bot-fly) and you develop the symptoms of a painful boil, make sure there is no maggot inside it. Tumbu and bot-flies cause what is known as myiasis, the ability to grow their larvae in human skin.

Symptoms

Tumbu lesions are usually very painful, hot, swollen and red, and sometimes give the feeling that something is moving inside. When your friends or family take a look they may see two small black dots or the head of a whitish larva writhing inside. The larva enters the skin from eggs laid by tumbu flies on clothes that have been left outside to dry. Bot-flies have a different mechanism of gaining access to the skin and are less easily prevented, but keeping covered and/or applying DEET to the skin when in affected areas reduces the risk.

Prevention

Hot-iron all clothes left outside to dry, including all creases and seams (this kills the eggs) in those parts of the tropics where it is common or – better – dry clothes inside or on a clothes line in full sun.

Treatment

The maggot is killed by placing a drop of oil or Vaseline on the lesian overnight, and then removing the maggot. Some local practitioners or experienced residents may be able to do this but it is better to see a doctor who can make sure the maggot is completely removed with sterile instruments as painlessly as possible. The wound is treated with antiseptic, and antibiotics are given for seven days to cure or reduce infection, which is commonly present. Flucloxacillin 500 mg four times daily can be used, or erythromycin 500 mg four times daily if allergic to penicillin.

Other biting insects and bugs

Here are a few more that can cause grief to travellers:

Nairobi fly

This insect (actually a blister beetle) is common in East Africa in the rainy season. It is about half a centimetre long and is red, black and dark green. You should flick it off the skin and not crush it because it can cause intense skin irritation when squashed on the skin, especially near the eye. Apply lacto calamine lotion or hydrocortisone 1 per cent cream to the skin and take antihistamines. Seek medical advice if the eye is severely inflamed.

Sandflies

These small insects cause itchy bites in hot climates. They can spread leishmaniasis (see pages 315–16) and the less serious sandfly fever.

Triatomine bugs (assassin bugs, kissing bugs, cone-nosed bugs, vinchucas)

These cause Chagas' disease in parts of South America (see pages 282–4).

Tsetse flies

These spread sleeping sickness in parts of West, central and East Africa (see pages 335–6).

For those either worried or fascinated, Table 31.1 on page 275 lists the vectors (carriers) of important infectious diseases, most of which are mentioned elsewhere in the book (see index).

21

How to survive an overseas assignment

Hopefully you will have read the section on preparing for an overseas assignment (pages 64–8), which discusses culture shock.

There is supposed to be a grave in India with the following epitaph: 'Here lies the body of a person who tried to hurry the East.'

Perhaps the main secret of coping with a new country is to identify an appropriate pace to life, and then adapt your personal rhythms accordingly. This will be based on your own happy mean between the laid-back fatalism of the local population on the one hand, and the reasonable goals and expectations of your job, expedition or travel plans on the other.

Take shopping, for example, or getting a visa, or even buying vehicle fuel. This may take half a day or even longer. You have a choice of staying on home time, being a frustrated foreigner and upsetting those around you, or just switching into a different gear, allowing the adrenalin to drain away and sitting or standing (un)comfortably, with a book and supply of safe drinks until your turn comes. You may make two or three new friendships before the day's finished – perhaps just as important as the project proposal or emails you haven't finished writing.

Here are some survival tips.

The climate

When first landing at a tropical airport children sometimes wonder why the pilot hasn't turned the aircraft engines off, only to discover that the blast of hot air comes from the country, not the plane. It takes two to three weeks for your body to partially adapt to the new temperature, longer if the climate is humid. Even then you are unlikely to be able to maintain the pace of life you are used to. So allow much longer than usual for normal physical and mental activities.

When first arriving in a hot country you will obviously lose large amounts of fluid through perspiration. This means you must replace both fluid and salt by drinking large amounts, more often, and adding salt to your meals. A good alternative is to make up your own rehydration solution (ORS; see pages 104–5) or just add a very small pinch of salt to any sweet drink. Although ORS is normally used to replace fluid lost in diarrhoea, it can be very reviving during a long, hot tropical day, especially in the absence of safe soft drinks. You should avoid using salt tablets. (If you have high blood pressure, have this checked regularly, remembering that excess salt can push your blood pressure higher.) For more on adapting to heat see pages 196–7.

Wearing appropriate clothes can also help you to acclimatize. They should be *loose-fitting*, so allowing air to circulate; *absorbent*, so allowing you to cool more easily (100 per cent cotton is ideal, silk for the rich and famous); and *pale in colour* so they reflect rather than absorb the heat. Acclimatization is slower in the elderly, the pregnant, the overweight or if you are very exhausted. Men acclimatize slightly quicker than women, in whom undiagnosed anaemia can slow the process further.

Language

For those living or working abroad there is nothing so frustrating as not being able to communicate with the people you have left home and luxuries to live alongside. Only the lucky few can fully learn a new language on the job. If you are going on an overseas assignment of, say, two years or more and communicating with local people is part of the job, you must ensure adequate time for language study before starting any official tasks. During this time language learning should take priority over everything else. Even after this phase is over, language slots must be built into your timetable so that you are able to continue studying. It is worth discussing this in detail with your agency or company at an early stage, so that everyone has the same expectations. An interactive CD-Rom or BBC course can help *before you go*, as can getting hold of a phrase book or user-friendly language manual. And courses are also available for children; see <http://www.muzzyonline. co.uk>.

Some survival tips

Work–life balance

Within the first week of arriving, work out a method for safeguarding your leisure. Set priority time for rest and recreation and write it into your diary, giving it equal priority to meetings and work deadlines. Establish a balance between your work and your time off. Draw boundaries so that work does not gradually take over everything else.

For those working overseas, the very minimum time off should be one, preferably one and a half days per week, one long weekend in six, five weeks per year. In refugee and civil war situations the weekend should become a week taken completely off-site. Of course, this advice may be tricky to arrange if work is very heavy, you are single and there is no obvious travelling companion, and also if there is hassle, danger, and it's a 48-hour trip to get anywhere you can really relax. In this case make sure when you do relax that you take a long enough break to recharge your batteries. The hidden dangers of just keeping going and running on adrenalin will catch up with you in the end.

If there is no obvious place to escape to and nothing to do when off-duty or away from work, it is even more essential early on in your assignment to devise ways of relaxing on-site and constructing a bolt-hole. Devise a system of protecting your personal privacy, or doing something that really relaxes you. For some this may be reading, for others parties, Salsa or amateur dramatics.

People who work all week, then use Sunday for church or voluntary activities, are high-risk candidates for burnout. Even backpackers and travellers will need at least one 'domestic' day per week or the delights of the road and new travel experiences will irritate rather than stimulate.

Leisure time needs to be built into both your contract and the understanding of your senior colleagues – even if it may not be understood in the local culture. It also needs to be programmed into your personal and family expectations. Mothers (and fathers) of young children are a priority sub-group!

Unless you give top attention to time out, exhaustion and burn-out will eventually occur, even though they may take time to declare themselves, often after a period of unproductive guilt-driven activity (see pages 173–87).

Here are three tendencies that spell 'Caution, take action': becoming an *alcoholic* (see below); becoming a *workaholic* – only too easy in the absence of any obvious alternative; becoming a *computerholic* – when on coming home in the evening you nod to the spouse and kids and then disappear into your 'cave' to play computer games or surf the net till midnight.

Have varied social contacts

In isolated postings it is common for everyone to work, play, relax and even pray together. Sooner or later (usually sooner), relationships and personal contentment begin to break down. Cultivate friendships outside your immediate circle, with local families and acquaintances and with expatriates who hold differing viewpoints or interests. Try to make it possible to take time out from the compound, campus or immediate surroundings.

Discover leisure interests

Many birdwatchers and collectors have first developed their interest overseas, as have mountaineers, geologists, novelists and painters. The customs, culture, music and art forms of many developing countries are a rich mine of interest. Board games, reading, the BBC World Service or BBC World TV, CNN, joining or starting a Scottish dancing club, reading your favourite weekly newspaper online or sent from home – all these help to keep you fresh and integrated, as does watching videos or DVDs. And then there are crosswords and Su Doku.

Take part in regular sport

Swimming is often ideal, crocodiles and bilharzia allowing. Walking, tennis, volleyball, squash and badminton may be possible. Many aid workers and longer-term residents go jogging, soon discovering the areas where stares from the local population and growls from the local dogs don't make the whole plan too much to cope with. Regular physical exercise, ideally at least once or twice a week of a sort that you enjoy and is possible locally, not only helps to keep you fit but is great at reducing stress. If you are in a dangerous or insecure zone, skipping or dance/aerobics to music works for some.

Become a writer

Some people find that at times of severe frustration, difficulty or excitement, adopting the mindset of a novelist or journalist can be helpful. Half-day waits in the visa office or close shaves at an armed roadblock or street demo become prime source material.

Accompanying dependents

For partners with no specific job description, expatriate life can at times become frustrating and boring. Caring for the children and the home may in large part be carried out by others; friends and relatives are on another continent, and you may have no official job or role. Moreover, your partner may be busy and fulfilled (and therefore insensitive to your needs) or very frustrated with an assignment that is not working out (and therefore needing to offload aggro).

Apart from following the commonsense tips above, a few other points may be helpful in this situation:

- Before you go, as far as possible define and clarify your likely role overseas with your company or agency, programme director and partner. You may be able to draw up a specific job description, task or appropriate expectation. If your role is to be left vague or you are to 'wait and see how things develop', this should be through an informed, planned decision and not simply by default.
- Develop your own outlets away from home, providing this is possible within the culture and with your visa type or work permit. This may mean voluntary help in the local community – through a church, voluntary organization, school or hospital. Many people find that their contribution in the informal sector is just as valuable as if they had gone out with a specific job description or pre-planned role.
- Invite friends from home, or elective students, local friends and expatriate volunteers living nearby, to stay or share meals.
- Determine to become really proficient in the local language. This is the best way of reducing social isolation.
- Learn about a new subject, either informally or by correspondence or through the Open University.
- Learn or re-learn to play a musical instrument. The local music and dance traditions may be every bit as rewarding as your favourite style of music, classical or rock. Resist the delights and dangers of too much booze, whether local or brought in from outside (see pages 221–2).
- Be open with your partner, who will need to understand the realities of your own life and the way you feel. Be proactive in establishing time off as a couple and as a family.

Professional update

For many working or serving overseas, professional opportunities can be exciting and challenging. Keep notes of interesting or significant discoveries, events, cases or ideas. Make sure you receive professional journals from home or can access them on-line. When on home leave try to fit in some continuing professional development (CPD) or attend a course or conference. Consider writing a paper or travel article or book. How about doing some research?

22

Alcohol

In some countries or particular communities, alcohol is forbidden or strongly discouraged. If this is the case it is only worth accepting a drink if this is both legal and acceptable with those among whom you live and work.

A greater problem is often the free availability of alcohol, including homebrew – which, added to tiredness, loneliness or stress, can bring to light a past, or new, drinking problem.

It is worth setting yourself some strict guidelines, as prevention is far easier than cure. Consider keeping a drink diary if you find it hard to keep your drinking under control. In this you list *when, where, how much* and *with whom* you drink each day of the week, and you fill it in every 24 hours, not in an inaccurate haze at the end of the week. Sometimes it is helpful for partners or close friends to do this together.

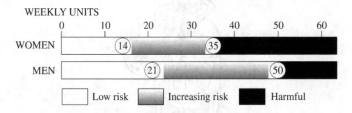

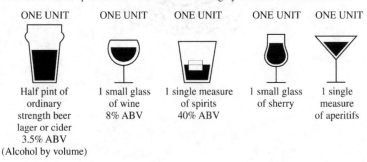

Figure 22.1 Units of alcohol

Sensible rules include: never exceeding an appropriate limit (e.g. 21 units per week for men, 14 units per week for women – see Figure 22.1), keeping at least two days per week alcohol-free, practising ways of saying no, never getting drunk or drinking alone, or drinking before sunset. Avoid making a habit of 'needing' a drink every evening in order to wind down. Never binge-drink. If this means avoiding mixing with certain people, fine. If you ever feel the problem is getting on top of you, tell someone appropriate and ask for help before it becomes known in the community or passes beyond your control.

And by the way, take great care in sampling the homebrew – there have been too many reports of contaminants causing death and blindness.

23

Accessing health care overseas

Background

Most of us travelling outside our own country are understandably concerned about becoming ill in a country where we may not know the system or where health care may be less reliable than we are used to.

Recent medical research indicates that, depending on destination, each day of travel carries a 3–4 per cent risk of illness, and that up to 8 per cent of all travellers and 12 per cent of those who become ill seek medical care when abroad. Of these 17 per cent receive an injection.

This means it is worth thinking ahead before you go abroad about what you might do if illness strikes or you have an accident. If you have any pre-existing medical condition which may cause you problems or require follow-up tests, this is even more important.

Of course, in many countries the standard of health care may be the same or even better (and often quicker) than the care you receive at home, especially in large cities. But in other situations health care may be substandard or, if you are travelling in remote areas, virtually non-existent.

Medical procedures abroad you should try and avoid

Of course, this will not always be possible and some of the following will be relatively safe in the best-equipped hospitals. However, normally you will have time to consider the best course of action. Where possible, seek the advice of a colleague, team leader, local host or expatriate before agreeing to any of the following. And if more seriously ill, contact the emergency helpline of your travel insurance company.

You should be very slow to accept any of the following:

- general anaesthetics;
- surgical procedures or operations;
- blood transfusions;
- drugs by injection via intramuscular or intravenous routes;
- accepting an intravenous infusion of fluids.

This may seem obvious, but often less experienced travellers, especially when worried about their health, subject themselves to unnecessary and sometimes unsafe procedures. In particular, injections and intravenous fluids are used in many developing countries when medication and fluids by mouth would be just as effective. Of course, it will be different in genuine emergencies, which are only a small proportion of the causes for seeking health care abroad.

Guidelines on the best procedures to follow

- Take all measures to minimize your risk of falling sick or being injured, e.g. sleep under a mosquito net, take your antimalarials, pay attention to food and water hygiene, avoid excessive alcohol and always wear seat belts when fitted.
- Take a first-aid kit (see pages 361–3).
- Take out comprehensive travel health insurance before departure. Keep a personal health list with you which includes any medicine you normally take, any antimalarials you are on, details of any allergies or past health problems, a copy of your health insurance and your emergency helpline number (which comes with your insurance policy) to ring if you are seriously ill or injured.
- Have access to emergency standby medicines to treat common illnesses, in particular standby malaria treatment and medication such as oral rehydration salts and ciprofloxacin (pages 356–60). Remember to read the Patient Information Leaflets that accompany most medicines so you are aware of possible side-effects.
- Find out the name and address of a good hospital or clinic and doctor when you first arrive in your destination, especially if you are travelling independently. And, for remote areas, find out about the nearest hospital or doctor you would try and reach in a medical emergency, and also how you might get there.
- Seek out health units that have a reputation of caring for foreigners. Local expatriates often know the best available facilities.
- If working for a company or as a volunteer, notify your manager, host, group leader or first-aider when you first start to feel unwell so that appropriate steps can be taken at an early stage. This is especially important if it could be malaria.
- Be prepared to travel a long distance to access good health care rather than simply going to the hospital or clinic nearby just because it is convenient. This means that you should plan ahead when you are well, rather than waiting until you are sick. Unless you are seriously ill, such journeys should ideally take place during daylight hours to minimize the risk of road traffic accidents.

- If you have to go to hospital, ask a friend or colleague to go with you; many hospitals are frightening or bewildering places, especially if you are ill and don't speak the language.
- Do not assume that the healthcare system is similar to the one you left at home – in particular, think carefully and take advice before agreeing to any of the list of procedures and treatments listed above.
- Have exit strategies that allow you to bow out gracefully from local healthcare providers if you are dissatisfied or alarmed.
- Unless seriously ill, clarify payment issues from the start. Act with courtesy with all medical staff you meet, as this will make it more likely you will receive the best treatment.
- Understand that in some countries questions from the patient or family are seen as challenges to the doctor's authority, so discuss your health problems and ask any questions with tact.
- Women and men should be aware that doctors in any country may occasionally fail to follow considerate or ethical practices. Be prepared to say no to an examination you feel is unnecessary or inappropriate.
- Consider setting up an emergency advice-line via email to a medical friend or colleague back home in case you wish to double-check advice you have been given. InterHealth members are entitled to use InterHealth for that purpose (<http://www.interhealth.org.uk>.)

Medicines and injections in developing countries

There is enormous variation in the availability of useful medicines. Although it may be difficult to find the most appropriate medicines according to the advice you have received, brand products are often available in abundance, under a wide variety of names. In most of Asia and Latin America and in the larger cities of Africa, many medicines are available without prescription from roadside pharmacies.

Before buying or using medicines overseas:

- Check that they are made by a reputable company, preferably a multinational, and that they look genuine. Fake drugs and substandard drugs are common, especially in West Africa and South Asia.
- Check the expiry date.
- Check the generic or scientific name (usually found somewhere on the bottle or packet, though in small print) to make sure it really is the preparation you want.
- Avoid preparations that contain steroids (e.g. prednisolone) unless this is definitely what you need. Never use eye drops with steroids unless prescribed by a doctor skilled in eye diseases.

- Avoid blood- or serum-based products, including locally made gammaglobulin. They can spread HIV infection.

Avoid injections, intravenous glucose and other widely used remedies *unless really indicated*. In many countries health workers, from doctors to traditional practitioners, use injections even for mild self-limiting illness. Often no treatment is needed at all, or medicines by mouth will be just as effective. If an injection is essential, go to a reputable health worker and provide your own needle and syringe.

24
Security

Although this varies widely, security is a problem in many parts of the world, as are the dangers of robbery, rape, kidnap and getting caught up in a local disturbance.

A few commonsense rules can greatly minimize your risks:

Personal possessions

Avoid ostentatious dress and gadgetry – wear clothes appropriate to the local culture. Travel with as little cash on you as possible. Wear a money-belt, preferably inside your clothes, or use a Tubigrip bandage to keep cash or tickets on the inner side of your leg. Watch your possessions with great care in crowds, on public transport, especially night trains, and on beaches. Keep any valuables close by, especially at night. Be on guard for pickpockets, especially in well-known tourist areas. In areas where mugging is common, consider keeping a small amount of local currency, dollars or pounds so you can easily hand them over.

Personal safety

Try to grasp the basic rules of how people relate and the words and mannerisms that cause offence or could be misunderstood. Especially important is to gauge the degree of intimacy between sexes that is considered acceptable. What might be considered a gesture of friendship in Latin America might cause great offence in Pakistan. Keep a low profile, understandably difficult for blondes in Africa or giants in East Asia. Avoid dark or lonely areas in city or country. Keep to well-worn routes.

If a car stops near you and asks instructions, or beckons for you to approach, act with extreme caution. Try to travel with a local resident who knows the best routes to take and how to cope with any difficult situation. Try not to use maps in public, but study the route in advance of setting out. Get to know your neighbourhood, the telephones that work, your nearest police station. Avoid excessive alcohol. If you find yourself on the edges of a disturbance or demonstration, beat a hasty retreat.

In many cultures single women will cause a great deal of interest, and may be asked continual and at times annoying questions. Try to keep your cool. By making sure people know you are not eligible you can increase your safety. Consider talking about 'your husband', having a photo to 'prove it' or wearing a fake wedding ring. For women, eye-to-eye contact is seen as a come-on in some cultures. Wearing dark glasses can help. Skimpy or tight clothing can be provocative and put you at extra risk, as well as causing offence. In Arab and Islamic countries it is especially important to wear modest clothes that cover arms and legs – also to wear a headscarf. If you feel you are in real danger and need to take action, deliver a crippling blow and make your escape. Consider going on a self-defence course before you travel.

A key rule is to act confidently as though you know where you are going.

You can get detailed advice on the safety of travel in any country of the world by accessing the UK Foreign Office website at <http://www.fco.gov.uk/> or checking the equivalent in your own home country.

Driving

Except in areas known to be safe, follow these rules.

- Never pick up a stranger.
- Avoid roads infrequently used.
- Try not to drive alone at night.
- Take extra care when your car is stationary and try to adjust your speed so you don't have to stop at traffic lights.
- Always stop at road blocks, do what you are asked without arguing and try to avoid eye contact; never lose your cool.
- Make sure someone else knows your destination and the route you plan to take.
- In built-up areas, keep the windows closed and the doors locked.
- When a car takes you home, ask the driver to wait until you are safely inside.

Domestic safety

Assess the likely risk of robbery, armed or otherwise, and take appropriate precautions. This may mean keeping a guard dog, building a perimeter fence, having an intercom with another nearby resident or employing a watchman. Consider using a time switch for lights or radios, calling a loud goodbye as you leave an empty house, fitting security locks and window bars and keeping a whistle handy. If your house looks as though it has been broken into, do not go in alone – summon help first. Only sleep with an open window if it is difficult to enter from the outside or if there are bars or grilles in place.

Thieving is often opportunistic, meaning you should not leave things lying around your garden or an open house, and that you should secure all doors and windows with care whenever you go out. Only employ domestic staff after making sure, preferably by reliable references, that the person is of good reputation.

Hotel safety

Before accepting any accommodation, ask to see it, and if you feel uncomfortable say so and request an alternative. (Double) lock your room, keep valuables with you and retain your key when leaving the building. Don't leave precious things lying around in your room. Remember that your passport may have a high value on the black market, and so may your identity.

If your door has a safety chain, use it, and never admit anyone unless you are sure you know who it is. Keep your door and balcony locked and curtains drawn. Avoid rooms that are easily accessible from the outside. If you receive a phone call never give away your identity until the caller has first made his or hers clear to you.

25

Pregnancy

Background

Parents-to-be often wonder if it is safe to travel or live in a developing country when pregnant. Before deciding on this it is important to understand the extra levels of risk at different times during pregnancy and then set this alongside your travel plans. Your doctor or midwife will probably be able to advise you, and if you are going on an overseas posting, your company or agency medical adviser may have guidelines.

- With the huge increase in overseas travel, pregnancy – both planned and unplanned – is an increasingly important and complex issue when travelling abroad.
- There are additional risks in pregnancy if you are travelling or living in a developing country, especially around the time of delivery.
- Because there are so many variables, if you are pregnant or pregnancy is a definite possibility, you need to do two important things.
    - The first is to seek specific medical advice before travel, when you can start to weigh the risks and to draw up plans.
    - The second is to become as informed as possible about the increased risks of pregnancy during travel and the details of any medical care which will be available at your destination.
- If you are planning an overseas delivery, certain conditions must be clearly in place (see below).

Parents-to-be must be satisfied and confident that there is no significant extra risk to either mother or newborn in having the delivery abroad compared to their country of origin.

Risks to pregnant travellers

It is helpful to consider the additional risks of pregnancy during travel under three separate though related headings:

- safety of travel during pregnancy;
- safety of living in a developing country when pregnant;
- safety of having a delivery overseas.

Safety of travel during pregnancy

The mere act of travelling during pregnancy carries small additional risks owing to the greater likelihood of illness, accidents and distance from good health care when away from home. However, for most healthy travellers with no previous problems during pregnancy this risk is small, providing you take certain extra precautions (see sections below).

- The safest time to travel is between 18 and 24–26 weeks. The least safe times are between 12 and 15 weeks (risk of miscarriage) and after 30 weeks (danger of late pregnancy complications, including bleeding and premature labour).
- Air flight is safe during pregnancy, and the slightly lower oxygen concentration and reduced pressure in the aircraft have no adverse effects on either mother or foetus.
- Airport security checks including radiation are not considered to pose any risk.
- In pregnancy you are slightly more likely to develop a deep vein thrombosis (see pages 72–4), so try if possible to choose an aisle or bulkhead seat.
- Indigestion and flatulence can be a greater problem during the flight and it is worth avoiding fizzy drinks. Keep up your fluid intake, and keep alcohol to a minimum.
- Your feet may swell more than normal: consider below-knee compression stockings, also helpful at preventing DVTs.
- Travel sickness may affect you: promethazine (Avomine) is effective and considered safe. In late pregnancy, e.g. from 32 weeks onwards, it is a good idea to travel with a companion; this is essential from 36 weeks.

Health problems which spell caution

If any of the conditions below apply to you, it means that travelling or living abroad, especially in a developing country, causes additional risks, so carefully weigh these risks with your doctor and draw up careful plans. Some of these apply to the whole of the pregnancy and some to certain times, especially from 30 weeks onwards. Only a few mean that you must avoid travel altogether.

- You have had a *medical condition* that adds to the risk of pregnancy. This would include heart disease, severe asthma or lung disease, diabetes, significant anaemia including sickle-cell disease, high blood pressure, previous deep vein thrombosis or pelvic infection, and any serious or long-term illness.

- You have had *problems in a previous pregnancy*. These would include an actual or threatened miscarriage, ectopic pregnancy (see note below), toxaemia, diabetes or hypertension, placental abnormalities, premature labour, any significant complication of birth likely to be repeated, and Rhesus incompatibility (see below).
- You have *problems in your present pregnancy*. These would include threatened miscarriage or any vaginal bleeding, foetal growth abnormalities, incompetent (weak) cervix, raised blood pressure, presence of twins or triplets. Also at extra risk are those aged 15 years or under and 35 years or over.

Most international flights will be unwilling to carry a passenger known to be 35 weeks pregnant or beyond, but many domestic flights make a cut-off point at 36 weeks. Check the exact regulations with the airline concerned and leave a margin of two weeks in case of last-minute changes of plan or cancellations. Always take a medical 'Safety for Flying Certificate' signed by a doctor, stating the expected date of delivery.

Note on ectopic pregnancy
If a woman has had one ectopic pregnancy she has about a one in four chance of this being repeated in a subsequent pregnancy.

Ectopics are dangerous. If you have previously had one, follow these guidelines:

- Use contraception before and during travel.
- If you opt not to do this, carry out a home pregnancy test immediately before any international travel. If this is positive, do not go abroad until it is confirmed that the pregnancy is not ectopic.
- If not taking contraception and not pregnant when leaving home, self-test for pregnancy each week when abroad, unless periods continue as normal.
- Return home if a pregnancy test is positive.

Safety of living in a developing country when pregnant
This will vary greatly depending on the country and your exact location. The main considerations will be the actual availability of good medical care and being within easy travelling distance of the best care available (therefore often restricting in-country travel).

Although most overseas pregnancies will pass without difficulty, if problems do arise or a tragedy does occur it's important that you have considered the risks in detail, leading to an informed choice.

Important risks include:

- *Miscarriage* There is a slight increased risk of this in the tropics because of fever, especially malaria, and possibly severe dehydration. If a miscarriage occurs or vaginal bleeding persists, medical facilities such as those for evacuation of the uterus (ERPC) or dilatation and curettage (D and C) may be less reliable – and less hygienic. Safe blood may be harder to get in the rare event of needing a transfusion.

- *Malaria* (see below).
- *Hepatitis E* This form of hepatitis is spread like hepatitis A. In some countries, such as Nepal, it is common. This form of hepatitis is dangerous in the second half of pregnancy. If you are in a country where it is known to be common or there is a current outbreak, take even more care than usual with food and water hygiene, or leave early (see pages 302–3).
- *Extra dangers from certain foods* This includes the risk of toxoplasmosis and Listeria. Take extra precautions with food and water hygiene; strictly avoid all salads, undercooked meats, unpasteurized milk, soft cheese and pâté. Take all precautions to avoid diarrhoea and use oral rehydration solution early, as dehydration may reduce placental blood flow. Boil water rather than using iodine to sterilize it, though this is probably safe to use intermittently for up to six weeks. A safe antibiotic for traveller's diarrhoea is erythromycin, though this is not effective against all organisms.
- *Medicines* Many medicines are best avoided in pregnancy, meaning treatment may need to be delayed until the baby is born. A bewildering number of drugs are available in many developing countries, either by prescription or over the counter. Some medicines are known to carry risks in pregnancy; the majority of medicines are probably safe, but best avoided because there is insufficient evidence; other medicines are so widely used that they are considered safe.[1]
- *Premature labour* Although in the absence of malaria this is no more likely when overseas, access to adequate treatment, such as safe blood for the mother and extra support for a premature baby, is greatly reduced.

Safety of having a delivery overseas

There is a potentially greater danger from complications at the time of delivery in a developing country, unless there are excellent, round-the-clock facilities within easy reach. In most resource-poor countries,

[1] For full information on this, see: *Prescribing Medicines in Pregnancy* (Australian Government Department of Health and Ageing, 2004), also available at <http://www.tga.gov.au/docs>; and *The British National Formulary*, updated annually and published by the British Medical Association and the Royal Pharmaceutical Society of Great Britain, available (but only on registration) at <http://www.bnf.org>.

facilities both for routine and for emergency care are less reliable. This means you need to make a careful choice, not through a haze of optimism but based on a cool look at what might happen in the worst scenario.

You can minimize health risks during pregnancy by setting up an ordered lifestyle, taking regular exercise and allowing more time than usual for rest, relaxation and routine tasks.

The following are suggested *minimum* requirements for an overseas delivery:

- a maternity unit, easily accessible at all times of the day or night and at all seasons, with 24-hour cover from an experienced doctor able to carry out forceps and vacuum deliveries and Caesarean sections;
- high standards of hygiene, fully trained midwives and the guaranteed use of sterile instruments;
- the ready availability of safe blood from a trusted donor with the same or a compatible blood group;
- resuscitation facilities for the newborn and a special care baby unit;
- the absence of any serious pregnancy-related problems in this or previous pregnancies, including Rhesus incompatibility;
- a personality that can cope with the added risks and anxieties of having a delivery away from home and support from the wider family;
- a partner or family member who can give practical support at the time of delivery, including organizing travel arrangements.

Before coming to a decision about having a delivery at home or abroad, carry out the following:

- Inspect the maternity unit and facilities for the newborn, preferably in the company of a doctor, nurse or midwife.
- Meet the doctor(s) or midwives likely to carry out the delivery.
- Ensure a doctor will be available 24 hours a day.
- Check with other expatriates who have used the facility. Ask whether the father can be present at the delivery.
- Ensure that any employing organization is satisfied with the arrangements.

Even if the minimum requirements are in place, the balance may still be tilted in favour of coming home if any of the following applies:

- this is your first delivery;
- you are over 35, or under 18;
- you are working in a country where HIV or malaria is prevalent;
- there is political instability, unreliable transport or the likelihood of heavy rains that could delay getting to hospital.

An alternative to coming home is to move nearer to a capital city or good-quality hospital at least two weeks before the delivery date, or to a nearby country with better health facilities.

For UK citizens, if both the baby's parents and/or two or more grandparents were born overseas, check citizenship rules with the Home Office.

Actions to be taken before travel

- If pregnancy is possible or planned, have your rubella antibodies checked, and if negative have a rubella immunization. In the USA the same is recommended for chickenpox.
- If you are pregnant have this confirmed by a clinician and preferably by a scan, and make sure an ectopic pregnancy is not present.
- Have a detailed antenatal examination if you are pregnant and an in-depth discussion with the obstetrician or midwife.
- Take folic acid, 0.4 mg from the time of trying to conceive, and 5 mg daily if pregnant, especially important if taking the malaria prevention tablet proguanil (Paludrine) or Malarone.
- Make long-term plans for pregnancy-related care while overseas, and a provisional decision about where the delivery will take place, based on the best information that can be obtained.
- Take out travel insurance which covers pregnancy-related health problems and any health issues affecting the newborn during or after delivery.

Malaria and pregnancy

Malaria, especially malignant malaria, which is common in sub-Saharan Africa and Southeast Asia, increases the risk of anaemia, premature labour, miscarriage and stillbirth. A severe attack can be life-threatening. The baby may be born with malaria. Women who are pregnant, or recently pregnant, are more attractive to mosquitoes – and more likely to get mosquito-borne illnesses, especially malaria. All this means that pregnant women are generally advised not to visit or live in high-risk malarious areas during pregnancy unless this is important or essential.

If you do, take the strictest precautions to avoid mosquito bites, including cover-up and the use of DEET-based insect repellents used at the normally recommended concentration: this is not harmful to mother or foetus. Chloroquine and proguanil (Paludrine) are considered safe in pregnancy but give less than 50 per cent protection. Mefloquine is now considered by most experts to be safe during pregnancy and at the time of conception. Malarone and doxycycline are not currently recommended in pregnancy.

Leisure pursuits and pregnancy

This is largely a matter of common sense, remembering that any accident may be harder to treat in a developing country, which means the risk to both mother and child is slightly greater. Avoid extreme sports, skiing, horseback riding and scuba diving (danger to foetus through pressure changes).

At moderate altitudes there is only a minimal reduction in the oxygen supply to the mother. Experts currently advise that pregnant women should avoid altitudes over 3,600 metres (about 12,000 feet), apart from brief stop-overs at high-altitude airports. Altitudes above 2,500 metres should be avoided in late or higher-risk pregnancies, and for delivery.

Immunizations during pregnancy

Although the risk of damage to the foetus from any vaccine given in pregnancy is extremely rare, as with all medical decisions risks and benefits have to be matched up.

Plan your immunizations in plenty of time, so that essential vaccines can be completed before conception. Tetanus and gammaglobulin for hepatitis A are safe (these are no longer readily available in the UK); other vaccines are best postponed, unless benefit clearly outweighs risk. Live vaccines should be avoided (these include yellow fever, mumps, measles, rubella (German measles), oral polio, oral typhoid, tuberculosis (BCG). So should Japanese encephalitis. Standard advice recommends that you should avoid becoming pregnant for 28 days after any live vaccine.

Make sure you have had measles and rubella immunizations – usually through MMR in childhood. If in doubt, a blood test can tell whether you have protection against rubella.

Rhesus incompatibility

There is a risk that Rhesus negative mothers who carry Rhesus positive children can have their own blood sensitized by their baby. The mother then develops Rhesus antibodies that can adversely affect any babies that she may have in the future.

The use of Anti D immunoglobulin helps prevent Rhesus illness in the newborn and is recommended for Rhesus negative mothers in the following situations:

- For use within 72 hours of birth. If facilities abroad allow the blood group of the newborn baby to be tested and the baby's blood group is confirmed Rhesus negative, an injection of Anti D immunoglobulin is not necessary. If the blood group is positive or testing is not possible, Anti D immunoglobulin should be given to the mother, whether or not any Anti D was given during pregnancy.
- For use within 72 hours of a miscarriage or threatened miscarriage, including vaginal bleeding.
- For use within 72 hours of external version, antepartum bleeding, trauma to the abdomen, amniocentesis or chorionic villus sampling.
- In some countries, e.g. the USA, guidelines recommend that Rhesus negative mothers should receive Anti D immunoglobulin at 28 weeks of pregnancy.

The vaccine should be kept between 2°C and 8°C, but can be taken in hand luggage during a flight, provided it is refrigerated on arrival. It should not be frozen. Rhesus negative women who may have further pregnancies overseas should consider taking Anti D immunoglobulin with them.

Breastfeeding and travel

There are few dangers or precautions – indeed, breastfeeding a child exclusively up to six months makes travel easier for a mother and is best for the infant. If this is not possible, mothers should seek advice on the best formula to use and its availability overseas, and must take every precaution to sterilize bottles and feeding equipment and to use boiled water.

In hot climates mothers will need to drink a greatly increased amount of fluid. This nearly always ensures adequate breast milk without the need to give supplementary water to the baby under six months.

Vaccinations

Most vaccinations are considered safe when breastfeeding but, again, it is better to postpone any that are not essential. The following should usually not be given: Japanese encephalitis; typhoid; and hepatitis A unless there is a high current risk of infection. Yellow fever should never be given.

Medicines

Most medicines are safe when breastfeeding, but always check with a medical adviser and read the Patient Information Leaflet. For malaria prevention, mothers should not use Malarone if breastfeeding children under 11 kg, and should not use it for treatment if breastfeeding children under 5 kg. Doxycycline and mefloquine are now generally considered to be safe to use when breastfeeding.

Summary of recommendations

1 Understand and act on the issues mentioned above.
2 Discuss your travel plans in detail with a medical practitioner if pregnancy is confirmed or possible.
3 Take out comprehensive travel insurance.
4 If planning a delivery overseas, check out the facilities in detail, according to the guidelines above.
5 Ensure immunizations are completed, if possible, before conception: avoid live vaccines during pregnancy and if possible delay pregnancy for 28 days after any live vaccine.
6 Take every precaution to avoid malaria: ideally, avoid living in malarious areas, especially where falciparum malaria is prevalent.
7 Report any pregnancy-related problems at once and take extra care to prevent illness.
8 If health problems arise and/or confidence diminishes in facilities available, consider an earlier return to your country of origin.

Further information

- Pregnant Traveller website: <http://www.pregnanttraveler.com>
- US Centers for Disease Control and Prevention: <http://www.cdc.gov/travel>

26

Children

This book contains a lot of information about children in different sections, so please check the index in addition to reading through the summaries below.

Most children enjoy living and travelling overseas, and many find returning home after several years in a tropical country harder than going out in the first place.

> You should not, however, assume that your children will always adapt easily. Some will find it much easier than others. Missing friends and family can be a major issue for some children, and some find coping with change much harder than others. So although going abroad with children is usually seen as a positive and life-enhancing experience, you will need to be very sensitive to their needs and to the way they react.

Overseas, problems are usually associated with illness, unhappiness at school, missing friends back home and and when one or both parents have to travel away from home, either often or for longer periods. Often children become unsettled when they perceive their parents do not have enough time to spend with them. This can, of course, happen just as easily back home.

Preparing for the adventure

> Give kids the vision! Enable older children to share 'ownership' of what you as a family will be doing. Involve them in your arrangements, excite them by what you will be involved with. In doing this, be careful not to raise false expectations or expect them to share the burden of making important decisions.

You can prepare very young children by selectively reading aloud about the country you are going to, and showing them photographs, films, DVDs or websites. Older children can be encouraged to do a project on the country, ideally at school. If the class teacher is involved and makes this a class project it can help to maintain links between children and their classmates over the coming months.

Sometimes it is worth children learning some of the local language before they go and when they arrive. The BBC do a language course especially for children under the title 'Muzzy' (see <http://www.muzzyonline.co.uk>).

If you can meet up with a family who have recently been to the place you are going to, so much the better, especially if they have children.

Usually, it is worth keeping plans to go abroad under wraps until they are reasonably firm. Continue normal school and family routines for as long as possible.

Children of all ages will need continuity with home throughout their time overseas. Encourage them to keep up friendships, send emails or even write regular letters. Favourite toys, cuddlies and books can make all the difference to the happiness of children during their first weeks overseas. Make sure there's space for toys, books and that favourite teddy. Keep a back-up trunk of other favourites not taken overseas for opening at home when you come back on leave, or for a visiting relative to bring at a strategic moment.

When overseas, try to arrange visits from friends, relatives and grandparents. These, if appropriately timed and not too long, can be enriching times – and give children a valuable sense of continuity. They can also be an opportunity (or an excuse) for an exciting family holiday.

If your assignment is remote and long-term, take extra sets of baby clothes of progressively larger sizes. Carefully think through what other things you may need to take with you, having first found out what is available from someone who has recently returned from the area you are going to. One important thing is a child car seat for any child less than four years of age. Also think about appropriate birthday and Christmas presents for at least a year ahead.

Some children worry about whether they will like the food overseas. Reassure them and take care that meals and mealtimes are enjoyable, and that you don't introduce too many new tastes and smells all at once. There is some value in alternating meals based on what your children are used to at home and local-style meals.

Finally, a word about how to handle any doting, anxious or elderly relatives or friends you will be leaving behind. They may think you are crazy or irresponsible to be going abroad, especially with children. It's worth spending time talking to them about this, reassuring them, giving them carefully thought-through information and making sure you have phone, fax and email connections sorted out to reduce the fear of isolation and what to do if 'something happens'. At the magic moment, suggest a trip so that they can come and see where you are living (if appropriate!).

Health care before leaving

Before leaving you will need to check the following:

- Vaccines will need to be updated with normal childhood vaccines, as well as getting any special vaccines needed for the trip or their time abroad (see Table 26.1 on page 243).
- Antimalarials, mosquito nets and other ways of protecting your child from mosquito bites are very important, as children can quickly become very ill with malaria. (See pages 134–5.)
- A medical check from your doctor may be needed, especially if your child has any ongoing health problems or has had a serious or significant illness in the past which may recur, such as asthma or eczema. Take full copies of any medical records with you.
- Take plenty of any medication your children need until you find out whether it is available where you will be living. If it is not, set up a system to get it sent out, plenty of time in advance.
- When designing or choosing your first-aid kit, think of the needs of your children.
- Arrange a dental check and, where relevant, an eye or hearing test.
- Know your children's blood groups if you are living in a developing country for any length of time, unless it's a relatively risk-free trip based largely in a major city.

Children's vaccines

Childhood vaccinations recommended in the UK as from 2006–7

Please note important changes from previous schedules with regard to Men C, Hib and pneumococcal vaccine.

The vaccines in Table 26.1 are given free at GP surgeries in the UK.

Chickenpox, flu vaccine, and hepatitis B are routinely used in some countries. Flu vaccine is recommended for specific groups of children in the UK.

BCG against TB is no longer routinely given, but is still recommended in certain parts of the UK where TB is common or to children of parents with TB, or brought up in high-prevalence countries.

Table 26.1 Childhood immunizations: current UK schedule

Age	Vaccine	Abbreviation
2 months	Diphtheria, tetanus, pertussis, inactivated polio	DTaP/IPV
	Haemophilus influenzae B	Hib
	Pneumococcal conjugate vaccine	PCV
3 months	Diphtheria, tetanus, pertussis, inactivated polio	DTaP/IPV
	Haemophilus influenzae B	Hib
	Meningitis C	Men C
4 months	Diphtheria, tetanus, pertussis, inactivated polio	DTaP/IPV
	Haemophilus influenzae B	Hib
	Meningitis C	Men C
	Pneumococcal conjugate vaccine	PCV
Around 12 months	*Haemophilus influenzae* B	Hib
	Meningitis C	Men C
Around 13 months	Measles, mumps, rubella	MMR
	Pneumococcal conjugate vaccine	PCV
From 3 years 4 months to 5 years	Diphtheria, tetanus, pertussis, inactivated polio	DTaP/IPV or dTaP/IPV
	Measles, mumps, rubella	MMR
From 13 to 18 years	Diphtheria, tetanus and polio	Td/IPV

Travel vaccinations in children

You should receive advice from your travel health adviser about which immunizations are recommended for all members of your family, including children, for the particular trip you will be making.

243

There is not full agreement on the lowest recommended ages, and different manufacturers of similar vaccines sometimes recommend different lowest ages.

The reason for setting a lower age limit is largely because certain vaccines are less effective below certain ages. Safety concerns are also a reason. Table 26.2 gives commonly recommended lower ages. A useful website is <http://www.immunisation.nhs.uk>.

Table 26.2 Immunizations: lowest recommended ages

Vaccine	Lowest recommended age
Cholera	2 years
Hepatitis A	Available from 1 year. We usually recommend from 5 years.
Hepatitis B	Birth, often in practice 6 weeks
Meningitis ACWY	Normally 2 years
Japanese encephalitis	12 months (unless risk is high)
Measles	13 months (as MMR)
Pneumococcal	2 months
Rabies	12 months upwards, unless high risk
Rubella	13 months (as MMR)
TB (BCG)	Birth
Tick-borne encephalitis	12 months to 12 years: paediatric dose. Over 12 years: adult dose.
Typhoid	2 years
Yellow fever	9 months

Notes: 1 There are differences in the recommended lower ages both between countries and depending on the manufacturer of the vaccine. This list should be taken as a guide only. Check with your travel health adviser.

2 With some vaccines, e.g. hepatitis B, there are differences between ages recommended in national immunization programmes and those advised for travellers moving from a low-risk to a higher-risk location.

Living overseas

Allow plenty of time at the beginning so you can get to know and understand your new environment together. Encourage your children to make friends with local children and families – but at their speed, not yours. Some children will react to the new situation with withdrawal and shyness. Give them space to develop relationships in the way and at the speed with which they feel comfortable.

If more serious withdrawal occurs, give additional home support and less contact with unfamiliar or frightening aspects of the culture around them. They may in addition be missing friends at home, but may not always say so.

After a period of withdrawal, gently encourage new friendships with other children and introduce them to enjoyable aspects of life in your new location.

If there are local customs that frighten young children – cheek-pinching in South Asia is a common example – explain that this is the normal way of greeting children and is not an act of hostility.

Monitor your children's experience of the schools they go to, making sure they are not getting academically behind compared to their contemporaries at home, and also that no unusual customs or patterns of discipline are causing unspoken anxiety.

You can help family bonding by making sure that each member is familiar with what the others do and the places where they work and study. In many cases, children will take an active and informed interest in the work you are involved with if you share it with them and give them a sense of ownership and involvement. If you travel out from home as part of your work, try to take the children with you from time to time.

Make plenty of time for family activities. Many children brought up overseas retain lifelong memories of family picnics, visits to safari parks, tropical beaches and mountains or just simple family days together. Holidays can take on new dimensions overseas, so never put them off in favour of all the really important things adults have to do.

Workaholics often come into their own when abroad – to everybody's disadvantage, especially their children's.

Finally: when travelling with small children take special care they don't get lost while they (or you) wander off to investigate the latest sight, sound or animal. They should carry with them identity and contact details. And take careful precautions in crossing any road.

Education overseas

Before confirming an overseas assignment, do careful research into school options and assess how suitable they will be for the likely duration of your time overseas. You will need to talk to other families who have had recent experience of the area you are going to.

A local school has many advantages for younger children as it helps them to feel part of the scene. This may be overshadowed, however, by variable quality of teaching and a sense of cultural isolation if your children are not accepted as ordinary members of the class. You will also need to make sure that local forms of discipline are OK for your children.

Home schooling is an option that suits some families well, but definitely not others. Check it out carefully, looking at different systems, preferably choosing one compatible with British educational requirements or those of your home country.

Children of secondary school age may do better at international schools, even if this means boarding. Boarding is hugely popular with some children, loathed by a few and agreeable to most. If children do board, visit as often as possible and be sensitive to any stress or unhappiness which may arise from bullying, loneliness, over-strict teachers or rare cases of abuse. Most international schools offer an excellent education, but try to find one that can prepare children for the exams they would normally be taking if back home.

If children board back in their home country, make sure they have guardians they – as well as you – approve of and like. During holidays, be especially careful to make them feel wanted and affirmed. This will mean pre-planning so that one or both parents have time free. Children who go to boarding school may subconsciously equate this with rejection, meaning that holidays or special visits are of great importance. Decisions by longer-serving expatriate families regarding when to come home are really important, and need to be thought about in advance on the basis of well-researched data.

Feeding children overseas

It is worth breastfeeding for one or even two years, if that fits in with your family and work routines. Apart from all the other benefits, it makes diarrhoea less likely.

Try to prepare feeds for the baby yourself (using carefully washed utensils), rather than leaving it to the cook, houseboy or ayah unless you have carefully trained them. It is better not to feed any reheated food to very young children (see page 88).

Make sure there is a cool supply of water at all times so that children don't have to make secret visits to the tap or well when arriving home thirsty.

Because of the heat, children may have less appetite than in the UK. This means that a balanced diet is especially important. Include a good source of protein – either eggs, meat, fish or lentils – as well as regular fresh fruit and vegetables. Keep a growth chart for children under five to monitor weight and height. These are usually available from the local clinic or health centre – it does not matter too much if they are not in English. Take seriously any unexplained fall in weight or flattening of the curve.

Illnesses abroad

By leaving Boston or Birmingham you do not necessarily leave behind sore throats, earaches, snuffles and coughs. As a parent you may worry that ordinary symptoms are caused by extraordinary illnesses. Usually, with the exception of malaria, they are not.

When young children become ill overseas it can be extremely worrying. This means that if you are planning a long stay, one of your first jobs is to identify the best local health facility (plus an appropriate back-up and better-equipped referral centre). Visit, meet the staff and find out what levels of care they can give. Then when illness does strike you will have Plan A and Plan B, which will reduce your fear and anxiety.

You should take special note of the following symptoms and situations:

Abdominal symptoms

Only the luckiest child (or adult) will escape diarrhoea. Start ORS at once (see pages 104–5); breastfed babies should continue to take breast milk. Giardia is common in children, and may be the cause of persistent diarrhoea or flatulence in any member of the family. Threadworms causing itchy bottoms are common, and all family members over the age of two should be treated with mebendazole 100 mg tablets (one tablet twice daily for three days) or a single 500 mg tablet if *any* family member has symptoms. Mebendazole kills four types of abdominal worm (round, thread, whip and hook). In fact, it is good practice to deworm the whole family every six months using the same dose (see pages 309–11). Abdominal pain, especially if it persists and is accompanied by fever, could be appendicitis, especially if it is central or in the lower right-hand side.

Accidents

These are among the greatest hazards overseas. A few days after arrival, do a risk assessment of the house and its environs and assess it creatively for any obvious or potential risks, never forgetting the family medicine shelf, probably groaning under a heavier weight than back home. Check the cooking area carefully, making sure that hot handles cannot be easily reached and pans pulled off the stove. Crossing roads in a developing country is a skill children should only acquire at the side of an adult, especially if driving is on a side opposite from the one you are used to at home, you live in a city or are visiting one from up-country. (See also pages 164–6.)

Cough or difficulty breathing

Beware of pneumonia, which you should suspect if the respiration rate starts to increase, and urgently if it reaches 50 or more per minute, or if there is in-drawing of the ribs or flaring of the nostrils on breathing. See a doctor and start antibiotics, such as amoxicillin or erythromycin at the correct dose for age. Asthma is common in children and may start for the first time when you are overseas. Any severe attack of wheezing needs skilled treatment quickly. Croup is common in children and can be serious, especially between six months and three years (see pages 284–5).

Dogs and animals

A family pet is often a vital member of the overseas family. Make sure the dog's rabies injections are always up to date (see page 99). Actively discourage your children from ever approaching, touching or stroking an unfamiliar dog or any other unknown animal. Make absolutely sure that children wash their hands with soap and water before eating, especially if they have been playing with animals.

Fever

This may be caused by malaria (see below) or by any common childhood illness. Treat high fever (over 38°C) by undressing (under a mosquito net), tepid sponging and paracetamol (not aspirin in children under 16). High fever or any fever that persists for more than eight hours, especially in a malarious area, means you should see a doctor. If this is not possible and you are in a malarious area or have recently come from one, treat for malaria as any delay can be dangerous. You must then seek advice if symptoms are not definitely improving within 24 hours (see pages 134–5).

Headache accompanied by vomiting or stiff neck

With or without a rash this spells immediate referral to a doctor – it may be meningitis (see pages 319–20).

Infected cuts and grazes

In hot and especially in humid climates, minor injuries easily get infected. Clean all breaks in the skin with care (removing all dirt and foreign bodies), then use antiseptic cream and keep covered with a light non-adherent dressing, frequently changed, until the skin is healed over (see pages 329–33). Boils are common (see page 330). Especially when outdoors, children should wear appropriate shoes to protect against both injury and acquiring hookworm. They should preferably wear shoes indoors as well.

Scorpion and snake bites

Scorpions like dark places. Teach your children to check their slippers and shoes before putting them on and to take care when putting their hands into boxes or into any dark place. If snakes are common, set up a family drill on how to avoid them and deal with them (see page 202).

Sleep problems

Children, like adults, may suffer from disturbed sleep when going to a new environment, especially if it is hot or there are unfamiliar smells and noises. Heat, the whining of mosquitoes or prickly heat may add to the problems. In addition, it is easy for children to be stimulated or alarmed by new and bewildering experiences. Often the best remedy is to allow the child to talk and play, even if it is beyond normal bedtime – extra contact with parents may be all that is needed. If this and other remedies fail, or if you are desperate for sleep, then promethazine (Phenergan) or trimeprazine (Vallergan) for a few nights at the recommended dose for age can help to break the cycle. Occasionally these stimulate rather than sedate. If you have children three or under, give a trial run before you travel, then take a small supply with you.

Sunburn

The combination of sun, light or absent clothing, excited children and distracted parents spells danger. Allow your children's skin to acclimatize gradually, starting with 15 minutes' exposure only, using high-factor sun lotion (SPF 25 or above). When swimming or on seaside holidays, take a long-sleeved shirt and stay in the shade during the middle of the day. If sunburn does occur, blame yourself and not your child, apply lacto calamine and watch out for any infection (see page 200).

Medicines

For all but the shortest trips it is worth taking one or more courses of standby antibiotics, an antihistamine, travel sickness pills, etc., especially if you are going to a resource-poor country or you are not sure if the medicines you need will be good quality and easily available (see Appendix C). Make sure you avoid medicines that are unsafe in children, and use the correct dose for age by consulting the Patient Information Leaflet. For medically or technically minded parents there is a Child Health Formulary online at <http://bnfc.org>. In a malarious area, never run out of prophylactics and keep a standby with you for treatment (see pages 131–2).

27

Physical disability

Please also read the section on pages 28–59 about travelling with pre-existing conditions.

Background

Provided you choose your destination and means of transport with care, physical handicap does not disqualify you from serious travel. Inhabitants and hosts in many countries are often very helpful. An 80-year-old relative of the writer recently made a three-week journey to a remote part of western China four months after a severe stroke had left him completely paralysed down one side and temporarily without speech. His secret? Determination, a sensitive travelling companion and careful pre-planning with airlines and accommodation.

Wheelchairs

A wheelchair should be robust, foldable, lightweight and as narrow as is comfortable. It should be well tested before the journey, and accompanied by a few simple repair tools. Battery-driven chairs are probably best avoided. A strong and considerate travelling companion for all but the hardiest is essential.

It is helpful to find out accurate details about both the flight and accommodation, not only to make travel as enjoyable as possible but also to reduce anxiety about the unknown. Useful information about the flight can be ascertained from the airline by using a simple questionnaire (see Table 27.1).

MEDIF forms

Under certain conditions you will need to complete what is known as a MEDIF form. This comes in two parts: you complete one part and your doctor the other. Some doctors will have a copy; otherwise you can usually obtain one from IATA, the International Air Transport Association, <http://www.iata.org>.

A MEDIF form usually needs to be completed in the case of recent severe or significant illness, injury, surgery or recent hospitalization: also if you need oxygen or other medical equipment.

Table 27.1 Questions to ask an airline about wheelchair access

1 Does the airline operate direct flights from your local airport? Are connecting flights necessary?
2 Facilities available at check-in:
   (a) Are check-in desks suitable for wheelchair users?
   (b) Is a member of staff dedicated to assist at the airport?
   (c) Is there provision of an alternative wheelchair, to allow the passenger's chair to be loaded on to the aircraft?
   (d) Is there assistance to dismantle the wheelchair (including battery operated), deflate tyres, etc?
3 Boarding the aircraft:
   (a) Is wheelchair access always possible?
   (b) If not, how does the passenger board the aircraft?
4 Access on aircraft:
   (a) Is a special wheelchair available?
   (b) Are toilets accessible?
5 Destination airport:
   (a) Is disembarkation by wheelchair always possible?
   (b) If not, how does the passenger disembark?
   (c) Is a member of staff dedicated to assist at the airport?
   (d) Is there assistance to collect luggage?
   (e) Is there assistance to reassemble the wheelchair?

Source: Modified from Occupational Health Department, SmithKline Beecham

General advice

Here are some commonsense guidelines:

- During the flight, exercise or massage your legs to prevent clot formation, and get advice from your doctor about how to prevent deep vein thrombosis (see pages 72–4).
- Continue to take medication (including diuretic pills). Keep all medication in your hand luggage (apart from a few spares) to avoid anxiety and in case of delays.
- Keep a list of any medication you are on, with a duplicate for your travelling companion or contact at home.
- Have a copy of your medical records and a recent letter from your doctor containing any advice or information you or a travelling colleague might need.
- Take out full travel insurance to cover any pre-existing conditions, even if it means paying extra premiums.

- Travellers who are severely hearing-impaired will need a companion who can pass on advice and information and interpret needs to hosts overseas.

Information about wheelchairs and mobility for the disabled is available from the Disabled Living Foundation, and information on other travel-related issues from Holiday Care (see Appendix H, page 374). Consider reading the book *Nothing Ventured*, a collection of travel vignettes by disabled globetrotters (see Further Reading).

The British Airways website has very useful information on the practical aspects of travelling with a disability: <http://www.britishairways.com/travel/healthmedcond/>.

SECTION 3
When you return

28

Illness on return home

There are two reasons why you may need to see a doctor when you return home. The first is because you have symptoms or health worries that you need to get checked out. The second is because you want to have a routine check even though you feel well, in case you may have picked up any tropical or other infection.

Symptoms that need to be checked out when you get home

> If you have been working hard or return after a long or stressful assignment, you can feel seriously tired when you arrive home and often your immunity is lowered. This makes it a common time to pick up colds, chest infections or other infectious illnesses. It also makes it more likely you may have a recurrence of malaria.

Some illnesses may show themselves for the first time after you get home, while others may have started abroad but become worse or more obvious when back in your home country. The list of illnesses and symptoms below is meant as a guide and is not fully comprehensive.

Bilharzia

If you have had any contact with fresh water in areas where this is known to occur, you may later develop symptoms. Katayama fever (acute schistosomiasis) causes fever and usually wheezy cough, itching and sometimes diarrhoea. It needs treating without delay. Bilharzia can also produce blood in the urine or stool – or not give any symptoms at all (see pages 277–81). The most commonly used blood test usually only becomes positive from about 60 days after you were infected.

Cough or chest symptoms

Chest infections often hit international travellers during or just after their return home. If this is the case you should see a doctor, who may suggest antibiotics. Also make sure that you report any cough that persists for more than three weeks (see pages 343–4). One rare but important cause of chest pain is a blood clot in the lung. This may cause sudden pain or shortness of breath, usually within seven to 14 days after a long flight. The small clots arise from a deep vein thrombosis (DVT) in your legs, meaning one of your calf muscles will usually feel sore if you press it (see page 74).

Diarrhoea and other bowel symptoms

Attacks of diarrhoea that started overseas may continue at home. Symptoms occasionally occur for the first time. There are many causes, including dysenteries (bacterial and amoebic), Salmonella, Campylobacter and Giardia. The last often causes persistent loose motions with flatulence (see pages 107–8). Diarrhoea usually disappears without treatment, but you should see a doctor and take a fresh stool specimen *either* if it persists for longer than seven days after returning home *or* if there is any blood or mucus in the stool. Continue to report symptoms until either your bowels have returned to their normal pre-travel state or you feel suitably reassured.

If certain organisms such as Salmonella, Shigella or Cryptosporidium show up on your stool test, you may occasionally be asked to have three clear tests before being allowed back into full social circulation. This especially applies to schoolchildren and food handlers, but practices vary from one part of the country to another, and from country to country.

Persistent diarrhoea, especially after returning from South Asia, may be a sign of malabsorption, in which case you will probably have lost some weight and have pale, floating stools. It is often associated with milk intolerance. This is easily treated, but you must report your symptoms to a doctor, preferably one with tropical experience (see pages 108–9).

Sometimes repeated bowel problems abroad can trigger an irritable bowel syndrome, or a variation of this called post-infectious irritable bowel syndrome (see pages 108–9) – a common and benign condition with irregular motions and abdominal pain. Again, this should be diagnosed by a doctor rather than by yourself.

Remember that diarrhoea or bowel symptoms after you get home may have nothing to do with your travels – see a doctor if abnormal symptoms persist, or if you are an older traveller.

Intestinal worms of various sorts may first come to light on return home (see pages 309–11).

Fever or malaria

A sensible rule is to assume that fever after returning home from a malarious area is malaria until proved otherwise. This is especially important in the first three months, when malignant malaria commonly recurs or even appears to occur for the first time. Benign forms may recur for months, occasionally years, after returning from the tropics.

If you develop a fever or symptoms that you think could be malaria, follow the advice given on pages 133–4. Although fever may have a variety of causes, *it is dangerous to ignore symptoms of fever after returning from a malarious area.* Sometimes a mild virus or even a cold may trigger malaria, and symptoms are often atypical, without the classic phases of shivering or sweating. Dengue fever, now found in most of the developing world, can mimic malaria; so can typhoid. There are several rarer causes of fever, some of which are very important to diagnose early.

Headaches

Get these checked if they are more severe than usual, come on for the first time or wake you in the morning. The commonest reason will be stress and overwork, but infections such as malaria can also be a cause, as can rarer tropical infections.

HIV and AIDS

If you have had unprotected sex or are a health worker or have had any at-risk incident, you may want an HIV test on return. This is more important than it used to be because drug treatment used early can greatly delay the onset of AIDS. So if you've been at risk, it's worth having an HIV test (see page 155). Many people worry about jeopardizing future insurance cover. Having an HIV test is unlikely to affect your premium, provided it is negative.

Persisting ill health, weight loss or unusual symptoms

If in doubt, check it out. Ill health of any sort starting during an overseas trip or persisting after return should always be investigated.

Psychological problems

Coming home can often be a time of stress, especially after a long or difficult assignment. A tropical check, if the doctor has time, can be a good opportunity to talk about any difficult experiences. Certain events overseas are known to make adjustment more difficult or to increase the risk of flashbacks or other unpleasant symptoms. For this reason we would recommend personal debriefing or a confidential review (see pages 262–4).

Sexually transmitted infections

An HIV check can be included as part of your tropical check-up either by your GP or in a tropical diseases centre. Alternatively, it can be carried out at a GUM (genitourinary medicine) clinic (also known as an STD – sexually transmitted disease – or, in the past, a VD – venereal disease – clinic). This is probably the best place if you are worried that you may have picked up another sexually transmitted infection, such as chlamydia.

Skin problems

Report any unusual skin symptoms. Groin itch, athlete's foot and other fungus infections are common. Persistent rashes, sores, ulcers or suspicious moles must be checked, as should any roughened skin patches in long-term tropical residents (see page 200). If you develop a sore that does not clear up and ulcerates, this could be cutaneous leishmaniasis from a sandfly bite. This is becoming commoner, especially in North Africa, the Middle East and western Asia (see pages 315–16).

Tiredness

This is almost universal after an overseas posting or mission or even after an active holiday. Sometimes it may persist for weeks, especially in the case of humanitarian aid workers who have worked hard with reduced sleep and no holiday for weeks on end. However, make sure you see a doctor and have this carefully checked if it is more severe than you would expect or persists for longer.

Urinary symptoms

If you have any symptoms such as passing urine more frequently or pain during urination, or you notice blood in your urine, see a doctor. Urinary tract infections are common overseas, and dehydration, bumpy journeys and increasing sexual activity can all add to the risk. Your symptoms may indicate a bladder infection (cystitis) or could be a sign of a sexually transmitted infection.

Career blank

It is very common, after taking a year out or after exciting or significant experiences abroad, to feel really confused about what you should do next. In this case it is worth arranging a career interview, either with your local careers service or privately (see page 373).

29

Having a tropical check-up

Who should have one?

If you are well with no symptoms, opinions vary as to whether a medical is necessary. Many people are worried that they may have some hidden illness that will declare itself, with mortal results, months or years later. Although this is rarely the case, you would probably benefit from a medical if you come into one of the following categories:

- if you are unwell or have any persisting symptoms, including unusual tiredness; also if you have loose bowels, which could indicate giardiasis, amoebiasis or another infection;
- if you may have picked up an illness that only shows itself later (bilharzia is probably the commonest (e.g. from Lake Malawi), while TB, HIV, Chagas' disease, sleeping sickness, hepatitis B and filarial infection are all much rarer);
- if you have lived in a developing country for more than 12 months;
- if your style of travel has put you at special risk (this includes any prolonged stay or adventure travel in remote or primitive locations, or work in refugee, famine or war situations);
- if you or your family continue to be worried that you have 'picked something up';
- if you continue to feel unduly stressed or depressed for more than a few weeks after returning home;
- if your company, mission or aid agency requires it;
- if you are a frequent traveller, e.g. you make two or more trips per year to a developing country or resource-poor area. Some specialists recommend a medical every two years for frequent travellers, especially if they are involved in high-pressure jobs at agency or company headquarters.

What does a tropical check-up consist of?

A tropical check-up usually involves filling in a personal health form, either on paper or online, followed by detailed questioning about any illnesses you have had, areas visited or health concerns. There will be an examination, which includes listening to the chest, checking for any enlargement of spleen, liver or lymph glands, feeling the abdomen, a careful check of the skin and an examination of the ears, eyes and mouth.

At some centres (including InterHealth) there is also a chance to talk through any difficult overseas experiences.

Investigations usually include a stool and urine test and, where appropriate, a haemoglobin and full blood count (including percentage of one of the white blood cells known as eosinophils – a useful marker of parasitic infections). Liver function tests can also be arranged – useful if you have been regularly exceeding a sensible alcohol intake, or have been taking mefloquine or doxycycline long term (e.g. more than six months) to prevent malaria. Tests can also be arranged for bilharzia, filaria, Chagas' disease (found in parts of South America only), HIV or any other condition you or your doctor are concerned about. Chest X-rays and ECGs are only rarely necessary. The most useful 'tropical tests' are stool examinations and full blood counts.

If you are a health worker or have previously had a course of hepatitis B immunizations, you can have your blood titres measured to see whether you need a booster or are immune for life (see page 384).

It is worth remembering that a single negative stool test does not mean your gut is necessarily free of parasites. If symptoms continue, consider having two further stool tests, preferably with fresh stools taken to the laboratory within two hours. Some laboratories can arrange a stool immunology test, sometimes known as an Enteric Organism Detection Test; this is more sensitive than many standard tests and can sometimes pick up a cause of infection which may otherwise be missed.

Many doctors recommend in addition that all those returning from an assignment in developing countries, either permanently or for pro-longed leave, should take a course of mebendazole 100 mg tablets for worms (one tablet twice a day for three days for adults or children aged two and over).

Who should carry out a tropical check-up?

If you are unwell or have symptoms, you should be carefully checked by someone trained or experienced in tropical or travel medicine. In the UK this might be your GP, university health centre, NHS tropical diseases unit or other centre specializing in travel medicine (see Appendix G). For any NHS referral you would normally need a letter from your GP. If you are wanting a check-up in another country where you are living or working, seek out a doctor or hospital with experience in tropical health or travel medicine. (See Appendix G.)

Personal debriefing or confidential review

Any difficult, dangerous or frightening experience overseas, either short term or long term, may have various effects that you feel after returning home. So can the cumulative hassles from lots of minor frustrations or endless often unsuccessful efforts to get on well with your colleagues (or friends). These effects may make adjustment more difficult, lead you to feel anxious or depressed, or cause gloomy thoughts, flashbacks or disturbing dreams that don't seem to go away. Occasionally they can lead on to a more serious condition known as post-traumatic stress disorder (PTSD) or bring to light underlying tensions or conflicts that may have been present before you went overseas.

Many of these problems can be greatly lessened by a chance to talk about any bad experience in a free-ranging debriefing interview on return home. If you have been on an assignment, your sending organization will normally arrange an operational debrief where you can discuss any work-related issues that need sorting out. Make sure you have one.

But in addition it is often helpful to have a *personal debrief* (sometimes known as a *confidential review* or *personal impact review*) during which you can talk about your feelings, fears and experiences.

The best time to do this is probably between three days and four weeks after arriving home – which gives you time to reflect, but not enough time to start endlessly recycling your experiences. If you've had a really traumatic experience, you should fix your debrief earlier.

Personal debriefing is best thought of as a chance to talk about 'normal reactions to abnormal situations'. We suggest you consider arranging one of these if you come into any of the categories below:

- You have been working in a situation of famine, war, conflict or danger.
- You have experienced actual or threatened kidnap, rape, assault, armed robbery or other frightening experiences.
- You have had any serious or long-standing conflicts with colleagues.
- You have had an assignment that has been cut short, has been especially difficult or has not worked out as expected.
- You are experiencing symptoms such as the following: recurrent bad dreams; flashbacks, panic or unexplained anxiety coming on for no obvious reason; the need to avoid situations, places or people because of the serious discomfort or anxiety they arouse. These symptoms can indicate PTSD which can be relieved or cured by skilled care.

These reviews give you a chance to talk in a relaxed setting with a trained debriefer or counsellor. You can talk freely about any aspect of your overseas experience. You should see these sessions as a confidential and routine review to help you reflect on your experiences, and to integrate them into your past, present and future life. Debriefs are distinct from counselling, though at the end of the session you may mutually agree that a series of counselling sessions might be helpful.

If you have been with a group of people who have all suffered a similar traumatic experience, a group or individual debriefing for two to three hours can sometimes be helpful. This is known as Critical Incident Debriefing, or CID. Ideally, it should take place three to five days after the incident. However, CID needs to be done in an appropriate way by someone with special skills and following careful guidelines, or there is a danger that experiences can be reinforced rather than relieved.

Finally, it is worth mentioning that some people find their religious faith challenged or threatened by experiences overseas, especially when this has included seeing severe or mass suffering. Often symptoms are more severe after manmade situations which have included brutality and suffering, rather than natural disasters, terrible as those can be. If this applies to you it is worthwhile seeing a spiritual counsellor, chaplain, pastor or minister for prayer and discussion. Many people find that once they develop a well-thought-through 'theology of suffering', their faith can grow rather than falter. See Further Reading on page 403.

Returning home from the viewpoint of children

Re-adapting

Periods of leave at home need to be arranged so that children do not feel squeezed out or of secondary importance. Make sure they see the people *they* want to see and do at least some of the things *they* want to do. Help them to understand the way their own country ticks, so that when they finally come home they are not strangers in their own land. In the event of an extended leave, one or two terms at school can be very beneficial.

If your children have had more than one or two years abroad it is not advisable to bring them straight back into a school year when they are preparing for important exams (e.g. GCSEs or pre-university exams in the UK),without at least a prior year to get adjusted.

Teenagers often find re-adaptation to their home country difficult, and will need the most favoured opportunities possible for re-entry. You will need to explain to class teachers (and head teachers) in detail about your child's overseas background, both academic and cultural, otherwise he or she may be seriously misunderstood and humiliated.

Children returning from a length of time overseas will often come across to their peers and also to their teachers as odd or different. They will probably feel outsiders themselves. Some of their experiences may not be believed or, even worse, be mocked or ignored.

There are some things you as parents can do to make things easier for your children.

- Make sure they have the latest style of footwear, trainers and school bags.
- Try to minimize any differences between them and their peers.
- Make sure they have the latest style of clothes and the latest gizmos.
- Knowing how to use mobile phones and to send text messages is essential.

You may groan at how much all this will cost, but it may turn out to be the best use possible of the limited amount you probably have to spend. It's especially important that your children don't feel the odd ones out if their normal tendency is to be shy or quiet, or if they don't mix easily.

Playing football (or another sport), being a club supporter and knowing the names of the team members can increase street-cred and help in the popularity stakes. When abroad it's easy to get familiar with the website of your favourite team. If you encourage your children to keep in touch with what is going on at home and with what their peers are interested in and talking about, then they will fit in much more quickly and feel much less like outsiders. That can do wonders for their self-confidence and eventual success.

For older children returning to their home country, it can be very helpful to meet up with other recently returned families and share experiences. Also, church youth groups, Sunday schools or other special-interest clubs, as well as the wider family (including grandparents), can be very helpful in giving children added security.

Third-culture kids

The term 'third-culture kid' or TCK is being increasingly used, and it is very important that this concept is understood by parents who have spent years living away from their own country. A TCK is a child from one culture who has grown up in one or more other cultures, and so really belongs to a third culture which is different from the others. TCKs have a number of special characteristics, both strengths and vulnerabilities. One is to recognize and feel an empathy with other TCKs, almost as though they belong to the same 'tribal group'. Often other TCKs will be the first friends children returning from overseas will make at school or university.

TCKs often feel uncomfortable and different, especially in their 'home' country, but often see no reason why and feel there must be something intrinsically the matter with them. Understanding this as parents and helping your children to understand these feelings while they are still teenagers can be very helpful for their later self-confidence and self-understanding.

If this rings bells for your family, see page 403 for further reading.

Health on return

Along with other family members, children should have a medical examination if they have lived in a developing country for longer than a year. There are more details about this on pages 261–2. It is sensible for all family members over the age of two to take a final course of worm medicine, as described on page 262. If children have swum in areas where bilharzia is known to occur they should have a blood test at least 60 days after their last exposure (and so should their parents). Malaria commonly occurs weeks or even months after coming home. Untreated malaria in children is *dangerous*. If you have been in a malarious area, do report any unexplained fever at once and ask for a malaria blood test (blood slide).

Doctors are not fully agreed whether routine health screening is needed on healthy children who have been living in a developing country. In terms of tests, the most useful ones are stool tests, blood counts (tests looking at red cells, white cells and platelets, often known as a full blood count) and a bilharzia blood test if there has been possible exposure.

Of course, if your child is unwell or does not seem to be thriving, putting on weight or displaying a normal amount of energy, a full medical check is essential, ideally by someone familiar with tropical or travel medicine.

Registering with a doctor

This section refers mainly to people who are based in the UK.

If you handed in your medical card on going overseas you should now re-register with a GP. If you are not sure how long you will be staying at your address, you can register as a temporary resident for up to three months, during which time you normally enjoy full NHS access. When registering permanently, your doctor or the practice nurse will want to see you for a brief medical, but this does not take the place of a tropical check-up. If you have previously been registered with either the same practice or a different one, it may take at least six weeks for your old notes to be retrieved. As a temporary resident your previous notes would not normally be sent for. The NHS is in the process of going over to electronic records, but this is likely to take several years and may make the situation with your notes either better or worse than previously.

NHS eligibility for UK citizens

Current guidelines are complex and less favourable than they used to be; see Appendix F.

Seeing a dentist

In the UK it is still possible to see a dentist under the NHS in many parts of the country. There are still charges to pay but they are much less than going privately. It is usually worth trying to see a dentist known to you from before or who looks after any members of your family or friends with whom you are staying. NHS Direct will tell you if there are any NHS dentists in your area (tel. 0845 4647).

Seeing an optician

As a general rule it is worth having an eye check at least every five years, and more often if you wear glasses or contacts. If there is any personal or family history of eye disease, especially glaucoma, you should have an eye check including a pressure check every year over the age of 40.

In the UK eye checks are free for those 60 or over, under 16, or under 18 if in full-time education, and also for those over 40 with a personal or close family history of glaucoma or a personal history of diabetes.

Being referred to a specialist

In the UK those coming home on short leave are having increasing difficulty getting specialist referrals within the UK National Health Service.

If you need a specialist referral, follow this procedure:

See your GP as soon as possible after getting home or, if you know your GP, write from overseas; explain the problem and your limited timescale, being sure to mention if you are serving with a charitable organization.

If you have been referred to a consultant and there is a delay in you getting an appointment, write a courteous note to the consultant to whom you have been referred, marked for his or her personal attention, explaining your circumstances. If there is still a delay make a weekly call to the consultant's secretary asking if there has been a cancellation.

If this fails, consider seeing the consultant privately. If you have a medical at InterHealth and need a referral, this can be arranged, though not usually through the NHS. Any Anglican clergy and their spouses or past or present mission partners of an Anglican missionary society are entitled to free specialist referral at St Luke's Hospital, London, and its associated consultants.

Some travel health insurance schemes cover the cost of urgent or essential health care on return home, especially if the problem first started overseas. In this case a private referral to a specialist is a good option. But check the terms of your insurance carefully.

30
Reverse culture shock

Even if you are one of the lucky ones who can quickly adapt from one culture to another and feel as comfortable after ten days in Taunton as after your ten weeks in Timbuktu, it may still be worth reading this.

What is it?

Many people who have lived, loved or worked abroad find settling back home really difficult. Often it seems harder and more complicated than the culture shock you experienced, or perhaps didn't experience, when you first went abroad.

When you go, you're geared up for change; when you come back, you are expecting to be familiar with everything – but *you* may have changed. Your life and those of your friends and relatives may seem to be going in different directions. You may feel you don't want to become like many of the people you are now seeing again. On the one hand you want to try to adapt and become 'normal', and on the other you don't want to lose the experiences and the wider outlook that is now – you.

The symptoms

When you first arrive home, are met at the airport and start to recount exciting experiences as the hero, or tramp, returning home, you probably *will* feel pretty good. But after a while this gradually seems to change. For no apparent reason you start feeling listless, anxious or depressed; you feel dismayed or angry at the materialism, decadence and pettiness of people's lives, the silly things they talk about; you feel confused about yourself and about your future.

Why do you feel the way you do?

You have the *normal* condition of reverse culture shock. You have left a country you have come to appreciate. You have left a lifestyle which, despite its frustrations, was often fulfilling – and sometimes exciting. Now you are mourning the loss of all this, and you are acutely missing the good friends, favourite places and significant experiences. Last week at this time I was ... Now I am looking out of a rainy bedroom window in Birmingham.

If you have ever lost a close friend or relative you may recognize the similarity of some of your feelings now.

Your feelings on returning home

Apart from experiencing sadness about what you have left behind, you may be shocked by what you find at home: the stifling materialism, the sense of embarrassment in some countries at any open display of emotion, not being able to be real with people.

You have moved on six months or six years in your life and so have your friends – but in a different direction. Even your best buddies, who should know better, ask foolish questions about why you are not more sun-tanned, or when you are going to get a proper job. They even forget which country you have been living in, and for reasons of ignorance or embarrassment ask hardly any questions about the real things you have been doing. They seem more interested in their latest pair of Adidas or Reeboks or their favourite soaps than in the concerns of the poor.

Shopping is a shock. For a start, there are far too many things in the shops. Is it morally justified for supermarkets to sell 47 different types of breakfast cereal, and 12 varieties of yoghurt? After all, you had no fresh milk in Uganda/Bolivia/Nepal, let alone a fridge!

Coping with your feelings

If you can identify with some or all of these feelings, relax – *you're normal*. If you can't, don't worry either. Those with certain personality types can cope with change much more easily than others and take all this in their stride.

Here are some suggestions which may help:

- *Recognize and don't deny the feelings you have.* Choose a good friend with whom you can really share your feelings. Rather than being shocked, he or she may be relieved you are human! Make the most of any debriefing opportunities if you went overseas with an agency or as a volunteer.
- *Keep in touch* with your overseas friends and any projects you've been involved with. Join any group where others who have returned meet to discuss, pray or raise support for people and projects you are familiar with. Go to any reunions, debriefing and reorientation weekends or get-togethers. Keep up with friends back home that you have known overseas, such as fellow team members, but don't cling on to them just to relive the past. Make new friends and trust that the future could be equally exciting and challenging whether in Reading, Edinburgh or Peru!
- *Let the process of coming to terms with your experience* take its own time. This may take days, weeks, even months, depending on your personality as well as how long and how deeply you were involved overseas. You will learn the knack of accepting the good, avoiding the bad and recognizing what you can usefully do to help bring change within the limits of your gifts and energies.
- *Join a social group* where you will feel comfortable and where you have a shared interest. It may be church, a language course, an evening class or a club. You may want to get involved in advocacy or raising support for a project you have been involved with.
- *Get some careers advice* if you are unsure about your future. Your local careers service may be able to supply you with free and relevant information about courses and jobs. If you are near London, you can book in to see an Adult Careers Consultant at InterHealth through our partner agency, InterChange (see page 373).
- *Enjoy a good break and have a check-up.* Spend time with your family and friends and ensure you have a medical check if you feel under the weather. You may be harbouring some bugs which require treatment.
- *Know when to see someone.* If your feelings of doom and gloom persist unduly or are very severe, or if your appetite and sleep pattern become markedly disturbed, don't hesitate to see someone who can help. Some sympathetic counselling, sometimes with temporary medication, will normally hasten a cure.

Getting on with your life

With time and practice it is possible to build on your overseas experience, whether it has lasted three weeks, three months or three years. Your time abroad, whether rich and hard to leave behind or bleak and difficult to understand, will always be potentially enriching provided you integrate the experience into your personality. Who knows? It may be the gateway for a longer period abroad in the future, or the means of helping you to understand and teach those of different cultures within your home country. One thing is sure, you will have become a more interesting person because of your time away from home.

SECTION 4
Notes on important conditions

31

Notes on important conditions

This section of the book is about the tropical and non-tropical conditions that are important to travellers. The descriptions of these start on the following page.

Table 31.1 Vectors (carriers) of important infectious diseases
(World Health Organization, 2005)

Vector	Main disease transmitted
Aquatic snails	Schistosomiasis (bilharzia)
Blackflies	River blindness (onchocerciasis)
Fleas	Plague (transmitted by fleas from rats to humans)
Mosquitoes	Dengue fever
Aedes	Rift Valley fever
	Yellow fever
Anopheles	Lymphatic filariasis
	Malaria
Culex	Japanese encephalitis
	Lymphatic filariasis
	West Nile fever
Sandflies	Leishmaniasis
	Sandfly fever (Phlebotomus fever)
Ticks	Crimean-Congo haemorrhagic fever
	Lyme disease
	Relapsing fever (borreliosis)
	Rickettsial diseases including spotted fevers and Q fever
	Tick-borne encephalitis
	Tularaemia
Triatomine bugs	Chagas' disease (American trypanosomiasis)
Tsetse flies	Sleeping sickness (African trypanosomiasis)

Anthrax

Background

Although anthrax is a tiny risk for travellers, outbreaks occur from time to time and there are concerns from some countries that it could be used in bioterrorism.

The disease exists in animals, e.g. livestock and game, in many parts of the world and most cases of human illness are caused by direct contact with animals or animal skins, including leather goods. The disease is caused by *Bacillus anthracis*, a tiny bacterium which produces spores which can remain infectious for years.

Symptoms

In humans there are three forms of the disease, causing completely different symptoms. They can start within seven days of being infected, but the time from infection until the start of symptoms (the incubation period) is very variable.

- *Cutaneous (skin) anthrax* starts as a blister, usually on the hands, which ulcerates and develops a black centre. It is caused when anthrax spores get on to your skin from an infected animal hide, including leather goods sold as souvenirs which come from infected animals. It's much the commonest form. It can take up to 60 days for skin pustules to develop.
- *Pulmonary (lungs) anthrax* causes flu-like symptoms, which rapidly become severe and may quickly become fatal. It is extremely uncommon, with symptoms usually starting within seven days of becoming infected.
- *Gastrointestinal (digestive) anthrax* gives severe abdominal pain and bloody diarrhoea, is very uncommon and usually comes from eating meat from an animal that is infected by anthrax or has died from it.

Prevention

This is largely a matter of common sense – avoid touching, eating or coming into bodily contact with infected animals. Also avoid any known source of spores, including souvenirs made from animal skins. Spores often get on to the hands through small cuts and abrasions, so take care handling leather souvenir items in local markets, especially in Africa. A vaccine is available but is hardly ever recommended except for those at highest risk. Person-to-person spread does not occur.

Treatment

If anthrax is suspected, immediate treatment is essential. Ciprofloxacin is the antibiotic of choice, but doxycycline and penicillin are alternatives. They are usually given for 60 days following a possible exposure.

For further details see infectious diseases websites in Appendix H.

Backache and sciatica

This is covered on pages 36–8.

Bilharzia (schistosomiasis, bilharziasis)

Freshwater swimmers in Africa beware!

Background

What is it?

Bilharzia or schistosomiasis is becoming increasingly common in travellers. It's caused by a worm, technically a 'fluke', with a smart life cycle. This is known as Schistosoma, and there are four species giving slightly different symptoms. In fresh water where certain types of snail are present, schistosome larvae penetrate your skin, do a grand tour of the body, and then settle down in the blood vessels surrounding your bladder or large intestine. Here they produce eggs, which when released cause irritation of the bladder or bowel before rediscovering the outside world.

Where is it found?

Most travellers pick up bilharzia in sub-Saharan Africa. Lakes Malawi, Victoria, Kariba and Volta are known trouble-spots but any fresh water, including lakes, rivers, ponds and irrigation canals, may be affected, especially if they are slow-flowing or stagnant. Sea water is safe, and so is any water smelling of chlorine or stored in a snail-free environment, e.g. a clean swimming pool, or in a water tank for at least 48 hours.

Travellers also occasionally pick up bilharzia in places outside Africa, such as northeastern Brazil, some islands in the Caribbean, and parts of the Middle East and the Far East, such as tributaries of the Mekong River or in the Philippines, Indonesia and southern China. The vast majority of travellers who pick up the disease do so in Africa. For distribution, see Figure 31.1 (overleaf).

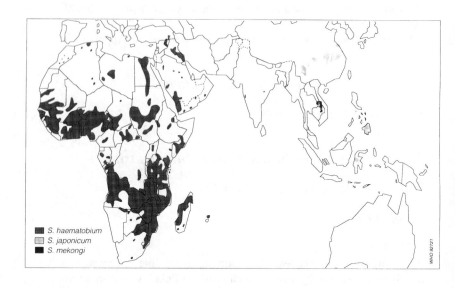

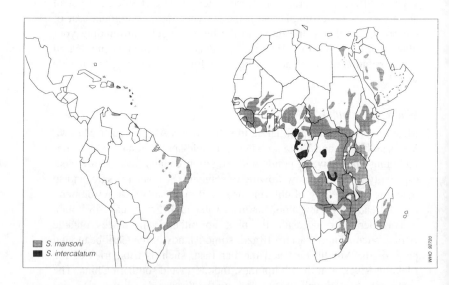

Figure 31.1 Areas where bilharzia (schistosomiasis) is found
(WHO, 1999)

Some people working internationally who were brought up in affected countries may have been infected. They should ideally have this checked out on a blood test if they are recruited to work with a company or agency.

Symptoms

- *Katayama fever or acute bilharzia* If you are very unlucky you will develop this, which can mimic malaria. Typical symptoms are fever, muscle ache, cough, wheezing, diarrhoea, sometimes with blood, and an itchy skin. This usually happens within one or two months of being exposed.
- *Chronic bilharzia* This is by far the commonest and often comes through repeated infection. However, a single exposure such as a swim in Lake Malawi may be enough to cause this or acute bilharzia. About half of all those with chronic bilharzia show no symptoms and the disease usually self-cures. The commonest symptom is tiredness, often very marked, whose cause often puzzles both the patient and the doctor. This is worth remembering because bilharzia can occasionally be incorrectly labelled as chronic fatigue syndrome.
- Blood can occur in the urine or semen from *S. haemotobium* and in the stool from *S. mansoni*, the two commonest species. Occasionally after months or years more serious symptoms occur (see below) which is why it's worth getting diagnosed and cured if you have been at risk.

Most people with bilharzia have this discovered on a routine blood test when they have a tropical check-up, and are usually unaware of symptoms.

Prevention

Prevent infection by avoiding any contact with infected water in areas where bilharzia occurs. That means you should give that alluring lake in sub-Saharan Africa a miss. Don't swim, wash, paddle, push vehicles or wade through rivers or water, especially if slow-flowing or stagnant. Don't drink water which could be infected without boiling it for one minute first. Wear protective footwear if you are walking through mud or damp areas near rivers or lakes. More obscure ways of getting bilharzia are: showering in infected water which has not been allowed to stand for at least 48 hours; and being baptized or baptizing others in rivers.

If you have foolishly exposed yourself, recent research shows that you can still reduce your risk. Preferably after a shower, apply 50 per cent DEET-based insect repellent over your whole body, excluding scalp and genitalia, 8 to 12 hours after exposure. This penetrates the skin and helps to kill larvae, which remain under the skin for some hours before moving on. Brisk rubbing down with a towel after a swim is also thought to reduce the risk.

But the advice still remains – avoid swimming in the lake!

Treatment

Bilharzia is treated by taking praziquantel (PZQ) at a total dose of 40 mg per kg, either swallowed all at one time or half in the morning and half in the evening on the same day. For people of average weight, that means four or five of the 500 mg or 600 mg tablets. Praziquantel is hard to get hold of in some countries, including the UK, but specialist travel centres will have it. Research shows that a single dose on one day is as effective as taking it for three days. PZQ cures the vast majority of infections and has little in the way of side-effects, slight dizziness, nausea and headache being the commonest.

How do you know whether you have bilharzia?

As mentioned above, you often don't know. The ELISA blood test is much the most accurate way of knowing whether you have caught it. Some laboratories can confirm this by looking for eggs in the stool and urine, but many cases are missed this way. The blood test becomes positive usually between 40 and 60 days after your last exposure. Therefore, we recommend that if at all possible you delay having the ELISA test until 60 days after your last swim, otherwise cases can be missed. Obviously, if you feel unwell in the meantime you need to see a doctor. In the midst of all your welcome-home parties, visiting your relatives, heading off to college or returning to work, don't forget to have the test if you have been at risk.

What are the long-term dangers?

If you have untreated bilharzia, and especially if you have had repeated exposures, there is a small risk that you may develop serious liver problems after many years (from *S. mansoni*) or, more commonly, changes in the bladder wall which occasionally become malignant (from *S. haemotobium*). That's one reason it's important to get checked out. More rarely, other serious health problems occur if you are infected.

How do you know if you are cured?

It is hard to confirm this. If you have used praziquantel 40–60 days after your last exposure it is extremely likely you will be cured, but using it earlier than that is not nearly so effective. So having a swim and then taking praziquantel is useless, though it may cure any infection caught from 40 days or more before.

One of the white cells, the eosinophil, is often raised in bilharzia and after you have been cured will fall down to a more normal level by about six weeks. It is worth having this rechecked, any time from six weeks after you have taken treatment.

The ELISA blood test does not help much in knowing whether you have been cured, or at least not for a long time. Recent research in over 1,000 cases of bilharzia seen at the London Hospital for Tropical Diseases shows that ELISA blood tests actually stay at the same level – or even rise to a higher level – three months after treatment in half of all travellers treated for bilharzia, and even after a year in one-third of cases. Eventually, sometimes after several years, the level on the ELISA test gradually falls. If you are worried about whether you still have bilharzia or you still have symptoms, see a specialist in tropical or travel medicine or if in the UK contact InterHealth or Edinburgh International Health Centre (see pages 369–71).

Summary

Avoid fresh water in African rivers or lakes. If you have been at any risk of catching bilharzia, arrange a blood test, ideally at least 60 days after your last exposure.

Brucellosis

Background

Brucellosis is mainly a disease of cattle, goats, sheep and camels, caused by the bacterium Brucella. Humans usually catch it through drinking infected milk or eating cheese (especially soft cheeses), butter or ice cream. It can also be caught by direct contact through the skin and mucous membranes from infected animals or animal carcasses, and through inhaling infected particles. It is common in West Asia, the Arabian peninsula and other parts of the Middle East, and scattered areas around the Mediterranean and in Africa. Agriculturalists, development workers and adventure travellers are at greatest risk.

Symptoms

These are variable and often vague, usually starting at least one month after exposure. At first there may be fever, general weakness and pain in muscles, back and joints, sometimes lasting a few weeks. Many cases then get better without treatment, but some continue, with intermittent (or 'relapsing') fever leading to profound tiredness, further muscle and joint pain and sometimes depression. In this form it can mimic chronic fatigue syndrome (see pages 183–7), or a depressive illness. Brucellosis can eventually affect almost any organ in the body. It is probably an under-diagnosed illness in travellers, and correct diagnosis and treatment as early as possible is something patients and doctors must aim for. The incubation period may be many weeks, and is nearly always three weeks or longer.

Prevention

Prevent it by making sure all non-powder milk (and milk products) are either politely refused or only drunk if pasteurized or boiled for at least one minute. Also avoid infected animals and animal carcasses; if they have to be handled, wear protective clothing. There is some evidence that infected milk as well as other infected animal parts can enter through small nicks and cuts in the skin. Those working with or in the vicinity of infected animals need to be well informed about preventing and recognizing brucellosis.

Treatment

Brucellosis is largely diagnosed by blood tests (the ELISA test is considered the most accurate) and treated under medical supervision with a combination of two drugs including doxycycline, rifampicin or a quinolone antibiotic such as ofloaxacin.

For further information see infectious diseases websites in Appendix H.

Chagas' disease
(South American 'sleeping sickness' or trypanosomiasis

Background

Though rare in travellers, this is a serious disease found in Central and South America where about 13 million people are affected. It is spread by a bug with a variety of names: assassin, kissing, triatomine, cone-nosed and vinchuca (see Figure 31.2). These creatures live in mud walls and bite at night, commonly on the face and in or on the eye. It is a risk for aid workers, adventure travellers and volunteers who sleep in mud or adobe huts in rural or poor urban areas, especially where chickens are common. Chagas' disease can also be spread through blood transfusions.

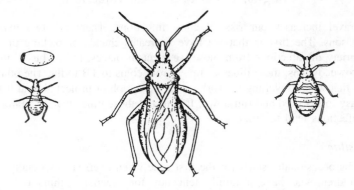

Figure 31.2 The cone-nosed bug, also known as the vinchuca, assassin or kissing bug, responsible for spreading Chagas' disease (1–4 cm long)

Symptoms

The bite is usually obvious, and the first symptom is a reddish nodule at the site of the bite, often with swelling of an eyelid. Fever commonly develops and lymph nodes become swollen. Symptoms may, however, be slight or non-existent, but serious disease, especially heart disease, heart failure and swelling of the colon or oesophagus, may occur, sometimes years later.

Prevention

This involves avoiding sleeping in the type of accommodation described above where the disease is common. If this is not possible, sleep in the middle of the hut away from the walls. An insecticide-impregnated mosquito net, if thoroughly tucked in, gives protection. Local blankets and rugs should not be used. Search your bed for hidden insects and apply DEET insect repellent to your face.

Treatment

The disease can be diagnosed by a Chagas' ELISA blood test and treatment must be started as soon as possible under expert supervision. About 50 per cent of cases can be cured if treated in the acute phase with either benznidazole or nifurtimox. This means that anyone who may have been exposed or has had an unscreened blood transfusion in affected areas of South America should request a Chagas' ELISA blood test at the time of their tropical check-up.

For further information see infectious diseases websites in Appendix H.

Coughs, colds and chest infections

Travel increases our risk of chest infections. There are two main reasons. The first is that we have a greater chance of picking up a variety of infections from those we meet in planes, trains, buses and crowded areas; these illnesses range from colds to TB to flu. The other is that when travelling or working hard on a job or project abroad it is easy to get tired and run down. It is just at those times that respiratory infections tend to strike.

Asthma

This occasionally starts for the first time when overseas, especially in children who have a family tendency for eczema, asthma or hay fever. If someone in the family develops severe or persistent wheezing or a stubborn night-cough, consult a doctor. Any episodes in a child should be discussed with a specialist or at your next home medical, to make sure you are recognizing and treating it in the best way. Wheezing is occasionally caused by tropical parasites, for example roundworms or bilharzia. There are detailed guidelines on asthma in travellers on pages 34–6.

Colds and coughs

Some people are surprised when told they can still catch a cold when living in a tropical climate. The majority of colds get better on their own, but those working long hours or following hectic international schedules frequently develop chest infections, especially at the end of an assignment or on returning home.

If a cold fails to clear up after a few days, and if in addition you are run down or have a tendency to bronchitis or sinusitis, see a doctor and consider starting on antibiotics such as amoxicillin (adult dose), 500 mg three times a day for seven days or, if allergic to penicillin, erythromycin 500 mg four times daily (see Appendix C).

Croup

This symptom in children is relatively common and always alarming. If a child develops difficulty breathing with a loud noise, or stridor, on inspiration, croup is the likely cause.

Treatment

Remain calm. Hold your child confidently and reassuringly in an upright position; remove any pets from the room. Try to steam up the room, for example by boiling a kettle or saucepan, using an umbrella or sheet as a canopy. Although there is no convincing evidence that this actually cures the attack, the comfort and sense of control it gives appears to be helpful to both children and adults.

Most attacks will gradually subside, but remain within earshot for the rest of the night as the attack may recur.

If symptoms are severe or continue to worsen, or your child is going blue around the lips, get immediate medical help. Discuss any attack of croup when you or your child next see a doctor or have a medical on return home.

Influenza

For details on flu, including avian flu, see pages 304–8.

Pneumonia

Pneumonia, especially in children, may develop fast, particularly after a cold or when very tired. Pneumonia usually leads to a high fever, shortness of breath, cough, sometimes pain in the chest and occasionally blood-stained sputum or phlegm.

A respiratory rate of over 50 breaths per minute in a child, and/or indrawing of the ribs or flaring of the nostrils, usually means pneumonia. Get medical help at once, but also start your child on an antibiotic, e.g. amoxicillin or erythromycin at the correct dose for age, if medical help is delayed.

A serious form of pneumonia known as Legionnaires' disease (legionellosis) is found in many parts of the world, including the tropics. It is spread by droplet infection mainly from hot water tanks, spa pools and air-conditioning systems in large buildings and cruise ships, contaminated by the Legionella bacterium. It is commoner in older people. The diagnosis is easy to miss but important. Erythromycin is the treatment of choice, under careful medical supervision, usually at a dose of 500 mg four times daily until symptoms subside.

SARS (Sudden Acute Respiratory Syndrome)

See pages 336–7.

Tonsillitis and sore throats

See page 339–40.

Tuberculosis

See pages 343–4.

Dengue fever

Background

What is it?

Dengue is a severe flu-like illness, caused by a virus and spread by an infected mosquito. Dengue fever comes in what are known as four subtypes, all very similar in the symptoms they produce. However, if you get dengue fever you only develop immunity against that sub-type, and sometimes if you then catch dengue fever again it may be more severe.

The female Aedes mosquitoes nearly always bite during the day, often the first half of the morning or second half of the afternoon. The incubation period, i.e. the time from when you get bitten to when you get symptoms, is usually between five and eight days, meaning it is quite common for short-term travellers to develop the illness after they return home.

Where and when is it found?

Dengue fever is a disease which has been rapidly spreading throughout the tropics, and 2.5 billion people now live in areas where they can catch it. It's one of the most common tropical illnesses affecting travellers. Dengue is found mainly in Southeast Asia, Central and South America, the Caribbean, the Pacific islands and parts of Africa (see Figure 31.3). It is more common in the rainy season, when epidemics often occur, but in many affected areas you can pick it up at any time of year. Dengue is rarely found above 600 metres (2,000 feet) as the mosquito is unable to survive or breed for long above that height.

The Aedes mosquito has developed a rapid life cycle so it can breed in old tyres, air conditioner vents and any area of standing water, meaning in practice you are more likely to get infected in a city than out in the country. Tourists in clean, well-kept resorts are less likely to get dengue than aid workers or those spending time in urban slums and poorer parts of the city.

Symptoms

Some or all of the following: severe muscle and joint ache (known as Breakbone Fever); pain behind the eyes; headache; fever; rash (usually starting on the trunk and spreading to the limbs); a rapid onset of illness.

However, many people get a milder version.

Dengue often seems to get better, then comes back again a few days later; so another name for it is Saddleback Fever. Usually the worst symptoms are over in a week, though it can take time, sometimes

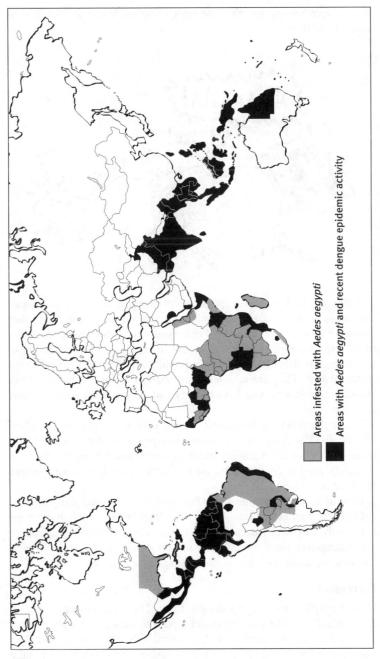

Figure 31.3 Areas where dengue fever is found
(Modified from a map by the US Centers for Disease Control and Prevention, 2005–6)

weeks, occasionally months, for your energy – and enthusiasm – to return to normal.

There are two more severe forms of dengue. The first is dengue haemorrhagic fever (DHF) with bleeding into the skin, gums and other organs. The second is dengue shock syndrome (DSS), rare, when the blood pressure rapidly falls and urgent treatment is life-saving. These forms tend to affect local people, especially children who are poor and malnourished. They are comparatively rare in travellers, but probably slightly commoner if you have already had dengue fever on a previous occasion.

In dengue fever the blood test usually shows low platelets and low white cells. The dengue fever blood serology test is often not available; in any case it usually takes several days for the result to be known, so it is mainly used to confirm afterwards whether your illness was dengue fever or not.

Dengue is a very real nuisance but once it has cleared and you have got over the tiredness it rarely leaves any long-lasting problems, though it is likely that it can occasionally trigger chronic fatigue syndrome.

Chikungunya fever is similar, but with severe joint pain. It is now common in India and the islands of the Indian Ocean.

Prevention

It's not easy to avoid getting dengue fever. The ideal answer is to keep covered and use DEET-based insect repellent – not a nice option when it is hot anyway. As mentioned, Aedes tend to bite for a few hours after dawn and a few hours before sunset, so these are the key times to take precautions. If you hear of an outbreak then take all the precautions you can. You can also spray your clothes with DEET or permethrin (Bug Proof) if you are in the middle of an epidemic. Always sleep under an insecticide-impregnated bed net, as although this may not prevent dengue it will help to prevent malaria. Trials are under way for a dengue vaccine.

Treatment

Because dengue mimics malaria you should see a doctor and get a malaria blood test, and also a full blood count which will measure your blood platelets, nearly always reduced in dengue fever. If the diagnosis of dengue seems likely, then rest, keep up your fluids, use oral rehydration solution, and take paracetamol, but *not* aspirin-based painkillers. And be very patient, not rushing back to work or on to the next part of your journey.

It's also important you are under good medical care, because of the small risk that you may become seriously ill with DHF – see above.

Get back to work and normal life slowly. It may take a month or more to get all your energy back, and sometimes you can feel very low afterwards. Warn your friends about this.

Ear problems

There are three ear problems which are common in travellers:

Infections of the ear canal

This is probably the commonest, and can be a serious nuisance, especially if you are tired and run down, or you are a keen swimmer or scuba diver.

Symptoms

The skin of the canal becomes itchy, swollen, produces pus and is sometimes very painful.

Prevention

Prevent this by having wax syringed before travel and at the same time having any eczema or infection of the ear canal well treated. This is important if you are likely to be swimming or doing any water sports. Also, dry your ears extremely carefully after swimming, and avoid polluted water, both sea and fresh.

Treatment

Get skilled medical advice. If that is impossible treat the infection with painkillers and by using antibiotic and steroid eardrops, e.g. Gentisone HC drops, after very cautious cleaning with cotton-wool buds. For severe infections, especially if there is pus and pain, you will also need antibiotics such as amoxicillin 500 mg three times daily or, if allergic to penicillin, erythromycin 500 mg four times daily, each for a week, though a variety of other antibiotics are also effective.

Sometimes a fungal infection is present, in which case different drops will be needed.

Infections of the eardrum

These are common, especially in children, following colds and coughs, but sometimes start with no warning.

Symptoms

Symptoms include severe pain, fever and deafness.

Treatment

Treat this by seeing a doctor who will usually recommend antibiotics, e.g. amoxicillin or erythromycin at the correct dose for age for five to seven days, along with painkillers such as paracetamol.

Ear pain during flights or as a result of other pressure changes

There are more details on page 71. This pain is caused by the tube between the back of the throat and the middle ear (called the Eustachian tube) being narrowed or becoming blocked so that equalization of pressure between your ear and the outside world can't happen. Swallowing, sucking a sweet or yawning may help, as can some medicines.

Ebola and other haemorrhagic fevers

Background

Ebola is one of several viral haemorrhagic fevers (VHFs) (others are listed below) and over the past few years has been the one causing most concern to travellers, largely because of sensational media stories.

However, all travellers should be aware of this group of illnesses. Although they are rare, they cause alarm, are dangerous, with death rates of 50 per cent or more, and can be prevented by taking sensible precautions.

What causes Ebola?

Ebola is caused by a filovirus and is spread through direct contact with the blood, secretions, organs or semen of infected people. Semen can be infected for up to seven weeks after recovery. The incubation period is two to 21 days. Health workers caring for infected patients are by far the highest risk group. Handling dead or infected chimpanzees occasionally causes the disease.

Where is Ebola found?

Outbreaks occur in sub-Saharan Africa, including the Democratic Republic of Congo, Uganda, Sudan and Gabon.

Symptoms

These include sudden onset of fever, weakness, muscle pain, headache and sore throat, followed by vomiting, diarrhoea and a rash. Bleeding both into the body organs and into the skin rapidly develops.

Treatment

There is no treatment apart from skilled health care in strict isolation.

How does this affect travellers?

You should only avoid travel if there is a confirmed and substantial outbreak in the part of the country you intend to visit. In the UK, the Foreign and Commonwealth Office advice line will advise you on this (see Appendix H).

In the extremely unlikely event of having any contact with a patient, you must report to a medical centre and take twice-daily temperature readings for three weeks; if these rise above 38°C you must be kept in strict isolation.

Other viral haemorrhagic fevers

These include the following, many of which have similar symptoms:

- Crimean-Congo haemorrhagic fever. This is caused by a bunyavirus and is spread by ticks. It is found in the steppe regions of central Asia, central Europe, and in tropical and southern Africa.
- Dengue haemorrhagic fever. This is described on pages 288–9.
- Marburg fever. This is caused by a filovirus and is spread by direct contact with infected cases in similar ways to Ebola. It occurs in sub-Saharan Africa including Angola.
- Lassa fever. This is described on pages 314–15.
- Rift Valley fever. This is caused by a phlebovirus, and can be acquired either through a mosquito bite or by direct contact with infected animals, mainly sheep, and from unpasteurized milk. It is found in Africa and Saudi Arabia.
- Yellow fever. This is described on pages 347–9.

There are other fevers in this same group, and some cause unexpected and sometimes explosive outbreaks which are unpredictable. Some VHFs have tended to spread to new areas recently. The majority are seized upon by the media, so information is usually available.

For further information see infectious diseases websites in Appendix H.

Eye problems

Background

Eyes are at greater risk in hot climates, especially if the air is dry and dusty or if you wear contact lenses. You can prevent most eye infections by regularly washing your face with soap and water, which reduces the number of germs that can enter your eye. Also be very careful not to rub your eyes.

These are the commonest conditions:

Contact lens problems

If you use contacts, discuss your trip with your contact lens practitioner, and take sufficient cleansing solution with you, using only sterilized water as an additive. At the first sign of any pain or irritation, take the lens out for at least 24 hours. Any persistent or severe discomfort needs medical advice. Take extra contacts with you, plus ordinary glasses, plus sunglasses, which can protect against sun, dust and wind. In unhygienic conditions, and in particular with soft lenses, an infection called Acanthamoeba can seriously damage the cornea. In dirty or dusty situations you would do better to wear glasses or at least take out your contacts at night.

Conjunctivitis

Symptoms

The eye becomes red, feels gritty and is sticky or stuck down on wakening.

Treatment

Apply antibiotic eye drops, e.g. chloramphenicol, every two hours until symptoms clear. Make sure the drops or ointment do *not* contain steroids unless prescribed by an eye specialist. If your eyes are not rapidly improving see a doctor or specialist.

Dry eyes

Symptoms

Your eyes get sore, dry and gritty. This is often caused by lack of tears, and can obviously get worse in a hot, dry or dusty climate, or in the plane.

Treatment

Use artificial tears, e.g. Hypotears, as often as you need to. Do not rub your eyes or touch them. If conjunctivitis develops, treat as above.

Styes

Symptoms

These are common, especially if you are tired or run down. They are usually caused by germs (often Staphylococcus) which cause boils in other parts of the body. You will notice a painful swelling on your eyelid or eye margin.

Treatment

Warm compresses can help the pain; antibiotic eye drops or antibiotics by mouth sometimes speed up the natural healing. Styes should not be squeezed.

Yellow eyes

Symptoms

If in the sober light of day you think your friend's eyes look yellow, it could be jaundice. You could have yellow eyes too, of course, but if you've read pages 302–3 and had your hepatitis jabs, it's much less likely.

Treatment

Assume it's a form of hepatitis (though there are also other causes) and immediately seek medical help.

Further advice

- *Eye check before you leave your home country* It's worth having this done before any long-term assignment (and during regular leave). If you are over 40 and there is glaucoma in the family, have your eye (intra-ocular) pressure checked yearly. You will need to ask your optician to include this. Also have an eye check before any serious or long-term travel if you are diabetic.
- *Glasses* Take at least one spare pair, and make a note of the prescription in case of loss. Glasses are often stolen.

- *High altitude or polar conditions* Snow blindness is a risk. Prevent this by wearing goggles. Wear sunglasses for protection in very bright light and at high altitude to lessen the risk of cataracts (see pages 189–90).
- *Report any symptoms that do not clear quickly* Eyes, especially if infected, can deteriorate rapidly in a tropical climate. See a doctor, preferably an eye specialist, if in doubt.

Fever

Fever in the tropics, unless mild or quickly self-limiting, should be taken seriously, even though most fevers will turn out to be neither serious nor 'tropical'.

However, if living in a malarious area or coming from one in the past three months, consider fever to be malaria until proved otherwise.

Common causes of non-tropical fever

In practice, many fevers in developing countries, just as in developed countries, are caused by unidentified viruses: they usually cause short, sharp rises in temperature and rarely last more than three to five days. They are common in children.

Other familiar diseases often start with a fever. Here is a partial checklist:

- *childhood illnesses* such as measles, chickenpox, rubella, also mumps, cytomegalovirus and glandular fever (this is also common in adolescents);

- *intestinal infections*: gastroenteritis, diverticulitis, appendicitis;
- *pelvic and gynaecological infections*;
- *renal tract infections* including pyelonephritis (kidney infection), prostatitis and cystitis;
- *respiratory infections, upper*: tonsillitis, throat, ear and sinus infections;
- *respiratory infections, lower*: influenza and related viruses, bronchitis and pneumonia;
- *skin infections*: boils, impetigo and cellulitis;
- *tooth infections* and abscesses;
- *miscellaneous causes* such as blood poisoning and (much more rarely) cancer, especially lymphoma.

Important causes of tropical fevers

Certain serious tropical diseases can cause fever, and sometimes there will be few other symptoms, especially to start with.

The list below shows the most common and the most serious. It is not fully comprehensive.

- *Amoebic dysentery* or *liver abscess* – the latter with severe pain in the liver (see pages 106–7).
- *Bacterial dysentery*, with bloody diarrhoea (see pages 101 and 103).
- *Brucellosis* from infected animals, mainly in Africa and around the Mediterranean (see pages 281–2).
- *Chikungunya fever*, resembles dengue (pages 286–9), mainly in the islands of the Indian Ocean and South India.
- *Dengue fever*, increasingly seen especially in South America and Southeast Asia (see pages 286–9).
- *Ebola* and other viral haemorrhagic fevers hit the headlines but are rare in practice (see pages 290–1).
- *Heatstroke* (see pages 196–7).
- *Hepatitis A, B, C or E*, with eyes soon becoming yellow (see pages 300–4).
- *HIV infection* (see pages 151–6).
- *Lassa fever*, severely ill, usually with ulcerated sore throat and muscle pains, in rural areas of western Africa – get treatment at once (see pages 314–15).
- *Legionellosis*, usually giving severe pneumonia (see page 285).
- *Leishmanisis (visceral)* caused by sandfly bites, rare in travellers (see pages 315–16).
- *Leptospirosis*, usually caught from water contaminated by rat urine: fever, headache, and severe muscle ache, often leading to anaemia and jaundice (see page 317).
- *Malaria*, probably the commonest (see pages 114–50).

- *Meningitis*, usually accompanied by severe headache, stiff neck and a non-blanching rash – no time to lose (see pages 319–20).
- *Q fever*, found in temperate and tropical countries, caused by Coxiella and spread by ticks, often causing a flu-like illness and caught by contact with infected animals.
- *Schistosomiasis*, acute (Katayama fever) (see pages 277–81).
- *Sexually transmitted infections* are an occasional cause of fever (see pages 157–60).
- *Sleeping sickness* – rare but possible in visitors to game parks, agricultural workers in eastern and western Africa (see pages 335–6).
- *Tick-bite fever* in Africa which can mimic malaria (see pages 338–9).
- *Toxoplasmosis*, often with symptoms like glandular fever.
- *Tuberculosis*, recurrent evening or night fever, usually with cough (see pages 343–4).
- *Typhoid* and paratyphoid fevers (see pages 345–6).
- *Typhus*, caused by Rickettsia, usually affecting trekkers or remote or rural travellers in Africa and Asia, especially Thailand, commonly with a rash (see pages 345–6).
- *West Nile fever*, worldwide but main risk North America, with symptoms similar to Japanese encephalitis (see pages 313–14).

For further information see infectious diseases websites in Appendix H.

Filariasis

Background

This, along with river blindness (see pages 328–9) and one or two other rarer conditions, is caused by a special type of roundworm, whose larval form is spread through the bite of an infected insect. This section refers to lymphatic filariasis (LF), which occurs throughout sub-Saharan Africa and in much of Southeast Asia. It is uncommon in travellers, but those living or working in remote areas are at some risk where it is known to be present. LF is spread by an infected Culex mosquito.

Symptoms

The classic symptom is 'elephantiasis', when the lower limbs become huge because of blockage to the lymph vessels. The disease is less severe in travellers but can cause fever, swelling of the lymph glands especially in the groin, and swelling of the legs and scrotum.

Prevention

Avoid mosquito bites in areas where it is known to occur, through the normal ways of cover-up, DEET-based insecticide and impregnated mosquito nets.

Treatment

This must be done by a specialist, who also needs to confirm the diagnosis through a special filarial antibody blood test. Two drugs are commonly used, diethylcarbamazine (DEC) and ivermectin. Often the eosinophil count (one of the white cells) is raised, and checking for filariasis is part of discovering the cause of a raised eosinophil count in returning travellers.

Gynae problems

There is more on the health care of women under pregnancy (see pages 230–3), security (see pages 227–9), and in other sections (see Index).

Background

These can be a real worry when away from home, first because it is often unsettling when unfamiliar symptoms occur, and also because many people are understandably reluctant to accept medical advice (and examinations) from unknown doctors.

Before leaving for any long overseas trip or going to live overseas, get yourself checked out if you have any symptoms you are worried about, including any concerns about your periods. Make sure you are up to date with your cervical (Pap) smear test.

Period problems

Light or absent periods

When travelling or going to live in a strange place, periods may get lighter or stop altogether, sometimes for months. This is very common, and you don't need to take any action unless pregnancy is a possibility, you have no period for more than about six months or you or your friends notice that you have lost a lot of weight.

Heavy or abnormal periods

Periods may also become irregular, abnormal or prolonged. There are many causes for this and although most are not serious, if such problems persist you should see a doctor.

Please note: it is worth reporting any prolonged heavy bleeding as soon as possible whenever it occurs, not least because of the increased risk of becoming anaemic or very occasionally needing a blood transfusion. Also check with your doctor when you next come home if any changes persist from your normal cycle.

Delaying a period

Often this is just what you will want to do, especially for a holiday or a short but important overseas assignment. You can simply continue taking your ordinary contraceptive pill without the normal seven-day break or start the pill and take it continuously. This does not work well for biphasic or triphasic pills. Talk to your doctor if in doubt, and make sure you take extra packs with you. Some experts suggest it is not wise to do this for more than two or three cycles (also see pages 24–5).

Periods and the local culture

Remember that tampons are luxury items in many developing countries and may be expensive or hard to obtain. Check with someone who knows the area you are going to and can give you up-to-date advice; otherwise take enough with you.

In some cultures, especially in Muslim countries, you should not enter places of worship if you are menstruating.

Finally, remember that sharks and other sea animals may be attracted by blood, as may some animals on wildlife safaris.

Vaginal discharge

This is often commoner in the tropics, especially in hot and humid conditions and if you wear tights or jeans.

Thrush

'Thrush', or Candida, usually causing an itchy discharge, is especially common. Using the antimalarial doxycycline can make this more likely. If you suspect thrush, use a clotrimazole (Canesten) suppository 500 mg for one night. A good alternative is to take diflucan 150 mg, as a single tablet. Don't take this if there is a chance you may be pregnant, or if you are also taking certain non-sedating antihistamines such as loratidine (Clarityn).

Trichomonas

Trichomonas is a common cause of discharge, often offensive. The treatment is metronidazole 200 mg tablets, two twice daily for seven days (again avoid if there is any possibility of pregnancy, and also avoid alcohol). See a doctor if your symptoms persist.

Sexually transmitted infections

Sexually transmitted infections (STIs, e.g. gonorrhoea or chlamydia) can cause a discharge, and if you think there is a possibility of an STI try to see a reliable doctor. Also encourage your partner to get checked. If this is not possible, self-treat as described on page 159, and make sure you see a doctor for a careful check-up as soon as you get home.

Hepatitis

Background

Hepatitis is an infection of the liver caused by a virus, usually leading to jaundice, in which the eyes and skin go yellow. Hepatitis A and B are preventable by immunization and, as far as travellers are concerned, *should* be diseases of the past.

There are at least five different forms, of which hepatitis A, B, C and E are important illnesses for travellers to know about.

Hepatitis A

This is the commonest form of jaundice in travellers, found almost worldwide and most often picked up in South or Southeast Asia or tropical Africa (see Figure 31.4, overleaf). It is spread by the faeco-oral route – in other words, germs from the faeces of an infected person contaminate the food and water drunk by another. It is therefore common wherever personal or public hygiene is poor. Those with hepatitis A usually make a full recovery, even though it may take time. However, it becomes more serious the older you get, with some figures suggesting that 2 per cent of those contracting it over the age of 40 die from it, and 4 per cent of those over the age of 60. Older people also take much longer to recover. This underlines the importance of having hepatitis A immunization for any travel to developing countries or where hygiene is poor.

Very young children brought up in areas where hepatitis A and B are common often catch either of these illnesses, and develop few or no symptoms but develop life-long immunity.

The interval between becoming infected and developing first symptoms (the incubation period) is two to six weeks. See pages 383–4 for details about hepatitis A immunization.

Hepatitis B

Previously also known as serum hepatitis, this is very common in Africa, Asia and South America (see Figure 31.5, overleaf). It is serious mainly because of its long-term effects. It is 100 times more infectious than HIV but is spread in a similar way, i.e. by having sex (with a

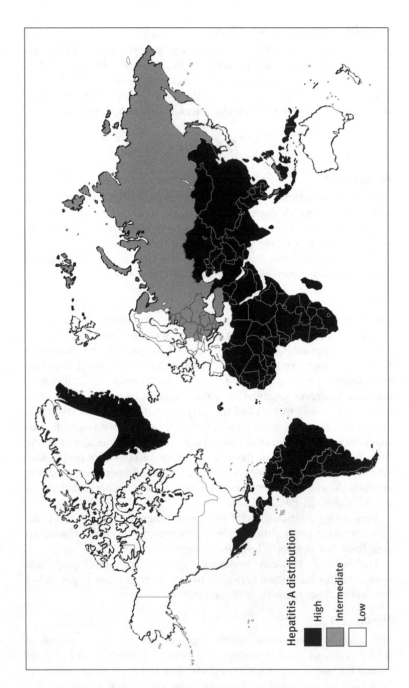

Figure 31.4 Areas where hepatitis A is found

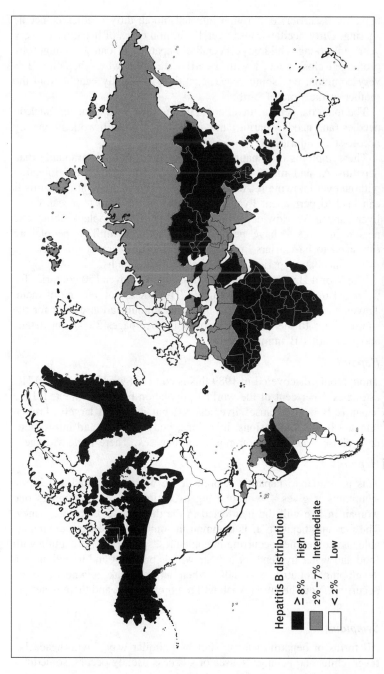

Figure 31.5 Areas where hepatitis B is found

(Modified from a map by the US Centers for Disease Control and Prevention, 2005–6)

Hepatitis B distribution

≥ 8%   High

2% – 7%   Intermediate

< 2%   Low

hepatitis B carrier) or through infected blood, dirty needles or needle sharing. Dirty needles cause over 12 million cases of hepatitis B every year. In young children especially, hepatitis B can be caught by prolonged close contact with a carrier. In areas where hepatitis B is very common, e.g. south Asia, hepatitis B is usually caught from the mother at the time of birth.

The main danger for travellers is through sex with a carrier, unclean needles (and needle-sharing) and, in the case of health workers, mainly needle-stick injuries.

The symptoms of hepatitis B usually come on more gradually than hepatitis A, and many children and some adults have the infection without ever knowing it. About 1 per cent of cases are fatal. Hepatitis B can lead to permanent liver damage, and in the long term can cause liver cancer. Worldwide, more than two billion people – about one person in three – have been infected, and 350 million people are estimated to be carriers, most of whom are unaware of this fact.

The incubation period is six weeks to six months.

The World Health Organization has signed up over 150 countries for universal immunization programmes. The UK is not yet one of them. Travellers are recommended to have this immunization except for the shortest trips to the lowest-risk countries. See pages 384–6 for details about hepatitis B immunization.

Hepatitis C

Though only discovered in 1989 this is common worldwide, and WHO estimates 3 per cent of the world's population has been infected. Like hepatitis B it also causes liver cancer, but is spread largely through infected blood transfusions, injections, body piercing and intravenous drug abuse – and less commonly through sex. There is no vaccine.

Hepatitis E

This is similar to hepatitis A both in the way it is spread and in the symptoms it gives – with one big exception: in some countries one woman in five will die if infected in the third trimester of pregnancy. The fact that hepatitis E is common in some countries, but unpredictable and sometimes occurring in epidemics, spells extreme caution with food and water hygiene for anyone who is pregnant and travelling in a developing country, especially when an outbreak is known to be occurring. Your hepatitis A jab will not protect you, and there is not yet a vaccine.

Symptoms

All forms of hepatitis tend to start in a similar way – with headache, fever, chills and aching. Nausea or sickness usually occurs, sometimes triggered by the smell of food or cigarette smoke.

There may be pain over the liver (the upper right side of the abdomen). The urine darkens and the eyes and skin usually become yellow. At this stage it is common to feel very ill, exhausted and nauseated. After days or sometimes weeks the symptoms gradually improve, though full health may not be restored for up to six months.

Children and some adults may have a much milder illness, or may even have hepatitis without knowing it.

For severe illness which is not improving, and especially if liver function tests are worsening, consider medical evacuation.

Prevention

Hepatitis A and E are prevented by good personal hygiene, and by following the advice on pages 85–96. Following HIV prevention advice largely prevents hepatitis B and C.

Immunizations are of great value. All those aged five or over (or younger children at very high risk), unless known to have hepatitis A antibodies on a blood test, should have a course of hepatitis A injections if going to a developing country (see pages 383–4).

When it comes to hepatitis B, all health workers serving in developing countries and all those travelling internationally, including children, should consider having hepatitis B immunization. If in doubt, discuss this with your travel clinic or a specialist in travel medicine (see pages 384–6).

Patients with hepatitis A are at their most infectious before the jaundice develops (i.e. during the incubation period), and are thought to stop being infectious within two weeks after the jaundice starts. They can mix freely after the jaundice has faded. Those with hepatitis A and E or hepatitis of unknown cause should use separate utensils and towels and take special care with personal hygiene. There is no need for strict isolation. Family contacts of those with hepatitis A not known to have immunity, or who have not had up-to-date immunizations, will gain some protection from hepatitis A vaccine (or gammaglobulin) given as soon as a family member develops jaundice. Gammaglobulin must come from a reliable (i.e. developed country) source.

Infection with hepatitis usually gives life-long immunity to that form of hepatitis.

Please see further details on vaccines in Appendix J, and also the infectious diseases websites in Appendix H.

Treatment

As with most viral illnesses, there is no specific treatment. The key to recovery is *adequate rest*, usually in bed to begin with. Provided the body rests sufficiently it is usually able to fight off the illness. Those who fail to rest or who return to work (or looking after their children) too quickly risk a longer illness or a relapse. Parents with young children will need maximum support, and in some situations unaffected partners will need to take time off work to look after the family. Older people need to take special care to get as much rest as possible.

Plenty of sweet drinks, especially those containing glucose, are claimed to ease the nausea. Intravenous glucose or fluids should be avoided unless vomiting makes it impossible to take fluids by mouth. There is no real evidence that special diets either help or hinder recovery.

Women who are on the pill are usually recommended to avoid it for about six months (and use alternative contraception!). It is also sensible to avoid alcohol until health has returned completely to normal, and ideally until liver function tests are also back to normal.

Blood tests that monitor liver function (LFTs) can usually be arranged; though useful, they are not essential except in severe illness. In high-quality labs, it is possible to confirm whether hepatitis A, B, C or E is the cause of the infection. Alternatively, this can be done at a routine medical examination back home.

Influenza (including avian flu)

Why is flu important for travellers?

Influenza is found throughout the world and kills many thousands of people each year. It is easy for travellers to catch flu, especially if they have no immunity to the type of flu circulating in the areas they are visiting.

Travellers visiting countries in either hemisphere during the influenza season are at special risk. In the northern hemisphere the season is mainly from November to March, and in the southern from April to September.

Planes, cruise ships and other crowded areas where people are in close contact are ideal for causing spread.

Flu is spread by droplet infection, i.e. by the virus passing through the air from an infected person to the lungs of another, e.g. through coughing and sneezing. It is also spread by contamination of the hands, meaning that regular hand washing helps to reduce spread.

International travellers should follow guidelines from their own country about whether to have flu immunizations before travel. See also details on pages 386–7.

At the time of writing it is assumed that the risk of avian flu will still be present and that regular updates will be available.

The details below apply specifically to this form of influenza.

Background

What is bird flu?

Avian influenza A (H5N1) or bird flu usually affects wild birds but also causes widespread disease and death among domestic poultry. Occasionally infected birds can pass this disease on to humans. At the time of writing, risks to humans remain low and sustained person-to-person spread has not been confirmed. This situation may change, however, and the concern remains that the virus may gain the ability to spread more quickly and unpredictably from human to human. Despite huge numbers of cases in birds and ongoing contact between birds and humans, there is no evidence at the time of writing that this has happened. Increasingly effective measures are in place to contain outbreaks among poultry and some measures are in place to try and minimize the spread if a human pandemic occurs.

A change from 'minimal risk' to humans to a 'pandemic risk' would probably first be noticed by a rapid increase in the number of human cases in a particular area, indicating the likelihood of person-to-person spread. If and when this happens, information will be disseminated and instructions are likely to be given by embassies, guided by the World Health Organization, as to what course of action is needed, including whether or not it is necessary to leave the area.

Current situation

The first cases of human H5N1 virus occurred in Hong Kong in 1997, but reappeared in Southeast Asia in mid-2003.

The current risk to travellers from avian flu is low at the time of writing, but vigilance is needed in case there are outbreaks. Check websites for the current situation and advice if you are visiting any countries which are currently reporting outbreaks.

Prior to travel

Be prepared before you go:

- Ensure you have adequate travel insurance which covers medical evacuation for any illness.
- Consider taking a first-aid kit, including a thermometer and alcohol-based hand gel for personal hygiene and frequent hand cleansing.
- Be up to date with all recommended travel immunizations.
- For individuals with chronic respiratory disease, chronic heart disease, chronic renal disease, chronic liver disease, diabetes, immunosuppression or previous history of pneumococcal disease or over 65 years of age, pneumococcal vaccine is recommended.

- Immunization with the influenza vaccine recommended in the UK or the country in which you are living will offer *no* protection against infection with avian influenza, until a specific avian flu vaccine is developed. However, the flu vaccine manufactured each year to protect against other strains of influenza should be used for all those currently falling within national guidelines.
- Obtain information from your home country about what to do when ill abroad. Follow their advice as to how to access supplies of oseltamivir (Tamiflu) or any other antiviral which may have some effect in case there is a rapid increase in the number of cases being reported and confirmed. For UK citizens this is the Foreign and Commonwealth Office. See website on page 308.

During travel to an infected area

- Avoid contact with poultry (chickens, ducks, geese, pigeons, quail) or any wild birds and the settings where they are present in numbers, i.e. commercial poultry farms, backyard poultry farms and live poultry markets. Do not visit or stay with families keeping domestic poultry in areas where bird flu is known to be currently present. Avoid contact with dead or sick poultry. Avoid contact with surfaces contaminated with animal faeces or secretions.
- These precautions apply to any people visiting affected areas, including friends and relatives going to countries that have current outbreaks.
- Be rigorous about personal hygiene measures – wash your hands frequently and thoroughly, especially when handling food. Use soap and water, or an alcohol gel if your hands are not visibly soiled.
- The routine use of masks or other personal protective equipment while in public areas is not currently recommended, but this advice may change.
- Do not eat uncooked or undercooked poultry or poultry products, including eggs. Do not eat poultry that has died or been sick, even if well cooked.
- There is no evidence at all that well-cooked poultry and eggs from birds showing no signs of illness cause any risk, and there is absolutely no reason not to continue eating these as usual.

When preparing food in an infected area

The advice below is good practice in any country you are visiting, but is especially important if you are visiting a country where cases of avian flu are being reported or known to occur.

- Separate raw meat from cooked or ready-to-eat foods. Do not use the same chopping board or the same knife for preparing raw meat and cooked or ready-to-eat foods.
- Do not handle either raw or cooked foods without washing your hands in between.
- Do not place cooked meat back on the same plate or surface as before it was cooked.
- All foods from poultry, including eggs and poultry blood, should be cooked thoroughly. Egg yolks should not be runny or liquid. Because influenza viruses are destroyed by heat, the cooking temperature for poultry meat should be at least 74°C (168°F).
- Wash egg shells in soapy water before handling and cooking, and wash your hands afterwards.
- Do not use raw or soft-boiled eggs in foods that will not be cooked.
- After handling raw poultry or eggs, wash your hands and all surfaces and utensils thoroughly with soap and water.
- Do not get involved in the slaughter, de-feathering and preparation of poultry for cooking. If you see any dead or sick wild swans, geese, ducks or domestic poultry, do not touch them but report to an appropriate person.

If you become unwell after possible exposure to avian flu

After any possible exposure, monitor your health for ten days.

It is highly unlikely that avian flu is the cause and much more likely that human influenza (or another illness) will be responsible, because normal influenza circulates in many areas of the world. However:

1 If you become ill with fever and develop a cough, sore throat or difficulty breathing, or if you develop any illness with fever during this ten-day period, consult a healthcare provider. Before you visit a healthcare setting, tell the provider the following:
(a) your symptoms;
(b) where you travelled;
(c) whether you have had direct contact with poultry, or a possible human case.

2 Do not travel while ill, unless travelling locally for medical care. Limiting contact with others as much as possible can help prevent the spread of an infectious illness.

3 The embassy of your country of origin may be able to assist with accessing medical advice.

Symptoms in humans

Most people infected have flu-like symptoms, become rapidly ill and develop a cough and fever (above 38°C). Sometimes, in addition to cough and flu-like symptoms, diarrhoea, vomiting, abdominal pain and occasionally bleeding from the nose and gums occur. Children appear to be the most easily infected, possibly because they have the greatest contact with infected poultry.

The incubation period (i.e. time between being exposed to infection to the time when symptoms first develop) ranges from two to 17 days, with ten days as a working norm. As human cases become more common, symptoms will become defined more accurately.

Treatment and prophylaxis

* At the time of writing there is no vaccine available to protect against avian influenza, though this situation is likely to change.
* Antiviral drugs probably offer some protection. The use of antivirals is not straightforward and always requires medical supervision. They should only be used for treatment of suspected cases following medical assessment or in those who have had direct contact with a confirmed case. Their effect will be even more limited if the virus develops resistance to the drugs.
* The antiviral drug oseltamivir (Tamiflu) is a recognized treatment for other types of influenza if used in patients who have had symptoms for two days or less. This drug works by stopping the growth and spread of some flu viruses within the body. Zanamivir (Relenza) is another such antiviral drug but is not available in tablet form.
* The use of oseltamivir should be started under medical supervision as soon as possible, ideally within 48 hours of any symptoms, but may be worth giving at any stage in the illness. The normal recommended dose for flu is 150 mg daily, given as two 75 mg tablets daily for five days. It is not currently licensed for use in children under one year. The dose could be increased to 300 mg daily for seven to ten days if there is no improvement. These guidelines may change if and when outbreaks among humans occur, and these will be posted on the WHO website (see below).
* At the time of writing it is not generally recommended that persons travelling to countries affected by avian influenza should carry their own supply of antiviral drugs.

Reference information websites

* http://www.fitfortravel.nhs.uk/general/AvianInfluenzaTravel.htm
* http://www.fco.gov.uk
* http://www.who.int/csr/disease/avian_influenza/en
* http://www.cdc.gov/travel/other/avian_influenza_se_asia_2005.htm
* http://www.nathnac.org/pro/clinical_updates/avian influenza/
* http://www.smartraveller.gov.au/zw-cgi/view/TravelBulletins/health
* http://www.hpa.org.uk/infections/topics_az/avianinfluenza/

Intestinal worms

Worms, or helminths as they are known medically, are an occupational hazard of all but the most fastidious travellers, and passing a roundworm or part of a tapeworm is perhaps the commonest cause of a traveller's scream from the toilet. Here are the most widespread.

Pinworms (threadworms, Enterobius)

You don't have to leave the UK to catch pinworms, which are very common, especially among children.

Symptoms

Pinworms are about 1 cm long, whitish and look like threads. They are often passed in the stool. They also cause anal itching, especially in children and especially at night. They are a nuisance, but not dangerous.

Prevention

This depends on good personal hygiene, washing hands after going to the toilet and before eating or preparing food, and keeping fingernails clean and short in all family members.

Treatment

Treatment is with mebendazole 100 mg tablets (Vermox), one tablet twice daily for three days (not in children under two, or in pregnancy) or a single 500 mg tablet. Piperazine (Pripsen) can be used in children under two, but the dosages are quite complex and you will need advice from a doctor or pharmacist, or at the very least to read the Patient Information Leaflet. Dosages of piperazine are different for pinworms and roundworms.

Roundworms (Ascaris)

These are found throughout the tropics, especially affecting school-age children and those living among the local population. Roundworms look rather like earthworms; they are 20–30 cm long, smooth, round and non-segmented.

Symptoms

These include abdominal pain, a distended abdomen and occasionally loss of weight. Often there are no symptoms, and a junior member of the household discovers one or more, often with great astonishment, on passing a stool or, even worse, during a vomiting attack. Eggs are often but not always found on stool tests.

Prevention

This depends on careful food and personal hygiene.

Treatment

Treatment is with mebendazole, as described above, or with piperazine.

Hookworm (Ankylostoma)

Hookworms occur quite commonly in international travellers, especially those who go barefoot or wear sandals or flip-flops.

Symptoms

Hookworms are not noticed in the stool, but their eggs may show up on stool tests. Heavy infection with hookworm is harmful, especially in children, because it leads to anaemia. Anyone who has symptoms of unexplained tiredness, shortness of breath or lack of energy should consider treating themselves for hookworm and having a haemoglobin test.

Prevention

This depends on wearing shoes when walking outside the home.

Treatment

This is with mebendazole, as described above.

Hookworm (Strongyloides)

This is another type of hookworm, spread and prevented in a similar way, which is found through most of the tropics and sub-tropics. The worms live in the upper bowel and can sometimes cause severe illness.

Symptoms

Many people show no symptoms. However, heavy infections can cause upper or mid-abdominal pain, tenderness, diarrhoea, nausea and vomiting. Weight loss and malabsorption can also occur. Occasionally skin symptoms develop, known as larva currens; these are itchy curly lines, usually on the buttocks, lower back and thighs, which slowly move, and cause great alarm. There is a rare form of this disease where massive infection results, often in those with poor immunity.

Diagnosis depends on showing eggs on stool tests or, more reliably, through special ELISA blood tests. Usually the eosinophils (one of the white cells) are present in high numbers, and Strongyloides is an important infection to look for when a high eosinophil count is picked up on a routine blood test in a returning traveller.

Treatment

Albendazole tablets, 400 mg twice daily for three days, with the same dose repeated after three weeks, usually cures it. An alternative is ivermectin 200 micrograms/kg daily for two days. Because Strongyloides is sometimes a serious disease, it should always be diagnosed and treated by a doctor, preferably a specialist in tropical or travel medicine.

Tapeworms (Taenia)

You can become infected with tapeworm by eating undercooked beef (*T. saginata*), fish (*Diphyllobothrium*) or pork (*T. solium*), or occasionally through poorly cooked food or salads contaminated with eggs. Tapeworms are long, flat, segmented worms, and sections may be noticed in the stool.

Symptoms

Often they cause no obvious symptoms but their eggs, or worm segments, are found on stool tests. They may lead to abdominal pain or loss of weight.

Pork tapeworm occasionally leads to cysticercosis, a condition in which cysts can develop in other organs causing, for example, epileptic fits if one lodges in the brain.

Prevention

Make sure that all meat, especially pork, is thoroughly cooked, meaning the centre of the meat should be brown or grey, not pink. Fish must be thoroughly cooked and, depending on the type, should normally be firmly white. Also be strict about food hygiene and, in areas where pigs are common, avoid eating salads unless you prepare them yourself at home.

Treatment

This is with praziquantel 20 mg/kg as a single dose after a light breakfast, or with niclosamide, but a doctor should confirm the diagnosis and supervise the treatment. Praziquantel also deals with the dwarf tapeworm (Hymenolepsis) and with Diphyllobothrium.

A final suggestion

For expatriate families or anyone living among the local population in a developing country, there is much to be said for a six-monthly 'worm-workout'. Dose yourself and any member of the family, unless under two or pregnant, with mebendazole 100 mg tablets, one twice daily for three days. Alternatives are mebendazole 500 mg, one tablet, or albendazole 400 mg, one tablet (200 mg dose in children between two and four). Then do a final purge when you eventually get home. These are effective against pinworms, roundworms, hookworm and whipworms (Trichuriasis).

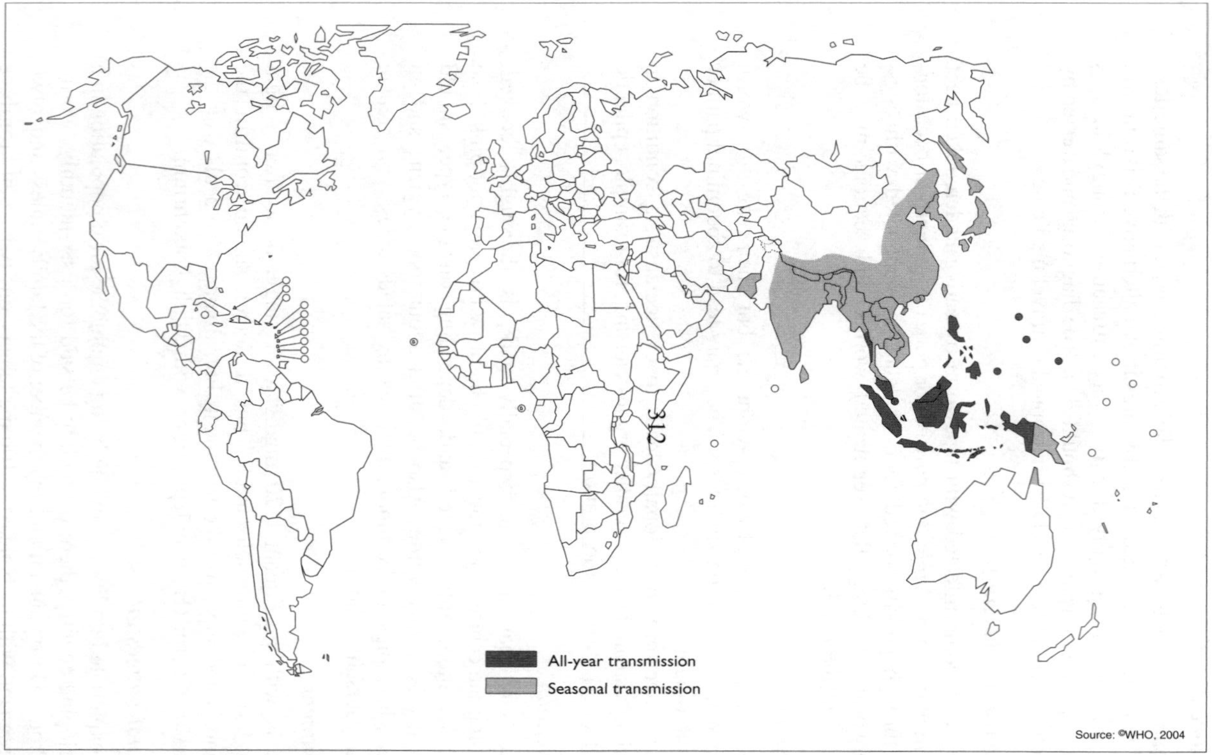

Figure 31.6 Areas where Japanese encephalitis is found (WHO, 2004)

All-year transmission

Seasonal transmission

312

Japanese encephalitis

Background

What is it?

Japanese encephalitis (JE) is a viral infection found in South and Southeast Asia and is caused by being bitten by an infected Culex mosquito.

Where is it found?

As the name suggests, this illness has its origins in the east. The main areas are India, especially the northern provinces, the low-lying areas of Nepal, northern parts of Myanmar (Burma), northern Sri Lanka, northern Thailand and low-lying parts of Laos and Vietnam (see Figure 31.6). Sporadic cases occur in the Philippines, Malaysia, Indonesia and Korea. In Japan the disease has been virtually eradicated.

The Culex mosquitoes often breed in flooded rice fields, especially where pigs are kept and where birds of the heron family are common. That's because of the complicated life cycle of the mosquito, which gets a boost when these species are present. You can also get JE in urban areas because rice paddies are often near or even within parts of cities.

How common is JE?

JE is becoming more common in many areas. In areas where JE is endemic, annual incidence ranges from one to ten per 10,000 people. Children under 15 years of age are principally affected. In many areas the disease is found year round; in others, such as northern India, it is more seasonal, occurring mainly during and after the monsoon rains (June through till November). Risk times are when the mosquitoes are most active, which is generally dusk until dawn.

Symptoms

Most people who get infected with JE get no symptoms. For those who do, the symptoms vary. Mild infections give you a fever and headache. More severe infections can have a rapid onset and give severe headache, fever and neck stiffness, with some nerves being affected. About half of all severe cases are fatal: deafness and fatigue can be long-lasting effects. The disease is commoner in children. The incubation period is usually 4 to 14 days.

What is the risk to travellers?

It is generally low, but risks vary greatly depending on the exact location, what you will be doing, how long you will be staying in rural areas and the time of year. This often makes it difficult to advise whether it is worth being immunized. You will need to discuss this with a travel health adviser (also see pages 387–9).

Prevention

- The key is to avoid being bitten. Use insect repellent, ideally containing DEET; cover up well; sleep in screened accommodation and under an insecticide-impregnated mosquito net.
- Make the environment near your home less mosquito-friendly, i.e. remove areas where mozzies can breed, such as any standing or stagnant water. If you live in an affected area, get rid of any breeding places in your garden or near your house. This will also help to protect you against malaria and dengue fever.
- Avoid outdoor activity during twilight hours when cases of JE are known to be occurring.
- Discuss vaccination with your travel health adviser.

Which vaccine is available?

Details on this are found on pages 387–9.

Lassa fever

Background

This is one of the severe viral haemorrhagic fevers (see also under Ebola, pages 290–1). It is a serious, often fatal disease which often leads to internal bleeding. It is confined to West Africa, where it is thought at least 100,000 people are infected each year. Aid workers, the military and adventure travellers passing through or working in affected areas are at some risk. Affected areas include Sierra Leone, Liberia, Guinea, parts of Nigeria and occasionally neighbouring countries.

Lassa fever is caused by a virus and is spread from a rodent known as the multimammate rat. The disease can be caught in several ways from the urine and droppings of these animals, which are often found in local homes and farms. You can catch it from areas where infected rats have deposited their faeces, e.g. from floors, beds, food or water. It can be caught by eating inadequately cooked, contaminated food. It can be caught by inhaling tiny particles in air contaminated by rodent excretions. It can be passed from person to person, through close contact (inhaling the virus from the infected person's throat); via blood; via secretions from the mouth or throat; from the urine of an infected person, either directly or through contaminated medical instruments; also through sex. The incubation period is three to 21 days, and the virus can be excreted in the urine of patients for three to nine weeks from the date the illness started, and in semen for up to three months.

Its serious nature and person-to-person spread make Lassa fever a dreaded illness.

Symptoms

Symptoms are gradually increasing fever, headache, sore throat, painful muscles, chest and abdominal pain. The throat and often the eyes are inflamed. Other diseases, e.g. malaria, cause similar symptoms, making diagnosis difficult. The disease can worsen as internal bleeding occurs, which in turn causes a fall in blood pressure. Most patients survive if well cared for (about 15 per cent of hospitalized patients die). After recovery, deafness can persist, sometimes for life.

Treatment

Treatment is through skilled nursing using strict barrier precautions. The antiviral agent ribavirin can be life-saving if started in the first week.

Action if you may have been exposed

If you have been in an area where Lassa fever cases are occurring, you should do two things. First, immediately report any suspicious symptoms and, second, check your temperature twice daily for three weeks after the contact, and report if it is raised above 38°C (even if other causes of fever are much more likely). You are very unlikely to catch Lassa fever unless you have been caring for patients with the disease or have been in close contact with an infected person or a carrier. It is very rare in international travellers.

For further information see infectious diseases websites in Appendix H.

Leishmaniasis

Background

Leishmaniasis has increased sharply since the early 1990s and now affects people in about 90 countries.

The disease comes in two forms:

- Kala-azar or visceral leishmaniasis is a serious illness affecting the whole body including bone marrow, liver and spleen. Though usually fatal if untreated, it is very rare in travellers. It is mainly found in Bangladesh, India, Nepal, Brazil and Sudan. In areas where HIV is present, the disease is often more serious.
- Cutaneous and mucosal leishmaniasis are becoming far commoner in travellers. Cutaneous leishmaniasis (CL), often known as oriental sore, affects the skin. Mucosal leishmaniasis (ML), often known as

Espundia, affects the mucous membranes of the mouth and nose. CL is commonest around the Mediterranean, western Asia, North Africa and Brazil. CL is found in Central and South America, e.g. Bolivia, Belize and Colombia.

Leishmaniasis is commoner in the countryside than the city but is increasingly invading the outskirts of cities.

All forms of leishmaniasis are caused by a one-celled parasite known as Leishmania, passed on by the bite of a sandfly (about one-third the size of a mosquito). Sandflies are active between dusk and dawn. This puts at risk those who may work through the night, such as soldiers, aid workers, ornithologists or those doing night-time research. Sandflies also bite during the day if disturbed.

Symptoms

Kala-azar leads to rapid loss of weight and a huge spleen. CL results in an ulcerating nodule following a sandfly bite on an exposed part of the body, especially the face, legs and arms. It may develop days, months or even years after the bite, though typically between four and six weeks. Though not serious it can leave a disfiguring mark. The bite often leaves a non-swollen red ring, but if left untreated tends to ulcerate and has been described as looking 'like a small pizza'.

ML gives a severe, ulcerating sore around the mouth and nose, again leaving permanent scarring.

Prevention

The key is to avoid being bitten by sandflies. They tend to live close to the ground, so sleeping in a hammock at least one metre off the ground, on the roof or in the upper storeys of houses gives protection. Also use DEET-based insect repellents, applying these all around the ankles and under the lower ends of the trousers. Sleep under a mosquito net. Sandflies can get through the holes in most nets but those impregnated with permethrin will usually kill sandflies before they get through the holes.

Treatment

This is specialized and is always done under medical supervision. Report any bite that persists or ulcerates, especially if on an exposed area such as the arm or leg. Paromomycin ointment applied for four weeks in CL cured two-thirds of patients in one recent clinical trial.

For further information see infectious diseases websites in Appendix H.

Leptospirosis (Weil's disease)

Background

This disease, caused by an organism called Leptospira, is found almost worldwide, but especially in the tropics. It is important for travellers because it can be picked up through contact with water contaminated by the urine of rodents, especially rats. This therefore includes ponds, ditches, canals, lakes, damp soil and especially any area affected by recent flooding. The disease enters the body through mucous membranes and skin, especially if there are any breaks in the skin or abrasions. It can also be caught from ingesting infected water or occasionally from eating food contaminated by rat urine. Aid and relief workers and water and sanitation engineers are at special risk. So are adventure travellers involved in aquatic sports in unclean fresh water. The incubation period according to the US Centers for Disease Control and Prevention (see Appendix I) is between 2 and 29 days, usually seven.

Symptoms

These are varied but usually there is sudden onset of fever, headache, muscle ache, chills, inflamed eyes and a rash. These symptoms can mimic other illnesses, such as malaria: one reason why it is important to get good medical advice as soon as possible. Also more serious symptoms including jaundice can develop rapidly.

Prevention

Avoid contaminated water, and be particularly careful if you have any skin cuts or abrasions. Avoid any contact with rodents, especially rats. If exposure to contaminated non-salt water is essential, wear a protective suit and consider taking prophylactic antibiotics. The current recommendation is doxycycline 200 mg *once per week*, starting one or two days before exposure, and continuing during the period of risk. Anyone also needing antimalarials would sensibly choose doxycycline 100 mg *daily,* which would protect against both diseases.

Treatment

This must be done by a specialist and started as soon as possible. Penicillin, amoxicillin and tetracyclines including doxycycline are the most effective antibiotics.

Lyme disease

Background

Lyme disease is found in parts of North America (especially the eastern and pacific coastal regions) and in parts of central, northern and eastern Europe (including the UK), extending into Asia. It may be found sporadically in other parts of the world. Lyme disease is caused by an organism called *Borrelia burgdorferi*, which is spread by infected Ixodes deer ticks. It usually occurs in summer.

Symptoms

The commonest symptom (present in about half of all cases) is a typical raised reddish rash, called Erythema migrans, which spreads outwards from the tick bite after two to six weeks, often leaving a clearer centre. Typical symptoms differ between cases in North America and Europe. European cases are often milder but both can cause lethargy, painful muscles and joints, headache and fever. Much later, heart or neurological symptoms may develop.

Chronic Lyme disease can also be a cause of unexplained tiredness and is worth considering in those with chronic fatigue syndrome as a rare but possible cause.

Blood tests are unreliable and remain negative in up to half of all patients, especially in the early stages of the disease. This means the diagnosis largely depends on a 'best-guess', i.e. having a tick bite in an area where Lyme disease is known to occur, accompanied by a typical rash. A positive blood test does, however, help to confirm the diagnosis.

Prevention

You can prevent Lyme disease by avoiding tick bites and, if walking in rural areas where it is known to occur, wearing boots, with trousers tucked into socks. If woollen or cotton socks are used, you can soak these in DEET solution (see page 22) or spray them with 100 per cent DEET insecticide. Permethrin in the form of Bug Proof can be sprayed on to any material.

Check your body for ticks and immediately remove any that you notice (which might also spread tick-borne encephalitis in Europe or Asia). The way to remove ticks is described on page 213.

A vaccine to protect against North American strains of Lyme disease has recently been withdrawn. Recent studies have shown that doxycycline 200 mg taken within 72 hours of a tick bite prevent the great majority of cases from developing.

Treatment

Lyme disease often disappears without treatment, but if you or your doctor suspect it, it is still worth treating, as this is simple if caught early but complex and prolonged if diagnosed later, when complications may have set in. Take doxycycline 100 mg capsules, usually at a dose of two daily for 14 days. The disease usually has an excellent outlook, especially in the European forms of the disease, but the earlier it is caught, the better.

For further information see infectious diseases websites in Appendix H.

Meningitis

Background

Meningitis is a serious infectious illness that causes inflammation of the brain lining. There are several forms, the mildest ones caused by viruses. They commonly lead to abdominal upsets and severe headache, which often settle without treatment.

However, there are several serious forms of meningitis, which need immediate diagnosis and treatment. Most of this section is about the most urgent form to treat, meningococcal meningitis. However, two other forms of bacterial meningitis also affect children, and sometimes adults:

- *Haemophilus influenzae* causes Haemophilus meningitis: the Hib vaccine (see page 243) protects against this.
- *Streptococcus pneumoniae* (pneumococcus) causes pneumococcal meningitis and the pneumococcal vaccine (Previnar, Pneumovax) can prevent this (pages 243 and 305).

Meningococcal meningitis

An organism known as Meningococcus, or *Neisseria meningitidis*, causes this, the most serious form of meningitis. It is spread by breathing in the germs from infected people or from healthy carriers. Meningococcal meningitis is found in many tropical countries, including the Sahel (countries bordering the southern Sahara, known as the 'Meningitis Belt'), though epidemics occur in countries to the south and the north of this area. There are outbreaks from time to time in other parts of the world, including the UK. Young children and adolescents are most at risk.

The disease comes in various strains, and vaccines have been developed against forms A, C, Y and W-135, which cause the most severe outbreaks. There is not yet any vaccine against form B. In the UK immunization against meningitis C is now routinely given to children, teenagers and adults (see pages 8, 243, 389–91). Meningitis tends to occur in the cool season when people crowd together – in the Sahel this coincides with the northern hemisphere winter. The incubation period is usually between two and ten days.

Symptoms

Many people who become infected with meningitis have no symptoms but still act as carriers. When symptoms do occur they start with a sudden onset of intense headache, neck stiffness, dislike of light, fever, nausea or vomiting. This is often preceded or accompanied by a blotchy rash. In meningitis this rash does not go white when you press it. One easy way of testing this is to press a glass against the skin. If it does not blanch, assume this is meningitis and get immediate medical treatment (see below). Often meningitis is known to be present in the area. Children are at special risk. Recently it has been reported that pale cold extremities in children can precede other symptoms by several hours and alert parents and doctors to the condition, especially when it is known there is a current outbreak.

Prevention

The illness caused by forms A, C, Y and W-135 can be prevented by a single quadrivalent immunization (see Appendix J, pages 389–91). Those visiting areas where the disease is known to occur, especially if working with children or in crowded communities, should be immunized with this, as should all children visiting affected areas. Anyone who has had their spleen removed must be immunized for any overseas travel. During epidemics, try to avoid crowded conditions. Anyone going on the Hajj pilgrimage to Saudi Arabia needs to be immunized with the quadrivalent form of the vaccine and must carry a certificate confirming it has been carried out in the past three years.

Treatment

This needs to be started immediately by a doctor, as the disease can cause death within hours. In an emergency, health workers can give penicillin G, two mega units, one injection intramuscularly into each buttock, to those not allergic to penicillin.

Please see further details on infectious diseases websites in Appendix H.

Migraine and headaches

Background

Migraine and other headaches sometimes become worse when working overseas. Stress, dehydration and missing meals can contribute to this; so can monosodium glutamate (MSG), present in meals in some parts of the world. Sudden changes of altitude can also make headaches worse.

Prevention

Most people with migraine know the best ways to prevent them. When working in hot climates, make sure you have plenty of fluids – enough to keep your urine pale. Avoid getting hungry, especially if working hard: a snack between meals can help. Chocolate, cheese and red wine can be contributing factors, especially if two of these, even in small quantities, are taken together. The contraceptive pill can worsen migraine, and some antimalarials make headaches worse. Although it is easy to say and much harder to do, learning to relax, setting up a good work–life balance and taking regular exercise will help some people.

If you have a tendency to migraine, discuss this with your doctor before travelling and take a supply of the most effective tablets with you.

Treatment

A good first-line treatment for migraine and also for other forms of headache, including tension headache, is one tablet of metoclopramide 10 mg (Maxolon – prescription needed in UK) or domperidone (Motilium – not in pregnancy), followed ten minutes later by either soluble aspirin total 900 mg (usually three tablets) or soluble paracetamol total 1,000 mg (usually two tablets) or ibuprofen 400–600 mg.

There is a range of treatments available for migraine, for both prevention and cure, which a surprising number of migraine sufferers – especially if they have been working overseas – are unaware of. Chief among these are the triptans, e.g. sumatriptan (Imigran) and – probably even more effective – zolmitriptan (Zolmig). However, these are very expensive if you need to send back for more supplies when overseas, and they are not yet available in many countries.

Further action

If headaches still seem to be getting worse, review your lifestyle and see if there are any changes you can make to reduce stress and overwork. Look at ways in which you can relax both on the job and at home, or how you might get away for a break or a holiday.

If headaches worsen for no obvious reason or they persist or start for the first time, this may be caused by a wide variety of infections and other conditions, including malaria. It would be sensible to consult a doctor.

Plague

Background

Plague, well known as the cause of the Black Death, still causes occasional outbreaks in parts of Asia, Africa and South America. The Democratic Republic of Congo, India, Madagascar, Mongolia and Vietnam regularly report cases. Although the risk to travellers and expatriates is extremely remote, the fear of plague can cause much anxiety and it is therefore worth knowing about its prevention. There have been recent reports of resistance developing in some areas, meaning that plague may be harder to treat in future. Some countries have concerns about the use of plague as a weapon in bioterrorism.

What causes it?

Plague is caused by a bacterium, *Yersinia pestis*, that affects rodents (especially rats) and occasionally other mammals, including humans. It is spread by fleas that come from an infected (often dying) animal and that are looking for another host. A bite from an infected flea causes *bubonic* plague, but a person so infected may pass on the germs (through coughing or breathing) to others, who then develop *pneumonic* plague. Pneumonic plague can also occur in patients with bubonic plague as the infection enters the lungs.

Symptoms

These develop within a week of exposure, and in the case of bubonic plague include severe shivering, high temperature and pain, as well as swelling in the groin or armpit, caused by inflamed glands (buboes). Untreated cases have a 50:50 chance of survival.

Pneumonic plague starts and progresses rapidly, with fever, cough and severe shortness of breath, death usually occurring within 48 hours.

Prevention

This consists of avoiding areas where outbreaks are known to be currently occurring. Avoid contact with live or dead rodents. If this is not possible, make every effort to avoid flea bites by applying insect repellent and sleeping with permethrin-impregnated sheets or bed nets.

Both bed nets and sheets must be well tucked in, as fleas can otherwise jump from the floor to the bed. Bed legs should ideally be stood in jars of salt water. Kill off any potentially infected rodents, especially rats in or near the house. Regularly treat domestic pets with flea powder. Plague vaccines are not currently recommended, except for vets and zoologists working in affected areas.

Consider taking preventative antibiotics in the following three situations: definite contact with a case of plague; being in crowded areas where pneumonic cases are occurring; and after a flea bite, in an area where plague is currently present.

Adults and children over the age of eight should take tetracycline or oxytetracycline 250 mg tablets four times daily for one week, if necessary repeating this if further contact occurs. Children between the ages of two and eight, if at high risk, can take ciprofloxacin 10 mg/kg daily in two divided doses for one week. (Ciprofloxacin is not otherwise normally used in children.) Children under the age of two and pregnant women should avoid areas where plague cases are occurring.

Treatment

If you develop any suspicious symptoms, you must start antibiotics immediately and be under medical supervision. The same antibiotics are used – twice the above dose of tetracycline or oxytetracycline, and 15 mg/kg of ciprofloxacin. Trimethoprim 200 mg twice daily has proved effective when resistance occurs, as in parts of Madagascar.

For further information see infectious diseases websites in Appendix H.

Rabies

Note: Even if you have had a course of three rabies injections before going abroad, you will still need further injections if you are bitten, licked or scratched by an animal that may have rabies (see below).

Background

What is rabies?

Rabies is an infection caused by a Lyssavirus, spread by a bite, lick or scratch from an infected mammal. Certain mammals are well known as 'reservoirs' of infection. Examples are the dog almost worldwide, the fox in Europe, vampire bats in South America and the Caribbean, and the silver-haired bat in North America. However, any mammal may be infected, and can in turn pass on the infection.

How common is rabies and where is it found?

The World Health Organization estimates (2005) that approximately 31,000 people die in Asia each year (the majority in India), and 24,000 in Africa. In Latin America the number of reported human cases is less than 100 per year.

Rabies is now very rare in western Europe, absent from the UK,

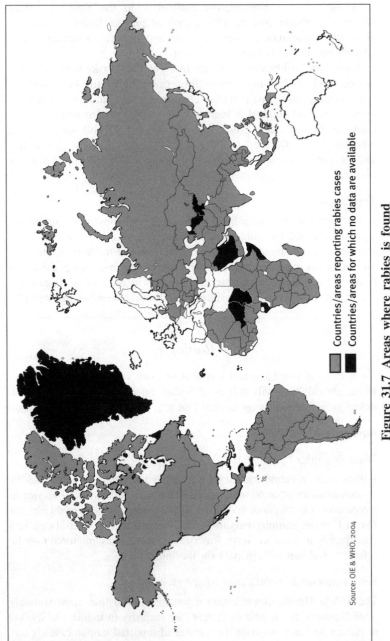

Figure 31.7 Areas where rabies is found
(Modified from a map by WHO, 2004)

Countries/areas reporting rabies cases

Countries/areas for which no data are available

Source: OIE & WHO, 2004

Australia, New Zealand, Norway, Sweden, Japan, probably Papua New Guinea and most Pacific islands. It remains very common in South and Southeast Asia and most of Africa (see Figure 31.7).

How do you catch rabies?

By being bitten, scratched, or licked on broken skin or the mouth by a rabid animal – usually a dog, sometimes a cat, monkey, squirrel, bear or raccoon. Bats can also spread it, often leaving no mark, and so occasionally can other mammals.

What is the risk to travellers?

As a traveller you have two risks, both of which need preventing: the small but important one of being infected with rabies, and the more common experience of anxiety following an encounter with a suspicious animal that you did nothing about. If you are well informed and fully vaccinated you will be well protected against both these risks. Your maximum danger times are usually when travelling in rural areas, trekking or jogging, or when you or your children touch an apparently friendly but unknown dog, monkey, squirrel or cat. There is also a risk from the pets of friends, especially dogs in areas where rabies is common, who have not had their rabies immunizations kept fully up to date.

What are the symptoms in animals and humans?

These are well known to most travellers. In animals there is often a change of behaviour, a dog becoming more aggressive or more docile than usual. There may be an aversion to water. Unprovoked attacks by dogs or by any mammal that behaves aggressively should ring alarm bells, especially if rabies is common in the area. *However, many infected (and infectious) mammals behave quite normally.*

Humans can develop symptoms any time from four days to two years after contact (usually 30 to 60 days).

The symptoms progress rapidly from fever and headache to paralysis, bouts of terror and aggression to coma and death. There is no cure once symptoms have started.

How do I protect myself from rabies?

The most important way is to try and avoid being bitten, licked or scratched by a dog, cat, monkey, squirrel or any other mammal. Children are at the most risk, and you need to keep a careful eye on them and explain why they should never touch an unknown animal.

Immunization is also important: see below and pages 392–4.

Who should be immunized?

This is a tricky question because the risk is low but the worry great. The expense of the vaccine also puts some people off. There are no universally agreed guidelines on this, and risk and benefit have to be carefully weighed. We believe the suggestions below represent a good commonsense approach.

The following travellers should be immunized:

- those staying longer than two weeks in sub-Saharan Africa or southern or Southeast Asia;
- those staying longer than one month in other areas of the world where rabies is known to occur, including central and southern America, and western Asia;
- those visiting an affected country for any length of time who will be travelling in remote areas which are more than 24 hours from the capital, or from a city known to have an equivalent level of health care.

> One important thing has tilted the balance in favour of having rabies immunizations before you go to a developing country in Africa or Asia. The vital Human Rabies Immunoglobulin (HRIG) or Equine Rabies Immunoglobulin (ERIG) is in short supply and is not available in many parts of the world if you have a risky incident. You need HRIG or ERIG if you have not had your pre-exposure injections before you set off on your travels. So if a dog bites you, it's a big problem (see below) unless you have been fully immunized before you go abroad.

What do I do if the worst happens?

If an incident as described above has happened, this is what you should do:

- Wash the wound carefully with soap and water, if possible under a running tap, to remove all saliva and dirt. Then apply tincture of iodine, povidone iodine or alcohol (ideally 70 per cent ethanol, but gin and whisky or other spirits will have some effect). Avoid scrubbing and do not have the wound stitched, certainly not within the first 48 hours. Assume any animal as potentially rabid which is either behaving strangely (many don't) or unknown, or which disappears. Try to observe the animal for ten days. If it is still alive on the tenth day you can relax and discontinue any treatment you have started.
- Be aware of WHO's definitions of categories:
  - *Category 1* Touching or feeding animals: licks on the skin. These need no treatment.
  - *Category 2* Nibbling of unbroken skin. Minor scratches or abrasions without bleeding. Licks on broken skin.
  - *Category 3* Single or multiple bites or scratches which pierce the skin. Contamination of mucous membranes by saliva from licking.
- Start post-exposure injections as follows for any Category 2 or 3 exposure:
  - If you have definitely had a course of two or three primary injections over a four-week period plus boosters every five years since (i.e. your rabies vaccines are up to date) all you need is the *Short Regime* of treatment. The Short Regime now consists of having two post-exposure injections of either HDCV, PCECV, PVRV or RVA vaccines (these different types of rabies vaccine can be used interchangeably (see page 392)). Have the first injection *as soon as possible* and the second three to seven days later. No rabies deaths have occurred in those who have followed this regime.
  - If you have not had a recent full pre-exposure course as described above (i.e. your rabies vaccines are not up to date) you will need the *Full Regime* of treatment. The Full Regime includes five post-exposure doses of HDCV, PCECV, PVRV or RVA with the first dose given *immediately* and the remainder on days 3, 7, 14 and about 28.
  - *Additionally for Category 3 exposures*: if not fully immunized before the incident, you will need either Human Rabies Immunoglobulin (HRIG) or Equine Rabies Immunoglobulin (ERIG) 20 units per kg of your body weight, injected into and around the bite site. You will need to start the HRIG or ERIG treatment *as soon as possible.*
- Make sure you also have a tetanus injection if you are not certain you are up to date, i.e. have had a full course of injections in the past

and a booster in the past ten years (five years if the bite is deep and dirty; see pages 394–5).

Special situations

Rabies and children

Children and toddlers with their love for furry beasts have a higher risk of being exposed to rabies. Actively discourage them from touching unknown animals. Prophylactic (pre-exposure) injections are only currently recommended from one year upwards, but post-exposure treatment is given regardless of age.

Rabies and pregnancy

Pregnant women are not normally given prophylactic injections, but they should plan to have these before conception if they come into the categories recommended above for preventative immunizations before travelling. If they have a Category 2 or 3 risk as above, full immunization as recommended is essential and no serious adverse reactions have been reported affecting the pregnancy.

Wrong advice

If a local doctor suggests that a single injection or tablet alone is sufficient, *do not accept such advice.* Follow the instructions above instead.

If you are worried, contact a specialist back home for advice or ring your travel insurance medical helpline. Medical staff at InterHealth can advise members of InterHealth at any time.

A useful website is <http://www.who.int/rabnet>.

Human Rabies Immunoglobulin is available by joining the Blood Care Foundation; for details see pages 170 and 376.

River blindness (onchocerciasis)

Background

This is currently found in about 25 countries, including scattered areas of central Africa and, less commonly, parts of Central America and the Yemen. It is a form of filariasis (see pages 296–7) caused by an organism known as *Onchocerca volvulus*, and is spread by the bite of infected female blackflies (2–4 mm long), appropriately known as *Simulium damnosum*. They usually breed near fast-flowing rivers. Untreated, the disease can eventually lead to blindness, rare in travellers unless repeatedly reinfected.

Travellers living for more than about three months in areas where this is present are at some risk. This includes missionaries, anthropologists, environmentalists and development workers.

Symptoms

These often start with an initial bite, often painful, which may be followed, usually after weeks or months, by an intensely itchy rash and skin nodules, especially over the lower trunk.

These symptoms may appear many months, or up to three years, after leaving the affected area. Eye symptoms, as mentioned, rarely occur in travellers.

Prevention

Cover the skin and use DEET-based insect repellents. Those working in high-risk areas can take prophylactic treatment under specialist advice.

Action if you have been at risk

If you have been working in an area where the disease is known to occur, you should have a blood test on return, especially if you develop itching within weeks or months, with or without a rash. Usually the eosinophil count will be raised and a filaria serology test may be positive. However, a skin snip at a tropical diseases centre clinches the diagnosis.

Treatment

Treatment is ivermectin (Mectizan), always under medical supervision, usually at a dose of 150 micrograms/kg, usually with re-treatment at intervals of six to 12 months until all the adult worms die out.

Skin conditions

The combination of sun, heat, biting insects and lack of hygiene means that skin problems are common in developing countries. Aid workers, adventure travellers, children and volunteers on low budgets need to take special care. So do those with diabetes. The following are some of the common problems.

Blisters

These can develop very quickly, may be slow to heal and often become infected.

Prevention

Wear well-fitting shoes and loose cotton socks. If trekking or walking any distance, *wear in your shoes or boots for several days before, and consider using two layers of socks.* Sandals, especially if worn without socks in dusty areas, quickly lead to blisters.

Treatment

If the skin is broken, wash carefully and apply antiseptic cream and a non-adherent bandage, secured with an adhesive dressing. If unbroken, leave intact if possible, otherwise pierce roof of blister with sterile needle, apply gauze covered with thin layer of Vaseline and secure with adhesive dressing. Various blister treatments can offer effective relief and are available at many outdoor shops and chemists. Avoid the offending footwear.

Boils and infected bites

These are very common in the tropics, often developing at times of overwork, stress or when due for home leave or a holiday. They often start as bites, which become infected through scratching.

Prevention

Develop a balanced lifestyle with adequate rest and relaxation; eat a well-balanced diet with fresh fruit and vegetables. Wash regularly with soap and water. Salt water is helpful, either through bathing in the sea (where unpolluted) or, if you are prone to boils, by adding a fistful of salt or an antiseptic such as Milton to bath water where possible. If living in an institution, make sure your sheets are properly cleaned and take care over your laundry.

Treatment

Wash gently with soap and water and apply antiseptic cream. Do not squeeze, especially if on the head and neck, but allow the boil to come to a point and burst naturally, at which time you can apply absorbent gauze with Vaseline. Larger boils, especially in the armpit, may need lancing by a doctor or nurse using a sterile blade.

Those with a tendency for troublesome boils should take flucloxacillin capsules 500 mg every six hours for a week or, if allergic to penicillin, erythromycin 500 mg every six hours for a week, in each case starting when the boil first develops. Because the germs causing boils often live in the nostrils, also gently insert a cream containing both an antibiotic and an antiseptic (e.g. chlorhexidine hydrochloride 0.1 per cent and neomycin sulphate 0.5 per cent, marketed in the UK as Naseptin) into both nostrils by using your cleaned little finger, twice daily for a week. Ideally also use this in all household members – especially children. If boils trouble you, take a supply of one of these antibiotics and Naseptin with you.

Boils are occasionally caused by tumbu flies (see pages 213–14).

Cellulitis

This is a common and important condition in travellers of all ages, but especially in older people or those with varicose veins, diabetes or reduced immunity. It is caused by a bacterial infection.

Symptoms

The tissues just under the skin become warm, red, often very painful and swollen. Symptoms often start in the feet or ankles and move rapidly up the legs, sometimes accompanied by red swollen lines. Cellulitis can develop extremely quickly, leading to fever and serious illness if untreated.

Prevention

Again, try to lead a healthy and balanced lifestyle and to avoid getting over-tired. Wash your feet regularly, treat any fungal infection, such as athlete's foot, and try to avoid injuries to your feet, especially on the beach or around the house and garden. Avoid going barefoot. Keep your toenails short. If you have swollen ankles or legs, consider support stockings or elevating your foot on a chair when sitting down.

Treatment

This needs to be started without delay. Take penicillin V 500 mg, one four times daily, or amoxicillin 500 mg capsules, one three times daily, or co-amoxiclav (Augmentin) 625 mg capsules, one three times daily. In addition, also start flucloxacillin 500 mg capsules, one four times daily. Fluclox is often hard to get hold of, in which case Augmentin alone is the best choice. All these antibiotics are penicillin-based, so if you are allergic to penicillin just take erythromycin 500 mg tablets, one four times daily. Continue antibiotics until all infection has gone – often one to two weeks – and rest with your leg up, taking painkillers as necessary. Sometimes these doses are insufficient and you will need antibiotics by injection or intravenously. Get seen by a doctor in any case, and urgently if self-treatment is not rapidly improving your symptoms.

If you have had cellulitis in the past, carry antibiotics with you and start them at the first sign of trouble.

Creeping eruption (Cutaneous larva migrans, sandworm)

This is usually caused by a larva from the dog tapeworm that penetrates the skin. It is often caught on tropical beaches, especially if a lot of dogs, or less commonly cats, are about.

Symptoms

The chief symptom is a red itchy line, usually on either the sole of the foot, the buttock or any other part of your body that has been resting on the beach or infected ground. The line moves slowly, a few millimetres a day. Sometimes it develops watery (vesicular) areas or becomes infected. Occasionally there are a number of lines, indicating multiple infections.

Prevention

Lie on a towel rather than directly on the beach, and don't walk barefoot above the high tide mark. This is because any contamination from dogs is usually washed away by seawater below the high tide mark. Ideally you should wear shoes when walking on the beach, unless splashing along at the water's edge.

Treatment

This condition often disappears on its own if you are patient, and is rarely serious. It can best be treated by taking albendazole 400 mg tablets, two daily for five days. Thiabendazole is often used but has more troublesome side-effects. Thiabendazole can also be used as an ointment, but this is usually less effective than albendazole tablets.

Fungal infections (Tinea)

Of the skin

Fungi like warm, moist conditions and are therefore very common in tropical climates.

Symptoms The main symptom of Tinea is a pink, slightly rough or raised itchy patch, often circular with a spreading edge.

Athlete's foot (*Tinea pedis*) causes itching between the toes; groin itch (Dhobie's itch, *Tinea cruris*) causes itching in the groin and between the legs. Other 'ringworm' infections occur in the scalp or anywhere on the body surface.

Thrush (Candida) is also a type of fungal infection, and in addition to causing vaginal discharge (see page 298) commonly causes a reddish line in the folds of the groin and the breast, especially in the overweight and those taking doxycycline as an antimalarial.

Prevention You can help prevent fungal infections by bathing regularly, wearing loose-fitting cotton underpants (Dhobie's itch) and open-toed shoes or sandals with cotton socks changed daily (athlete's foot). Trainers or any shoe with an internal rubber sole are likely to make athlete's foot worse.

Treatment You can treat athlete's foot by applying an antifungal dusting powder, e.g. zinc undecenoate 20 per cent, undecenoic acid 5 per cent (Mycota), between the toes and into the socks, or by applying clotrimazole cream (Canesten). This also works well for many other Tinea infections if rubbed in well three times daily and continued for two weeks after symptoms have cleared. Fungal infections that fail to clear up respond to itraconazole (Sporanox) capsules 100 mg once daily for 15–30 days or 200 mg twice daily for seven days. For treatment of Candida, see page 298. Avoid these drugs in pregnancy, and read the Patient Information Leaflet, as there are situations where they are not safe to use. Also see below.

Of the fingernails or toenails

Fungal nail infections, especially of the toes, are very common in those who live or work in hot or humid conditions.

Symptoms Nails become yellowish, brittle, thickened or crumbling, though there are other causes for this; if in doubt, arrange to have nail clippings tested in a good-quality laboratory.

Treatment This is only worth doing if the problem becomes a real nuisance or you are back from the tropics for good or a long break. This is for two reasons: treatment takes a long time, and the condition often recurs in a hot climate.

The most effective treatment is itraconazole (Sporanox) 100 mg capsules, two capsules twice daily for seven days. For fingernails, repeat once after a three-week drug-free interval. For toenails repeat twice with three-week drug-free intervals between each course. Alternatively, try terbinafine (Lamisil) 250 mg tablets, one daily six weeks minimum for fingernails, and 12 weeks minimum for toenails. All these antifungal tablets must be taken under medical supervision, and liver function tests need to be monitored during and after longer-term treatment: they also interact with some other medicines. Milder infections sometimes respond to amorolfine (Loceryl) nail lacquer applied twice weekly for three to six months, used according to manufacturer's instructions.

With any treatment of a fungal infection by mouth, make sure a doctor supervises your treatment, as antifungals are powerful and have some side-effects and serious interactions with other drugs.

Fungal infection (Pityriasis)

Travellers often notice a scaly rash with paling, or occasionally some darkening of the skin. It usually occurs over the back and trunk. This is known as *Pityriasis versicolor*, a superficial fungus. It is not serious and is unlikely to be passed on from person to person, unlike many forms of Tinea. It can look unsightly and often worries travellers that they have caught something more serious.

Treatment

There are several effective treatments, including selenium sulphide 2.5 per cent which is applied for seven days, and then repeated on the first and third days of the month for six months to prevent recurrence. It should be left on for five to ten minutes and then washed off. Other antifungal creams, such as terbinafine, applied for two weeks also work well. Itraconazole 20 mg capsules or tablets daily for seven days can be used if creams are not available.

Patches that continue to look pale usually regain their pigment over time, especially if you go back cautiously into the sun.

Impetigo (infected skin)

This is a common bacterial infection of the skin that tends to occur when you are tired, hot or run down.

Symptoms

Impetigo is a spreading, slightly itchy rash that weeps golden-coloured pus. It is very infectious.

Prevention

This is by regular washing in soap and water and by taking extra care if another member of the household also has it.

Treatment

Gently remove any crusts with povidone-iodine (or another antiseptic) or salty water, and apply a topical antibiotic cream or ointment such as fucidic acid (Fucidin) or mupirocin. If the impetigo continues to spread, or you develop red, hot skin in patches or streaks, with or without swollen lymph nodes, start oral antibiotics such as flucloxacillin 500 mg four times a day, amoxicillin 500 mg three times a day or, if allergic to penicillin, erythromycin 500 mg four times daily, in each case for seven days. You should see a doctor. The condition is common in children, who can use the same antibiotics at the correct dose for age.

When removing crusts or rubbing in cream, either use gloves or wash your hands with soap and water immediately afterwards.

Prickly heat

This is an itchy condition caused by the blocking up of sweat ducts. It is common in children and those not acclimatized to hot and humid climates.

Symptoms

Prickly heat consists of small reddish spots, on a pinkish skin, which develop mainly on the upper trunk, armpits, waist and the backs of the knees and neck. It disturbs sleep and can be very irritating, especially for children.

Prevention

Wear loose-fitting cotton clothing and avoid excessive soap. Dust talcum powder into clothes that rub against the skin.

Treatment

It can be soothed by applying lacto calamine lotion (unsightly, so not popular with school-age children) and keeping as cool as possible. Air-conditioning helps to reduce it, but most international travellers find it improves anyway after acclimatization.

Scabies

See pages 210–11.

Skin cancer

Those most at risk from skin cancer include long-term residents of the tropics, the fair-skinned and anyone exposed to prolonged or excessive sun in childhood. Make sure you take sensible precautions to avoid too much sun. There are details about this important condition on page 200.

Sleeping sickness (African trypanosomiasis)

Background

African sleeping sickness is caused by a parasite injected by a bite from an infected Tsetse fly (see Figure 31.8). There are two forms of sleeping sickness: western or gambiense, mainly in West and central Africa; and eastern or rhodesiense, mainly in eastern Africa. Travellers are at low risk but need to be cautious on safari trips, or if working outdoors or involved in aid or development projects in affected areas.

Symptoms

A sign that you have been bitten by a Tsetse fly is often the development of a painful boil-like swelling at the site of the bite. Fever and headache may then develop within days or weeks (eastern form), but often months later (western form). First symptoms usually include severe headache, insomnia, enlarged lymph nodes (especially in the neck), a rash and anaemia. Later, severe sleepiness and weight loss usually develop.

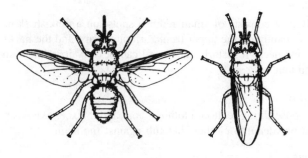

Figure 31.8 Tsetse fly (about 1 cm long)

Prevention

This is not entirely straightforward and depends on being aware of the risk. Tsetse flies can bite through clothing and insect repellents have little effect. Avoid wearing the colour blue (a favourite colour of Tsetses) and be alert in areas where sleeping sickness is known to occur.

If you have suspicious symptoms, consult a doctor experienced in tropical diseases without delay. Sleeping sickness can be quite hard to diagnose in travellers, but specific blood tests are increasingly accurate.

Treatment

This must be under medical supervision as soon as possible, as it is otherwise fatal. Eflornithine and melarsoprol are the main drugs used.

For further information see infectious diseases websites in Appendix H.

Sudden acute respiratory syndrome (SARS)

Background

This first came to light in 2002 and, thanks to clever and careful control measures coordinated by the World Health Organization, was eradicated. At the time of writing no cases are occurring. However, the fear remains that it could easily recur.

It is caused by a coronavirus and is thought to spread from infected animals, probably civet cats and raccoon dogs in southeastern China.

Symptoms

These develop two to ten, average five, days after contact and consist of fever, often high, with headache, muscle pain, chills and rigors. After three to seven days a dry cough and shortness of breath develop. The illness can persist for many days. About 10 per cent of cases die, but more than half of those over 60 died in the 2002–3 outbreak. These symptoms mimic many other illness, including flu and avian flu.

Prevention

In the case of a further outbreak, information on this will be quickly made available and posted on websites. At the present time no special precautions need to be taken apart from avoiding close contact with live food markets in China. (In the case of avian flu it is specifically live poultry markets that pose the chief danger.)

Treatment

Apart from high-quality medical and nursing care there is no treatment.
For more information see <http://www.cdc.gov/ncidod/sars>.

Tick-borne encephalitis (TBE)

Background

TBE is a serious viral infection usually spread by the bite of infected Ixodes ticks. It cannot be passed on from person to person.

The complex distribution of TBE mentioned below is taken from latest advice from the Centers for Disease Control and Prevention, USA.

TBE occurs in areas correlated with the distribution of the tick vectors in the temperate regions of Europe and Asia between latitudes 39° and 65°, extending from western France to Hokkaido in Japan. The countries most heavily impacted are Austria, Belarus, Czech Republic, Estonia, Germany, Hungary, Kazakhstan, Latvia, Lithuania, Poland, Romania, Russia, Slovakia and the Ukraine. There are also foci in the southern portions of Finland, Norway, Sweden and the island of Bornholm in Denmark, as well as the northern portions of Albania, Bosnia, Croatia, Italy, Greece and Slovenia. Sporadic cases have also been reported in Turkey. In China the known endemic areas are Hunchun in Jilin province and western Yunnan near the Burmese border.

The disease has recently become more common in many areas, possibly because of global warming. It occurs mainly during the summer months in rural forested areas, forest margins, meadows and shrubberies, up to an altitude of 1,000 metres.

Symptoms

Most people bitten by an infected tick develop no symptoms. For those who do, symptoms resemble a flu-like illness starting seven to 14 days after the tick-bite. About one person in ten develops a second phase of the illness with severe headache, and confusion. This can lead to paralysis and death. TBE becomes more serious with age.

Prevention

This depends on trying to avoid tick bites. Wear boots in affected areas, with trousers tucked into socks. If made of wool or cotton these can be soaked in a DEET solution (see page 22) or you can spray socks with either 100 per cent DEET or permethrin in the form of Bug Proof (permethrin can be used on any type of clothing).

Check your body regularly, including the groin and scalp hairline, for the presence of ticks and remove any at once (for details on how to do this see pages 213–14).

Cover the ground with a protective sheet when picnicking.

Avoid unpasteurized dairy products in affected areas as occasionally you can pick this up from infected animals.

A vaccine is available (see page 396), recommended only for those staying long term in affected areas. Ramblers, environmentalists, aid workers, soldiers and those trekking, camping or picnicking in affected areas are at definite risk and should consider vaccination.

Treatment

In severely affected areas of Europe a hyperimmune globulin has been available but is no longer recommended because of side-effects. Report to the nearest hospital if you are worried. There is no treatment for TBE but skilled care in hospital improves chances of survival.

For further information see infectious diseases websites in Appendix H.

Tick-bite fever (TBF)

Background

African tick-bite fever is caused by an organism called *Rickettsia africae* or *R. conorii*. Tick-bite fever is found in sub-Saharan Africa, and commonly in southern and eastern Africa. The disease is spread by the bites of infected ticks which tend to live in forested, brush or grassy areas and get on to skin or clothing when you are trekking or going on walking safaris in affected areas.

TBF is one of a complex group of Rickettsial infections found in different forms in different parts of the world, some of which are serious, but African TBF is rarely so. (See under typhus, pages 345–6.) African TBF should not be confused with a much less common disease known as tick-borne relapsing fever, caused by an organism called Borrelia.

Symptoms

These can be non-specific and mimic malaria. Common symptoms are fever, sometimes a faint rash, swollen lymph nodes and the presence of a dark skin lesion, sometimes several, often with surrounding swelling of the skin, known as an eschar (described on page 345 in the section on typhus). Symptoms usually last for four to seven days.

Prevention

When walking in affected areas, follow the instructions under prevention of typhus on page 346. Check yourself and colleagues for tick bites; ticks usually have to feed for some hours before passing on any infection. See page 213 for how to remove ticks.

Treatment

This is with doxycycline 100 mg once or twice daily for one week (not in pregnancy or those under 16). However, most cases of TBF cure themselves, and because the illness is usually short-lived and rarely causes serious symptoms, it is frequently not confirmed by blood tests and usually self-cures without treatment.

However, symptoms should first be treated as for malaria, unless this has been excluded on a blood slide, because the two diseases can easily be confused.

Tonsillitis and sore throats

Background

If you have suffered from tonsillitis before going abroad, you may well find it recurs, especially at times of stress, overwork or exhaustion.

Many sore throats and most attacks of tonsillitis are caused by a germ called Streptococcus (Strep throat), and any sore throat, especially if accompanied by swollen neck glands and a fever, is worth treating with antibiotics; see below.

Sore throats, especially if accompanied by neck glands and marked tiredness, can be caused by glandular fever (see below and page 184). A condition known as Vincent's angina or ulcerative gingivitis can affect both the throat and gums. Very occasionally throat infections may be caused by diphtheria (foul breath, greenish membrane on throat).

Symptoms

Symptoms of tonsillitis, usually obvious, are fever, sore throat and often swollen lymph glands, usually just under the skin at the angle of the jaw.

Prevention

This is to give priority to holidays, one or two days off in seven, and trying to achieve a balanced lifestyle. If you have a tendency to tonsillitis, consider starting antibiotic treatment *as soon as symptoms start.*

If you have had several severe attacks in the recent past, or a tonsillar abscess, discuss with your doctor whether you should have your tonsils removed before any long-term assignment abroad or on your next home leave.

Treatment

If symptoms are severe or persistent, treat for seven to ten days either with penicillin V 250 mg four times daily or 500 mg three times daily, or with amoxicillin 500 mg three times daily. If you are allergic to penicillin, try erythromycin 500 mg four times daily. Some people find that gargling with aspirin can soothe the pain, but this should not be used in those under 16. Treat children with the same antibiotics at the correct dose for age.

Remember, however, that many sore throats are caused by viruses, and although antibiotics will cause no harm, neither will they make any difference.

Note on glandular fever (infectious mononucleosis)

This is a common cause of sore throat, especially in younger travellers. Often neck glands are present, you feel very tired, and are sometimes low in spirits. The symptoms can persist for a long time.

Very few local doctors will know about this condition because it is apparently uncommon in most developing countries. If you think this may be the cause of your problems, see a doctor used to seeing international travellers and foreigners. A blood test known as a Paul Bunnell Test or Monospot will sometimes confirm it. Glandular fever needs treating with care, and you will need plenty of rest until symptoms disappear and energy returns. Two other conditions can mimic glandular fever – cytomegalovirus infection and toxoplasmosis. There is no specific treatment.

Tooth and mouth problems

Reasons for taking tooth care seriously

Severe toothache and dental abscesses are surprisingly common in those living overseas. It is worth giving your teeth a high degree of priority, for the following reasons:

- Severe toothache can ruin a visit, an important programme or a holiday.
- Tooth abscesses often occur when you are tired or run down, as for example during a tough assignment or at the end of a volunteer year.
- Dental care overseas is often unreliable, may be very expensive and carries a small but definite hepatitis B and HIV risk in some countries.
- Severe or recurrent toothache is a common reason for having to cut short a visit or assignment.
- The water used as a coolant or to rinse your mouth may be contaminated.
- Chronic tooth infection can cause tiredness and recurrent fever and malaise.
- Gum disease (gingivitis) can become more troublesome if you are tired or run down when working abroad.

Preventing tooth problems

Have a thorough dental check well before you leave. Have any fillings attended to, any ill-fitting dentures replaced and any pre-emptive treatment of impacted or painful wisdom teeth completed. Ask your dentist about gum disease and whether you need to take any further action to reduce it. Whenever you come home on leave, have a further check.

Continue to clean your teeth regularly when overseas – not always easy if living in the back of beyond with an unreliable water supply. Make sure the water you use is either boiled or sterilized, and keep a supply in the bathroom or wherever you clean your teeth. Otherwise just use toothpaste (and saliva).

Dental floss is useful. If your teeth are prone to decay, avoid excessive sweets and too much oversweetened tea or soft drinks, unless there is nothing else safe to drink.

A small amount of fluoride helps prevent tooth decay; too much leads to tooth mottling and discoloration. Natural levels of fluoride in the water tend to be higher in tropical countries. Use fluoride tablets only if local levels are known to be very low or absent. Fluoride toothpaste can still be used, but make sure children don't eat it.

Choose any dentist overseas with care and on personal recommendation. Check as far as you are able that all needles and syringes are sealed, disposable and not reused; also that all instruments are steam-sterilized.

Consider taking an emergency dental kit and a supply of antibiotics (see below and Appendix C).

Common dental problems

Toothache

This may be caused by injury, the loosening of a filling, or a dental abscess that is starting to form. If pain becomes severe or prolonged, try to find a reliable dentist and in the meantime start treatment with antibiotics, as detailed below. Oil of cloves can ease the pain, as can aspirin placed at the base of the tooth. In children, give paracetamol tablets or syrup by mouth, rather than aspirin.

Tooth abscess

This is usually obvious because of severe pain on moving the tooth or pressing the root. Sometimes you may develop a swollen cheek or jaw (which may be painful or painless).

Treat an abscess by taking antibiotics such as co-amoxiclav (Augmentin) 625 mg three times a day for seven days (not if allergic to penicillin) or erythromycin 500 mg four times daily. Sometimes metronidazole (Flagyl) is very effective, especially in a deep-seated or chronic abscess, at a dosage of 200 mg three times daily for five to seven days. Be aware of the side-effects mentioned on page 107. See a dentist, who may either remove the tooth or recommend root canal treatment. In the case of the latter, enquire carefully how many treatments are likely and the cost of each.

Lost dentures

Consider taking a spare pair, and try to remove dentures before any attack of vomiting.

A broken front tooth

If clean, soak in salty boiled water and replace within half an hour, pressing in firmly the right way round. Get to the dentist as soon as possible.

Known heart problems

If you have known heart problems, such as a past history of rheumatic fever, heart valve disease or the presence of prosthetic valves, antibiotic cover will be needed for all dental work – discuss this with your dentist before going overseas. Widely used is amoxicillin 2 gram by mouth 30 minutes before and 1 gram six hours after any dental work or, if allergic to penicillin, erythromycin 1.5 grams before and 1 gram after.

A dental kit

These are available and widely used by those living in remote conditions or where dental facilities are unreliable. They usually contain equipment for temporary replacements of crowns, bridges and caps, as well as material for temporary fillings. After using a kit, see a reliable dentist as soon as you can. If you take a kit, make sure you also have a supply of antibiotics.

Mouth ulcers

Background

These can be a real nuisance among longer-term travellers. Often proguanil (Paludrine) and Malarone, which contains proguanil, contribute to mouth ulcers, as can doxycycline or chloroquine if taken for several weeks or months. Only change to another antimalarial if your mouth really causes you grief. Mouth ulcers can also develop if you are tired, run down or have repeated bowel problems. Sometimes they just occur for no reason.

Treatment

They are best treated by making sure you eat a well-balanced diet, getting any bowel infection diagnosed and treated, and making sure you have enough sleep and leisure. Some people find that taking vitamin B complex daily or folic acid 5 mg for a month seems to help. Try using an antiseptic mouthwash (e.g. chlorhexidine or povidone iodine) or carbenoxolone gel (Bioral) or hydrocortisone 2.5 mg lozenges (Corlan).

If any single ulcer or mouth problem lasts longer than three weeks, a doctor should check you out.

Tuberculosis (TB)

Background

International travellers sometimes develop TB, usually if they have been working with infectious cases, e.g. as health workers or prison visitors, or if living or working longer term in areas where TB is common. With the spread of HIV, TB is becoming commoner in many countries, and this also means that those working in HIV-affected areas are at an increased risk. Multi-drug resistant cases (MDR-TB) are on the increase, especially in the Russian federation and former countries of the Soviet Union.

Tuberculosis is most commonly a disease of the lungs, caused by germs spreading from an infectious case or from reactivation of a previous (often unknown) lesion (latent TB, see below).

Symptoms of active TB

These include cough for more than three weeks, especially if accompanied by coughing up sputum (sometimes blood-stained), pain in the chest, evening fever and loss of weight. Children may simply lose weight or fail to gain it, only developing specific symptoms later. Many people have what is known as latent TB, from a previous infection which has never caused symptoms but which can become active during periods of exhaustion, stress, overwork or other illness, in particular HIV infection.

TB can affect other parts of the body, but this is comparatively rare in travellers and difficult to diagnose. Persisting ill health and recurrent fever are sometimes caused by chronic TB infection.

Prevention

Obviously this is by avoiding close or prolonged contact with active cases of TB, which may include colleagues, patients or those being visited in prisons, or if frequently travelling on public transport. In addition to minimizing contact, keep fit, eat nutritious food, take regular exercise, get regular sleep and maintain a good work–life balance, especially if working in high-risk situations. Of course, this helps to prevent many infectious illnesses and to minimize stress.

TB in children is also partly prevented by having a BCG vaccination (see pages 380–1).

Treatment

If TB is caught early it can usually be fully treated using multi-drug therapy under careful medical supervision. However, multi-drug resistant (MDR) TB is on the increase and treatment for this, though usually possible, is more complex and prolonged.

Action

If you have been knowingly exposed to TB or have been living long term overseas, especially in high-risk occupations, you should consider having a tuberculin test when you return home. A test which becomes strongly positive may indicate you have developed TB, especially if previous tests did not register a strong reaction. However, if you have previously had a BCG vaccination the tuberculin test can be hard to interpret. If you develop suspicious symptoms either abroad or after you come home, consult a doctor as soon as possible. You should then ideally have a sputum test, tuberculin test or blood ELISPOT test if available and chest X-ray.

For further information see infectious diseases websites in Appendix H.

Typhus fever

Background

This is a group of diseases caused by an organism known as Rickettsia. Rickettsial infections cause a large variety of localized illnesses in different parts of the world (21 are currently described in the 'Yellow Book' of the US Centers for Disease Control and Prevention). Some of these illnesses have more than one name and they are spread by a variety of vectors (including fleas, ticks, mites, lice and sandflies). Each of these feed off an animal host and then bite a human, causing infection. Rickettsial illnesses are not generally spread from person to person.

Most are of little importance to the majority of travellers, unless going to very specific areas (e.g. the Rocky Mountains for Rocky Mountain spotted fever) but three are probably more common than is thought. They include the two forms of typhus fever described below and African tick-bite fever, described separately on pages 338–9.

Scrub typhus

This is found in rural Asia, especially the Indian subcontinent and central, eastern and Southeast Asia, and some Pacific islands. It is spread by small red mites called chiggers (not to be confused with jiggers, see pages 208 and 211). The mites feed off infected rodents and are found in a variety of habitats, including long grass and jungle areas. Their presence is seasonal and hard to predict.

Murine or endemic typhus

This is found almost worldwide and is spread by the rat flea, which passes the infection through bites or skin abrasions.

Symptoms

These usually start four to 14 days after being bitten and include fever, headache, sweating, tiredness, muscle ache, enlarged lymph nodes and a rash, usually starting on the trunk. An eschar is often present at the site of the bite – that is, a dark-coloured mark with a reddish border at the place you were bitten (also known as a tache-noire). This is often on the ankle or lower leg, where there may be localized swelling. Lymph nodes may develop in the groin. Typhus can cause serious illness, especially murine, scrub and above all Rocky Mountain spotted fever.

345

Prevention

Be aware of the risk and protect your lower limbs by wearing trousers, strong shoes or boots, and tucking trousers into long socks. If you are on serious walking safaris or expeditions in affected areas, you can soak your socks (if they are made of wool or cotton) in DEET solution or spray on DEET insecticide at 100 per cent concentration. Or you can use permethrin on your clothes in the form of Bug Proof (see page 22).

Treatment

This is usually by doxycycline 100 mg capsules, two daily for a week. Increasingly, scrub typhus is resistant to doxycycline and an alternative is rifampicin 900 mg daily for seven days. Your symptoms may baffle not only you but also your doctor, so it is worth being aware of this condition, which is being seen more commonly, especially in travellers returning from rural holidays in Thailand. A special blood test usually confirms the diagnosis, but often takes too long to be of much value.

For further information see infectious diseases websites in Appendix H.

Urinary tract infections (UTI)

Background

Infections of the bladder (cystitis) are common when travelling. Hot, bumpy journeys, dehydration and increased sexual activity all make this common in travellers. For long-term residents living in hot climates, urinary infections may be associated with a kidney or bladder stone. UTIs can also spread up the ureter to the kidney leading to a kidney infection, also known as pyelonephritis.

Symptoms

Symptoms of a *lower* urinary tract infection (cystitis), involving bladder and urethra, are usually but not always obvious: an urge to pass urine frequently, accompanied by pain or a burning sensation.

Symptoms of an *upper* urinary tract infection (pyelonephritis) may lead to fever, nausea, worsening symptoms, rigors (uncontrollable shivering) and pain in the lower back in one or both loins (to the side of the spinal column). Simple bladder infections can lead on to kidney infections, especially if you are tired and run down or don't treat lower UTIs when symptoms persist.

If you develop an agonizing pain in the bladder or loin area, this could be a kidney stone.

Women tend to get urinary infections more commonly than men. UTIs are common in pregnancy but symptoms may be less obvious.

Children who start, or restart, wetting their bed for no obvious reason may have a urinary infection. A urinary tract infection may also be the cause of an unidentified fever.

Prevention

This is largely by drinking large amounts of fluid in hot climates. Of course, if you are going on a long hot bus journey this may not be very convenient, but do so whenever you can. Cranberry juice has been shown to help prevent UTIs in some people if you can get hold of it. If cystitis in women is associated with having sex, careful washing before sex and taking an antibiotic either at the time of sex or the following morning can help to prevent it. One option is a single ciprofloxacin 100 mg or 250 mg tablet.

Treatment

Simple UTIs can be self-treated. An ideal antibiotic is ciprofloxacin, which you may have with you to treat diarrhoea. The dose for a UTI is 100 mg twice daily (or 250 mg daily if this is the strength of tablet in your medical kit) taken for three days. This should not be used in children under 16. Amoxicillin is also effective at a dose of 250 mg three times daily for five days, or 250 mg, six tablets taken together followed by a further six after 10–12 hours, providing you are not allergic to penicillin. If symptoms persist get medical advice. UTIs in children should not be self-treated and any antibiotic must be taken in the correct dose for age. Amoxicillin is safe in children and also in pregnancy.

Warning

Symptoms of a UTI can sometimes be caused by a sexually transmitted infection (see pages 158–9). If this is a possibility, try and see a doctor as soon as possible in addition to getting specially tested when you arrive home. Also make sure your partner seeks treatment.

If you have any urinary infection overseas it is sensible to have a urine test on return home, to make sure no infection persists.

Yellow fever

Background

Yellow fever is a viral infection found in the tropical belt of Central and South America, and in Africa, especially West Africa (Figure 31.9, overleaf). The number of outbreaks has increased since the 1980s, making yellow fever vaccination of worldwide importance to prevent the spread into other regions as yet unaffected, as well as to minimize

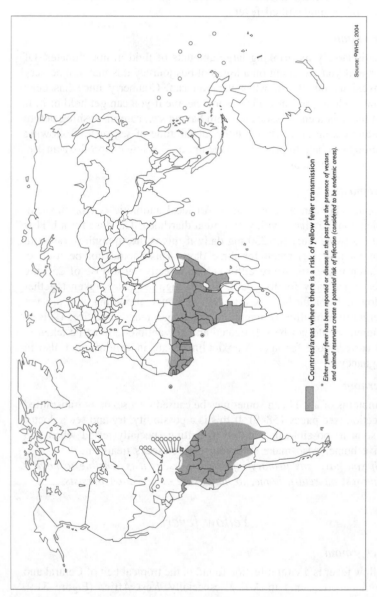

Figure 31.9 Areas where yellow fever is found (WHO, 2004)

Countries/areas where there is a risk of yellow fever transmission*

* Either yellow fever has been reported or disease in the past plus the presence of vectors and animal reservoirs create a potential risk of infection (considered to be endemic areas).

Source: ©WHO, 2004

local outbreaks in areas where it is currently found. It is so far unknown in Asia.

Yellow fever is found in rural areas where outbreaks tend to be small or sporadic and where infection is usually caused by bites from mosquitoes which have been in contact with infected monkeys. It is also found in urban areas where infection is spread from person to person by infected mosquitoes, sometimes leading to epidemics. The risk to travellers is small but those most at risk are visitors who enter affected forested areas. The mosquitoes bite during daylight hours and can survive at altitudes up to 2,500 metres. The incubation period is three to six days, i.e. symptoms do not develop longer than six days after an infected mosquito bite.

Symptoms

There are two phases. Initially, there is fever, muscular pain, headache, nausea or vomiting, often with a slow pulse. About one-fifth of patients develop a second phase after a few days with worsening of symptoms, abdominal pain, jaundice and signs of a haemorrhagic fever (see pages 290–2).

Prevention

This is mainly by immunization (there is more important information on yellow fever vaccine on pages 398–9). YF vaccination is of great importance but nevertheless carries a small risk in those over the age of 60. Avoiding mosquito bites is essential for all, if a known outbreak is occurring. This is through cover-up and using DEET-based repellents during the day, and at night by sleeping under an impregnated mosquito net. Those unimmunized, or whose immunization has lapsed or is uncertain, need to avoid areas where outbreaks are occurring. Check current outbreaks with a travel health specialist, or the website listed under infectious diseases websites (pages 374–5), before visiting any country in the yellow fever zone.

Treatment

There is no specific treatment apart from excellent medical and nursing care.

For further information see infectious diseases websites in Appendix H.

Appendix A
A stress self-help tool

Stress – good and bad!
Know the difference, know yourself and keep well

A short time spent doing this exercise will help you to know yourself – know the difference between the energizing feeling of good pressure and the anxious, draining feeling of bad stress.

We need the good pressure which comes from inside ourselves, our desires and motivations, and the good pressure which comes from outside ourselves in the form of the assignment to be undertaken. There are the diverse requirements of our work, the challenge to persevere in tough times and the drive to stretch ourselves and achieve our objectives.

If you are 'just' travelling, backpacking or visiting, this still applies to you! This chapter will help you get through any difficult patches and get you back on track.

Rule of thumb
Check at a glance

How are you?

Most of the time – 70 per cent – excited, enthusiastic, buzzing, eager, interested, amazed, challenged, thoughtful?

Then you're probably under just the right amount of pressure.

But if you're:

Most of the time – 70 per cent – overloaded, overanxious or overwhelmed, fearful, exhausted, unwell, unhappy ...

Then you're probably stressed and you need to attend to it without delay.

It looks like this!

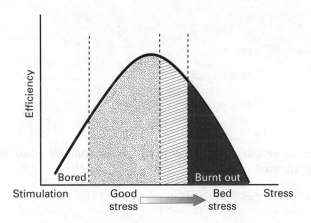

Figure A.1 Graph showing efficiency, stimulation and stress

Now answer these questions to get a picture of how you keep yourself well

1 What gives me energy is:

2 What relaxes me is:

3 I take care of my body by:

4 What I most enjoy about my work overseas is:

5 I switch off work by:

Answer these questions to get a picture of yourself when you're getting stressed

1 What really makes me start to get stressed is:

2 The last time I was really stressed was:

3 When I'm starting to get stressed I change in these ways:
(a) In my body:

(b) In my thinking:

(c) In my behaviour:

(d) In my feelings:

4 The warning signs that stress is getting bad for me are:

5 When I'm getting stressed I change towards other people in these ways:

If these things are happening you need to do something about it now!

Here's how you might get back on track

1 Very basic – try to get enough sleep, eat healthy food, take some exercise and seek out fun or laughter.
2 Keep in touch with family and friends.
3 Review your expectations. Are they too high or too low? Are they realistic?
4 Check out any areas of uncertainty. Clarify as much as possible.
5 Tell your line manager or field co-ordinator clearly that you want to talk things over. Confront the work-related causes of mounting stress and get some solutions in place.
6 Look at a picture of yourself when you are not feeling stressed and reinstate the things that are good for you that you've allowed to slip.
7 Don't turn to or depend on alcohol, painkillers, sex, nicotine, porn, drugs, sugary, fatty foods or anything else addictive. For a fleeting moment of relief they store up more trouble for you in the long run.
8 Do take time off if this is possible. Take it as soon as you can without causing unfair strain on your colleagues. Don't leave it until you *have* to take time off.
9 Do seek appropriate help and support from those around you. If your health or personal well-being is deteriorating, do consult a doctor or other health professional.

Whatever you do, don't delay! Do it now!

Annie Hargrave
Head of Psychological Health Services Team at InterHealth

Appendix B
Checklist of items for your trip

Travel health supplies

- ☐ Aftersun
- ☐ Antibacterial handwash
- ☐ Antimosquito clothes spray
- ☐ First-aid kit or sterile kit (for suggested contents see Appendix D)
- ☐ Flight socks
- ☐ Insect-killer room spray
- ☐ Insect repellents
- ☐ Malaria prevention medication (if required)
- ☐ Medicine kit if going to remote locations (see Appendix C)
- ☐ Mosquito net impregnated with permethrin
- ☐ Mosquito net hanging or fixing kit
- ☐ Mosquito net re-treatment
- ☐ Personal medication
- ☐ Sunscreen and lipbalm with SPF
- ☐ Thermometer
- ☐ Travel health book (*The Traveller's Good Health Guide* or *Travel Health in Your Pocket* – see Further Reading)
- ☐ Treatment medicines (e.g. antibiotics, antihistamines; for diarrhoea, malaria, travel sickness) or kit
- ☐ Water bottle (e.g. Platypus bottle)
- ☐ Water purifier and/or iodine tablets and neutralizing tablets

Documents and information

- ☐ Embassy or high commission contact details
- ☐ Emergency contact details
- ☐ Flight and travel tickets
- ☐ Medical details, including list of recent investigations, doctor's letters and list of names and doses of any medicine currently being taken
- ☐ Passport and photocopies
- ☐ Passport photos (spare)
- ☐ Travel insurance documents including emergency helpline number
- ☐ Travellers cheques and record of serial numbers
- ☐ Vaccination booklet and photocopy
- ☐ Visas (as appropriate)

Other useful items

- ☐ Ear plugs

- [ ] Medic Alert bracelet or identification
- [ ] Money belt
- [ ] Sandals or flip-flops
- [ ] Swiss army knife or equivalent
- [ ] Sun hat
- [ ] Sunglasses
- [ ] Travel padlocks
- [ ] Travel towel
- [ ] Travel wash and peg-free washing line
- [ ] Universal adaptor
- [ ] Universal sink plug

Appendix C
Checklist of useful medicines

A supply of medicines or a medical kit is worth taking with you if you are working in a remote area or a place where you cannot easily obtain or trust essential medicines.

Pre-packed kits are available (see Appendix E for suppliers). Alternatively you can make up your own.

Please consult Patient Information Leaflets enclosed with most medicines and the text in this manual for further details, notes of side-effects, interactions with other drugs, safety in pregnancy and when breastfeeding, and for exact dosages.

Dosages given are those commonly used for adults.

In the UK items marked # are available on prescription only. They can be obtained from your doctor, usually on a private rather than on an NHS prescription. Drugs not so marked are available from chemists under the supervision of a pharmacist.

Generic (scientific) names are given first; common brand names are in brackets.

P = avoid in pregnancy; **B** = avoid if breastfeeding.

Basic list

This is a suggested list of standard items for a tropical kit (some common alternatives are given).

Name	What used for	How used (normal adult dose)	P or B
AMOXCILLIN # 250 mg caps (Amoxil)	General-purpose antibiotic Avoid if allergic to penicillin	One, three times daily for one week Double the dose in severe infections	
Alternative: CO-AMOXICLAV # *625 mg (Augmentin)*	*General-purpose antibiotic*	*One, three times daily for one week*	P
ANTACID tablets (various brand names)	Indigestion, heartburn	One or two as needed	
ANTISEPTIC CREAM (various brand names)	To prevent and treat skin infections	Rub in as needed. Start antibiotics by mouth if skin infection severe	
Alternative: ANTIBIOTIC CREAM e.g. *FUSIDIC ACID # (Fucidin) or* *MUPIROCIN # (Bactroban)*			
CHLORAMPHENICOL # eye drops *Alternative: GENTAMICIN # (Genticin)* *eye drops*	Eye infections, especially conjunctivitis *See a doctor if no rapid improvement*	Use one–two drops every two hours, then gradually reduce Continue 48 hours after infection cleared	P

Name	What used for	How used (normal adult dose)	P or B
CHLORPHENAMINE 4 mg tabs (Piriton)	Allergy, hay fever, itching. May cause drowsiness; take care driving	One, four-hourly as needed. Double dose if severe allergic reaction	
CINNARIZINE 15 mg tabs (Stugeron)	Travel sickness. May cause drowsiness	Two, two hours before travel, then one every eight hours if needed	
CIPROFLOXACIN # 250 mg tabs (Ciproxin)	To treat severe diarrhoea and dysentery; avoid in children under 16 unless very ill	Two taken together for one day in mild to moderate diarrhoea; continue for two further days in severe diarrhoea or dysentery	P, B
	For treating urinary tract infections	250 mg daily for three days or 100 mg twice daily for three days	
CLOTRIMAZOLE cream (Canesten)	Fungal infections of the skin, including athlete's foot, vaginal thrush	Rub in as needed. Pessaries (500 mg) also needed for vaginal thrush	
Alternative: MICONAZOLE cream (Daktarin)			
ERYTHROMYCIN # 250 mg tabs	General-purpose antibiotic for those allergic to penicillin	One, four times daily for one week. Double if infection severe	
HYDROCORTISONE 1% cream	For bites, eczema, itchy skin conditions. Avoid if infected	Rub in twice daily for up to seven days	
INSECT REPELLENT containing DEET 50% (various brand names)	To repel mosquitoes, sandflies and other biting insects. Do not use in children under two months	Apply frequently to exposed areas but beware rare cases of skin sensitivity	

Name	What used for	How used (normal adult dose)	P or B
LOPERAMIDE 2 mg tabs (Imodium)	Emergency treatment of diarrhoea Avoid in children under four	Two, then one every four hours until diarrhoea controlled: do not use in dysentery	P
MEBENDAZOLE # 100 mg tabs (Vermox)	Treatment of pin, round, whip and hookworm. Not in children under two	One, twice daily for three days Same dose for children	P
METOCLOPRAMIDE # 10 mg tabs (Maxolon)	Nausea, sickness	One, three times daily as needed	
Alternative: DOMPERIDONE # 10 mg (Motilium)			*P, B*
METRONIDAZOLE # 400 mg tabs (Flagyl, Zadstat)	Amoebiasis, giardiasis	Usually two, three times daily for five days, but see text for specific doses if diagnosis known	P
Alternative: TINIDAZOLE 500 mg (Fasigyn)	*Amoebiasis, giardiasis*	*For amoebiasis four daily for three days, for giardiasis four taken together, repeat four together after two weeks*	*P, avoid in first trimester*
ORAL REHYDRATION SALTS (Dioralyte, Rehidrat)	Diarrhoea, dehydration	One sachet with water, frequently	
PARACETAMOL 500 mg tabs (Panadol, Tylenol) **PARACETAMOL** liquid suspension (Calpol) is very useful in children	Pain, fever	Two, four to six-hourly Never more than 8 in 24 hours Children's dose as per instructions	
SENOKOT tabs	For prevention and treatment of constipation, along with plenty to drink	One increasing up to four tabs at bedtime as needed	

Additional list

You should also consider whether you need any of the following:

Name	What used for	How used	P or B
ANTIMALARIALS	See text	For prevention/treatment	
ACETAZOLAMIDE # 250 mg tabs (Diamox)	To help prevent and treat acute mountain sickness	Dosage, see text	P
CALAMINE lotion or lacto calamine	Sore, inflamed, itchy skin	Apply as needed	
CLOTRIMAZOLE # 500mg pessaries (Canesten)	Vaginal thrush	Insert one for one night	P, B
Alternative: FLUCONAZOLE 150 mg cap (Diflucan)	*Vaginal thrush*	*One capsule*	*P, B*
FLUCLOXACILLIN # 250 mg caps (Floxapen)	To treat recurrent boils early if known tendency, and cellulitis Avoid if allergic to penicillin	Two, four times daily for seven days	
ITRACONAZOLE # 100 mg tabs (Sporanox)	Fungal skin infections Avoid if taking antihistamines, erythromycin. Avoid grapefruit and grapefruit juice	One daily for 15 days	P, B
OIL OF CLOVES	Toothache	Apply to painful tooth and gum	
ORAL CONTRACEPTIVE PILL #	To prevent conception, delay periods, reduce menstrual flow	As instructed	P, B
ZOPICLONE # 3.75 mg (Zimovane)	Difficulty sleeping	One or two per night for short-term use only	P, B

Appendix D
Suggested contents of first-aid kits

See pages 13–16 for further details of the types of kit recommended. A wide variety of kits is available from suppliers (see Appendix E) to cover the varying needs of travellers. Alternatively you can make up your own.

A simple first-aid kit

A simple kit could contain some or all of the following:

- Basic first-aid leaflet
- Clinical thermometer (preferably non-mercury)
- Contents list
- Cotton wool rolls
- Crepe bandage
- Documentation for customs
- First-aid instructions
- Gauze swabs
- Mediswabs
- Micropore tape
- Non-adherent dressings, e.g. Melolin
- Plasters or Band-Aids
- Rubber gloves
- Safety pins
- Savlon antiseptic cream
- Scissors (but some airlines will not allow these)
- Skin-closure strips, e.g. Steristrips
- Sterile dressings (Melolin)
- Triangular bandage
- Tweezers
- Wound dressing (medium)
- Zinc oxide tape 1.25 cm wide

Add an Ambulance Dressing if going to a war zone or insecure region.

A needle and syringe kit

You may also wish to take this kit for sterile supplies in an emergency. It could include some or all of the following:

- Adult intravenous cannula
- Butterfly needles for children
- Malaria lancets

- Needles – small, medium, large
- Skin suture with needle
- Syringes – 2 ml and 5 ml

An AIDS protection kit

If you plan to travel extensively in areas where HIV disease is common, you may wish to take an AIDS protection kit, which in addition to the above would include one or two intravenous giving sets and fluid such as Hartmann's solution – at least one litre.

Table D.1 compares first-aid kits available from InterHealth. (Correct at time of writing – August 2006.)

Table D.1 How InterHealth first-aid kits compare

Contents of kit	Holiday first-aid kit	Traveller's first-aid kit	Frontliner's first-aid kit	HIV/hepatitis B protection kit
2 ml syringes		3	5	2
5 ml syringes		2	3	2
21 g needles		3	4	2
23 g needles		4	6	2
25 g needles		2	3	2
Malaria blood lancets		3	5	
Green adult IV drip needle (cannula)		1	2	2
Medipreps	5	5	10	5
Small sterile dressings (Melolin)	1	1	2	5
Large sterile dressings (Melolin)	1	1	2	
Gauze swabs	5	5	10	2
Medium wound dressing	1		1	
Micropore tape	1	1	1	1
Zinc oxide tape (1.25 cm)	1	1	1	1

Table D.1 How InterHealth first-aid kits compare (cont'd)

Contents of kit	Holiday first-aid kit	Traveller's first-aid kit	Frontliner's first-aid kit	HIV/hepatitis B protection kit
Suture and needle kit			1	1
Steristrips for wound closure	6	6	9	3
IV administration kit				2
500 ml bottles of IV fluid (Hartmann's solution)				2
Pairs of gloves	2	2	4	2
Pairs of scissors	1	1	1	1
Plasters	30	20	30	
Fabric dressing strip	1	1	1	
Crepe bandage	1	1	1	
Triangular bandage	1		1	
Safety pins	6	6	6	
Savlon antiseptic cream	1	1	1	
Pair of tweezers	1	1	1	
Disposable face shield	1	1	1	1
Disposable thermometer	1	1	1	1
Customs card	Yes	Yes	Yes	Yes
Basic first-aid leaflet	Yes	Yes	Yes	Yes
Padded nylon packaging with handle and belt loop	Yes	Yes	Yes	Yes

Appendix E
List of suppliers

InterHealth

157 Waterloo Road
London SE1 8US
Tel (general): +44 (0)20 7902 9000
Tel (supplies line): +44 (0)20 7902 9090
Fax: +44 (0)20 7902 9091
Email: supplies@interhealth.org.uk
Website: www.interhealth.org.uk

InterHealth supplies a wide range of first-aid and medicine kits, mosquito nets, water filters, medicines and antimalarials. Also a catalogue with detailed descriptions of items provided, combined with health information, available free on request and also on website. All supplies can be ordered online from anywhere in the world.

Mission Supplies Ltd

Airport House
Kings Mill Lane
South Nutfield
Surrey RH15 5JY
Tel: +44 (0)1737 823812
Fax: +44 (0)1737 823771
Email: enquiries@missionsupplies.co.uk
Website: www.missionsupplies.co.uk

Provides a range of both small and large equipment needed by people and programmes overseas.

Nomad

3–4 Wellington Terrace
Turnpike Lane
London N8 0PX
Tel: +44 (0)20 8889 7014
Fax: +44 (0)20 8889 9529
Email: orders@nomadtravel.co.uk
Website: www.nomadtravel.co.uk

Provides clothing, equipment, kits. Also runs a pharmacy and immunization clinic. See page 369.

In addition many high street, camping and outdoor retailers sell a variety of useful travel health items. In the UK these include Blacks, Cotswold Camping, Field and Trek, YHA Adventure Shops, Tiso, etc.

Appendix F
NHS eligibility for UK citizens working abroad

Rules, procedures and documentation on access to hospital and primary health care, NHS charges and exemptions

Note: Details are complex, have recently been revised and need to be read and followed with special care by any UK citizen who has been working or living abroad for longer than five years. Details below are correct at the time of writing but subject to change, so access the website listed at the end of this appendix for further information.

Who is eligible for free hospital treatment while in the UK?

Under the current regulations, certain people who have lived in the UK who are currently working overseas may be entitled to free National Health Service (NHS) hospital treatment in the UK. The following groups of people would be fully exempt from charges for NHS hospital treatment in the UK:

- anyone who at some point has lived lawfully in the UK for ten continuous years and has not worked abroad for longer than five years;
- anyone who is employed in an EEA member state and contributing compulsory UK National Insurance contributions (Class I or II);
- anyone who is a member of Her Majesty's United Kingdom armed forces;
- anyone who is a Crown servant employed by Her Majesty's Government and recruited in the UK;
- anyone recruited in the UK who works for the British Council or Commonwealth War Graves Commission;
- anyone who is working in employment that is financed in part by the government of the UK and by arrangement with the government or a public body of some other country or territory.

These exemptions also apply to the spouse and children (under the age of 16, or 19 if in further education) of such a person if they are living with you in the UK on a permanent basis.

In common with those ordinarily resident in the UK, anyone who meets the criteria of ordinary residence or is exempt from charges for hospital treatment will have to pay statutory NHS charges, e.g.

prescription charges, unless they also qualify for exemption from these, and will have to go on to waiting lists for treatment where appropriate.

If I should need hospital treatment, what documents will I need?

The regulations place a responsibility on individual hospitals to determine whether, in accordance with the regulations, a patient is liable to be charged for treatment or not. In order to establish entitlement, hospitals can ask you to provide documentation that supports your claim that you are a former UK resident currently working overseas. It is for you to decide what to supply; however, examples of evidence could include:

- documentation to prove you are entitled to live in the UK such as British passport, permission from the Home Office;
- confirmation of diplomatic position in the UK, letter from embassy confirming posting;
- valid HM forces ID card;
- proof of employment and where recruited, e.g. letter from employer confirming employment and stating where recruitment took place;
- letter from employer confirming employment and funding arrangements.

Am I entitled to access primary care services?

Any person living here lawfully and on a settled basis is regarded as resident in the UK and therefore entitled to free primary medical services. On taking up residence in the UK, it is advisable to approach a GP practice and apply to register on to its list of NHS patients. The practice may choose to accept or decline your application. An application may be refused if the practice has reasonable grounds for doing so, such as if you are living outside their practice area. A practice would not be able to refuse your application on the grounds of race, gender, social class, age, religion, sexual orientation, appearance, disability or medical condition.

Do I have to pay for emergency treatment if I have an accident?

Regardless of residential status or nationality, emergency treatment given at primary care practices (a GP) or in accident and emergency departments or a walk-in centre providing services similar to those of a hospital accident and emergency department is free of charge.

In the case of treatment given in an accident and emergency department or walk-in centre, the exemption from charges will cease to apply once the patient is formally admitted as an in-patient (this will include emergency operations and admittance to High Dependency Units) or registered at an outpatient clinic.

Am I entitled to help with the costs of non-emergency NHS treatment?

Information about help with health costs is detailed in leaflet HC1 'Are you entitled to help with health costs?' This is available from main post offices and hospitals, by phoning 08701 555 455, or from <http://www.dh.gov.uk/assetRoot/04/06/77/85/04067785.pdf>.

What are the other exemptions from charge for NHS hospital treatment?

Please see details on the website listed below.

What if I do not meet one of these exemptions from charges?

If you are not ordinarily resident or exempt under the regulations, charges will apply for any hospital treatment you receive and cannot be waived. If this is the case you are strongly advised to take out private healthcare insurance that would cover you for the length of time you are in the UK. There is no facility to purchase healthcare insurance from the NHS, therefore any necessary insurance must be organized privately.

Please note: the above information gives general guidance only and should not be treated as a complete and authoritative statement of law. In all cases the regulations place the responsibility of deciding who is entitled to receive free hospital treatment with the hospital providing treatment.

For more details see <http://www.dh.gov.uk/PolicyandGuidance/International/OverseasVisitors>.

Appendix G
Travel health centres

United Kingdom and Ireland

In the UK the following clinics and centres offer pre-travel advice and immunizations and/or health care on return from abroad. NHS health centres and GP clinics also offer many travel immunizations.

For details of the nearest MASTA travel health clinic near you (these charge private rates), phone 020 7291 9333.

London

InterHealth

157 Waterloo Road
London SE1 8US
Tel: +44 (0)20 7902 9000
Fax: +44 (0)20 7902 9091
Email: info@interhealth.org.uk
Website: http://www.interhealth.org.uk
InterHealth sees anyone travelling overseas but has discounted rates for all those involved in charitable work overseas, including aid workers, missionaries and volunteers, providing they or their organizations join as members.

Hospital for Tropical Diseases

Mortimer Market Building
Capper Street
London WC1E 6AU
Travel clinic: +44 (0)20 7388 9600
General line: +44 (0)20 7530 5000
Fax: +44 (0)20 7383 4817

Nomad

Website: http://www.nomadtravel.co.uk
See details below and on page 364. Nomad runs travel clinics in London, Bristol and Southampton.

Trailfinders Ltd

194 Kensington High Street
London W8 7RG
Tel: +44 (0)20 7938 3999
Fax: +44 (0)20 7938 3305

Travel health centres in other cities

Birmingham

Department of Infection and Tropical Medicine
Birmingham Heartlands Hospital
Bordesley Green East
Bordesley Green
Birmingham B9 5SS
Tel: +44 (0)121 424 2000

Bristol

Nomad
38 Park Street
Clifton
Bristol BS1 5JG
Tel: +44 (0)117 922 6567

Dublin

The Tropical Medical Bureau runs a network of clinics in Ireland, including Dublin, offering a wide range of services. For details see <http://www.tmb.ie>.

Edinburgh

Edinburgh International Health Centre
Elphinstone Wing
Carberry, Musselburgh
Edinburgh EH21 8PW
Tel: +44 (0)131 653 6767
Fax: +44 (0)131 653 3646
Email: admin@eihc.org
This centre specializes in those returning from abroad who have been serving in the charitable sector, including aid workers, missionaries and volunteers.

The Travel Clinic
RIDU, Ward 41 OPD
Western General Hospital
Crewe Road South
Edinburgh EH4 2XU
Tel: +44 (0)131 537 2822
Fax: +44 (0)131 537 2879

Glasgow

The Brownlee Centre
Gartnavel General Hospital
Glasgow G12 0YN
Tel: +44 (0)141 211 1089/75

Liverpool

Liverpool School of Tropical Medicine
International Travel Health Clinic
Pembroke Place
Liverpool L3 5QA
Tel: +44 (0)151 708 9393

Worldwide

The International Society of Travel Medicine lists clinics worldwide
run by its members with details of the facilities they provide. Visit their
website at <http://www.istm.org> and click on the country. This is an
open access website.

For details of English-speaking doctors abroad and tropical health
information, contact the International Association for Medical Assistance to Travellers (IAMAT), 1623 Military Road, Niagara Falls, NY
14304-1745, tel: +1 (0)01 716 754 4883; email: <info@iamat.org>;
website: <http://www.iamat.org>.

Appendix H
Sources of specialist advice

The following apply to the UK unless otherwise stated.

Aid workers – best practice in their management and support

People in Aid
Development House
56–64 Leonard Street
London EC2A 4JX
Tel: +44 (0)20 7065 0900
Fax: +44 (0)20 7065 0901
Email: info@peopleinaid.org
Website: http://www.peopleinaid.org
People in Aid is an international organization dedicated to provide help and support to aid agencies and other voluntary organizations which second people overseas. They provide a range of information, advice, publications and seminars as well as benchmarking best practice. It is possible to join either as a corporate or as a personal member.

The following useful booklets are available from them: *Staff Health and Welfare*; *Prevent Accidents*; *Work Life Balance*; *Health and Safety*.

AIDS

The *Sexual Health* helpline is 0800 567123.

The UK NGO AIDS Consortium
Tel: +44 (0)20 7324 4780
Email: ukaidscon@gn.apc.org
Website: http://www.ukaidsconsortium.org.uk
The Consortium provides advice on funding and technical assistance for projects and employers and employees.

Alcohol

The Alcoholics Anonymous helpline is 0845 7697 555.

Asthma

The National Asthma Campaign helpline is 0845 7010203.
Website: http://www.asthma.org.uk

Back pain

The Back Care helpline is 0845 1302704.
Website: http://www.backcare.org.uk

Blood donation

The National Blood Service will tell you how and where to give blood (and find out your blood group if you become a donor). Tel: 08457 711711.

Careers and job vacancies

InterChange specializes in careers information, advice and counselling for those returning from overseas. Appointments can be made via *InterHealth* on +44 (0)20 7902 9000.

RedR-IHE specializes in job vacancies and training in the humanitarian aid sector. See <http://www.redr.org/london>.

Christian Vocations
St James's House
Trinity Road
Dudley DY1 1JB
Tel: 0870 745 4825
Email: info@christianvocations.org
Website: http://www.christianvocations.org
Christian Vocations matches jobs with personnel available for the Christian sector. It publishes annually *The Short-Term Service Directory* and *Mission Matters*.

REACH
Tel: +44 (0)20 7582 6543
Fax: +44 (0)20 7582 2423
Email: mail@reach-online.org.uk
Website: http://www.volwork.org.uk
REACH has lists of vacancies in part-time charitable work for professionals of all ages.

Counselling

The British Association for Counselling and Psychotherapy
Tel: 0870 443 5252
Website: http://www.bacp.co.uk

InterHealth can arrange counselling for anyone who has been working overseas. See details above.

Diabetes

Diabetes UK
Tel: +44 (0)20 9424 1000
Careline: 0845 120 2960
Email: info@diabetes.org.uk
Website: http://www.diabetes.org.uk

Diabetes UK (formerly the British Diabetic Association) has useful information on travel.

Disability

The Disabled Living Foundation
Helpline: 0845 1309177
Website: http://www.dlf.org.uk
Specializes in mobility aids and equipment.

Holiday Care
Tel: 0845 124 9971
Website: http://www.holidaycare.org.uk
Provides information for disabled people travelling abroad.

Expeditions

British Mountaineering Council
177–179 Burton Road
Manchester M20 2BB
Tel: 0870 010 4878
Website: http://www.thebmc.co.uk
The BMC's website has useful information on health problems at high altitude.

Expedition Advisory Centre (Royal Geographical Society)
Tel: +44 (0)20 7591 3030
Fax: +44 (0)20 7591 3031
Email: eac@rgs.org
Website: http://www.rgs.org/eac
This centre provides a wide range of advice and should be contacted by anyone going on or leading an expedition.

First-aid courses for overseas workers

In the UK these are run by the *British Red Cross*.
Tel: +44 (0)24 7630 4200
Email: arobinson@redcross.org.uk

Foreign and Commonwealth Office advice line

Tel: 0845 850 2829
Information on safety and security when travelling in any country of the world.

Infectious diseases websites from the World Health Organization

- General plus disease-specific information sheets: http://www.who.int/healthtopics

In addition:

- Avian flu: http://www.who.int/csr/disease/avian_influenza
- Malaria: http://www.rbm.who.int
- Rabies: http://www.who.int/rabies/rabnet
- Tuberculosis: http://www.who.int/gtb/
- Outbreaks: http://www.who.int/csr/don

Also see:

- http://www.cdc.gov/travel/yb

This is the website for the 'Yellow Book' published and updated regularly by the Centers for Disease Control and Prevention, USA.

- http://www.who.int/ith

This is the website for International Travel and Health published and updated regularly by the World Health Organization.

For further travel health websites see Further reading and websites on travellers' health, pages 401–4.

Malaria

There are pre-recorded messages on antimalarials from the *London School of Hygiene and Tropical Medicine* on +44 (0)906 5508908.

Maps

Stanfords
Website: http://www.stanfords.co.uk
For maps and travel books.

Marriage guidance

Relate (previously the Marriage Guidance Council)
Tel: +44 (0)1788 573241
Website: http://www.relate.org.uk
Has trained counsellors throughout the United Kingdom. Contact them at local centres or through the national office.

Medical Advisory Service for Travellers Abroad (MASTA)

Traveller's health line: +44 (0)906 8224100
MASTA provides detailed briefs on immunizations, recommended antimalarials and health hazards for each country of the world.

MedicAlert

Tel: +44 (0)20 7833 3034
Website: http://www.medicalert.org.uk
Provides bracelets and necklets for those with allergies or special conditions.

Rape and personal safety

The Suzy Lamplugh Trust
Tel: +44 (0)20 7091 0014
Website: http://www.suzylamplugh.org
Provides details on the awareness and avoidance of situations involving
personal danger.

Safe blood

The Blood Care Foundation
PO Box 588
Horsham
West Sussex RH12 5WJ
Tel: +44 (0)1403 262652
Email: chairman@bloodcare.org.uk
Website: http://www.bloodcare.org.uk
Safe blood arranged for most places in the world (and also Human
Rabies Immunoglobulin).

Travel health insurance

Banner Financial Services Group Ltd
Tel: +44 (0)1342 710600
Email: info@bannergroup.com
Website: http://www.bannergroup.com

We recommend you receive quotes from two or more sources, and
make sure your full insurance needs are met.

In the UK the following give special rates for older travellers and
those with pre-existing conditions.

Older travellers
RIAS: 0800 0681655
Saga: 0800 056 5464
Help the Aged: 0800 413180
Age Concern: 0845 6012234
Stroke Association: 0845 3033100
British Heart Foundation: 08450 70 80 70

Specialists in pre-existing medical conditions
All Clear: 0870 777 9339
Free Spirit: 0845 230 5000

Travel agents

Key Travel
1st Floor, 28–32 Britannia Street
London WC1X 9JF

Tel: +44 (0)20 7843 9600
Fax: +44 (0)20 7278 8035
Email: reservations@keytravel.co.uk
Website: http://www.keytravel.co.uk
Specializes in economic fares for members of charitable organizations.

Trailfinders
Europe: 0845 050 5940; worldwide: 0845 058 5858
Website: http://www.trailfinders.com
Arranges low-cost prices worldwide for any traveller.

South American Experience
Tel: +44 (0)20 7976 5511
Website: http://www.southamericanexperience.co.uk
Specializes in flights to and from Latin America.

Appendix I
Incubation periods of important illnesses

The incubation period is the time between being infected by an organism (e.g. from the bite of a mosquito, the swallowing of a diarrhoea-causing organism) until the first symptoms appear. Knowing the incubation period can be useful as it may help you work out what disease may be causing (or not causing) your symptoms.

The incubation periods for some illnesses are very variable and among experts there are wide differences for the incubation periods of certain illnesses. So this list is an approximate guide only.

Amoebiasis	At least 7 days, sometimes weeks or months
Anthrax	7 to 60 days, depending on type
Avian flu	2 to 17 days, often 8 to 10
Bacillary dysentery	12 hours to 4 days
Bilharzia (schistosomiasis)	4 weeks or more
Brucellosis	3 weeks, sometimes much longer
Chagas' disease	7 to 10 days from being bitten, 20 to 40 from blood transfusions
Chickenpox	2 to 3 weeks
Chikungunya	5 to 7 days
Cholera	A few hours to 5 days
Dengue fever	5 to 8 days usually; can be 3 to 14
Diphtheria	1 to 5 days
Ebola	2 to 21 days
Filariasis	6 months or more
Food poisoning (bacterial)	Variable: 1 hour to 12 days
German measles (rubella)	2 to 3 weeks
Giardiasis	Very variable, usually from 1 to 3 weeks, commonly between 7 and 10 days, sometimes much longer
Gonorrhoea	2 to 7 days
Hepatitis A	2 to 6 weeks
Hepatitis B	6 weeks to 6 months
Hepatitis E	Usually longer than 60 days
Herpes (genital)	2 to 12 days
HIV infection	2 weeks to 10 years or more
Japanese encephalitis	4 to 14 days
Lassa fever	3 to 21 days
Legionnaires' disease	2 to 14 days

Leprosy	Usually 2 to 4 years; occasionally shorter or much longer
Leptospirosis	2 to 29 days; usually 7
Lyme disease	Usually 2 to 6 weeks
Malaria	Usually about 2 weeks. May be much longer; is never less than 7 days
Measles	1 to 2 weeks
Meningococcal meningitis	2 to 10 days
Mumps	2 to 3 weeks
Norovirus diarrhoea and vomiting	24 to 48 hours
Plague	Usually less than 1 week
Polio	10 to 15 days
Rabies	4 days to 2 years, usually 30–60 days
River blindness (onchocerciasis)	1 year or more
SARS	Up to 10 days, typically 5
Scabies	2 to 6 weeks
Sleeping sickness	2 weeks to 2 months
Syphilis	10 days to 10 weeks
Tetanus	Usually about 2 weeks; may be much quicker or much longer
Tick-borne encephalitis	7 to 14 days
Typhoid	Usually about 10 days. Can vary between 1 and 40
Typhus	1 day to 1 month depending on type, often 4 to 14 days
Visceral leishmaniasis	3 months or more
Yellow fever	3 to 6 days

Appendix J
Notes on individual vaccines

The range and recommendations on vaccines for international travel continually change. It is becoming more complex as a greater range of vaccines are produced and as different manufacturers recommend different dosage schedules. Countries vary in what they recommend and the types of vaccine they have available. International experts are not always agreed about the exact dosage schedules, and there are many minor variations between different official sources of advice.

For these reasons the information below needs to be checked against the specific recommendations in your country of origin and for the places where you will be travelling.

We have attempted to include information from a worldwide perspective as well as recording what is currently available, and recommended, in the UK at the time of writing (April 2006).

BCG (for tuberculosis)

For more information on TB see pages 343–4.

Note: there is no widespread agreement about the use of BCG in travellers; some countries do not use it at all. It has very limited effectiveness.

Type of vaccine: live, injected intradermally. BCG gives very limited protection to adults, but partially protects young children from some of the worst complications of TB.

A tuberculin test (also known as a Mantoux, Heaf or Tine test) should be given to adults before they are offered BCG, and if the reaction is greater than 5 mm BCG should not be given. Prior testing is not usually recommended in children, but some countries still advise it.

Countries where TB is a risk: see page 343.

Risk to travellers: those with no immunity, i.e. who are tuberculin negative, are at risk especially if working or living in close contact with the local population.

Number and spacing of doses: one only.

Precautions: BCG should not be given to anyone seriously ill, with high fever, who is pregnant, taking steroids, has a positive tuberculin test or who is HIV-positive. See note about tuberculin tests above.

How obtained: this can often be difficult to obtain. Ask your family doctor or travel health specialist, who may be able to arrange it.

Reaction with other vaccines: can be given at the same time as other killed or live vaccines. If not given on the same day as other live vaccines, four or more weeks should ideally be left between them. In the case of having a tuberculin test and reading the result, other live vaccines can confuse the interpretation so this must be completed at least one week before having other live vaccines.

Certification: none necessary.

Recommendations: current advice from the World Health Organization (2005–6) regarding BCG in travellers suggests that it should be considered for the following: infants under six months of age travelling from low-risk to high-risk countries; health workers and others working in close contact with TB patients such as prison visitors. BCG does not need to be repeated. It is still advised for all infants in developing countries.

Some countries will give official advice different from the above.

Cholera vaccine

For information on cholera, see pages 110–11.

Common trade names: Dukoral.
Note: this comparatively new vaccine, known as a whole cell recombinant vaccine, is effective and increasingly used. Previous cholera vaccinations are no longer recommended.

Type of vaccine: oral, non-live.

Countries where cholera occurs: this is found either sporadically or in epidemics in resource-poor countries of Asia, Africa, Central and South America. It is more common during war and chronic complex emergencies but not usually after natural disasters: also among internally displaced people and in refugee camps. Its exact distribution is frequently changing.

Risk to travellers: this is generally low except where travellers are working in areas with known outbreaks and are involved closely with the local population, as aid workers, health workers or volunteers.

Number and spacing of doses: to protect against cholera adults and children over six years should receive two doses; children between two and six years should receive three doses. It is not used in children under two years of age. Doses, which are given as liquid drinks, should be at least one week and less than six weeks apart. If more than six weeks elapse the full course should be repeated.

Single booster doses can be given to children between two and six years of age after six months and to adults and children over six years of age after two years.

No food or drink should be taken one hour before and one hour after the vaccine, and antibiotics should be avoided for one week before and one week after the vaccine. Immunization should be completed at least one week before possible exposure to cholera, but protection probably takes effect shortly after the second dose.

Precautions: it should not be used in anyone who has had a significant reaction to a first dose, nor to anyone with fever or acute gastrointestinal illness. It should be avoided in those with sensitivity to formaldehyde. Consult the Patient Information Leaflet for other precautions. It should only be used in pregnancy and breastfeeding in high-risk situations. Side-effects are uncommon, but include occasional diarrhoea, abdominal pain or fever.

Degrees of protection: Dukoral gives protection of between 65 per cent and 85 per cent against the common form of cholera 01 El Tor for up to three years, but none against the 0139 Bengal strain found in parts of southern Asia.

It also gives about 50 per cent protection against the commonest form of traveller's diarrhoea (ETEC, see page 101) but immunity wanes over the following three months.

Reactions with other vaccines: there are no known interactions but oral cholera and oral typhoid vaccine should be separated by at least eight hours.

Storage: it should be stored between 2° and 8°C but can be kept up to 27° for a single two-week period.

Recommendations: the vaccine should be advised for those mixing with the local population in areas where the disease is endemic, i.e. where cases can occur at any time, and also when epidemics are occurring. It is important to check that the majority of cases at the traveller's destination are not caused by 0139 strains (common in parts of South Asia) as then there is no value in giving the vaccine.

It can also be used for short-term protection against traveller's diarrhoea in those with gastrointestinal disease for whom diarrhoea is best avoided, and in those with important journeys needing to minimize their risk of illness. Discuss this with your travel health adviser.

Hepatitis A vaccine

For details about hepatitis A see pages 299–300.

Trade names: for adults, Havrix Monodose, Avaxim, Vaqta; for children, Havrix Junior, Vaqta Paediatric.

Hepatyrix and Viatim are combined hepatitis A and typhoid vaccines.

Twinrix and Twinrix Paediatric are combined vaccines against hepatitis A and B; see under hepatitis B below.

Note: in the UK, hepatitis A vaccine has now superseded the use of gammaglobulin even in pregnancy and for those who are immunocompromised.

Type of vaccine: inactivated, given by intramuscular injection.

Countries where hepatitis A occurs: see page 299.

Risk to travellers: all those travelling from industrialized to developing countries are at risk, especially adults and older children. Younger children if infected often have a milder disease, with few or no symptoms, and then develop lifelong immunity.

Number and spacing of doses: one dose of hepatitis A vaccine provides coverage for up to one year, taking effect two weeks after immunization and probably much sooner. A booster dose six to 24 months (ideally at about one year) after the first gives persistent immunity probably for 20 years. Evidence now suggests immunity lasts for much longer than the original ten years originally recommended. Children from one to 16 can be given the junior version, with a booster six to 24 months later.

Precautions: should not be given to anyone who has had a significant reaction to a previous dose, or who has a feverish illness. Side-effects are usually mild, with slight soreness and redness at the injection site, and less often fever, headache and nausea. Pregnant women and the immunocompromised were formerly recommended to have gammaglobulin, but the vaccine is now recommended instead.

It is better to arrange to have hepatitis A immunization prior to conception rather than during pregnancy.

Reactions with other vaccines: none. May be given at the same time but at a different site.

How obtained: is usually available in the UK on the NHS for those travelling to developing countries. Can also be given at travel clinics. Some doctors will want to check your hepatitis A antibodies before giving it (see below).

Storage: should be kept between 2° and 8°C and should be protected from light. Should not be frozen. Is thought to retain its potency if briefly warmed in transit for up to about seven days. Has a short shelf life of two years.

Recommendations: hepatitis A vaccine is recommended for those aged 16 and over travelling to developing countries. If travelling for more than 12 months, and in frequent travellers, an additional booster should be given (see above). Children between one and 15 should receive the junior form, though children under five are only immunized for trips to high-risk areas or for longer periods of travel.

Note: anyone in an industrialized country born before about 1945, brought up in a developing country or with a history of jaundice may have natural immunity and can be tested for antibodies to see if immunization is necessary.

See note on Twinrix under hepatitis B, below, which gives combined cover against hepatitis A and B, and under typhoid vaccine, which is combined with hepatitis A under the trade names Hepatyrix or Viatim.

Hepatitis B vaccine

For information on hepatitis B see pages 300–2.

Common trade names include: Engerix B, HB Vax 11, HBvaxPRO, Engerix B Paed (ages 0–12), HB–Vax 11 Paed (ages 0–15).

Type of vaccine: inactivated, given by intramuscular injection into the deltoid muscle.

Countries where hepatitis B is a risk: worldwide, but most common in Africa, South and Southeast Asia, China, the Pacific islands and parts of South America, eastern Europe and the former Soviet states. (see page 301).

Risk to travellers: generally (though not exclusively) spread in a similar way to AIDS, therefore blood transfusions, dirty needles and having unprotected sex with carriers are the main methods of spread. Health workers have an increased risk, as do very young children, who can catch it through close contact with a carrier. Infants can catch it from mothers who are carriers.

Number and spacing of doses: there are three methods:
- *Regular course*: three injections, leaving at least one month between the first and second, five months between the second and third (0, 1, 6), given by intramuscular route.

- *Accelerated course* if insufficient time for regular course: three injections at intervals of at least one month, followed by a booster six to 12 months later (0, 1, 2, 6–12).
- *Super accelerated course* used in many European countries: injections at days 0, 7, 21 followed by a booster after six to 12 months.

Most travellers will gain a degree of protection after the second dose of any schedule and the course can be completed on return, but it is better to complete the course before travelling.

Degree of protection: the vaccine normally gives protection immediately after the third dose, or after any booster. It can be given at any age.

Experts do not fully agree about how long protection against hepatitis B persists. Current recommendations in the UK suggests that if a protective level of 100 iu/ml or more is confirmed on a blood test at least eight to 12 weeks after the final course is complete or any booster has been given, immunity persists for life. In the USA and many other countries the protective level is set at 10 iu/ml and this is likely to soon become the norm. WHO currently states that a primary course of immunization lasts for at least 15 years.

A small proportion of those receiving hepatitis B immunization do not show any protective level on blood tests, meaning that additional doses are usually recommended. Discuss this with your travel health adviser. It is important for health workers and others at high risk to have had their protective levels checked to make sure they are at or above the levels recommended in their country of origin.

Precautions: hepatitis B vaccine should not be given to anyone who has had a significant adverse reaction to a previous dose. The Patient Information Leaflet of the vaccine used should be consulted for any other precautions, as different types of vaccine are used. It should be avoided in pregnancy unless the risk is high, and should not normally be given to those unwell or with a fever. Side-effects include local soreness, occasionally with nodule formation, and fever, nausea and headache. There is no confirmation of any serious long-term side-effects.

How obtained: the vaccine is available from a variety of sources including travel clinics and, in the UK, on the NHS for accredited health workers and those in training. In many countries hepatitis B is part of the childhood or national immunization programme.

Storage: if you need to take doses abroad with you, the vaccine should be kept between 2° and 8°C. It is thought to remain effective if temporarily heated up to 25°C for between four and six days, provided it is then re-refrigerated. It should not be frozen.

Reaction with other vaccines: none. May be given at the same time but at a different site.

Recommendations: frequent travellers, all health workers and those working with drug abusers, the mentally handicapped, street children or in institutions, including orphanages, should be protected, regardless of their length of stay. Others, including children, living or working in developing countries for more than one month, should be immunized. Further advice can be obtained from your travel health adviser.

A combined hepatitis A and hepatitis B vaccine is available under the name Twinrix and Twinrix Paediatric. This is not more economical, but will mean fewer injections if you need protection against both hepatitis A and hepatitis B. Twinrix is useful for those previously unimmunized against both hepatitis A and B who need both immunizations because of frequent travel or a prolonged trip abroad. However, hepatitis A protection only takes place after the second dose, unlike with hepatitis A vaccine used on its own. Twinrix can be used for either the regular or the accelerated course.

Three doses are given, at day 0, one month and six months, i.e. with four weeks between the first and second, five months between the second and third. Then to maintain immunity a hepatitis A booster needs to be given after ten to 20 years and a hepatitis B booster after five years.

Note for those brought up in developing countries: one person in three has had the disease hepatitis B, and the great majority then develop lifelong immunity. This can often be checked on a blood test before a course of injections is given, as often vaccination will not be necessary.

Influenza vaccine

For information on influenza, including avian flu, see pages 304–8.

Common trade names: Aggripal, Begrivac, Fluarix, Fluvirin, Inflexal, Influvac, Mastaflu. Names change frequently.

Type of vaccine: inactivated, injected by subcutaneous or intramuscular injection.

Countries where disease occurs: worldwide, especially in winter months, i.e. November to March in northern hemisphere, April to September in southern. Vaccine composition is different for each hemisphere and therefore travellers going from one hemisphere to another may receive only partial protection.

Risk to travellers: significant, especially if travelling during winter months and in crowded conditions such as cruise ships. Also for those at high risk; see below.

Number of doses: a single dose each year, which must be constituted according to World Health Organization current guidelines. Strains of flu alter each year and so the make-up of the vaccine has to be regularly updated. The composition for vaccines between northern and southern hemispheres is different.

Precautions: avoid in anyone who has had a significant reaction to a previous dose; also in those with a significant allergy to eggs or poultry. Not generally recommended in pregnancy. Side-effects include tenderness at the injection site in about 20 per cent of people and sometimes slight malaise and fever.

How obtained: in the UK, available on the NHS for those 65 or over, those with chronic lung conditions and in a few other high-risk categories, see below. Others will normally be charged.

Reaction with other vaccines: none. Can be given at the same time but at a different site.

Recommendations: because a serious flu epidemic could occur at any time and spread rapidly, current advice is for travellers from the northern hemisphere in high-risk categories to be immunized prior to travel in the northern hemisphere winter, or if travelling to the southern hemisphere winter to have a dose of the southern hemisphere vaccine on arrival. It is especially important for high-risk groups which includes those aged 65 or over, those with cardiac or respiratory conditions, or diabetes, any who are immunocompromised, and healthcare workers.

For further details see the Flunet website, <http://www.who.int/globalatlas/autologin/flunet>.

Japanese encephalitis vaccine

For information on Japanese encephalitis (JE) see pages 312–14.

Common brands and trade names: Biken and Green Cross.

Type of vaccine: inactivated, given by subcutaneous injection.

Countries where the disease occurs: see page 312. JE is spread by Culex mosquitoes and can cause a dangerous illness with severe headache, sometimes leading to death or long-term disability. It is, however, rare in travellers, though children are at greater risk than adults.

Risk to travellers: see pages 313–14.

Number and spacing of doses: there are two manufacturers. Biken recommend three doses, on days 0, 7–14 and 28, with a booster every two to three years. Green Cross recommend either three doses given on days 0, 7 and 28 with a booster after one year, or two doses at an interval of seven to 14 days, a third after one year and then boosters every three years. Protection starts ten to 14 days after completing the course and immediately after any booster. Children aged one to three years or under should receive half the dose. Children under 12 months are not recommended to receive this, except in special circumstances.

Precautions: the vaccine should not be given to anyone who has had a serious reaction to a previous dose, nor to anyone with a fever, cancer or with any serious illness, especially of the heart, liver or lungs. It should not be given in pregnancy. Side-effects include local soreness, occasionally fever and headache, vomiting and abdominal pain. More serious reactions have occasionally been reported, sometimes hours or days after the injection: reactions seem less likely after boosters. Side-effects after the first vaccine usually occur between 12 hours and three days later. Reactions after subsequent doses may occur from three days to two weeks after having the vaccine. This is the main reason we recommend you complete the course of JE ten days or more before travelling. We also suggest you wait in the clinic for 30 minutes after having the jab.

How obtained: expensive, and in the UK not available on the NHS. It is available from travel clinics, and some UK GPs will order it and give it privately. It is available in many countries where JE is found and immunization can often be arranged or completed on arrival, though we recommend where possible this is completed before travelling.

Reaction with other vaccines: none. Can be given at the same time but at a different site.

Recommendations: should you have the vaccine or not? You need to weigh the risks and benefits carefully with your travel health adviser. We generally recommend it in the following situations:

- for those planning to live in risk areas for four weeks or longer (WHO recommends two weeks);
- for those making frequent trips to affected areas;

- for those going on shorter trips if there is a known outbreak occurring or if engaged in extensive outdoor activities;
- for those who have a possibility of unexpected travel to high-risk areas, such as humanitarian aid workers or the military on standby duty.

Consult your travel health adviser to help you weigh up risk, cost and benefit.

Note: avoiding mosquito bites is as important as having the vaccine, see page 314.

Meningitis vaccine

For information on meningitis see pages 319–20.

Trade names: ACWY VAX, Meningitec, Mengivac and AC Vax (the latter two are no longer available in the UK).

Note: Immunization against meningitis is quite complex owing to the different strains, vaccines and requirements of different countries. Discuss your specific needs with your travel health adviser.

Mengivac and AC Vax protect only against meningococcal meningitis strains A and C, two of the most serious forms of meningitis. They are no longer used in the UK. ACWY VAX protects against strains A, C, W-135 and Y and is increasingly becoming the vaccine of choice; it is essential for those going on the Hajj pilgrimage to Saudi Arabia.

Meningitec is a common trade name for the monovalent conjugate vaccine against meningitis C, currently part of the childhood immunization programme in the UK and many other countries.

Protection: the World Health Organization currently states that vaccines against groups A and C are 85–100 per cent effective, in older children and adults. Standard group C vaccines (as opposed to the conjugate vaccine, see below) do not protect children under two years of age, and the effectiveness of the group A component in children under one year is unclear. Group Y and W-135 confer immunity on most children over the age of two.

The monovalent group C conjugate vaccine now given to young children and adolescents is effective in children under two years of age. Protection from all vaccines starts within ten days.

Type of vaccine: inactived, given by injection.

Countries where these strains of meningitis occur: see page 319.

Risk to travellers: an appreciable risk occurs during outbreaks or when visiting the Meningitis Belt during the dry season. Children or those working with children are at greatest risk. In addition there are outbreaks of meningitis, often of the group C strain, among children and adolescents in many countries.

Number and spacing of doses: normally a single dose of A and C vaccine or, in the UK and increasingly in other countries, the quadrivalent vaccine at least three weeks before departure, with boosters every five years.

Different manufacturers give varying advice. Form AC Vax can be given from two months of age and needs boosters every five years, form Mengivac from 18 months, needing boosters every three years. Immunization as mentioned above is less effective in those under two years of age and a booster should be given after one year. ACWY vaccine can also be given to children from six months to two years, but protection may be suboptimal so a booster can be given after one year.

There should be a minimum period of two weeks between the conjugate C vaccine and any of the others (which are all polyvalent vaccines), regardless of which one was given first.

Precautions: meningitis vaccine of any type should not be given to anyone who has had a significant reaction to a previous meningitis vaccination. It is best avoided in pregnancy unless risk is very high. Side-effects are usually mild and include local soreness as well as occasional chills and fever in the first 24 hours.

How obtained: in the UK the quadrivalent vaccine is not normally free under the NHS, though many GPs will obtain it or write a prescription for you to collect. Otherwise it is available in travel clinics. The C conjugate vaccine for children and adolescents is free in the UK and in many other countries.

Reactions with other vaccines: none. Can be given at the same time but at a different site.

Recommendations: those travelling to affected areas should either be immunized against strains A and C or, ideally, receive the quadrivalent vaccine against strains A, C, Y and W-135. Anyone going to Saudi Arabia on the Hajj pilgrimage or for the Umrah must have a current certificate confirming immunization by the quadrivalent vaccine, which from the point of view of certification needs to be given every *three* years.

All those who have had their spleen removed must be immunized against meningitis (quadrivalent vaccine) regardless of country of travel. The distribution of meningitis changes frequently. Consult your travel health adviser a few weeks before departure.

Polio vaccine

Type of vaccine: live, oral (OPV) has been the standard vaccine used worldwide including industrialized countries. However, in a number of countries IPV vaccine, which is an inactivated vaccine given by injection, is now used instead. This is the case in much of Europe, including the UK and in the USA (see page 244).

Countries where polio occurs: polio is rapidly disappearing after a worldwide immunization programme, though from time to time it has reappeared in areas where vaccination programmes have been interrupted. At the time of writing there are still cases occurring in parts of Africa and Asia. Until polio has been officially confirmed by the WHO as no longer occurring, all travellers to developing countries must ensure their polio immunizations are up to date.

Risk to travellers: extremely low, except if travelling to or working among communities where polio is still occurring.

Number and spacing of doses: most children and those brought up in the UK and born after 1956 (when the vaccine was introduced) should have received a primary course of three polio vaccinations. For such people a single one-off booster is needed.

Those who have not had a primary course of three in the past, or who are unsure, should do so if visiting areas where polio is still known to occur. In the UK the course is three IPV at intervals of one month or more.

Worldwide IPV is generally recommended for those who have not previously been immunized and in those who are immunocompromised. Otherwise either OPV or IPV can be used.

Protection takes place four weeks after the primary course or immediately after any booster.

Precautions: oral polio should not be given to anyone with fever, serious illness, diarrhoea and vomiting, or those with low immunity, including HIV infection. It should not be given in pregnancy. There are usually no side-effects. OPV very occasionally causes vaccine-associated paralysis (about one case in three million, a reason IPV is increasingly recommended instead of OPV. IPV should be used in those who are immunocompromised.

How obtained: in the UK polio vaccine is generally free on the NHS, though adults requiring a primary course may be charged. It remains part of the WHO worldwide immunization programme, and is therefore available in most countries.

Reactions with other vaccines: may be given on the same day as any other vaccine, live or killed. In the case of other live vaccines, oral polio should ideally be given either on the same day or separated by an interval of four weeks or more.

Recommendations: all travellers should be in-date for polio. This is essential for countries where cases are still occurring. Varying recommendations are provided by different clinics, and clear guidance is awaited from WHO after the full worldwide eradication of the disease.

Rabies vaccine

For information on rabies and action to be taken if bitten by a suspect animal see pages 323–8.

Note: contrary to some people's fears, modern rabies pre-exposure vaccine is both simple and safe. However, *it does not give full protection*, and after any encounter with a potentially rabid animal further doses are needed.

Type of vaccine and trade names: there are several inactive vaccines, which are largely interchangeable and are given by intramuscular injection (IM), or in some clinics and countries by intradermal injection (ID). Commonly used vaccines are Human Diploid Cell Vaccine (HDCV, Imovax), Purified Chick Embryo Culture Vaccine (PCECV, also known as Rabipur or RabAvert), PVRV (Verorab) and RVA. These injections are given before exposure, i.e. before you travel, but the same ones are in addition used after an at-risk exposure, see pages 326–8. All these forms of the vaccine are normally given by intramuscular injection which should be into the deltoid muscle (upper arm) or for children the antero-lateral aspect of the thigh. The gluteal (buttock muscle) should not be used. If the intradermal technique is used the vaccine is usually given in the upper arm, but see below.

Countries affected by rabies: see page 324.

Risk to travellers: the risk to most careful travellers is relatively low, but intrepid travellers, rural workers, vets, zoologists and children are at higher risk. Many travellers and expatriates worry that their last encounter with a suspicious dog might lead to an untimely death.

Number and spacing of doses: three injections are needed with seven days between the first and second, and 14 to 21 between the second and third (0, 7, 21–28). Current advice is that repeat primary courses of three injections do not need to be repeated, but that a first booster should ideally be given after three years and subsequently every five years. An alternative regime of two intradermal injections, 28 days apart, gives almost as good protection and is sometimes used, but a booster is needed after 12 months.

Those working with animals should ideally have their antibody levels regularly checked.

For further details see pages 326–8.

Protection: The vaccine gives protection as soon as the courses detailed above of two or three pre-exposure injections are completed. Injections given to those who are currently taking chloroquine should be by the IM route, as chloroquine may reduce the effect of the intradermal injection. This also means intradermal injections must be completed before starting chloroquine. There is no consensus yet about whether mefloquine reduces the effectiveness of intradermal rabies, or how many days should be left between completing ID rabies and starting chloroquine or mefloquine. Seek advice from your travel clinic.

The vaccine is thought to retain its potency for a cumulative total of 14 days if unrefrigerated. It should, however, be kept as cool as possible, ideally in a vacuum flask. It must not be transported in the aircraft hold, where freezing may destroy it.

Rabies injections in children under the age of 12 months may not be fully effective (though they are sometimes used from six months onwards). For this reason, if going to live with your family abroad you should take enough rabies vaccine with you so that children can be immunized from the age of one year upwards, unless you know reliable supplies are available at your destination.

Rabies vaccines are increasingly becoming available in developing countries.

Precautions: rabies vaccine should be avoided in anyone who has had a significant reaction to a previous dose, and in anyone with a high fever or who is seriously ill. Pregnant women should only receive it if their risk is very high, though after any possible exposure it is essential. Side-effects are few, and include local swelling and redness and occasionally fever and headache, or more general allergic reactions.

How obtained: not usually available in the UK on the NHS. It is available from travel clinics and privately from many family doctors.

Reactions with other vaccines: none. Can be given at the same time but at a different site.

Advantages of having rabies injections before going abroad

- It reduces from five to two the number of further HDCV or equivalent injections you need after an encounter with a suspicious animal.
- It means you will not need a special immunoglobulin (HRIG or ERIG) injection as well. Both of these can be hard to obtain, and contain some risk of contamination.
- It limits the risk of delays in obtaining vaccine when in remote areas, allowing you up to 48 hours before having post-exposure injections.

Recommendations: please see the details on pages 325–6.

Special note: under certain situations, e.g. those at very high risk, such as veterinarians, or those who are unsure if they have completed their course or who have had reactions to previous doses, it is possible in some well-resourced countries to arrange a blood test to confirm whether or not you have a protective level of rabies antibody in your blood.

For more details of what post-exposure injections you need after an at-risk incident with a suspicious animal, see page 327.

Tetanus and diphtheria

Common names: Tetanus toxoid vaccine (TT) or tetanus with low-dose diphtheria (Td). Diftavax is not now available in the UK and Revaxis is used instead, which also covers against polio.

Type of vaccine: inactivated injectable. Tetanus with low-dose diphtheria (Td) is used for those aged seven and above according to the latest WHO recommendations.

Countries where tetanus occurs: worldwide, but commoner in the tropics; rarer at high altitudes. *Diphtheria* occurs in many developing countries, the former Soviet states, the Russian Federation and in parts of eastern Europe.

Risk to travellers: in the absence of completed immunization, any wound, even a trivial one, may cause tetanus. So also may delivery, surgery, middle-ear infections, bites and boils. The risk of diphtheria to travellers is extremely low.

Number and spacing of doses: those born after 1961 and brought up in the UK will normally have received a course of DPT in childhood, and those who have served in the armed forces a course of TT. Others should make sure they have completed a primary course of three injections before travelling abroad. DPT or an equivalent vaccine is part of the worldwide vaccination programme of the WHO, but those working internationally need to check that they have definitely had these.

The best spacing for immunizations against tetanus and diphtheria is six to eight weeks between the first and second, four to six months between the second and third, but three injections at monthly intervals will confer full immunity. In the UK this is now given as Revaxis (combined IPV diphtheria and tetanus). Boosters are needed every ten years. If, however, you have had a tetanus booster alone in the past ten years, you can receive a single low-dose diphtheria injection instead, though again this is not available in the UK and Revaxis is used instead.

Protection takes effect immediately after the third dose or any booster.

Precautions: should not be given to anyone who has had a previous significant reaction to a TT, Td or Revaxis injection, or to anyone with a feverish illness. Side-effects: may cause fever and pain at the injection site, especially if fewer than five years have elapsed since last booster. This is not a reason for withholding further immunizations. It is safe in pregnancy.

How obtained: Revaxis is usually available in the UK on the NHS. Protection against tetanus, diphtheria and polio are part of the WHO worldwide immunization programme and preparations are available in virtually all countries, either as DPT, TT (tetanus only), Td or Revaxis.

Reactions with other vaccines: none. Can be given at the same time but at a different site.

Recommendations: all those travelling overseas should have completed a primary course of three Td, TT or DPT injections at some time in their lives, and have had a booster within the past ten years; currently in the UK Revaxis is used for this.

Note: current WHO guidelines are that after a clean wound there is no need for any booster tetanus injection if you have completed a primary course in the past and had a booster in the past ten years. For a dirty wound it is recommended that those receiving such a wound or injury during travel should have a booster TT or Td or Revaxis if they have not been immunized in the past five years.

Tick-borne encephalitis (TBE) vaccine

For further information on TBE see pages 337–8.

Trade names: Encepur, FSME-IMMUN.

Type of vaccine: non-live, injectable.

Countries where TBE occurs: for latest detailed information see page 337.

Risk to travellers: low unless camping, trekking or working in forested areas in summer where the disease is known to occur. Take precautions to avoid tick bites (see pages 213 and 338).

Number and spacing of doses: two doses from four weeks to 12 weeks apart protects for one year. A booster can be given five to 12 months after the second dose and protects for a further three years. Subsequent boosters are given every three years for those who remain at risk. There are slight variations depending on the brand being used: follow the manufacturer's instructions. If using the Encepur brand, two dosages are given four weeks apart. Encepur also has summer and winter dosage regimes. Enquire at your travel clinic. FSME-IMMUN is currently the licensed TBE vaccine used in the UK.

Precautions: avoid if there has been any significant reaction to a previous dose, or if allergic to the preservative, thiomersal. It should not be given to anyone allergic to egg protein. Side-effects: headache, local soreness and mild symptoms may occur for 24 hours, and occasionally a mild rash, swollen lymph nodes and a marked fever. There are very rare more serious side-effects.

How obtained: from travel clinics. In the UK it is not available on the NHS. TBE vaccine is available in many countries where the disease is common, such as Austria and Germany.

Recommendations: see above. Obtain specialist advice from a travel clinic. Whether you need it or not will depend on exactly where and when you will be travelling, and what you will be doing.

Typhoid vaccine

For information about typhoid fever see pages 112–13.

Trade names: Typhim Vi, Typherix.
Hepatyrix and Viatim includes hepatitis A vaccine.

Type of vaccine: killed, injectable. (There is also an oral vaccine, see below.)

Countries where typhoid occurs: the Indian subcontinent, Indonesia and other parts of Asia, tropical South America and Africa.

Risk to travellers: there is an appreciable risk.

Number and spacing of doses: a single injection gives substantial protection for three years. Boosters are needed every three years. Protection takes effect seven to ten days after the injection. This vaccine does not protect against the similar paratyphoid group of illnesses, nor does it give full protection, meaning it is still essential to take care with food and water hygiene, especially in South Asia.

Precautions: should not be given to anyone who has had a serious reaction to a previous typhoid vaccine or to those with a fever or who are seriously ill. It is not usually given to those under two years of age. It should only be given in pregnancy if the risk is high. Side-effects include minor pain, swelling and redness at the injection site for two to three days, with occasional mild fever or headache. Side-effects are less marked than with the previously used vaccines.

How obtained: In the UK usually available on the NHS and from travel clinics.

Certification: not normally required.

Reactions with other vaccines: none. May be given at the same time but at a different site.

Recommendations: travellers to developing countries, eastern Europe, Russia and the former Soviet states from age five upwards should be immunized, except for trips of less than one month to high-quality accommodation and with low-risk lifestyles. Children between two and five years, and pregnant women, should only be covered if the risk of catching the disease is considered high. Precautions with food and water are essential. Immunization is still needed even if you have had typhoid fever in the past.

Note on oral typhoid vaccine: live oral typhoid vaccine Ty 21a (Vivotif) is used in some centres as an alternative to the injectable Typhim Vi described above. Three doses are necessary, taken on alternate days with a cool drink on an empty stomach. It gives protection seven days after the final dose. Doses must be kept in the refrigerator. For regular travellers or those at high risk, a three-dose booster course is needed annually. It should not be used in children under six or in pregnant women. Proguanil, mefloquine and antibiotics should be stopped for one week before having the oral vaccine and for one week after.

Yellow fever vaccine

For information on yellow fever (YF), see pages 347–9.

Type of vaccine: live, injectable.

Countries where yellow fever occurs: tropical Africa between approximately 16° north and 16° south; tropical South America between 10° north and 20° south (see map page 348).

Some countries within this belt are reportedly free, but there are many more cases than are officially reported.

Risk to travellers: there is an appreciable risk in several countries in the YF zone, especially to rural travellers.

Number and spacing of doses: a single injection to those over nine months of age, with a booster every ten years.

Precautions: should not be given to anyone who has had a significant reaction to a previous dose, or anyone with fever, who is seriously ill, has depressed immunity or is allergic to neomycin, polymixin or hens' eggs. YF vaccine should not be given to children under nine months (unless going to very high-risk areas, when it can be used from six months) or to pregnant women, who should avoid travel in high-risk areas. Those with any history of thymus disorders must not receive the vaccine. Older travellers, especially over the age of 60, are more likely to have serious reactions and should only be given the vaccine if they will be travelling to areas where there is a significant risk, otherwise they should be given an exemption letter. Side-effects, which affect about one person in ten, include local pain, headache and fever, five to ten days after the injection. Very occasionally there are more serious reactions, especially in older people.

How obtained: from yellow fever vaccination centres, including some GP clinics in the UK and from nearly all accredited travel clinics and many hospitals worldwide. Your travel health adviser or family doctor will advise you where you can obtain it. In the UK it is not available on the NHS.

Reactions with other vaccines: can be given at the same time as any other vaccine but at a different site. Being a live vaccine, if not given on the same day as other live vaccines it should be given at an interval of four weeks or more.

Certification: an international certificate should be filled in and carried when travelling abroad. It is valid for ten years, taking effect ten days after the first vaccination and immediately after any further dose. Some countries outside the YF zone will demand to see a valid certificate if you have travelled from or passed through a country within the YF zone in the past ten days. It is important you get up-to-date specialist advice about which countries are currently demanding certificates, as these vary and do not always follow WHO recommendations. An exemption letter should be carried by anyone who for any reason cannot be vaccinated.

Recommendations: there are two reasons for having a yellow fever immunization:

1 for entry into certain countries if you have passed through a region where yellow fever is present in the past ten days;
2 to protect you against the risk of catching yellow fever if you visit an affected area.

Anyone nine months or over coming into either of these categories should be immunized. Frequent travellers should keep their yellow fever immunization up to date. Note the exemptions listed above.
    If in doubt get specialist advice.

See Table J.1 (overleaf) for a summary of common minor vaccine reactions.

Table J.1 A summary of common minor vaccine reactions

BCG	Local reaction (pain, swelling, redness)	Common
Cholera	Oral presentation – none	
DTP	Local reaction (pain, swelling, redness)	Up to 50%[a]
Hepatitis A	Local reaction (pain, swelling redness)	Up to 50%
Hepatitis B	Local reaction (pain, swelling, redness)	Adults up to 30%, children up to 5%
	Fever	1–6%
Hib	Local reaction (pain, swelling, redness)	5–15%
	Fever	2–10%
Japanese encephalitis	Local reaction, low-grade fever, myalgia, gastrointestinal upset	Up to 20%
Measles/MMR	Local reaction (pain, swelling, redness)	Up to 10%
	Irritability, malaise and non-specific symptoms, fever	Up to 5%
Pneumococcal	Local reaction (pain, swelling, redness)	30–50%
Poliomyelitis (OPV)	None	
Poliomyelitis (IPV)	None	
Rabies	Local and/or general reaction depending on type of vaccine (see product information)	15–25%
Meningococcal vaccines	Mild local reaction	Up to 71%
Tetanus/Td	Local reaction (pain, swelling, redness)[b]	Up to 10%
	Malaise and non-specific symptoms	Up to 25%
Tick-borne encephalitis	Local reaction (pain, swelling, redness)	Up to 10%
Typhoid fever	Depends on type of vaccine use (see product information)	
Yellow fever	Headache	10%
	Influenza-like symptoms	22%
	Local reaction (pain, swelling, redness)	5%

Notes: More serious reactions can occur, for example with Japanese encephalitis vaccine and with yellow fever, especially in those over the age of 60. Seek advice from your travel health adviser.

[a] With whole-cell pertussis vaccine. Rates for acellular pertussis vaccine are lower.
[b] Rate of local reactions likely to increase with booster doses, up to 50–85%.
Source: *International Travel and Health*, World Health Organization, Geneva, 2005.

Further reading and websites on travellers' health

Except where otherwise indicated, the following may be bought or ordered from bookshops or bought online from Amazon (<http://www.amazon.co.uk>).

On healthcare while abroad

Books

Travellers' Health, Dr Richard Dawood, Oxford University Press, fourth edition 2002. A standard and very detailed reference book for the serious traveller.

Health Advice for Travellers, UK Department of Health, 2005 and updated regularly. Basic information directed at tourists and concentrating on Europe. Free from post offices and available online at <http://www.dh.gov.uk/policyandguidance/healthadvicefortravellers/>.

International Travel and Health, World Health Organization, Geneva, 2006 and updated annually. Available from WHO Distribution and Sales, 1211 Geneva, and online at <http://www.who.int/ith/en>. Mainly designed for those giving health advice, but also useful for the traveller.

Health Information for International Travel (the 'Yellow Book'), Centers for Disease Control and Prevention, Atlanta, USA, 2005–6. The Yellow Book is published every two years and has authoritative information useful for travellers as well as for health providers; <http://www.cdc.gov/travel/yb>.

Travel Safe: Know Before You Go, UK Foreign and Commonwealth Office in association with Lonely Planet, 49 pages, 2006. A useful booklet for the inexperienced traveller with some information on travel health. We recommend the FCO's Know Before You Go initiative, of value to international travellers.

International Travel Health Guide, S. Rose and J. Keystone, Elsevier, 13th edition 2006. An annually updated and authoritative book on travel health written from a US perspective.

The Traveler's Medical Guide, G. Fujimoto, M. Robin and B. Dessery, Prairie Smoke Press, third edition 2003. A very useful guide, directed more towards American audiences.

Travel Health in Your Pocket, Ted Lankester, Berlitz Publishing, due for publication 2007. A passport-sized guide written in informal language and directed towards short-term and younger travellers. Also available from InterHealth.

Bugs, Bites and Bowels, Dr Jane Wilson-Howarth, Cadogan, 1999. An enjoyable and informative read, though some areas now slightly outdated.

How to Shit Around the World: The Art of Staying Clean and Healthy while Travelling, Dr Jane Wilson-Howarth, Travelers' Tales Guides, 2006. Seriously useful information from a well-known travel health expert.

New Practical First Aid, British Red Cross, Dorling Kindersley, 2003. An excellent, easy-to-follow manual, recommended and designed for the general traveller, and for all teams working abroad.

Websites

A number are given throughout the book and on pages 369–77. In addition the following are useful:

Health Protection Scotland: http://www.fitfortravel.scot.nhs.uk
Provides valuable information on travel, including country specific risks.

National Travel Health Network and Centre (NaTHNaC): http://www.nathnac.org
The UK government's travel health specialist organization, with increasingly valuable information for both travellers and providers.

UK Health Protection Agency: http://www.hpa.org.uk/infections/topics_az/travel
Provides useful information, slanted towards health providers.

University of Minnesota Department of Medicine: http://www.tropical.umn.edu
Pre-travel handouts on key health topics produced by the University of Minnesota in a number of languages.

For expeditions and adventure travel

Expedition Medicine, D. Warrell and S. Anderson (eds), Royal Geographical Society, revised edition 2004. An excellent guide for those travelling to inhospitable areas or planning adventure travel.

The High Altitude Medicine Handbook, A. Pollard and D. Murdoch, Radcliffe Medical Press, Oxford, third edition 2003. Essential for serious climbers.

For the disabled and elderly

Nothing Ventured: Disabled People Travel the World, A. Walsh (ed.), Rough Guide Series, Penguin, 1991. An inspiring read for anyone, and still relevant.

For those with children

Your Child's Health Abroad, J. Wilson-Howarth and M. Ellis, Bradt Publications, 2004. The kids' and parents' survival kit, giving practical and comprehensive information for parents and families, all of whom should obtain a copy if living abroad.

Families on the Move: Growing Up Overseas and Loving It, M. Knell, Monarch Books, 2003. A very useful book for expatriate families on bringing up children overseas. Written from a broadly Christian perspective but with valuable insights for any family.

The Third Culture Kid Experience: Growing Up Among Worlds, D. Pollock and R. Van Reken, Intercultural Press, 1999. An interesting and practical book looking at issues facing expatriate children, especially those from missionary families.

For those in stressful situations

Honourably Wounded, M. Foyle, Monarch, second edition 2001. Invaluable insights and suggestions, written specifically for those involved in church-related work overseas, all of whom should consider obtaining a copy before leaving. Translated into many languages.

On safety and security

Staying Alive, D. Roberts, International Committee of the Red Cross, Geneva, second edition 2006. A must-have book for anyone working or travelling in high-risk areas and war zones. Chapter on health care provided by InterHealth staff.

Your Passport to Safer Travel, M. Hodson, Thomas Cook Publishing, 2001. Personal health and safety, especially for the woman traveller. See also entry on Suzy Lamplugh Trust on page 376.

Index

*Page numbers in **bold** print indicate key or primary references.*

INDEX